Contents

10   Scene Design   292

11   Theater Architecture   329

12   The Audience   360

General Bibliography   381

Glossary   383

Index   389

Preface

Theatrical production, like all creative expression, is a reminder that a culture is not to be judged by its material accomplishments alone, but also by the aspirations and ideals that motivate conduct. In dealing with significant choices and actions, dramatists have at their disposal special means of illuminating the human condition. Thus, a play is more than an evening's diversion in the theater, more than pages of a text; it is a personal statement of the playwright and a clue to the culture that produced it. The objective of this work is to provide students with the tools of analysis that will give them insight into the total imaginative process that makes up theater.

I wish to express my gratitude to my students over the years, from whom I have learned so much. I am grateful to the following persons and institutions for their cooperation in the preparation of this book: Werner Hecht of the Berliner Ensemble; Dr. Jaromir Svoboda of the Prague National Theater; Dr. Eckehart Nölle of the Munich Theatermuseum; Jerzy Grotowski of the Polish Laboratory Theater; the Victoria and Albert Museum; the New York Public Library; Dimitrios A. Harissiadis; Will Swalling; Joyce Miller; and to my associates and colleagues in regional and educational theaters for their generosity in supplying photographs of their works. I am also indebted to individual theaters and publishers for permission to reprint copyrighted materials.

Thanks to my wife, Dorcas Hatlen, without whose assistance and encouragement this revision would never have come to print.

Acknowledgments

TEXT CREDITS

9, 42: From *Death of a Salesman* by Arthur Miller. Copyright 1949, renewed ©1977 by Arthur Miller. Reprinted by permission of Viking Penguin, Inc.

11, 51, 314: From *A Soldier's Play* by Charles Fuller. Copyright ©1981 by Charles Fuller. Reprinted by permission of Hill and Wang, a division of Farrar, Straus and Giroux, Inc.

12: From *Anna Christie* by Eugene O'Neill. Copyright 1922 by Random House, Inc.

12: From *The Caucasian Chalk Circle* by Bertolt Brecht. Copyright ©1947 by University of Minnesota Press. Translated by Eric Bentley and Maja Apelman.

15, 233: From *Look Back in Anger* by John Osbourne. Reprinted by permission of S.G. Phillips, Inc. Copyright ©1957 by S. G. Phillips.

16: From *The Collection* in *Three Plays by Harold Pinter*. Copyright 1962 by Methuen London Ltd.

18: From *Curse of the Starving Class* in *Seven Plays* by Sam Shepard. Copyright 1981 by Bantam Books.

31: From *Our Town* by Thornton Wilder. (New York: Coward-McCann, 1938.) Reprinted by permission of Miss Isabel Wilder.

32: From *Talley's Folley* by Lanford Wilson. Copyright ©1979 by Lanford Wilson. Reprinted by permission of Hill & Wang, a division of Farrar, Straus and Giroux, Inc.

34, 52, 174: Specified excerpts from pp. 1-2, 15-16, and 25-26 from *Amadeus* by Peter Shaffer. Copyright ©1980, 1981 by Peter Shaffer. Reprinted by permission of Harper & Row, Publishers, Inc.

39, 54: From *'Night Mother* by Marsha Norman. Copyright ©1983 by Marsha Norman. Reprinted by permission of Hill & Wang, a division of Farrar, Straus and Giroux, Inc.

43: From *The Little Foxes* by Lillian Hellman. Copyright 1939 by Random House, Inc.

49: From *A Streetcar Named Desire* by Tennessee Williams. Copyright 1947 by Tennessee Williams. Reprinted by permission of New Directions Publishing Corporation.

50: From *A Raisin in the Sun* by Lorraine Hansberry. Copyright 1959 by Random House, Inc.

54: *Hedda Gabler* by Henrik Ibsen. Translated by Edmund Gosse and William Archer. Copyright 1907 by Charles Scribner's Sons.

59, 201: From *The Birthday Party* by Harold Pinter. Copyright 1959 by Methuen London Ltd.

70: From Aristotle's *On the Art of Poetry*, translated by Ingram Bywater. Copyright 1920 by Clarendon Press.

75, 78: From *The Antigone of Sophocles* by Sophocles, translated by R.C. Jebb. Copyright ©1939 by Harcourt Brace Jovanovich, Inc.

84: From *Antigone* by Jean Anouilh, translated by Lewis Galantiere. Copyright 1946 by Van Loewen, Inc.

97: From *The World of Melodrama* by Frank Rahill. Copyright 1967 by Pennsylvania State University Press.

121: From *Noises Off* by Michael Frayn. Copyright 1982 by Methuen London Ltd.

124: From *Fiddler on the Roof* by Joseph Stein. Copyright ©1964 by Joseph Stein. Used by permission of Crown Publishers, Inc.

132, 155: From *Crimes of the Heart* by Beth Henley. Copyright ©1981 by Beth Henley. Reprinted by permission of Viking Penguin, Inc.

148: From *Major Barbara* by George Bernard Shaw. Copyright by Dodd, Mead & Company, 1941. Reprinted by permission of The Society of Authors, Ltd.

149: From *Travesties* by Tom Stoppard. Copyright 1975 by Fraser & Dunlap.

176: From *Equus* by Peter Shaffer. Copyright 1974 by Avon Books.

186: Kurt Schwitters, "Green Child," quoted in John Elderfield, *Kurt Schwitters*. Copyright 1985 by Thames & Hudson, Ltd.

201, 205: From *Waiting for Godot* by Samuel Beckett. Copyright 1954 by Faber & Faber Ltd.

204: From *The Bald Soprano* from *Four Plays by Eugene Ionesco*, translated by Donald M. Allen. Copyright ©1958 by Grove Press, Inc. Published by Grove Press, Inc.

224, 243: Peter Brook, "Introduction to *Marat/Sade*" by Peter Weiss (New York: Atheneum, 1965). From the Introduction by Peter Brook to the play, *The Persecution and Assassination of Jean-Paul Marat as Performed by the Inmates of the Asylum of Chareton under the Direction of the Marquis de Sade*, by Peter Weiss. Copyright ©1965 by John Calder, Ltd. Reprinted by permission of Atheneum Publishers.

235: From *Stanislavski Produces Othello* by K.S. Alekseev, translated by Helen Nowak. Reprinted by permission of Geoffrey Bles, Ltd., London, 1948.

239: From *On Directing* by Harold Clurman. (New York: Macmillan, 1972). Originally appeared in *Directing the Play*, edited by Toby Cole and Helen Krich Chinoy (Indianapolis: Bobbs-Merrill, 1953).

241: From "An Audience of One" by Tyrone Guthrie in *Directors on Directing*, ed. by Toby Cole and Helen Krich Chinoy. Copyright 1964 by the Bobbs-Merrill Company.

244: From a review of *A Midsummer Night's Dream* by Clive Barnes in *The New York Times*, August 28, 1970.

247: From Michael Steele, review of *The Tempest* in *The Minneapolis Star*, 1981. Reprinted by permission.

248: From Brendan Gill, review of *The Marriage of Figaro*, in *The New Yorker*, October 28, 1985.

251: Lucian Pintilie quoted in Mike Steele's "TK" in *American Theater*, July-August, 1985.

259: From Clive Barnes, review of *Death of a Salesman*, June 27, 1975. Copyright ©1975 by The New York Times Company. Reprinted by permission.

275: From Lillian Ross, "Profiles: The Player," *The New Yorker*, October 21, 1961, October 28, 1961, and November 4, 1961. Reprinted by permission. Copyright ©1961 by The New Yorker Magazine, Inc., October 28, 1961.

277: From *The Basic Training of Pavlo Hummel* and *Sticks & Bones* by David Rabe. Copyright ©1969, 1972, 1973 by David Rabe. Reprinted by permission of Viking Penguin, Inc.

279: From Roger Planchon, interviewed by Michael Kustow, "Creating a Theater of Real Life," in *Theater Quarterly*, 2, no. 5 (January-March 1971).

282: From Jack Kroll, review of Al Pacino in *The Basic Training of Pavlo Hummel,* May 9, 1977. Copyright ©1977 by *Newsweek.*

288: From Arthur Holmberg, review of *Mother Courage and Her Children,* Bertolt Brecht, Boston Shakespeare Co., February 1984, in *Theater Journal,* December 1984.

296: From *Arthur Miller's Adaptation of An Enemy of the People by Henrik Ibsen.* Copyright 1951, renewed ©1979 by Arthur Miller. Reprinted by permission of Viking Penguin, Inc.

306: From *Designing and Painting for the Theater* by Lynn Pecktal. Copyright ©1975 by Lynn Pecktal. Reprinted by permission of CBS College Publishing.

307: From *Scenery Then & Now* by Donald Oenslager. (New York: W.W. Norton & Co., Inc., 1936.) Reprinted by permission of the author.

316: From *Wild Honey* by Anton Chekhov and Michael Frayn. Copyright 1984 by Methuen London Ltd.

352: From *The Theater & Its Double* by Antonin Artaud. Copyright ©1958 by Grove Press. Translated by Mary Caroline Richards. Reprinted by permission of the publisher.

358: From Jerzy Grotowski, quoted in *Time,* October 24, 1969. Reprinted by permission of Time, Inc. and the author.

PHOTOGRAPH CREDITS

Chapter 1: 1: D. A. Harissiadis. **2:** D. A. Harissiadis. **4:** From C. Walter Hodges' *Shakespeare's Theater.* **7:** Peter Smith, courtesy of Stratford Shakespeare Festival, Ontario. **9:** University of Missouri Theater. **13:** University of California, Santa Barbara. **14:** courtesy of Berliner Ensemble. **16:** courtesy of Cleveland Play House. **18:** Gerry Goodstein. **21:** Martha Swope. **22:** courtesy of Jarka Burian. **25:** Gerry Goodstein.

Chapter 2: 28: D.A. Harissiadis. **32:** University of Kentucky Theater Department. **34:** D.A. Harissiadis. **36:** Wayne State University, Department of Theater. **37:** Will Swalling, University of California, Santa Barbara. **38:** Portland State University Theater. **40:** Angus McBean. **41:** Dr. Jaromir Svoboda, courtesy of Prague National Theater. **44:** courtesy of Ahmanson Theater. **45:** Gary Sweetman, courtesy of Asolo State Theater. **48:** courtesy of Cleveland Play House. **49:** courtesy of North Carolina Playmakers' Repertory Company. **52:** Martha Swope. **53:** Martha Swope. **57:** Brigitte Lacombe, Goodman Theater. **60:** University of Missouri Theater. **63:** Martha Swope. **66:** Ruth Walz.

Chapter 3: 69: D.A. Harissiadis. **71:** American Shakespeare Festival, Connecticut. **73:** Stanford University Theater. **74:** D.A. Harissiadis. **75:** Purdue University Theater. **77:** Dr. Jaromir Svoboda, courtesy of Prague National Theater. **81:** D.A. Harissiadis. **82:** American Shakespeare Festival, Connecticut. **83:** courtesy of Royal Shakespeare Theater. **85:** Mark Taper Forum. **86:** courtesy of Munich Kammerspiele. **87:** *The London Stage.* **89:** Wayne State University Theater. **91:** Wayne State University Theater.

Chapter 4: 94: Harvard Theater Collection. **96:** University of Minnesota Theater. **97:** *The London Stage.* **108:** Nineteenth century theater poster. **101:** Daumier print. **103:** Pacific Conservatory of Performing Arts. **105:** Nineteenth century theater poster. **108:** *The London Stage.* **111:** Martha Swope. **111:** University of Toledo Theater. **112:** Martha Swope. **113:** Gary Sweetman, Asolo State Theater. **114:** American Conservatory Theater. **115:** Gary Sweetman, Asolo State Theater.

Chapter 5: 117: Ilse Buhs. **119:** Wayne State University Theater. **120:** South Coast Repertory Company. **121:** Program Cover. **122:** Cleveland Play House. **123:** Syracuse Stage. **124:** Clarke College. **126:** Purdue University Theater. **126:** Cincinnati Playhouse in the Park. **129:** Will Swalling, University of California, Santa Barbara. **129:** University of West Virginia. **130:** Gary Sweetman, Asolo State Theater. **131:** Martha Swope. **135:** Texas Christian University Theater. **138:** American Conservatory Theater. **141:** D.A. Harissiadis. **142:** Utah Shakespeare Festival. **144:** Repertory Theater of St. Louis. **148:** Joan Marcus, Arena Stage. **150:** Mark Taper Forum. **152:** Goodman Theater.

Chapter 6: 154: University of Toledo Theater. **157:** Gary Sweetman, Asolo State Theater. **158:** Munich Theatermuseum. **160:** Guthrie Theater. **164:** Clarke College. **165:** Guthrie Theater. **171:** Munich Theatermuseum. **172:** Clarke College. **173:** Henry May, University of California, Berkeley, Theater. **175:** Munich Theatermuseum. **177:** New York Public Library. **181:** Will Swalling, University of California, Santa Barbara. **183:** Museum of Modern Art. **184:** Martha Swope. **186:** Museum of Modern Art. **187:** Dr. Jaromir Svoboda, courtesy of Prague National Theater. **189:** Munich Theatermuseum. **192:** Ilse Buhs. **199:** Ilse Buhs.

Chapter 7: 200: courtesy of Royal Court Theater. **202:** courtesy of Buffalo Arts Festival. **203:** courtesy of Studio Théâtre Elysee, Paris. **204:** Will Swalling, University of California, Santa Barbara. **207:** Goodman Theater. **211:** courtesy of Living Theater. **212:** University of California, Berkeley. **213:** photo courtesy of Elizabeth Le Compte. **215:** photo courtesy of Ted Shank. **218:** courtesy of Walker Art Center, Minneapolis.

Chapter 8: 225: Munich Kammerspiele. **227:** D. A. Harissiadis. **228:** Victoria & Albert Museum. **229:** Munich Theatermuseum. **230:** New York Public Library. **240:** courtesy of Ahmanson Theater. **241:** Gary Sweetman, Asolo State Theater. **242:** courtesy of Roundhouse Theater, London. **245:** courtesy of Royal Shakespeare Company. **247:** Bruce Goldstein, Guthrie Theater. **250:** photo by M. Franck/Viva, courtesy of Theatre du Soleil. **263:** Guthrie Theater.

Chapter 9: 258: Mark Taper Forum. **261:** Martha Swope. **263:** Asolo State Theater. **264:** courtesy of Guthrie Theater. **266:** Harvard Theater Collection. **267:** American Conservatory Theater. **270:** courtesy Théâtre d' Orsay, Paris. **271:** courtesy Berliner Ensemble. **273:** courtesy of Royal Shakespeare Theater. **275:** Hartford Stage Company. **278:** Miami University Theater, Ohio. **280:** Guthrie Theater. **281:** photo by Michael Edwards, Cleveland Play House. **282:** Guthrie Theater. **286:** courtesy of Polish Laboratory Theater. **288:** Repertory Theater of St. Louis.

Chapter 10: 292: Martha Swope. **294:** Munich Theatermuseum. **295:** Munich Theatermuseum. **297:** Richard Bashky. **299:** Munich Theatermuseum. **300:** New York Public Library. **303:** Munich Theatermuseum. **305:** New York Public Library. **308:** New York Public Library. **310:** Victoria & Albert Museum. **311:** Wesleyan University Press. **313:** photo courtesy of Jarka Burian. **315:** Dr. Jaromir Svoboda, courtesy of Prague National Theater. **317:** courtesy of Arena Stage. **318:** Martha Swope. **319:** courtesy of Munich Kammerspiele. **320:** Dr. Jaromir Svoboda, courtesy of Prague National Theater. **323:** courtesy of Royal Shakespeare Company. **324:** photo courtesy of Jarka Burian. **325:** Ruth Walz. **326:** Ruth Walz. **327:** Henry May, University of California, Berkeley.

Chapter 11: 329: drawing by Gerda Becker With, courtesy of William Melnitz. **330:** D.A. Harissiadis. **332:** Victoria & Albert Museum. **333:** Richard Leecroft, *Theater and Playhouse.* **334:** courtesy of Oregon Shakespeare Festival. **335:** Munich Theatermuseum. **336:** Munich Theatermuseum. **338:** Munich Theatermuseum. **340:** Architectural Press, Ltd., London. **345:** courtesy of Guthrie Theater. **346:** courtesy of Festival Theater, Ontario. **347:** courtesy of Arena Stage. **349:** courtesy of Arena Stage. **350:** courtesy of University of Michigan Drama Department. **351:** courtesy of Royal Shakespeare Company. **352:** Architectural Press, Ltd., London. **353:** Architectural Press, Ltd., London. **355:** courtesy of International Center for Theater Research. **355:** sketch by R. Moscosco, courtesy of Théâtre du Soleil, Paris. **356:** photo by M. Franck/Viva, courtesy of Théâtre du Soleil.

Chapter 12: 360: Gary Sweetman, Asolo State Theater. **361:** Will Swalling, University of California, Santa Barbara. **362:** Daumier print, Munich Theatermuseum. **365:** D.A. Harissiadis. **366:** D.A. Harissiadis. **367:** from *Shakespeare's Theater* by C. Walter Hodges. **368:** *Theater Annual,* 1906. **367:** Munich Theatermuseum. **371:** Architectural Press, Ltd., London. **372:** courtesy of J. Grotowski, Polish Laboratory Theater. **375:** courtesy of Trinity Square Repertory Company. **376:** Munich Theatermuseum.

CHAPTER OPENERS

Chapter 1: Greek drama began when the hero emerged from the choric odes honoring Dionysus. In *Oedipus at Colonus*, Sophocles shows Oedipus, who has blinded and exiled himself for his crimes against his father and mother, as he finds sanctuary and tranquility at Colonus. (D.A. Harissiadis.)

Chapter 2: The opening scene in *Agamemnon*, by Aeschylus, shows the watchman on the tower alerting the citizens that the King is returning from the Trojan Wars. His expository monologue sets the scene for Agamemnon's entrance. (Greek National Theater, Epidaurus. Photo: D.A. Harissiadis.)

Chapter 3: Tragedy deals with active, positive protagonists caught up in significant conflicts. In Aeschylus' *Agamemnon*, the King makes a spectacular return from the Trojan War to confront his estranged Queen, Clytemnestra, who plots his death. (Greek National Theater at Epidaurus.)

Chapter 4: Eugene O'Neill's father, James O'Neill, made a fortune playing the swashbuckling hero in *The Count of Monte Cristo*, which he began in 1883 and continued to play for almost 6,000 performances. He appears in the duel scene in a forest of painted trees. (Harvard Theater Collection.)

Chapter 5: Even in tragedy there can be traces of comedy, as in this grave digger's scene from Hamlet. (Schiller Theater, West Berlin. Directed by Fritz Kortner. Photo: Ilse Buhs.)

Chapter 6: The realist brought to the theater the environment of the domestic interior and the problems of daily life. In Ibsen's *A Doll's House*, Nora shocked her husband and many theatergoers by walking out on her family. (University of Toledo. Directed by George Back; designed by William R. Smith.)

Chapter 7: Beckett's *Waiting for Godot* was a pivotal play of the post World War II theater. In this landmark of absurdist drama, Estragon and Vladimir dramatize the act of waiting. (University of California, Santa Barbara. Directed by Frederick Thon. Photo: Will Swalling.)

Chapter 8: Brecht was one of the most influential theater practitioners of modern times. Here, he directs his play *Mother Courage* at the Munich Kammerspiele.

Chapter 9: Sean O'Casey creates marvelous acting roles in his plays, such as these three in *Juno and the Paycock*. Walter Matthau as "Captain" Jack Boyle, Maureen Stapleton as Juno, and Jack Lemmon as "Joxer" Daly. (Mark Taper Forum, Los Angeles.)

Chapter 10: A recent Broadway musical success, *A Sunday in the Park with George*, depended a good deal on its visual appeal, since it dealt with French pointillist painter Georges Seurat and one of his famous works. (Photo: Martha Swope.)

Chapter 11: A reconstruction of a Greek theater, based on the fourth century B.C. remains at Epidaurus. The full orchestra circle is typical of the fifth century B.C., but the raised stage is thought to be a century after the Golden Age of drama. (Photo: D.A. Harissiadis.)

Chapter 12: The audience as seen during the curtain call at the Asolo State Theater, Sarasota, Florida. (Photo: Gary Sweetman)

1

The Background

THESPIS

The time: Sixth century B.C. It is the vintage season.
The place: A circular threshing floor of hard-packed earth, just outside the city wall in Icaria, near Marathon.
The cast: A chorus of fifty men and boys performing before their fellow citizens.

The onlookers gather about the circle; some stand at the sides, but most of them sit on the sloping hillside. All eyes are on the chorus, singing and dancing in unison—their voices clear and bright in the crisp morning air, their familiar steps performed with an easy grace, the flow of the dance and the rhythm of the music and movement felt by all who watch.

Suddenly, a solitary figure breaks away from the chorus and mounts an altar stone in the center of the circle. The crowd is startled when he begins to speak, his voice cutting off the chant of the chorus. Instead of the cadence of the dancing and singing, he speaks in the accents of a storyteller,

The tragic hero Hippolytus, who was wounded when his horses were frightened by a sea monster, is carried by the chorus during the exodus from the orchestra circle.

(Greek National Theater at Epidaurus. Directed by Spyros A. Evangelatos.)

recalling the adventures of an ancient hero. The sunlight catches the chalky white makeup of his face; his body is animated and his voice is charged with emotion. This is the hero himself, brought by the audacious act of impersonation from the distant past into the living present. This is no ordinary storyteller.

The chorus, momentarily transfixed by the miraculous appearance of the hero, now draws toward him as he enacts the ordeal of suffering. He seems to be wounded; he struggles mightily and dies. The chorus responds in mimetic action, sometimes singing and dancing, bodies and voices following the hero. During his suffering, the chorus sings a hymn of supplication; and when he dies, they gather about the altar in lamentation, take up his body, and move in a solemn recessional, circling the ring, while the onlookers are involuntarily caught up in the stirring atmosphere of the performance.

So it may have been with Thespis in ancient Greece—Thespis, who is thought to have been the first actor. After he perfected his art and wrote plays to suit his innovation, he took his show to Athens, where he quickly won approval and the flattery of imitation. Others followed his example; and the ruler, Pisistratus, was so impressed by "tragedies," as they now came to be called, that he set up contests in them in 534 B.C. as a part of the City Dionysia, a festival in homage to Dionysus, god of wine, vegetation, and fertility. Most appropriately, Thespis was the first to win the prize.

AN EASTER TROPE

Move ahead to the tenth century at Winchester, England. It is Easter morning and the cathedral is filled with worshipers. As the Mass begins, the faithful notice that something different has been added. A tomb has been placed before the altar steps, but it is open. All at once, from the side of the altar, two figures appear—angels, so their folded wings seem to say. Next come three women down the aisle, carrying cloths and ointments. These must be the three Marys. As they near the tomb, one of the angels steps forward, puts up a restraining hand, and speaks:

First Angel: Whom do you seek in the tomb, worshipers of Christ?
The Women: Jesus of Nazareth who was crucified, O dweller of Heaven.
Angel: He is not here, he has risen as he foretold; go announce that he has risen, saying:
The Women: Hallelujah! The Lord has risen today, a brave lion, Christ the son of God.
First Angel: (*Pointing to the tomb*) Come and see the place where the Lord was laid, hallelujah! hallelujah!
Second Angel: Go quickly and tell the disciples that the Lord has risen, hallelujah!

The three Marys meet the angels and discover the empty tomb during an Easter Trope at a performance in the church.

(From C. Walter Hodges' Shakespeare's Theater.)

> **Women:** (*Singing in unison with shouts of joy*) The Lord was hung upon the cross for us, has risen from the tomb, hallelujah!

Now the congregation joins in singing "Hallelujah, hallelujah, He is risen." This little trope, known as *Quem Quaeritis* (whom do you seek?), the oldest fragment of liturgical drama, shows how the biblical tale came alive: The word became flesh. Salvation is based on victory over death, and one of the strongest discoveries of the gospel is the discovery of the empty tomb. So on Easter morning, when the three Marys approach the tomb to anoint the body, their hearts are heavy after the agony of the Crucifixion. At the sight of the angels, they might at first be apprehensive, but when they hear the good news and see the evidence, sorrow is turned to joy. The discovery brings a reversal that shows the change of fate for the hero.

In the medieval church, the clergy's objective was to convey to their flocks the message of salvation; but since most of the people were illiterate and services were conducted in Latin, the impact of the worship service left something to be desired. Attempts were made to present graphic representations of the gospel in mosaics, sculptures, and stained glass windows. The introduction of enacted material into the Mass was an extension of the effort to make the biblical story more compelling.

The dramatic action of the tropes in medieval times led to the evolution of full-scale theatrical pieces, until some cycle plays required three days for performances and included dozens of incidents and characters. As liturgical plays grew more complex and secular, medieval drama broke away from the church and developed a remarkably flexible style of playwriting and staging, which was to profoundly influence the nature of English Renaissance theater.

These two instances illustrate the beginnings of theater in the Western world. When Thespis made the daring leap from narration to impersonation, he changed the *manner* of presentation from recitation to enactment. Before Thespis, when Greek rhapsodists recited stories of legendary heroes, primarily from Homer, their performance was comprised of description and narration. With Thespis, the performer became the character; he assumed a complete identity. The effect was to create dramatic action that seemed to be happening here and now. Theatrical performance ever since has had the quality of an ongoing experience. Similarly, when the angels and the three Marys acted out the discovery at the tomb, the incident came to life before the eyes of the worshipers. The event was given immediacy by dramatic action.

Thespis' innovation had a profound influence on the chorus, too, because when the hero appeared in the flesh, it was compelled to respond to him in a new way. Its lamentation was not for some remote figure in the dim past but for a living character, suffering before its eyes. In essence, the chorus became actors, too, and although the members did not become distinct, individualized characters, they did assume roles of elders, handmaidens, warriors, suppliants, and so on; and they also responded and reacted as actors involved in the fate of the hero.

After Thespis, Aeschylus in the fifth century B.C. added a second actor, and Sophocles a third. Athenian playwrights developed their mastery of dramatic language and action to produce one of the most prodigious outpourings of creative effort known to the Western world—the rich legacy of Greek tragedy and comedy.

HAMLET'S "MOUSETRAP"

Thus far we have seen elementary examples of dramatic action. Now let us turn to a more complicated situation, in which Hamlet tried his hand at playwriting. Hamlet is grieved by the sudden death of his father and the hasty marriage of his mother to his uncle, Claudius. Early in the play, Hamlet confronts his father's ghost, who tells him that he has been murdered by Claudius. The dead king gives Hamlet the burden of avenging his murder. For a time Hamlet delays, not altogether sure of the new king's guilt. So when the traveling players arrive to perform at court, Hamlet persuades them to play *The Murder of Gonzago,* to which he adds "a dozen or sixteen lines" of his own. This interjection, which he calls "The Mousetrap," shows a reenactment of the murder of King Hamlet by pouring poison into his ears. Hamlet devises this scene to see whether or not Claudius is actually guilty of murder. "The play's the thing/Wherein I'll catch the conscience of the King."

At the performance before the court, Hamlet stations himself so that he can see Claudius' face. Here then is a dramatic action performed to produce a very specific effect on one member of the audience.

The play begins with a dumb show in which the poisoning is enacted, but Claudius does not respond. Then Lucianus recites the lines that Hamlet wrote:

Lucianus: Thoughts black, hand apt, drugs fit, and time agreeing,
  Confederate season, else no creative seeing,
  Thou mixture of rank, of midnight weeds collected,
  With Hecate's ban thrice blasted, thrice infected,
  Thy natural magic and dire property
  On wholesome life usurps immediately.

(Pours the poison in his ears)

At this action, King Claudius blanches, rises, and flees from the room. Hamlet's play has produced the desired effect. The bait was taken. The trap was sprung.

"The Mousetrap" is a major advance over *Quem Quaeritis.* Both are discovery scenes, but the medieval trope is relatively passive, for we do not see the climactic moment when Jesus breaks the seal and emerges from the tomb. Instead, we are presented with the circumstantial evidence of his departure.

In *Hamlet,* the discovery is a double one: Claudius' murder of King Hamlet is apparent from his guilty reaction to the simulated poisoning. He discovers that his crime is known, which means that he must take action against the prince. Hamlet also discovers what he needed to know. The ghost of his father was an honest one; his Uncle Claudius did indeed commit murder. The revelation of Claudius' guilt culminates the rising tension that preceded it. The audience, as well as Hamlet, is in on the psychological am-

In "The Mousetrap," the play within the play, Hamlet catches the guilty
conscience of King Claudius by reenacting the murder when poison was poured in
the victim's ear.

bush of Claudius, and once the discovery is made, the emotional momentum
surges forward toward the next action.

Hamlet's "Mousetrap" is a good example of the dramatic method. A
sequence of words and actions is created to be performed to evoke a response.

EMPATHY

Response in the theater is *empathic*. *Empathy* means "feeling into." It may be
defined as "imitative motor response." Notice the word *motor*. An empathic
response is not mere sympathy; it involves physical identification and participation. Watch bystanders trying to help a high jumper over the bar. Or
feel the tension in your own body as you attempt to help a tailback cross the
goal line. We have listened to an unsure soprano, trying desperately to hit
a high note beyond her own range, and have felt some of her tension in our
own throats. The largest crowds are attracted to those sporting events that

involve vigorous physical action to which the spectator responds empathi-
cally. Similarly, film and television fare that exploits vigorous action, such
as in melodramas and farces, is the most popular because the audience is
called on for strong empathic response.

HISTRIONIC SENSIBILITY

Another way of describing theatrical response is found in Francis Fergusson's term "histrionic sensibility"—the theatergoer's ability to perceive and
discriminate actions and visual symbols, just as the trained ear discriminates
sounds. It is a learned process that we employ when we judge behavior. For
example, in the stands we may not hear the dialogue between an umpire
and an enraged second baseman after a close play, but even at a considerable distance, we understand the feelings of the adversaries because of the
way they act. When we communicate with one another on important issues,
we prefer face-to-face contact, which enables us to make judgments about
the speaker and the speaker's manner.

Consider a familiar episode from life that may have the quality of
drama: You apply for a job. You go through a process of action that generates a certain amount of tension because the outcome is in doubt. The
action may be intensified if it is critically important to you to succeed. You
may have a rival who is also desperate to land the job.

In any case, you are obliged to follow a specific procedure. You fill out
a form, perhaps submit letters of recommendation or your service record
elsewhere; you make an appointment for an interview. You are prompt for
your appointment, and when you meet your prospective employer you
make every effort to create a favorable impression so that your words and
actions will help you to achieve your objective. The employer consults what
you have written on the forms and your other papers and listens to your
answers. With a bit of luck, the job is yours.

Why the interview? Because it gave the employer and you an opportunity to assess one another. When you entered the boss's office, you got
certain impressions from the room, the furniture, the décor, the things on
the desk. And you made tentative judgments about the person, based on
appearance, manner of speaking, and way of looking at you as you replied
to questions.

What you were both doing during this sizing-up process was evaluating one another by histrionic sensibility. We have learned to read "body language"; we are responsive to others' "vibrations"; we communicate on a
subliminal or visceral level that sometimes can be more intense than the spoken word.

This kind of communication is essential for understanding the impact
of the theater. The actors' shrug of a shoulder, the lifting of an eyebrow,

the anger which they try to conceal in their voice, the reaction of a listener or the lack of response, the pace of the action, the cadence of the sounds, the way in which characters interact—all constitute an eloquent vocabulary of a universal language, even though the signals may be ephemeral and ambiguous, vanishing at the moment of creation.

Experienced playwrights are aware of these multifaceted forces, and they create their actions to make optimum use of them. Here, in the opening scene of Arthur Miller's *Death of a Salesman*, you see a dramatist making full use of theatrical materials:

(A melody is heard, played upon a flute. It is small and fine, telling of grass and trees and the horizon. The curtain rises.

Before us is the Salesman's house. We are aware of towering angular shapes behind it, surrounding it on all sides. Only the blue light of the sky falls upon the house and forestage; the surrounding area shows an angry glow of orange. As more light appears, we see a solid vault of apartment houses around the small, fragile-seeming home. An air of the dream clings to the place, a dream rising out of reality.

From the right, Willy Loman, the Salesman, enters, carrying two large sample cases. The flute plays on. He hears but is not aware of it. He is past sixty years of age, dressed quietly. Even as he crosses the stage to the doorway of the

An exhausted Willy Loman comes home to his wife, Linda, from an unsuccessful trip in *Death of a Salesman.*

(University of Missouri. Directed by James Hooks.)

house, his exhaustion is apparent. He unlocks the door, comes into the kitchen, and thankfully lets his burden down, feeling the soreness of his palms. A word-sigh escapes his lips—it might be "Oh boy, oh boy." He closes the door, then carries his cases out into the living-room, through the draped kitchen doorway. Linda, his wife, has stirred in her bed at the right. She gets out and puts on a robe, listening.)

Linda: *(Hearing Willy outside the bedroom, calls with some trepidation)* Willy!
Willy: It's all right. I came back.
Linda: Why? What happened? *(Slight pause)* Did something happen, Willy?
Willy: No, nothing happened.
Linda: You didn't smash the car, did you?
Willy: *(With casual irritation)* I said nothing happened. Didn't you hear me?
Linda: Don't you feel well?
Willy: I'm tired to death. *(The flute has faded away. He sits on the bed beside her, a little numb.)* I couldn't make it. I just couldn't make it, Linda![1]

This brief excerpt shows how Miller combines dramatic action with dialogue to create a specific effect. In just eight lines, the playwright raises the question about his protagonist: What is wrong with Willy? It takes the entire evening to answer this question and to reveal the *subtext* through words and actions.

Constantin Stanislavski, one of the most influential directors and actors of the modern theater, defined subtext this way:

> The subtext is a web of innumerable, varied, inner patterns inside a play and a part, woven from "magic ifs," given circumstances, all sorts of figments of imagination, inner movements, objects of attention, smaller and greater truths and a belief in them, adaptations, adjustments, and other similar elements.[2]

Stanislavski goes on to say, "The whole text of the play will be accompanied by a subtextual stream of images, like a moving picture, constantly thrown on the screen of our inner vision, to guide us as we speak and act on the stage."

In a recent Moscow production, director Yuri Lyubimov wanted to show in dramatic action the subtext of the scene in Anton Chekhov's *Three Sisters* in which one of the frustrated daughters, Masha, meets the attractive army officer, Vershinin, for the first time. Masha is half-heartedly reading a book. She shows her boredom by drumming on the table with her fingers and jiggling her leg. Vershinin enters, stops, and sees Masha, who is now motionless. Their eyes meet, and the room begins to revolve. The subtext has been revealed by concrete actions, just as Willy shows his exhaustion and despair when he enters, carrying his two heavy sample cases: He sets them down, rubs his hands and murmurs, "Boy, oh boy."

During your interview for a job, you and the boss were looking at one another for overt signs that would tell you whether or not your relationship would be compatible.

When you read or see plays and films, you will be looking for meaning behind the façade of words and actions, searching for the subtext. It has been said that it is the job of the playwright to put the spectator to work. You are called on to respond to a network of words and actions created to produce specific effects—and the ability to respond is one of the pleasures of theatergoing.

DRAMATIC ACTION

In its simplest form, *action* refers to the physical movement of the play: the entrances and exits; the stage business of the characters; the larger movements of the ensemble; the quarrels, love scenes, reunions, and partings—all the overt action essential for the plot. Like every other element of the play, the dramatist includes this kind of action because it is significant and pertinent.

The playwright may use a strong action to set the plot in motion. Charles Fuller began his Pulitzer Prize-winning play, *A Soldier's Play*, with a violent action, which becomes the focus of attention for all that follows.

The scene is at Fort Neal, Louisiana, in 1944.

(*As the play opens, the stage is black. In the background, rising in volume, we hear the song "Don't Sit Under the Apple Tree," sung by the Andrews Sisters. Quite suddenly, in a sharp though narrow beam of light, in limbo, Tech/Sergeant Vernon C. Waters, a well-built, light-brown-skinned man in a World War II winter army uniform, is seen down on all fours. He is stinking drunk, trying to stand and mumbling to himself.*)

Waters: (*Repeating*) They'll still hate you! They still hate you. . . . They still hate you!

(*Waters is laughing as suddenly someone steps into the light. We never see this person. He is holding a .45 caliber pistol. He lifts it swiftly and ominously toward Water's head and fires. Waters is knocked over backward. He is dead. The music has stopped and there is a strong silence onstage.*)

Voice: Let's go!

(*The man with the gun takes a step, then stops. He points the gun at Waters again and fires a second time. There is another silence as limbo is plunged into darkness, and the barracks is just as quickly lit.*)[3]

From this initial action, the play is developed as an investigation of the murder, which turns out to have more to do with the character of the victim than with finding the guilty party. *A Soldier's Play* is more than a whodunit; Fuller has written a biting exploration of racial tensions among blacks and between blacks and whites.

Action is often used to indicate character. Eugene O'Neill establishes the character of the leading role in *Anna Christie* clearly and economically with her first entrance. The setting is a waterfront saloon:

> (*There is a ring of the family entrance bell. Larry [the bartender] comes to the door and opens it a trifle—then, with a puzzled expression, pulls it wide. Anna Christopherson enters. She is a tall, blond, fully developed girl of twenty, handsome after a large, Viking-daughter fashion, but now run down in health and plainly showing all the outward evidences of belonging to the world's oldest profession. Her youthful face is already hard and cynical beneath its layers of makeup. Her clothes are the tawdry finery of peasant stock turned prostitute. She comes and sinks wearily in a chair by the table, left front.*)

Anna: Gimme a whiskey—ginger ale on the side. (*Then, as Larry turns to go, forcing a winning smile at him*) And don't be stingy, baby.[4]

Although Bertolt Brecht, the remarkable creator of the "epic theater," denied any interest in evoking an emotional response, many of the actions in his plays, which reveal the nature of his characters, also arouse feeling.

In *The Caucasian Chalk Circle*, Grusha, a kitchen maid, rescues the governor's abandoned child during a rebellion, after the governor has been slain and his head impaled on a lance before the palace gates. Everyone leaves except Grusha and the child. She tries to tear herself away.

The Story Teller:

> (*She walks a few steps toward the child and bends over it.*)

>   . . . she went back for one more look at the child.
> Only to sit with him for a moment or two,
> Only till someone should come,
> Its mother, perhaps, or anyone else.

> (*Leaning on a trunk, she sits facing the child.*)

>   Only till she would have to leave, for the
> danger was too great,
> The city was full of flame and crying.

Grusha, a servant girl in Brecht's
Caucasian Chalk Circle, cannot resist the
temptation of goodness and rescues the
Governor's abandoned child.

*(University of California, Santa Barbara.
Directed by the author.)*

(The light grows dimmer, as though evening and night were coming on.)

Terrible is the seductive power of goodness!

(Grusha now settles down to watch over the child through the night. . . .)

A long time she sat with the child
Till evening came, till night came, till dawn came.
Too long she sat, too long she saw
The soft breathing, the little fists,
Till toward morning the temptation grew too strong
And she rose, and bent down and, sighing, took the child
And carried it off.

(She does what The Story Teller says as he describes it.)[5]

Brecht shows his audience that even waiting is an action. Samuel Beckett, of course, built an entire play on waiting in his *Waiting for Godot.* He makes the point that the two lonely tramps are waiting because there is no place for them to go. The meaning comes from *inaction,* from the excruciatingly painful ordeal of two lost souls, with no resources of their own, trying to ignite a spark of faith in the empty darkness.

Since plays are brought to their completed form by directors, actors, and designers, playwrights are at the mercy of those who interpret their work, and although their text and directions may be faithfully followed, playwrights cannot possibly control the production of their plays, even if they direct them themselves. Actors bring the text to life, and their legitimate contribution to their performance is their way of speaking, moving, and reacting, as they (and the director) interpret the play. The actors enter, walk, sit, argue, make love, eat, drink, and exit—and all these movements reflect the performers' way of responding to the playwright's text. Indeed, the *manner* in which the actors perform is their creative contribution to the production—the legitimate and necessary extension of the playwright's script in theatrical terms. Thus, the physical action of the play is a combi-

Two views of Ekkeherd Schall in the Hitlerian role, when his speech inflames the crowd in Brecht's *The Resistable Rise of Arturo Ui* at the Berliner Ensemble.

nation of the dramatist's original creation and the enrichment of the actors' and director's interpretation.

Speech itself is a form of action. It can be a way of doing, of creating tension and momentum to move the play forward. Implicit in most dramatic dialogue is an underlying pattern of action as a character strives for a goal, seeks to influence the behavior of others, searches for the meaning of his or her experience, or becomes embroiled in a vigorous clash of wills. Good dramatic dialogue is action.

John Osborne's *Look Back in Anger* (1956) was a pivotal play in postwar British theater because of its scathing attack on class distinctions and social inertia in general. Jimmy Porter, the protagonist, was the first of the "angry young men" who brought about sweeping changes in playwriting, acting, and production. As the play opens, Jimmy and his friend Cliff are reading the Sunday paper, while Jimmy's wife, Alison, is ironing. Jimmy, who castigates everyone and everything, turns his attention to Alison in this verbal assault, which nearly has the effect of physical blows:

Alison: Really, Jimmy you're like a child.

Jimmy: Don't try and patronize me. (*Turning to Cliff*) She's so clumsy. I watch for her to do the same things every night. The way she jumps on the bed, as if she were stamping on someone's face, and draws the curtains back with a great clatter, in that casually destructive way of hers. It's like someone launching a battleship. Have you ever noticed how noisy women are? (*Crosses below chairs to L.C.*) Have you? The way they kick the floor about, simply walking over it? Or have you watched them sitting at their dressing tables, dropping their weapons and banging down their bits of boxes and brushes and lipsticks?

(*He faces her dressing table.*)

I've watched her doing it night after night. When you see a woman in front of her bedroom mirror, you realise what a refined sort of a butcher she is. (*Turns in*) Did you ever see some dirty old Arab, sticking his fingers into some mess of lamb fat and gristle? Well, she's just like that. Thank God they don't have many women surgeons! Those primitive hands would have your guts out in no time. Flip! Out it comes, like the powder out of its box. Flop! Back it goes, like the powder puff on the table.

Cliff: (*Grimacing cheerfully*) Ugh! Stop it!

Jimmy: (*Moving upstage*) She'd drop your guts like hair clips and fluff all over the floor. You've got to be fundamentally insensitive to be as noisy and as clumsy as that.[6]

Jimmy's dialogue reveals the deep, smoldering rage that animates him.

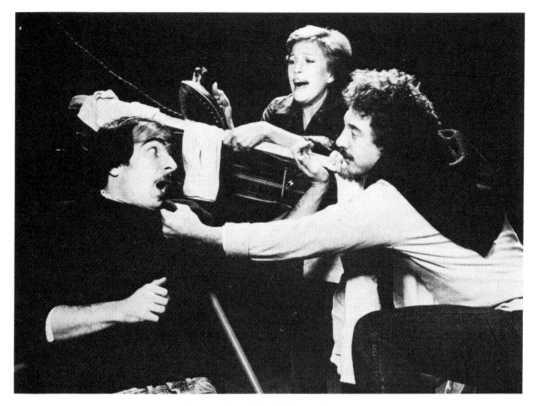

In Osborne's pivotal play, *Look Back in Anger,* a bit of friendly horseplay turns sour when Alison burns herself.

(Cleveland Play House.)

Among contemporary playwrights, Harold Pinter's dialogue is particularly distinctive because of the emotional freight it carries. His speeches, often clipped and hackneyed, possess a sinister ambiguity that conveys a strong sense of aggression. Beneath the surface of the spoken word are suggested layers of meaning, full of latent menace.

This is evident in Pinter's *The Collection,* first presented by the Royal Shakespeare Company in 1962. It is a suspenseful sort of psychological play, based on the relations between two couples, one heterosexual, the other homosexual. In the following excerpt, the dialogue carries the force of physical aggression. James suspects that his wife has had an affair with Bill and now confronts his rival.

(*James stands, goes to a fruit bowl, picks up fruit knife. He runs his finger along the blade.*)

James: This is fairly sharp.
Bill: What do you mean?

James: Come on.
Bill: I beg your pardon?
James: Come on. You've got that one. I've got this one.
Bill: What about it?
James: I get a bit tired of words sometimes, don't you? Let's have a game. For fun.
Bill: What sort of game?
James: Let's have a mock duel.
Bill: I don't want a mock duel, thank you.
James: Of course you do. Come on. First one who's touched is a sissy.
Bill: This is all rather unsubtle, don't you think?
James: Not in the least. Come on, into first position.
Bill: I thought we were friends.
James: Of course we're friends. What on earth's the matter with you? I'm not going to kill you. It's just a game, that's all. We're playing a game. You're not windy, are you?
Bill: I think it's silly.
James: I say, you're a bit of a spoilsport, aren't you?
Bill: I'm putting my knife down anyway.
James: Well, I'll pick it up.

(*James does so and faces him with two knives.*)

Bill: Now you've got two.
James: I've got another one in my hip pocket.

(*Pause*)

Bill: What do you do, swallow them?
James: Do you?

(*Pause. They stare at each other. Suddenly*)

Go on! Swallow it!

(*James throws the knife at Bill's face. Bill throws up hand to protect his face and catches knife by blade. It cuts his hand.*)

Bill: Ow!
James: Well caught! What's the matter?[7]

This excerpt is a good illustration of Pinter's ability to externalize the subtext. Underneath the spare dialogue, one senses the menace, almost as if one were watching a physical combat. James, despite the tight rein he

While Wesley cleans up the debris from his father's drunken spree, he recalls his boyhood memories of similar escapades.

(Yale University Repertory Theater.)

keeps on his inner rage, lets off enough steam so that we sense his turbulence.

Among contemporary American playwrights, Sam Shepard is known for his graphic monologues, which are patchworks of striking images fashioned from everyday material.

The setting of *Curse of the Starving Class* is on a deteriorating farm, which an indolent family is in danger of losing to confidence tricksters. It is early morning, and Wesley is cleaning up the ruins of a door that his drunken father kicked in the night before. Wesley recalls the action:

Wesley: (*As he throws wood into wheelbarrow*) I was lying there on my back. I could smell the avocado blossoms. I could hear the coyotes. I could hear stock cars squealing down the street. . . . I could feel the space around me like a big, black world. I listened like an animal. My listening was afraid. Afraid of sound. Tense. Like any second something could invade me. Some foreigner. Something undescribable. Then I heard the Packard coming up the hill. From a mile off I could tell it was the Packard by the sound of the valves. The lifters have a sound like nothing else. Then I could picture my Dad driving it. Shifting unconsciously. Downshifting into second for the last pull up the hill. I could feel the headlights closing in. Cutting through the orchard. I could see the trees being lit one after the other by the lights, then going back to black. My heart was pounding. Just from my Dad coming back. Then I heard him pull the brake. Lights go off. Key's turned off. Then a long silence. Him just sitting in the car. Just sitting. I picture him just sitting. What's he doing? He's plastered and can't move. He's plastered and doesn't want to move. He's going to sleep there all night. He's slept there before. He's woken up with dew on the hood before. Freezing headache. Teeth covered with peanuts. Then I hear the door of the Packard open. A pop of metal. Dogs barking down the road. Door slams. Feet. Paper bag being tucked under one arm. Paper bag covering "Tiger Rose." Feet coming. Feet walking toward the door. Feet stopping. Heart pounding. Sound of door not opening. Foot kicking door. Man's voice. Dad's voice. Dad calling Mom. No answer. Foot kicking. Foot kicking harder. Wood splitting. Man's voice. In the night. Foot kicking hard through door. One foot right through door. Bottle crashing. Glass breaking. Fist through door.[8]

The total play may be regarded as an action, or perhaps a "system of actions," to use Aristotle's term—an organic whole with nothing missing or irrelevant, a cohesive beginning, middle, and end. Until recent years, such unity was considered essential for structuring a play. And although an orderly progression of incidents no longer describes the form of many current plays, the need for action, for a dynamic quality to the shaping of material, is still fundamental to playwriting.

Playwrights create organized patterns of words and movement. Although initially they set down the play in written terms, what they actually produce is a barrage of sensory stimuli—concrete, objective signals that can come to life in the theater. The audience can only respond to what it sees and hears in performance. And what it sees and hears are actions.

Consider Hamlet's problem of revealing Claudius' guilt. The inner psychic condition of the King must be conveyed by outward signs. The evidence of his guilt must be triggered by some kind of stimulus that will cause him to respond in an overt fashion. The dramatist's solution was to confront Claudius with a mimetic reenactment of the murder. His guilt is shown in specific, tangible signs. When he witnesses the poisoning, Claudius blanches, rises from his throne, calls out "Give me some light; away!" and storms out of the room.

The spectator watching the play within the play, Act III, Scene 2, is confronted with a very complex set of signals. The traveling players must have a place in the foreground, where their actions can be seen by the audience and the court, but the central focus is on Claudius and the effect on him of the simulated poisoning. So the King will probably be in an elevated position, facing the audience. Near him are the Queen and Polonius, who are deeply concerned about the strange behavior of Hamlet. He must be positioned in a prominent place at the side, so he can see the King and in turn be seen by the audience. At the precise moment of discovery, set off by the mock act of poisoning, the spectators see this action and the consequences simultaneously. They see the guilty start of the distraught Claudius and Hamlet's response to the King's reaction. They are also aware of the players' shock at the sudden disruption of their performance, of Queen Gertrude's anxiety over her husband's condition, of Polonius' fear for the King, of Ophelia's astonishment at the King's action and Hamlet's behavior, and of Horatio's reaction as he, too, sees the evidence of Claudius' guilt. These actions of the performers are enhanced by other theatrical stimuli—the scenery, costumes, lighting; the use of tempo, rhythm, sound, and space.

Most plays are not as complex or layered as *Hamlet*, but all drama is created in the form of action, and its full effect is not realized until it is presented as it was intended—in the theater before an audience.

APPEAL OF THE THEATER

Why do people go to the theater?

Why did the citizens of ancient Athens arise in the cold hours of dawn, scale the steep slope of the Acropolis, and sit on the hard seats of the Theater of Dionysus while they watched a trilogy such as Aeschylus' *Oresteia*—three plays of unrelieved suffering and seriousness? Why did a London chimney sweep of Elizabethan times make his way across the Thames to the Globe Theater to stand for hours in the pit to see a play like *Hamlet*—a work so perplexing in language and content that literary scholars still argue about its meaning? Why did our forefathers find the lure of theatrical performance so appealing that they journeyed for several days to see second-rate actors in a makeshift showboat production of *The Rivals*? Why do people today, after a hectic day's work in the office, submit themselves to the ordeal of fighting their way through snarled traffic, rushing through dinner, and paying for expensive seats in a dark cavern so they can see the latest Broadway hit? What is the secret of theatrical appeal so compelling that we find it necessary to install electronic boxes in nearly every living room so that we can huddle in the dark, night after night, giving ourselves to make-believe characters going through make-believe actions?

The sources of the theater's appeal are many, and no doubt the theatrical experience is often a blend of several. Let us suggest four.

First, the theater offers an effective means of telling a story. People have always delighted in hearing tales of adventure and excitement. From

The story appeal of Dickens' *The Life and Adventures of Nicholas Nickelby* was captured in this Royal Shakespeare Company production that involved 42 performers and played for eight and a half hours to audiences that paid $100 per ticket.

very primitive times, storytellers have entertained their companions around the fire with vivid accounts of heroes' exploits and warriors' triumphs over adversity. Likewise, in the theater, we enjoy a stirring contest between two well-matched opponents. We become involved vicariously with the participants, and we are concerned about the outcome. We are moved by the give and take of the struggle, the excitement of the chase, the discovery, the denouement.

Most plays rely heavily on story appeal, particularly film and television fare, which is calculated to attract the widest possible audience. Hence, most drama is journalistic and, like a newspaper, intended for immediate popular consumption. But this does not mean that great dramatists have been unconcerned about shaping a compelling narrative; one of the distinguishing marks of a fine play is that it provides satisfactions on many levels—one of which may be narrative.

Second, the audience finds pleasure in the skill of execution. Sports enthusiasts at the Olympic games may marvel at a pole-vaulter as he swings his body up and over the bar more than nineteen feet above the ground. Or they may enjoy the incredible balance and timing of a gymnast working on the parallel bars, or the precision of a diver as she lofts her body into the air, executes a complicated figure, and enters the water with scarcely a splash.

Skill of execution is one of the appeals of musical comedy, such as in Andrew Lloyd Webber's *Cats*, which featured exciting dancing, singing, and spectacular effects. Here, Old Deuteronomy is borne aloft on a giant tire.
(Directed by Trevor Nunn. Scenography by John Napier.)

In the arts, one derives pleasure from the mastery of materials—the painter's brushwork, the sculptor's ability to shape stone and metal, the musician's control of a voice or instrument, the dancer's use of space. We enjoy the repetition of familiar music, at least in part, because of the skills of those who play it. Certainly, one of the chief attractions of musical comedy comes from the excellence of the dancing and singing. In more serious drama, the connoisseur enjoys comparing performances of outstanding actors and actresses, such as Laurence Olivier, George C. Scott, Maggie Smith, Jason Robards, Jessica Tandy, Dustin Hoffman, and Colleen Dewhurst. In Japan, for example, the spectator of the Kabuki theater may compare an actor's performance in a role with that of his father or grandfather, as each generation follows precisely the footsteps of the one before. As a knowledgeable spectator, you learn to note the effectiveness of the ensemble acting, the director's adroit use of pace and rhythm, the actor's ability to react as well as to speak, the appropriateness of the setting in providing a suitable environment, the expressive use of movement and business, the emotional content implied by the groupings of characters, and the dramatist's use of symbols and metaphors to communicate ideas and feelings. The enjoyment informed spectators feel at a performance of a great play stems in part from their recognition of the skills of the cast and production staff in translating into theatrical terms the essential values of the play.

A third satisfaction of the theater is the opportunity it affords us for gaining fresh perceptions. Aristotle suggested that humankind's greatest pleasure is in learning. The theater is an excellent way to extend ourselves beyond the narrow circle of everyday existence. We become acquainted with people and cultures quite foreign to us. Oedipus, on stage, is no murky, legendary king but a man of flesh and blood, torn asunder by his guilt and suffering. *Equus* gives us insight into the life and motivations of a boy whose psyche has been disturbed by his fixations on horses, as do the distorted personalities of Tennessee Williams' Blanche du Bois, Henrik Ibsen's Hedda Gabler, and August Strindberg's Miss Julie. We spend an hour or two becoming acquainted with characters we would probably not meet in real life—kings and beggars, geniuses and outcasts, leprechauns and ghosts. We even meet quite a representation from the animal kingdom—horses, lizards, rhinoceroses, wasps, birds, insects, flies, frogs, and roosters. The theater offers extraordinary opportunities for insightful experiences.

Fourth, the dramatic experience can also be a spiritual one. As Aristotle suggested, comedy may show us to be worse than we are, but tragedy shows us to be better. It is serious, elevated in scale, and of a certain magnitude. At its best, tragedy evokes a catharsis—a purging away, a cleansing of the ignoble, the mean, the base. Great works of drama depict great characters exploring the great issues of life. In them humans are tested to the utmost, and although their bodies may be broken, their spirit triumphs. Through suffering, they transcend their physical limitations and affirm the dignity of humankind and its resilient spirit. Greek tragedy was a declaration of faith; it exalted humankind. "Wonders are many, and none is more wonderful than man," sang Sophocles. The trials and sufferings of Antigone, Oedipus, and Prometheus were positive statements about the Greek view of life and of a human's potential grandeur. Our loftiest ideas and aspirations have been the significant content of drama, and spiritual stimulation one of its enduring achievements. Comic writers like Molière and George Bernard Shaw have attacked and exposed hypocrisy and chicanery. Likewise, those concerned with humans as a social animal, writers like Ibsen, Miller, and David Rabe, have stripped away the façade of social pretense and have forced us to see reality. The theater has often been a salutary social weapon for dealing with the truth.

In addition to these venerable appeals, the new theater has given many of us fresh insights into ways of responding to extraordinary stimuli. We have been exposed to audacious use of language and astonishing images, sometimes shocking, sometimes painful, sometimes fabulous. We have been battered by sounds, temporarily blinded by lights, and startled by the assaults on our nervous system. Although on occasion we may be bewildered by the symbols, actions, and images that come at us in spurts and spasms and that we cannot readily identify with or relate to, we enjoy expanding our awareness, stretching our minds and emotional capacities, and sharing in the excitement of exploring new territory.

THEATRICAL CONVENTIONS

Theatrical production, like all forms of art, is conventionalized. That is, there are certain common agreements between spectator and theater worker concerning the manner of creation and production—certain "ground rules" that determine how the game is to be played. In easel painting, there is the convention that colored pigments are applied to a flat surface within a regular framework. Music is a conventionalized combination of sounds and rhythms, which make almost no pretense of imitating nature. Spectators, as they enter the theater, become a partner to conventions governing time, space, and the manner of playing.

The conventions of realistic production that dominated the theater during the latter part of the nineteenth century, and for much of the twentieth, attempted to foster the illusion of actuality through lifelike representation of characters and setting. There was tacit agreement that performer and spectator would remain separate from one another. The separation was facilitated by the darkened auditorium and the lighted stage and by the architectural features of the raised stage, which could be closed off by a curtain and the proscenium arch. There was also a psychological barrier known as the "fourth wall," a convention in which the actors pretended that the audience did not exist and avoided direct communication across the footlights. Dramatic structure was usually linear and tied to a story line. Scenery was designed to give the illusion of a genuine environment, with practical doors and windows and properties and furniture that seemed a part of real life. Actually, there was a good deal of license in the arrangement of furniture and exits and entrances so that the setting would "open out" to the audience and the actors could be readily heard and seen.

Artistic conventions are susceptible to change. Just as we had remarkable innovations in painting and music in the twentieth century, we have had rebellion in theatrical conventions. Many theater workers have rejected the limitations of the proscenium arch and are finding ways, such as the thrust or arena stages, to bring the spectator and the performer into a closer relationship. More recently, performances are given in "found spaces," such as warehouses, garages, store buildings, and street corners, abandoning conventional theaters altogether. Scenery has become frankly theatrical instead of illusionistic. As an example of this tendency, a fragment of a wall or a skeletal framework picked out of the darkness by light serves as a setting, which a generation ago would have required a complete interior with

Gospel at Colonus, performed at the American Music Theater Festival, was an updated version of *Oedipus at Colonus* (see page 1). The blinded hero is now a musician and the chorus a gospel singing choir.

three walls, ceiling, and a room full of furniture. Playwrights have rejected the conventions of realism in an effort to gain more freedom. Acting is often quite stylized; the separation between spectator and performer has broken down. Indeed, in some instances, the theater worker actively seeks to involve the audience in the action. Modern theatergoers are no longer sure how much of the performance will be onstage or in their lap. Nor does the play necessarily have a well-defined plot or even clear language and sharp delineation of character.

Fashions in theatrical conventions have differed from time to time, and to understand the drama of any period, it is essential to know the conventions that influenced the production. In the Greek theater, for example, only three speaking characters appeared at one time; there was little or no violence onstage; actors wore masks, special footgear and headpieces; the plays were written in verse, dramatizing ancient legends and myths; and they were presented usually in a single permanent setting, with a simple story that occurred in a short space of time.

In the Elizabethan theater, like the Greek, all roles were played by male actors in an outdoor theater in the daytime, with little or no illusionistic scenery. The plays written in verse were quite different in form and content from Greek drama. The play usually was a complicated one, involving several plot lines; comedy matter was mixed with serious, highborn characters with low; and the playwright ransacked history and literature for material that would tell an exciting story. The plays were performed by professional actors in theaters whose dimensions and arrangement placed the actor in close proximity to the spectator and allowed the subtleties of the language to be exploited. The convention of the large unlocalized platform gave the dramatist a great deal of freedom in staging an animated and complicated narrative.

In each age, theater conventions have varied according to the influences of the playwrights, actors, audience, and physical theaters, and in turn, the conventions have affected all elements of the drama. It is essential to recognize these conventions in evaluating any drama because of their pressure in shaping the play and its production.

YOU AND THE PLAY

It is unfortunate that initial contact with the theater is made through the printed page. Understanding a play by reading it is like trying to make a journey by looking at a map, or like visualizing a ball game from the box score or looking at a stuffed animal instead of going to the zoo or on a safari. Playwriting is not the art of putting words together; it is one of inventing sequences of images, actions, and dialogue to project the play that the writer has in his or her head.

If your acquaintance with the theater is through film, you should be aware that motion pictures are primarily a visual medium that emphasizes action. At times, it can be a great art form, when talented people make use of the film's unique facility for cutting from one image to another and exploiting the juxtaposition and interrelationship of dramatic actions of infinite variety.

Television, relying mostly on tape, has the advantage of coming into your living quarters at little cost. It has the intimacy and most of the values of motion pictures, except for the small screen; however, too often it suffers from the pressure of packaged, formula material diluted to suit what the sponsors think the public wants.

For many of us, genuine theater exists only with living actors before an audience. It is their presence that illuminates the text and sets up a circular response so that performer and spectator come together in sharing a theatrical experience.

Responding to a play is an active process, a fascinating exploration. You are invited to participate with such sensitivity and imagination as you possess. You will need to respond and make judgments from a welter of words, signals, and actions that are constantly in flux; and you must keep track of the action, as the eye follows a moving object. You are called on to respond to your fellow human beings—to their follies, problems, and aspirations—when they are caught up in the most telling moments of their lives. As you see and hear the action onstage, you are challenged to search out the meanings behind the characters' actions and words. Theatergoing is an opportunity to come to terms with life.

PLAYS TO READ AND SEE

F = Film available; V = Videotape available.

F		O'Neill, *Anna Christie* (Garbo)
		Pinter, *The Collection*
F	V	Miller, *Death of a Salesman*
F	V	Shakespeare, *Hamlet* (Olivier/Williamson)
F	V	Osborne, *Look Back in Anger*
F	V	Fuller, *A Soldier's Play* (*Story*)

BIBLIOGRAPHY

FERGUSSON, FRANCIS. *The Idea of a Theater.* Princeton, N.J.: Princeton University Press, 1949.

GASSNER, JOHN, and RALPH G. ALLEN. *Theater and Drama in the Making*, 2 vols. Boston: Houghton Mifflin Company, 1964.

MATTHEWS, BRANDER. *The Principles of Playmaking.* Freeport, N.Y.: Books for Libraries Press, 1970.

NAGLER, ALOIS M. *Source Book in Theatrical History.* New York: Dover Publications, Inc., 1952.

NICOLL, ALLARDYCE. *The Development of the Theater.* New York: Harcourt Brace Jovanovich, Inc., 1966.

ROWE, KENNETH THORPE. *The Theater in Your Head.* New York: Funk & Wagnalls, Inc., 1960.

STYAN, J. L. *The Dramatic Experience.* Cambridge, Eng.: Cambridge University Press, 1965.

WILLIAMS, RAYMOND. *Drama in Performance.* London: F. Muller, 1954.

NOTES

1. Arthur Miller, *Death of a Salesman* (New York: The Viking Press, 1949).

2. Constantin Stanislavski, *Building a Character,* trans. E. R. Hapgood (New York: Theater Arts, Inc., 1949).

3. Charles Fuller, *A Soldier's Play* (New York: Hill & Wang, 1981). (The film version is entitled *The Soldier's Story.*)

4. Eugene O'Neill, *Anna Christie* (New York: Random House, Inc., 1922).

5. Bertolt Brecht, *The Caucasian Chalk Circle,* trans. Eric Bentley and Maja Apelman (New York: Grove Press, Inc., 1947).

6. John Osborne, *Look Back in Anger* (Chicago: The Dramatic Publishing Company, 1959).

7. Harold Pinter, *The Collection* in *Three Plays by Harold Pinter* (New York: Grove Press, Inc., 1962).

8. Sam Shepard, *Curse of the Starving Class,* in *Seven Plays* (New York: Bantam Books, Inc., 1981).

2

The Play and Its Parts

When playwrights create plays, they must visualize them in action in the theater before an audience. As they work with the relevant dialogue and movement, they are somewhat like trial lawyers who present evidence, witnesses, and exhibits to persuade the jury of the validity of their case. Playwrights are not involved so much with the factual aspects of a past action; they are, rather, creating the effect of an ongoing experience that is occurring before the eyes of the spectators, but they, too, present concrete evidence of human experience in words and actions.

Since most theater begins with the text, let us look first at the play and its parts.

Aristotle, in the fourth century B.C., was the first to write on the theory of dramatic criticism. Although he lived a century after the golden age of Greek drama and some of his views may seem arbitrary, his *Poetics* is the fountainhead of dramatic criticism and one cannot discuss dramatic theory very long without referring to him. We will use some of his ideas and terminology to discuss the elements of drama.

His analysis of tragedy listed these six parts in order of importance:

1. Plot
2. Character
3. Thought
4. Diction
5. Music
6. Spectacle

We will follow this hierarchy as a framework for discussion, bearing in mind that Aristotle's terms have special meanings and that they are subject to endless controversy.

PLOT

Plot is the structural element of the play that gives the action its form. Plot is to the playwright what composition is to the painter and the musician. Although most plays tell stories, the plot is not the narrative itself, but the *shape of the story*. The plot is made up of a series of incidents selected and arranged to produce a response.

Over the years critics have attempted to formulate a pattern for drama. A widely known theory by the French critic Ferdinand Brunetiére was that the essence of drama is conflict. What we require in the theater, said Brunetiére, "is the spectacle of a will striving toward a goal." Audiences in the theater, like fans in a stadium, gather to see a contest—a conflict. It may be a conflict between two men striving for fame or for the same woman; it may be a conflict between an individual and society; or it may be a struggle between conflicting motivations in the same character. In Ibsen's *A Doll's House,* several kinds of conflicts are going on at once. Nora is opposed to Krogstad; she is also in conflict with her genuine and assumed nature, with her husband, and also with her ideals and those of conventional society. *Hamlet* offers a welter of conflicts: Hamlet versus the King, his mother, Ophelia, Laertes, Polonius, and the pirates, and his inner conflicts as he is torn between self-doubt and his sworn obligation to his father. Comedy, as well as serious drama, depends on a network of conflicts, often involving a love triangle.

It is true that the conflict theory does not fit all plays—sometimes the dramatist is more interested in creating a mood or revealing character, or simply in defining a social situation—but in general most of the plays that have endured make use of plots rooted in conflict. In *Amadeus,* Salieri's ambition to achieve fame conflicts with the brilliance of Mozart; in *'Night Mother,* Mama tries desparately to keep her daughter Jessie from committing suicide; Tootsie, an obnoxious, unemployed actor, is rejected until he disguises himself and auditions for a female role.

The classic view of dramatic structure, as expressed by Aristotle and followed by many playwrights and critics ever since, was a unified plot of organically related elements in which there was "a beginning, a middle, and an end," following "a necessary and probable" order with no extraneous material.

In practice, Greek tragedy of the fifth century B.C. was simple in structure, consisting of a few episodes involving a small number of characters and usually occurring in a single place over a short period of time.

On the other hand, medieval dramas, built around biblical stories or the lives of saints, used complex plots because the playwrights wished to put all the significant action before the spectators. Thus, there were dozens of incidents, scores of characters, and a great variety of locales. This kind of drama was unified by its theme, or in the case of the Passion Play, by the central figure of Christ. Episodic plotting also characterizes the Kabuki plays of Japan, the traditional dramas of India and China, and the modern parables of Brecht and many other recent innovators.

Shakespeare and his contemporaries and eighteenth-century romanticists were influenced by the loose structure of the medieval plays, but their plots centered on major characters.

The neoclassicists of France endeavored to follow their version of the simple, unified structure of the Greeks, but only Jean Racine was successful in working with this format. Writers of melodramas in the nineteenth century aimed at involving their audiences in exciting action, so the plays were highly contrived sequences of sensational scenes. With the coming of naturalism and realism, the general trend was toward a compact structure in which all the parts fit together as a "well-made play," with skillful exposition, logical progression, and a strong conflict leading to a powerful climax. Ibsen perfected this structural pattern in his plays, showing characters caught and rebelling against the conventions and strictures of nineteenth-century society.

Our current dramatists are no longer bound by rigid patterns but use all manner of plot-making techniques, although a play with a strong story line is still popular at the box office.

Another way of looking at plot is to examine its technical machinery, which provides a method of analyzing the content. The basic aspects of plot are

1. Exposition
2. Discovery
3. Reversal
4. Point of attack
5. Foreshadowing
6. Complication
7. Climax
8. Crisis
9. Denouement

Exposition

As the curtain opens, the dramatist faces the problem of capturing the audience's attention and providing the necessary background so that they can follow the subsequent action. The playwright must present the characters in such a way that the audience becomes concerned with what happens to them—vicariously sharing their suffering, trials, and triumphs. The function of *exposition* is to acquaint the spectator with the characters—their relationships, background, and present situation. Expository devices vary with theatrical conventions.

Very often in classical and oriental drama characters present exposition directly to the audience. In *Our Town* (1938) Thornton Wilder startled theatergoers by opening his play with no curtain and no scenery. The Stage Manager appears and sets two tables and several chairs downstage. He leans against the proscenium pillar and says,

Stage Manager: This play is called "Our Town." It was written by Thornton Wilder. . . . The name of the town is Grover's Corners, New Hampshire—just across the Massachusetts line: longitude 42 degrees 40 minutes; latitude 70 degrees 37 minutes. The First Act shows a day in our town. The day is May 7, 1901. The time is just before dawn. (*A rooster crows.*)[1]

The Stage Manager continues to comment throughout the play and assumes several roles.

This use of direct address to the audience is now very common. It not

Talley's Folly is a romantic story dramatizing Talley's engaging suit to win his bride. The plot begins with a lengthy monologue in which Talley provides the necessary exposition and creates the light atmosphere for the action.

(University of Kentucky.)

only has the advantage of telling the audience immediately what they need to know but also enables the playwright to establish some sense of character. Lanford Wilson begins *Talley's Folly* with an effective monologue:

> ***Matt:*** *(Enters in front of the stage. Matt Friedman is forty-two, dark, and rather large. Warm and unhurried, he has a definite talent for mimicry. In his voice there is still a trace of a German-Jewish accent, of which he is probably unaware. He speaks to the audience.)* They tell me that we have ninety-seven minutes here tonight—without intermission. So if that means anything to anybody; if you think you'll need a drink of water or anything. . . .
>
> You know, a year ago I drove Sally home from a dance; and while we were standing on the porch up at the house, we looked down to the river and saw this silver flying thing rise straight up and zip off. We came running down to the river, we thought the Japanese had landed some amazing new flying machine, but all we found was the boathouse here, and—uh, that was enough.[2]

A standard expository device is a "feather duster" scene in which two minor characters bounce information off of one another in preparation for the appearance of the important figures. Other means are the use of choruses, confidants, prologues, monologues, and visual aids, such as slides, films, and charts. The stage setting is, of course, a very important means of presenting environmental material. The most accomplished dramatists weave the exposition into the fabric of the play, often using the major characters, as in Willy Loman's first entrance.

Discovery

Throughout the play, the dramatist reveals a constant flow of information about the characters, their feelings, motivations, and relationships. In the first chapter we saw how the medieval trope *Quem Quaeritis* was built around the significant discovery of the empty tomb; and in Hamlet's play within a play, "The Mousetrap," the discovery of Claudius' guilt is a major turning point in the action. As a matter of fact, *Hamlet* is built around a series of discoveries: the ghost's revelation of the murder, the madness and death of Ophelia, the plot to slay Hamlet, the poisoned sword and drink. Many comedies are built around mistakes, pretenses, and misunderstandings, so that the element of discovery is fundamental to the unraveling of the plot. One of the most notable discovery scenes occurs in Molière's *Tartuffe*, in which the title character masquerades as a priest and worms his way into Orgon's household, scheming to steal not only his fortune but also his wife, Elmire. She unmasks the imposter by getting her husband to hide under a table while she pretends to respond to Tartuffe's advances.

Discovery scenes may be those of recognition; for example, in Aeschylus' *Libation Bearers*, Electra recognizes her brother, Orestes, by a lock of his hair and by their matching footprints. In Sophocles' *Electra*, Orestes is recognized by his father's signet ring; and in the Euripidean version, a tutor recognizes Orestes by a scar. Comedy often has recognition scenes between long-lost relatives and lovers based on signs and tokens such as rings, lockets, and distinguishing scars. In the zany production of *The Comedy of Errors* by the Flying Kharamazov Brothers, the separated twins finally recognize each other because they both have moles (*live moles!*) on their shoulders.

The use of discoveries is also very important in murder mysteries, in which playwrights contrive a tangle of clues to keep the audience from discovering the identity of the culprits until the end of the play.

Discovery in serious drama may often involve self-discovery, when the characters in the moment of truth come to know themselves, as in *Oedipus Rex, King Lear, Macbeth, Hamlet, Othello, Ghosts,* and *The Crucible.*

One of the outstanding examples of a discovery scene in recent dramatic literature occurs in *Amadeus* when Salieri first meets Mozart at the Emperor's palace. Salieri has composed a "March of Welcome," which he plays as Mozart enters. It is banal and vague. A few moments later, when they are about to part, this exchange takes place:

In Euripides' *Bacchae*, Agave recognizes her son's head after she has participated in a ritual ecstasy in which he was killed.

(Greek National Theater)

Mozart: You're a good fellow, Salieri! And that's a jolly little thing you wrote for me.

Salieri: It was my pleasure.

Mozart: Let's see if I can remember it. May I?

Salieri: By all means. It's yours.

Mozart: *Grazie, Signore.*

(*Mozart tosses the manuscript onto the lid of the fortepiano, where he cannot see it, sits at the instrument, and plays Salieri's March of Welcome perfectly from memory—at first slowly, recalling it, but on the reprise of the tune, very much faster.*)

The rest is just the same, isn't it? (*He finishes it with insolent speed*)

Salieri: You have a remarkable memory.

Mozart: (*Delighted with himself*) Grazie ancora, Signore! (*He plays the opening seven bars again, but this time stops on the interval of the fourth, and sounds it again with displeasure.*) It doesn't really *work*, that fourth, does it? . . . Let's try the third above. . . . (*He does so—and smiles happily.*) Ah yes! . . . Good!

(*He repeats the new interval, leading up to it smartly with the well-known military-trumpet arpeggio which characterizes the celebrated March from* **The**

Marriage of Figaro, *"Non piu andrai."* Then, using the interval—tentatively, delicately, one note at a time, in the treble—he steals into the famous tune itself.

On and on he plays, improvising happily what is virtually the March we know now, laughing gleefully each time he comes to the amended interval of a third. Salieri watches him with an answering smile painted on his face.

Mozart's playing grows more and more exhibitionistic, revealing to the audience the formidable virtuoso he is. The whole time he himself remains totally oblivious of the offense he is giving. Finally, he finishes the march with a series of triumphant flourishes and chords. An ominous pause)

Salieri: *Scusate.* I must go.
Mozart: Really? (*Springing up and indicating the keyboard*) Why don't *you* try a variation?
Salieri: Thank you, but I must attend on the Emperor.
Mozart: Ah.
Salieri: It has been delightful to meet you.
Mozart: For me too! . . . And thanks for the march!

(*Mozart picks up the manuscript from the top of the fortepiano and marches happily offstage. A slight pause. Salieri moves toward the audience. The lights go down around him.*)

Salieri: (*To audience*) Was it then—so early—that I began to have thoughts of murder?[3]

Salieri has made a momentous discovery—he has a gifted rival. This discovery precipitates the action and leads Salieri to plan and execute Mozart's destruction.

Reversal

Many plays follow a pattern of *reversal,* in which the fortunes of the leading character turn from good to bad or vice versa. A protagonist apparently enjoying the fruits of power and prosperity plunges into disaster. In *Oedipus Rex*, the Shepherd expects to bring good news, but his message has the opposite effect, resulting in catastrophe. King Lear intends to divide his land equitably, but when his daughter Cordelia is unable or unwilling to compete with her sisters in flattering their father, the King in his anger initiates a chain of action that reverses his intention and leads to a series of calamities.

In comedy, turning the tables is one of the most common devices, often showing a humble person attaining status, such as a woodchopper becoming the King's physician in *The Doctor in Spite of Himself* or a clerk becoming the boss in *How to Succeed in Business Without Really Trying*. Shaw's

George Bernard Shaw's *Pygmalion* is constructed around a reversal as Professor Higgins transforms a cockney flower girl into a lady of quality by improving her speech and social graces. *My Fair Lady* was based on *Pygmalion*.

(Directed by Margaret Spear, Wayne State University.)

Pygmalion, which became the book for the musical *My Fair Lady*, tells the story of the conversion of a flower girl into a "lady of quality." Other familiar uses of comic reversal occur when young lovers, separated and thwarted by authority figures, overcome the opposition and unite to make a new society in which the pattern is repeated.

Point of Attack

In a linear plot, the playwright creates a chain of events that constitutes the main action. The *point of attack* refers to that moment when the mechanism is set in motion—the first pitch is thrown, the football is kicked off, the first blow is landed, the battle is joined. Disequilibrium is created, resulting in a change that continues until a new equilibrium is established, usually at the end of the play.

In *Romeo and Juliet*, the point of attack occurs in the very opening of the play, when the quarrelsome servants of the Capulets confront the servants of the Montagues and immediately become embroiled in a street brawl. This initial encounter not only reveals the bitter conflict between the two houses but also begins the turbulence that spreads from minor characters to engulf entire families in succeeding waves of violence and suffering.

The point of attack may occur with the arrival of a person whose presence disrupts the situation. Blanche comes to visit her sister and brother-in-

The point of attack occurs in Duerrenmatt's *The Visit* when Madame Zachanasian returns to her hometown to seek revenge against the man who betrayed her in her youth.

(Directed by the author; design by N. Vichodyl. University of California, Santa Barbara.)

law in New Orleans and threatens their marriage; Madam Zachanasian, once an outcast from her impoverished village but now a wealthy widow, returns to avenge her ill treatment at the hands of her former lover; Petruchio arrives in Padua and determines to tame the shrew Kate and make her his obedient wife.

Another way of triggering the point of attack occurs when a character makes an important commitment: Hamlet swears to avenge the murder of his father; Oedipus promises the citizens of Thebes to rid the kingdom of the plague; the psychiatrist, Dysart, accepts the case of a seventeen-year-old stableboy who has blinded six horses with a steel spike; Captain Davenport, a black lawyer, has been assigned the investigation of a murdered sergeant in a segregated camp; an obnoxious New York actor disguises himself as a woman and auditions for a female role.

The point of attack relates directly to theatrical conventions. In medieval drama, a flexible stage was needed to accommodate the desire for long and complex plots, such as those showing the life of Christ or the lives of the saints or presenting many episodes from Bible stories. Therefore, medieval drama frequently used an early point of attack. Elizabethan practice often followed the medieval one so that complex stories could include

In Peter Shaffer's *Equus,* the point of attack occurs when the psychiatrist Dysart
agrees to investigate a young boy's bizarre attachment for a horse.
(Portland State University. Directed by Jack Featheringill.)

a good deal of history, as in Shakespeare's *Henry IV,* Parts One and Two;
Richard II; Richard III; and *Julius Caesar.* In contrast, the Greek conventions
of the "unities of time, place, and action," and the limitation of no more than
three speaking characters at one time, required a late point of attack, with
the play beginning near the major climax and including only a few episodes
and a simple plot. French drama and the realistic plays of the late nineteenth
centuries tended to follow the classic pattern of a late point of attack and a
concise plot; however, the experimental dramas of expressionism, the epic
plays of Bertolt Brecht, and much of modern drama are no longer con-
strained to an organic structure or to limitations of time and space, and the
point of attack is not bound by conventions. For example, in *Amadeus* the
action takes place in November 1823 but includes flashbacks to the decade
1781–1791, and there are thirty-one scenes in the play.

Foreshadowing

Foreshadowing is the playwright's way to prepare for the action that is to follow. It serves several purposes. It makes the subsequent action credible, builds suspense and tension, and carries the momentum of the action forward. It may also reveal character, aid in the development of complications and climaxes, prepare for an entrance, and create atmosphere.

Within the first thirty lines of *Hamlet,* the guards speak of the "dreaded sight" that has appeared twice before—which foreshadows the ghost's entrance and provides the appropriate eerie atmosphere. In *Agamemnon,* the watchman, during the Prologue, sees the signal fires that indicate the return of the King, but his joy is tempered with apprehension because of the hostility of Clytemnestra. In Ibsen's *A Doll's House,* Nora's deception with the macaroons on her first appearance prepares for the discovery of the larger deception of forging her father's signature.

Marsha Norman's *'Night Mother,* the Pulitzer Prize-winning play of 1984, dramatizes the action of a mother's attempt to change her daughter's decision to commit suicide. The following excerpt is an example of foreshadowing and the point of attack:

> (*Jessie sits down with the gun and starts cleaning it, pushing the cylinder out, checking to see that the chambers and barrel are empty, then putting some oil on a small patch of cloth and pushing it through the barrel with the push rod that was in the box. Mama goes to the kitchen and washes her hands, as instructed, trying not to show her concern about the gun.*)

Mama: I shoulda got you to bring down that milk can. Agnes Fletcher sold hers to somebody with a flea market for forty dollars apiece.

Jessie: I'll go back and get it in a minute. There's a wagon wheel up there, too. There's even a churn. I'll get it all if you want.

Mama: (*Coming over, now, taking over now*) What are you doing?

Jessie: The barrel has to be clean, Mama. Old powder, dust gets in it . . .

Mama: What for?

Jessie: I told you.

Mama: (*Reaching for the gun*) And I told you, we don't get criminals out here.

Jessie: (*Quickly pulling it to her*) And I told you . . . (*Then trying to be calm*) The gun is for me.

Mama: Well, you can have it if you want. When I die, you'll get it all, anyway.

Jessie: I'm going to kill myself, Mama.[4]

The playwright values tension and suspense more than surprise, and the traditional practice has been to establish a background to prepare the

Strindberg's *Miss Julie* dramatizes an encounter between Miss Julie and her father's manservant during a Midsummer Eve's celebration. He is about to chop off a bird's head, foreshadowing Julie's suicide.

audience for the action that follows. But many contemporary writers, who regard life as illogical and incomprehensible, do not feel obligated to give the audience clear clues to their characters or their motivations. Harold Pinter, Max Frisch, and Friedrich Duerrenmatt have written striking plays whose plots reflect a nameless dread and an overpowering sense of unidentified evil, using ambiguous language and actions, which the spectators are left to sort out for themselves.

Complications

Most plots are made up of a series of *complications*. A complication is any force that affects the direction of the action. Comedy very often shows a character striving after a goal but being thwarted by obstacles. The hero falls in love with a woman, but he is kept from her by a series of complications—there is parental disapproval or economic or political differences; he is put in jail or sent overseas; she is ill or involved with another suitor; and so on. In tragedy, the hero frequently becomes committed to action that tests him to the utmost. The suffering and hardships of the testing process are the complications.

Usually a play has a pattern of increasing intensification from the first complication (the point of attack) to the major climax, when the fate of the protagonist is settled or the dramatist has given the spectator an insight into the characters and their experience. Complications create a "straining forward of interest," to use George Pierce Baker's apt phrase. Their purpose is to intensify the emotions, create suspense, provide the building blocks of the play's structure, and illustrate and determine what happens to the characters.

Romeo falls in love with Juliet, but the situation is complicated by the enmity between the two families. This hostility is aggravated when Romeo slays Tybalt, causing a new complication, the banishment of Romeo. Another complication is raised when Juliet's father insists that she marry Paris immediately. To avoid the marriage, a plan is devised for Juliet to feign

The first complication and the point of attack begin when Romeo and Juliet fall in love with one another, despite their parents' animosity.

(Prague National Theater. Scenography by Joseph Svoboda.)

death through the use of a magic potion. But the letter to Romeo disclosing the plan is not delivered, further complicating the action. Romeo learns of Juliet's apparent death, goes to her, and takes poison. Juliet awakens to find her lover dead—another complication. She joins him in death. Shakespeare, like most playwrights, begins with a character trying to reach an objective, but complications intervene and require the character to readjust as the play gathers momentum and intensity. It is through complications that the playwright constructs the plot.

Climax

The climax is the culmination of the course of action; it is "the maximum disturbance of the equilibrium," "the moment of most intense strain," "the crisis of maximum emotion and tension." In Hamlet's "The Mousetrap," the climax occurs when Claudius rises from his chair at the sight of the simulated murder of King Hamlet. In *Quem Quaeritis*, the climax is the discovery of the empty tomb.

In Miller's *Death of a Salesman* the conflict between Willy and his son Biff finally comes to a head when Biff attempts to make his father face reality.

Willy: (*With hatred, threateningly*) The door of your life is wide open!
Biff: Pop! I'm a dime a dozen, and so are you!
Willy: (*Turning on him now in an uncontrolled outburst*) I am not a dime a dozen! I am Willy Loman, and you are Biff Loman!

(*Biff starts for Willy, but is blocked by Happy. In his fury, Biff seems on the verge of attacking his father.*)

Biff: I am not a leader of men, Willy, and neither are you. You were never anything but a hard-working drummer who landed in the ash can like all the rest of them! I'm one dollar an hour, Willy! I tried seven states and couldn't raise it. A buck an hour! Do you gather my meaning! I'm not bringing home any prizes any more, and you're going to stop waiting for me to bring them home!
Willy: (*Directly to Biff*) You vengeful, spiteful mut!

(*Biff breaks from Happy. Willy, in fright, starts up the stairs. Biff grabs him.*)

Biff: (*At the peak of his fury*) Pop, I'm nothing. I'm nothing, Pop. Can't you understand that? There's no spite in it any more. I'm just what I am, that's all.

(*Biff's fury has spent itself, and he breaks down, sobbing, holding on to Willy, who dumbly fumbles for Biff's face.*)

Willy: (*Astonished*) What're you doing? What're you doing? (*To Linda*) Why is he crying?

Biff: (*Crying, broken*) Will you let me go, for Christ's sake? Will you take that phony dream and burn it before something happens?[5]

Another strong climactic scene takes place in Lillian Hellman's *The Little Foxes* when the ruthless, egocentric Regina goads her ill husband, Horace, into a heart attack during their argument over their unhappy marriage.

Regina: No. No, it wasn't what I wanted. (*Pauses, leans back, pleasantly*) It took me a little while to find out I had made a mistake. As for you—I don't know. It was almost as if I couldn't stand the kind of man you were. (*Smiles, softly*) I used to lie there at night, praying you wouldn't come near—

Horace: Really? It was as bad as that?

Regina: (*Nods*) Remember when I went to Doctor Sloan and I told you he said there was something the matter with me and that you shouldn't touch me any more?

Horace: I remember.

Regina: But you believed it? I couldn't understand that. I couldn't understand that anybody could be such a soft fool. That was when I began to despise you.

Horace: (*Puts his hand to his throat, glances around at bottle of medicine on table, then to her*) Why didn't you leave me?

Regina: I told you I married you *for* something. It turned out it was only for this. (*Carefully*) This wasn't what I wanted, but it was something. I never thought about it much, but if I had, (*Horace puts his hand to his throat*) I'd have known that you would die before I would. But I couldn't have known that you would get heart trouble so early and so bad. I'm lucky, Horace. I've always been lucky. (*Horace turns slowly to medicine.*) I'll be lucky again.

(*Horace looks at her. Then he puts his hand to his throat. Because he cannot reach the bottle he moves the chair closer. He reaches for medicine, takes out cork, picks up spoon, tries to pour some in the spoon, the bottle slips out of his shaking fingers and crashes on the table. He draws in his breath, gasps.*)

Horace: Please. Tell Addie—the other bottle is upstairs. (*She has not moved. She does not move now. He stares at her. Then, suddenly as if he understood, he raises his voice. It is a panic-stricken whisper, too small to be heard outside the room.*) Addie! Addie! Come—

(*Stops as he hears the softness of his voice. He makes a sudden, furious spring from the chair to the stairs, taking the first few steps as if he were a desperate*

Maureen Stapleton and Elizabeth Taylor
in Lillian Hellman's *The Little Foxes* at the
Ahmanson Theater.

(Directed by Austin Pendleton.)

*runner. On the fourth step he slips, gasps, grasps the rail, makes a great effort
to reach the landing. When he reaches the landing, he is on his knees. His knees
give way, he falls on the landing, out of view. Regina has not turned during
his climb up the stairs. Now she waits a second. Then she goes below the landing,
speaks up)*

Regina: Horace. (*When there is no answer, she turns, crosses to door L., opens
door, calls*) Addie! Cal! Come in here.[6]

Actually, in many plays there are series of climaxes, with moments of
stability and adjustment in between. The action surges forward and upward
in mounting tension through minor climaxes until it reaches the major climax, when the emotional impact of the play is strongest. The structure, in
this respect, resembles a boxing match between two opponents of similar
strength and skill. In each round, there are moments of climactic action with
first one fighter gaining the advantage and then the other. In between the
peaks of action there are relatively quiet moments and rest periods. In the

frantic last round, the major climax is reached when one boxer succeeds in knocking the other one out.

Climaxes occur at the moments of greatest turbulence, as when Mama, in *'Night Mother,* is unable to prevent Jessie from escaping to her room to commit suicide; or when the villagers, in *The Visit,* kill one of their own people to obtain one billion marks from a wealthy widow who demands vengeance; or when the fatally ill Mozart recognizes Salieri as the instigator of his destruction. In melodrama, the climax is the time of maximum violence or jeopardy—hero and villain fight at the edge of a cliff, the spaceship is out of control, the ammunition is all gone. In comedy, the climactic scenes often depict the characters embroiled in the maximum amount of mix-ups.

Crisis

Although the terms *crisis* and *climax* are often used interchangeably because they may occur at the same time, we shall consider a crisis to mean a time

A crisis in *Hamlet* occurs when the armed Prince has the opportunity to avenge the death of his father by killing Claudius at prayer. Hamlet hesitates and desists, thus setting up his own destruction.

(Asolo State Theater, Sarasota, Florida.)

of decision, a turning point, a crossroads. After an accident (which may be a climax), a patient hovers between life and death. He is at a moment of crisis. A batter steps to the plate with the score tied and the bases loaded. The count reaches three balls and two strikes. The game is at a point of crisis. (It is probably at the climax, too.)

A crisis involves a clash of interests. The protagonist is faced with alternatives that will determine his or her fate. Hamlet, sword in hand, must decide whether or not to slay the praying Claudius; Juliet must decide whether or not to take the sleeping potion; Nora must decide whether or not to leave her husband.

Sometimes characters make their own decisions; sometimes decisions are thrust on them. A crisis may lead to good fortune or catastrophe, depending on the nature of the play and the author's intent.

A dramatist creates situations that dramatize the characters at critical moments of their careers. For a while the outcome is in doubt. The protagonist teeters on the brink of success or failure. A decisive action occurs that settles the fate of the hero. The moments of decision are the crises.

In the traditional drama of the past, characters have some freedom of choice, but many modern playwrights have created characters who have no chance to assert themselves—their wills are paralyzed and their destinies are imposed on them from the outside. They are victims of unseen or external forces rather than active agents. These plays avoid crises, and instead, the characters are acted on with no compelling sense of choice.

Despite Brecht's rejection of traditional dramatic structure, he has an excellent sense for creating strong crises within the episodes of his plays. For example, *The Caucasian Chalk Circle* is a sequence of critical actions:

> During the palace rebellion, Grusha rescues and escapes with the governor's child.
> Grusha saves the child from the Ironshirts.
> Grusha escapes from the Ironshirts by crossing the Rotten Bridge.
> Grusha marries a peasant who feigns dying.
> An outcast, Azdak, becomes the judge.
> Azdak's wisdom gives Grusha custody of the child.

Denouement

The *denouement* is the final resolution of the plot, the untying of the knot that the complications have formed. Romeo and Juliet are united in death; the blinded Oedipus goes into exile; Hamlet, Laertes, the Queen, and Claudius die and order is restored in Elsinore. In mystery plays, the guilty person is identified and brought to justice; in romantic comedies, the lovers are united and the problems are solved; in old-fashioned melodramas, the good are rewarded and the bad are punished; in tragedies, the protagonist preserves his integrity and achieves his spiritual goal, even though he suffers physical destruction. The denouement indicates the ultimate disposition of the major characters. Its function is to restore order and to unify and complete the cause of the action.

The absurdist playwright who rejects the traditional format of a clearly defined linear plot may leave the resolution ambiguous or incomplete. In Samuel Beckett's *Waiting for Godot*, Vladimir and Estragon look forward to the arrival of Godot from the very beginning, but he does not come. The act of waiting is the force that animates the play and allows the dramatist to reveal the characters and their ideas. Eugene Ionesco, in the denouements of *The Chairs* and *The Leader*, tricks expectancy by negative endings. In *The Chairs*, an old couple await the coming of the orator who will deliver a significant message; but when he arrives, he can only babble, and he writes on the blackboard, "Angelfood, adieu." Those who look forward to the appearance of the leader are shocked when he appears—without a head.

Luigi Pirandello, one of the foremost dramatists of the twentieth century, engages his characters in *Right You Are if You Think You Are* in an intellectual chase to learn the true identity of a family who tell conflicting stories. In the denouement, curiosity is not satisfied, and the audience leaves the theater without knowing the answers. Pinter's plays are famous for their ambiguity, not only of the dialogue but also of the characters and their actions, since the playwright does not spell out the answers but allows the spectators to find meanings for themselves. Generally, however, the denouement brings about a clear and ordered resolution.

CHARACTER

Aristotle, in his *Poetics*, regarded character as secondary to plot, thus beginning an argument that continues to this day. Actually, the controversy is a fruitless one, since plot and character are interrelated. Character is defined by what the character says and does. Plot is character in action.

Like other aspects of drama, characterization has varied with fashion. In Greek, Elizabethan, and Japanese drama, the roles of women were played by men. Medieval drama often had allegorical figures representing single attributes of character, such as Wisdom, Greed, and Gluttony. Medieval characters ranged from God to the Devil, from purest saint to most abject sinner. Some characters have been drawn on a heroic scale, masters of their fate, working out their destinies by their own resources; other characters have been treated as hapless victims of an unfortunate heredity and environment, incapable of taking action, defeated, frustrated, and resigned. Modern dramatists of realistic and naturalistic persuasions have endeavored to create the illusion of complicated character by piling up a wealth of physical details, by capitalizing on the significant trifle, and by searching for the psychological meaning beneath the act. The expressionists have ex-

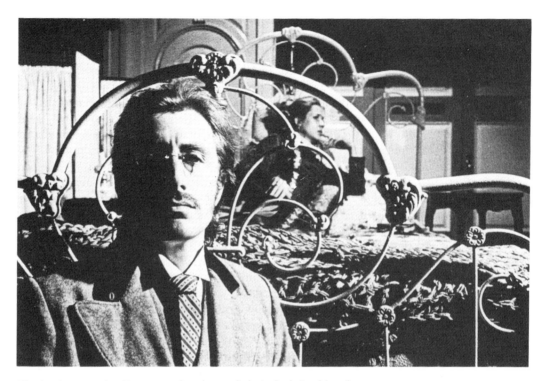

The development of realism centered on the psychological relationships of characters. Ibsen exposed the complications of differing points of view in a series of clashes between Nora and her husband Torvald.

(Cleveland Playhouse.)

perimented with split personalities or have taken from characters all aspects of individuality, reducing them to X or Mr. Zero. Dramatic literature is filled with a wide variety of portraits.

Novelists can create characters by using a broad range of actions over many years and under many conditions. They can directly express the thoughts coursing through the heads of their creatures, and they have great freedom with time and space. In sharp contrast, the playwrights' work is compressed in time and restricted in scope. Generally, they have felt obliged to limit themselves to relatively few characters since they have only a short time to present them to an audience.

Playwrights define and delineate characters by their words and actions, which reveal their inner lives. If a character is meant to portray a hero, that heroism must be established in word and action before the audience. Concrete signs are essential if the theatergoer is to believe in or identify with the character. Miller, in *Death of a Salesman*, gave us an immediate sense of

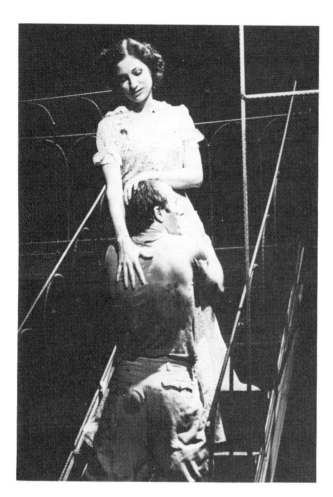

The close relationship between Stanley and Stella is threatened when Blanche appears.

(Playmakers' Repertory Company, Chapel Hill, North Carolina. Directed by Bill Ludel.)

Willy by his entrance and first few lines. Williams, in *A Streetcar Named Desire*, quickly reveals the characters of Stanley and Stella in their first appearance:

> *(Two men come around the corner, Stanley Kowalski and Mitch. They are about twenty-eight or thirty years old, roughly dressed in blue denim work clothes. Stanley carries his bowling jacket and a red-stained package from the butcher's. They stop at the foot of the steps.)*

Stanley: *(Bellowing)* Hey there! Stella, baby! *(Stella comes out on the first floor landing, a gentle young woman about twenty-five, and of a background obviously quite different from her husband's.)*

Stella: *(Mildly)* Don't holler at me like that. Hi Mitch.

Stanley: Catch!
Stella: What?
Stanley: Meat!

> (*He heaves the package at her. She cries out in protest but manages to catch it; then she laughs breathlessly. . . .*)[7]

During the last quarter of the nineteenth century, progress in scientific methods and psychology led playwrights to delineate characters with complicated inner lives and complex motivations, often concealed behind a façade of conventional behavior. One of the appeals of such plays was the gradual revelation of the true characters beneath the surface, such as in the plays of Ibsen, Strindberg, and Chekhov.

Many twentieth-century plays depend for their appeal on substantial characters who are psychologically complex, as in Eugene O'Neill's *A Long Day's Journey into Night,* Williams' *A Streetcar Named Desire,* and Miller's *Death of a Salesman.*

Some contemporary writers and theorists now reject the psychological aspects of drama in favor of plays that emphasize philosophical or political content that subordinates the individual identity to the larger social scene. The characters may not be defined at all, and little attempt is made to create credible, complex people or to probe beneath the surface. Actors become agents of the action without revealing their inner life, so they perform more like dancers or musicians. In expressionistic plays, actors may represent states of mind or one aspect of character rather than a complete person. In innovative productions of the classics, one actor may play several parts or the character may be entirely changed: Hamlet is played by a woman; Macbeth's witches become three punk teenagers; Peer Gynt is played by six different actors.

The mainstream of drama, however, relies on credible characters who are recognizable human beings with whom we can relate.

Characterization may be delineated in five ways:

1. By appearance. The character's physical presence is an immediate stimulus to the spectator because it offers clues to his or her age, occupation, economic level, social status, health, disposition, and so on—all of which have been carefully considered by the director when casting, as well as by the costume and makeup designers. Often the playwright prescribes a specific image.

Lorraine Hansberry in *A Raisin in the Sun* describes in detail the matriarch of the family:

> (*Mama enters. She is a woman in her early sixties, full-bodied and strong. She is one of those women of a certain grace and beauty who wear it so unobtrusively*

that it takes a while to notice. Her dark-brown face is surrounded by the total whiteness of her hair, and, being a woman who has adjusted to many things in life and overcome many more, her face is full of strength. She has, we can see, wit and faith of a kind that keep her eyes lit and full of interest and expectancy. She is, in a word, a beautiful woman. Her bearing is perhaps most like the noble bearing of the women of the Hereros of Southwest Africa—rather as if she imagines that as she walks she still bears a basket or a vessel upon her head. Her speech, on the other hand, is as careless as her carriage is precise—she is inclined to slur everything—but her voice is perhaps not so much quiet as simply soft.)[8]

2. By speech. The kind of language used by a person defines a character, as does the manner of speaking, voice quality, inflection pattern, pitch, rate, and general vitality. Most playwrights take great care to write dialogue that establishes character.

   For a long time it was a convention in realistic plays for the actor to pretend that the audience did not exist and to refrain from addressing them directly, but that convention is no longer observed. For instance, in dramas that generally follow the format of realism, characters act as narrators and make comments directly to the spectators in *Brighton Beach Memoirs, A Soldier's Play, Talley's Folly,* and *A Nightingale Sang.* The commentary also helps to characterize the speaker.

   In *A Soldier's Play,* Captain Davenport's first speech gives us a clear indication of the type of man he is:

   (*Captain Davenport walks across the stage from the wings, dressed sharply in an M.P. uniform, his hat cocked to the side and strapped down, the way airmen wear theirs. He is carrying a briefcase, and we are aware of a man who is very confident and self-assured. He is smiling as he faces the audience, cleaning his glasses as he begins to speak.*)

   Davenport: Call me Davenport—Captain, United States Army, attached to the 343rd Military Police Corps Unit, Fort Neal, Louisiana. I'm a lawyer the segregated Armed Services couldn't find a place for. My job in this war? Policing colored troops. (*Slight pause*) One morning during mid-April 1944, a colored tech/sergeant, Vernon C. Waters, assigned to the 221st Chemical Smoke Generating Company, stationed here before transfer to Europe, was brutally shot to death in a wooded section off the New Post Road and the junction of Highway 51—just two hundred yards from the colored N.C.O. club—by a person or persons unknown.[9]

3. By action. Behavior and body language offer clues to character. We are apt to judge people by what they do rather than by what they say.

Playwright Peter Shaffer, in his *Amadeus,* immediately characterized two leading players in a scene of comic action that surprised the audience's expectations about the musical genius, Mozart.

Peter Shaffer, in *Amadeus,* introduces Mozart to the audience in a startling fashion. The following action takes place in the Emperor's palace:

(*Offstage, noises are heard.*)

Constanze: (*Off*) Squeak! Squeak! Squeak!

(*Constanze runs on from upstage: a pretty girl in her early twenties, full of high spirits. At this second she is pretending to be a mouse. She runs across the stage in her gay party dress, and hides under the fortepiano. Suddenly a small, pallid, large-eyed man in a showy wig and a showy set of clothes runs in after her and freezes—center—as a cat would freeze, hunting a mouse. This is Wolfgang Amadeus Mozart.*

As we get to know him through his next scenes, we discover several things about him: he is an extremely restless man, his hands and feet in almost continuous motion; his voice is light and high; and he is possessed of an unforgettable giggle—piercing and infantile.)

Mozart: Miaouw.
Constanze: (*Betraying where she is*) Squeak!
Mozart: Miaouw! . . . Miaouw! . . . Miaouw!

(*The composer drops on all fours and, wrinkling his face, begins spitting and stalking his prey. The mouse—giggling with excitement—breaks her cover and dashes across the floor. The cat pursues. Almost at the chair where Salieri sits concealed, the mouse turns at bay. The cat stalks her—nearer and nearer—in its knee breeches and elaborate coat.*)

I'm going to pounce-bounce! I'm going to scrunch-munch! I'm going to chew-poo my little mouse-wouse! I'm going to tear her to bits with my paws-claws!
Constanze: No!
Mozart: Paws-claws—paws-claws—paws-claws! *Ohh!* (*He falls on her. She screams.*)[10]

In *'Night Mother*, Mama's and Jessie's characters are delineated by small talk and trivial actions that conceal the desperate struggle going on beneath the surface as the mother tries to save her daughter's life.

In *'Night Mother*, Mama's character is immediately established as the curtain rises:

(*Mama stretches to reach the cupcakes in a cabinet in the kitchen. She can't see them, but she can feel around for them, and she's eager to have one, so she's working pretty hard at it. This may be the most serious exercise Mama ever gets. She finds the cupcake, the coconut-covered, raspberry-and-marshmallow-filled kind known as a snowball, but sees that there's one missing from the package. She calls to Jessie, who is apparently somewhere else in the house.*)

Mama: (*Unwrapping the cupcake*) Jessie, it's the last snowball, sugar. Put it on the list, O.K.? And we're out of Hershey bars, and where's that peanut brittle? I think maybe Dawson's been in it again. I ought to put a big mirror on the refrigerator door. That'll keep him out of my treats, won't it? You hear me, honey? (*Then more to herself*) I hate it when the coconut falls off. Why does the coconut fall off?[11]

One of the most famous actions in *Hedda Gabler* occurs at the end of Act III when the protagonist reveals her destructive, neurotic nature by burning a valuable manuscript—the product of Lövborg and his helper, Thea.

(*Hedda listens for a moment at the door. Then she goes up to the writing table, takes out a packet of manuscript, peeps under the cover, draws a few of the sheets half out, and looks at them. Next she goes over and seats herself in the armchair beside the stove, with a packet in her lap. Presently she opens the stove door, and then the packet.*)

Hedda: (*Throws one of the quires into the fire and whispers to herself*) Now I am burning your child, Thea! Burning it, curly-locks! (*Throwing more quires into the stove*) Your child and Eilert Lövborg's. (*Throws the rest in*) I am burning—I am burning your child.[12]

4. By what others say about or how they react to a character. Sometimes the playwright uses comment about an absent character as a method of revealing the truth. In Ferene Molnar's *Liliom*, for example, the true character behind the blustering, swaggering barker, Liliom, is indicated by Julie's line: "It is possible, dear, that someone may beat you, and beat you, and beat you—and not hurt you at all." Willy Loman in *Death of a Salesman* is a man who never saw himself or his motivations accurately. His son Biff expresses the truth about Willy when he says, "He had the wrong dreams. All, all wrong. . . . The man didn't know who he was."

The playwright may deliberately mislead or perplex the spectator by having characters say ambiguous or controversial things. Molière begins *Tartuffe* with a domestic quarrel in which he exposes two entirely different points of view about his leading character. Pirandello delighted in making the point time and again in his plays that it is difficult, if not impossible, really to comprehend the character of anyone. Hence his plays are filled with conflicting statements about the characters. In his *Right You Are if You Think You Are,* he dramatizes a series of incidents in which the leading characters tell conflicting stories about one another so the audience never knows the truth—thus illustrating the problem of separating illusion from reality.

The sharpness of a character's image is in part dependent on the structure of the drama. Plays written for a theater that permit most of the essential action to appear onstage give the playwright a greater opportunity to create more vivid and complex characters than plays that are confined to a minimum of action. One reason Hamlet is such a rich and interesting character is the number of views of him we see through his relationship to the ghost, Horatio, Ophelia, the Players, Gertrude, Polonius, Claudius, and Rosencrantz and Guildenstern. When we contrast this variety of exposure to that of Agamemnon or Orestes or Antigone, we realize how restricted the Greeks were in delineating complex characters. Some playwrights, notably Shakespeare, have the ability to sketch memorable characters in a very few lines, but most dramatists develop their major characters' roles at length to create distinctive and believable personalities.

In most dramas, the purpose of showing people in action is to enlist our interest and involve our emotions in the fortunes of the characters. To accomplish this purpose, the dramatist creates characters with whom we have some kind of bond, either through temperament, condition, or destiny. If we cannot empathize with them, we remain passive and indifferent, and the action does not fulfill its function. Hence, it is important for us to believe in the characters. Sometimes they leave us cold. Their motivations and sense of values seem incredible; they are confused and incomprehensible; they make no effort to decide their fate; they are too self-centered or too short-sighted. On the other hand, a good playwright can kindle our interest and sympathy for all kinds of characters by giving us understanding, particularly if these characters are well played by skillful performers.

THOUGHT

The third element cited by Aristotle is *thought,* or *dianoia,* by which he meant the intellectual aspect of the play as shown by the characters' speech and actions whenever they argue, plead, or reason. Thought is the rationale for behavior.

One does not go to the theater primarily for information. Plays are not objective debates nor mere presentations of factual data and logical arguments leading to a clear decision; but as in the experiences of life itself, characters make decisions out of a network of feelings and thoughts. Like all forms of literature, good drama usually is meaningful. A play is a unified organization of an imaginative experience and insight, and while it provides emotional outlets, it also engages the mind. We go to the theater for delight and discovery. As Eric Bentley says, the effect of seeing a great play is "of a veil lifted, the scales falling from the eyes, in a word, something momentous exhibited—and said."[13]

As indicated earlier, a basic ingredient in the theater from the very beginning to the present day has been conflict—the "good guys" against the "bad guys," husband versus wife, children clashing with parents, lovers' quarrels, and rebels against society. In dramatizing such collisions, the playwright has found it necessary to show both sides of the argument. Even in medieval drama, written specifically to show the rewards for following the straight and narrow path to salvation, the clergy were obliged for dramatic reasons to include the Devil as well as God, vices as well as virtues, sinners as well as saints. In most plays, the dramatist presents a variety of thoughts and views. Antigone is in conflict with Creon, and Oedipus with Tiresias. Blanche's sensitivity is opposed by Stanley's brutality; Major Barbara's religious convictions are challenged by her father's capitalistic views as a munitions manufacturer; the El Teatro Campesino of Luis Valdez shows Chicanos against white growers and extortionists; the disillusioned war veteran in David Rabe's *Sticks and Bones* is shown in opposition to his family's determined efforts to resist his intrusion into their superficial lives. The rationale for conflicting points of view constitutes one aspect of thought in drama.

In addition to the varied views of individual characters, thought concerns a play's theme—a "golden text" that summarizes the moral and indicates the symbolic meaning of the play as a whole, such as "love conquers all," "murder will out," and "niceness pays." But drama does not always lend itself to such neat copybook maxims. A given play may convey a variety of interpretations to an audience. Most of Ibsen's contemporaries were profoundly shocked at Nora's decision in *A Doll's House* to leave her husband and children, although her action is entirely credible to most of us today. Some people regard Antigone as headstrong and foolish in openly defying Creon and thus deliberately choosing to die. In his notes while directing *A Streetcar Named Desire*, Elia Kazan clearly shows that he intended to express Williams' point of view: "If we don't watch out, the apes will take over." But in production, the impression conveyed to many spectators by the actors' performance was that Blanche threatened the Kowalski home, and Stanley's brutal treatment of her was justified. The ideas of great dramas have, of course, been sources of endless academic contention. What is the true interpretation of *Hamlet*? Is Shylock a comic or a tragic figure? Is the tragedy of *Antigone* really the tragedy of Creon? Varied interpretations of a play's

David Mamet's *Glengarry Glen Ross* is concerned with a group of real estate men engaged in savage competition for financial rewards. The playwright's abrasive, rough vernacular is one of his major weapons in dramatizing the struggle to survive.

(Goodman Theater. Directed by Gregory Mosher.)

meaning indicate that the dramatist has not been explicit in stating a theme. Many great plays have a depth or richness, making them susceptible to all kinds of interpretations. One of the most interesting aspects of the contemporary theater is the astonishing variety of experimental revivals. Inevitably, individual readers and spectators are challenged to search their own minds and experiences in evaluating a play.

Whatever the purpose of the playwright, the action of significant drama is as meaningful as an experience in life itself. The choices that the characters make, their motivation and behavior, their dialogue and the subtext, and the sequence of action are rewarding subjects for investigation. The content of a play is a valid reflection of the time in which it was written. Current drama very often mirrors the world in a vivid and compelling way, focusing on our life-styles, the shifting sense of values, our loss of philosophic roots, the plight of minorities, alienation, and the struggle for power, recognition, and security.

We can see how many plays in the American theater reveal the social viewpoint of the times. In the 1930s, during the Depression, there was the bittersweet realization that life can be ironic—"progress" is not without its suffering. In the 1940s there was the growing realization of the threat of war and a nostalgia for the "good old days." After the war, disillusion set in. The view of our society became one of doubt and despair. In the 1960s, during the times of protest, the theater, like every other institution, was shaken by misgivings and hostility. In some cases there was blatant attack on all aspects of production—the plays and their content and structure, the style of acting and design, even the architecture of the theater. Dramatists found the stage a powerful platform from which to articulate their opposition to the establishment. In the 1970s dramatists became concerned with illness and death. Although the commercial theater has traditionally been timid about presenting controversial material, the social climate has made an impact that cannot be denied. The thought content of drama reflects the culture that produced it.

DICTION

The fourth element of drama is diction—the language of the play, the dialogue the actors speak. The diction provides a system of verbal signs that set the characters and their actions before an audience.

Spoken language in the theater must be immediately apprehended by the listener; pages cannot be turned back, nor can there be pauses to weigh and consider a line before continuing to the next. The dialogue must be interesting despite the need for simplicity and economy. It should capture the spirit of life and character. As the Irish playwright J. M. Synge said, "In a good play, every speech should be as fully flavored as a nut or an apple." The diction must be appropriate for the character and the situation. Lines do not exist in the theater as separate entities. They are always in context, growing out of the emotionally charged incidents of the plot. The language of drama must be dynamic. As already suggested, speech is a form of action. Dialogue shows the characters' relationship to others; reflects the progression of the action; indicates what is happening inside the characters; reveals their suffering, growth, or decline. It is a means of articulating the clash of wills and conflicting motivations.

The dramatist needs the poet's feeling for language—a rich imagination; a facility with provocative imagery; and awareness of the weight, texture, and arrangement of words. Dramatic dialogue is not contemplative or static; it is harnessed to action and change. Even in the Japanese Noh dramas, which are often plays of reminiscence, the dialogue pulses with the life of the remembered event. It must be speakable so that it gives the performers sounds and cadences that help them project the thoughts and feelings of the characters. For the audience the dialogue must be audibly intelligible so that the words are arresting, evoking images that are not only immediately comprehensible but set up emotional reverberations as well.

Much of the serious drama before the nineteenth century was linked to poetry. The Greek and Elizabethan masters of drama were poets as well as playwrights. Their works, therefore, have an added literary value, and their use of verse seems particularly appropriate for their elevated tragedies of high-born characters. In modern times poetry has given way to prose as the naturalist and realist bring onstage commonplace figures in everyday pursuits. Many people have lamented the absence of poetry in the modern theater; attempts have been made to recapture some of the enrichment of the poetic speech, notably by Maxwell Anderson, Christopher Fry, Brecht, T. S. Eliot, and Federico Garcia Lorca. Although modern drama lacks elevated language, it would be a mistake to think that all plays written in the poetic form were notably successful. Indeed, the use of verse in the past was often puerile and ostentatious. Many poets had no sense of dramatic form or theatrical awareness. Often their plays were not stageworthy; the preoccupation with the language retarded the action, and the drama became bogged down with linguistic clutter.

Over the years, a great variety of dialogue devices has been used. One of the most interesting, devised by the Greeks, is called *stichomythia,* in which short bursts of dialogue are delivered in alternating lines. It is a means of building tension in the way that a motion-picture editor uses rapid intercutting of film clips to intensify the action. In the seventeenth century, Molière used *stichomythia* in scenes of tension, such as in the clash between Toinette and Argan in *The Imaginary Invalid.*

Pinter's language has the capacity for setting up echoes and vibrations far beyond the façade of words. His use of rhythm and silence opens up unexpected associations and a surreal sense of menace. As John Lahr says of Pinter, "The story on stage is deeper than the words that explain it, the language mere signposts for an immense and inaudible despair.[14]

The following passage indicates Pinter's remarkable ability to create theatrical effects with the colloquial idiom. In *The Birthday Party,* Stanley has sought refuge at a seaside resort, but he has been followed by two sinister strangers, McCann and Goldberg, who undermine and destroy him. As they are about to take him away in their long, black car, this dialogue occurs:

McCann: He looks better, doesn't he?
Goldberg: Much better.
McCann: A new man.
Goldberg: You know what we'll do?
McCann: What?
Goldberg: We'll buy him another pair. (*They begin to woo him, gently and with relish. During the following sequence, Stanley shows no reaction. He remains with no movement, where he sits.*)
McCann: Out of our own pockets.

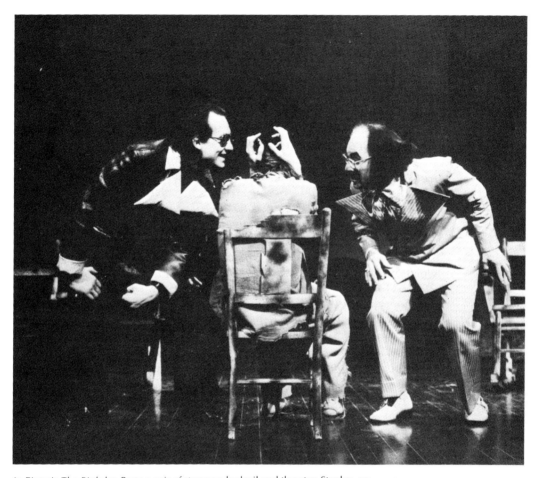

In Pinter's *The Birthday Party* a pair of strangers bedevil and threaten Stanley, an innocuous appearing young man who has tried to find a quiet sanctuary at a summer resort.

(University of Missouri, Columbia. Directed by Weldon Durham.)

Goldberg: It goes without saying. Between you and me, Stan, it's about time
        you had a new pair of glasses.
McCann: You can't see straight.
Goldberg: It's true. You've been cockeyed for years.
McCann: Now you're even more cockeyed.
Goldberg: He's right. You've gone from bad to worse.
McCann: Worse than worse.
Goldberg: You need a long convalescence.
McCann: A change of air.
Goldberg: Somewhere over the rainbow.

McCann: Where angels fear to tread.
Goldberg: Exactly.
McCann: You're in a rut.
Goldberg: You look anaemic.
McCann: Rheumatic.
Goldberg: Myopic.
McCann: Epileptic.
Goldberg: You're on the verge.
McCann: You're a dead duck.
Goldberg: But we can save you.
McCann: From a worse fate.
Goldberg: True.
McCann: Undeniable.
Goldberg: From now on, we'll take the hub of your wheel.
McCann: We'll renew your season ticket.
Goldberg: We'll take twopence off your morning tea.
McCann: We'll give you a discount on all inflammable goods.
Goldberg: We'll watch over you.
McCann: Advise you.
Goldberg: Give you proper care and treatment.[15]

Another contemporary playwright with a special flair for diction is Tom Stoppard, who creates a kind of intellectual vaudeville. In his *Rosencrantz and Guildenstern Are Dead, Jumpers,* and *Travesties,* he puts together dazzling pastiches of puns, double entendres, alliterations, and quotations.

As we shall see in Chapter Seven, the new theatricalism often regards language as a subordinate element in production. Following Artaud's edict, "no more masterpieces," a revolt began, not only against "great plays" but against language. Innovators have worked with improvised dialogue, invented languages, and nonverbal communication.

Extended soliloquies and monologues, which were a part of drama until the advent of realism, are again a part of the playwright's techniques.

The use of prose in the modern theater has often resulted in speech that is flat, pedestrian, and vulgar, filled with clichés of commonplace conversation. As Elder Olson has said, "The drama has increasingly sought to be articulate in the language of the inarticulate."[16] He goes on to lament the loss of subtle expression and profound thoughts available when poetic diction was more flexible.

On the other hand, the current emphasis on the vernacular has eliminated the straining for effect in "purple passages" of pretentious rhetoric. With the poet's feeling for language, some contemporary playwrights have created speech that is vivid and evocative. One thinks, for example, of the texture of Shepard's plays, utilizing the imagery of the rock and car and road cultures, and the graphic local color in the work of Beth Henley, Marsha Norman, Preston Jones, and Lanford Wilson. Others have created passages of words and pauses that have the power of stimulating the imagination and suggesting hidden and unsuspected meanings.

MUSIC

The fifth element mentioned by Aristotle is music, which refers to all the auditory material, including sound effects.

The Greek drama, in its early association with dithyrambs, made full use of musical potential in the singing and dancing of the chorus. Sound patterns were also important in the acting of the major characters, who sang, chanted, danced, and spoke with great variety in cadence, texture, and tempo. In the oriental theater, music has always played an important part. In the Noh and Kabuki theaters of Japan and in the traditional as well as modern plays of China, an orchestra is an essential aspect of the performance. Elizabethan drama was rich in lyricism that broke into song. Later English drama continued the use of music, and in burlettas, comic operas popular in the latter half of the eighteenth century, the entire performance was sung or chanted. Melodrama was originally linked to music, and even though the spoken word came to dominate the genre, musical backgrounds were used to accompany exits and entrances of major characters and to reinforce the mood of emotionally loaded scenes, such as chases, fights, escapes, love scenes, and deaths.

America's major theatrical invention, the musical comedy, grew out of popular entertainment of the nineteenth century. The minstrel show appealed to a wide audience from 1840 onwards; its male ensembles usually played in blackface in a melange of comedy, song, and dancing. The first musical comedy to become a hit was *The Black Crook* (1866), an extravaganza that featured spectacle and scantily clad chorus girls. Other early influences were the operettas by European composers that were built around sentimental stories about charming people in make-believe places which provided opportunities for picturesque scenery and tuneful music—for instance, Franz Lehar's *The Merry Widow* (1907) and Oscar Strauss' *The Chocolate Soldier* (1910). From France came the influence of "leg" shows like the Folies-Bergère, which combined vaudeville, comedy, and beautiful women in lavish costumes and scenery. Florenz Ziegfeld set the fashion for such display in America.

George M. Cohan added the patriotic note in his bright, energetic musicals, such as *Forty-Five Minutes from Broadway*. In 1927, a major change occurred when Jerome Kern and Edna Ferber produced her book *Showboat*, linking literary material with music. George and Ira Gershwin introduced sophisticated musical forms in early works like *Lady, Be Good* (1924), but their landmark was *Porgy and Bess* (1935), a play about the Southern black that created the first successful native folk opera. In 1931, the Gershwins, with Morrie Ryskind, produced the political satire *Of Thee I Sing*, the first musical to win the Pulitzer Prize. In 1943, Richard Rodgers and Oscar Hammerstein made another significant change in the musical with *Oklahoma*, based on Lynn Riggs' folk play *Green Grow the Lilacs*. The dancing of chorus girls was replaced by Agnes de Mille's ballet, and the story and music were melded organically in a plot that dealt with simple, lively country folk instead of dramatizing frivolous, upper-class love affairs of big-city dwellers. Other memorable musicals produced by Rodgers and Hammerstein were *South Pacific* (1949) and *The Sound of Music* (1959). Leonard Bernstein and Stephen Sondheim combined serious subject matter with sophisticated music in *West Side Story* (1957). In the late 1960s the "American Tribal Love-Rock Musical" *Hair*, a brash, formless protest against the established culture, created a new style of show. In 1964, *Fiddler on the Roof* became a phenomenal hit with its warm-hearted treatment of the stories of Shalom Aleichem.

Musical comedies have always been the biggest drawing card at the box office. More than two dozen musicals have enjoyed runs of over a thousand performances on Broadway. The formula of popular music, spectacular scenery and costuming, and lively, imaginative choreography continue as

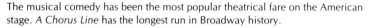

The musical comedy has been the most popular theatrical fare on the American stage. *A Chorus Line* has the longest run in Broadway history.

standard fare in the commercial theater in such hits as *Cats, Forty-Second Street,* and *A Chorus Line.*

Although the motion picture has always exploited the evocative power of music to heighten its effects, naturalistic and realistic drama has usually rejected music as an artificial intrusion. But even in realistic drama, playwrights have used sound to enhance the mood of their plays. For example, Chekhov was very conscious of the use of sound in *Uncle Vanya.* In the final act of the play, a melancholy atmosphere is reinforced by the click of the counting beads, the scratch of the pen, the churring of a cricket, the tapping of the night watchman's cane, the soft strumming of a guitar, and the bells of the carriage when Dr. Astrov departs.

As the theater has become freer in recent years, music and sound have often played an increasingly important part in performance. In Jack Gelber's *The Connection,* a jazz orchestra is a part of the acting company and actually plays approximately thirty minutes of music in each act. Brecht, with his lyrical gifts, uses music as an important part of his epic theater—for example, in *The Caucasian Chalk Circle,* which follows the oriental practice of having an orchestra onstage and injecting songs freely into the dialogue.

In C. P. Taylor's play *Good,* a mild German scholar is gradually transformed into a Nazi execution camp administrator. Throughout the action a five-piece band sits onstage and plays appropriate music, sometimes underscoring the action and sometimes as counterpoint to it. Taylor's *And a Nightingale Sang* also makes use of expressive music during the action when one of the characters at the piano plays songs from World War II. In *The Elephant Man,* a cellist in evening clothes is stationed near the wings and intermittently plays music from Elgar and Bach. He is not a character involved in the plot, but his appearance and performance seem aesthetically right.

Another of the present-day dramatists with a keen sense of the power of music in drama is Peter Shaffer. In *Equus* he called for an "Equus Noise"—"a choric effect made up of all the actors sitting around upstage and composed of humming, thumping, and stamping"—an effect that was particularly striking during the scene in which the boy is wounding the animals. Of course, Shaffer's stunning use of Mozart's music lifted the action of *Amadeus* to a very high level of production.

The influence of rock, jazz, and country music is pervasive as an integral part of Shepard's work. It is evident, not only in the songs and incidental music, but also in Shepard's language, which is often strident and jumpy, recalling rock jargon.

Jean-Louis van Itallie in his *America Hurrah!* (1965), a satire on traditional values, uses highly theatricalized techniques, including nonsense language, impersonal automatons instead of characters, and stylized sound. For example, in the first episode, *Interview,* the Telephone Operator suffers from a stomach cramp. She falls over the seat in pain.

(The whistling of the telephone circuit becomes a siren. Three actors carry the Telephone Operator over to the boxes, stage left, which now serve as an operating table. Three actors imitate the Telephone Operator's breathing pattern while four actors behind her make stylized sounds and movements as surgeons and nurses in the midst of an operation. The Telephone Operator's breathing accelerates, then stops. After a moment the actors begin spreading over the stage and making the muted sounds of a cocktail party: music, laughter, talk. The actors find a position and remain there, playing various aspects of a party in slow motion and muted tones. They completely ignore the First Interviewer who, as a Girl at the Party, goes from person to person as if she were in a garden of living statues.)[17]

In the experimental work of the new theater, many other innovators make a sharp break from traditional dramatic practice by placing most of their emphasis on music, sound, and spectacle. Often, conventional dialogue is replaced by disparate fragments, some of which may be recorded. Very often a complex sound track accompanies a series of striking images and actions that do not follow a plot line but serve instead to evoke moods and feelings through their sensuous appeal.

SPECTACLE

The sixth dramatic element, *spectacle*, includes all visual aspects of the production—scenery, lighting, costumes, makeup, and the stage business of the performers. It also includes the environment of the action, whether an actual playhouse or an adapted site, such as a Greek hillside, a Japanese shrine in a dry river bed, an opulent hall in a Renaissance palace, an open marketplace, an inn yard, a factory warehouse, or a street. The audience is also a part of the celebration we call theater because spectators often come to be seen as well as to see, and the communal experience of being eyewitnesses to a stirring event has its effect. Because drama is often thought of as *dialogue*, that aspect threatens to dominate the audience's experience. But there is rebellion against this dominance, and today we are more than ever conscious of the need to make a theater of images—even at the expense of subordinating the diction and rejecting the conventional playhouse and scenery. By its very nature, dramatic action results in compelling visual experiences. Think of the images evoked in Chapter One, even without the benefit of performance, when the three Marys see the miracle of the empty tomb; or imagine the manner in which Hamlet's "Mousetrap" reveals Claudius' crime; or call to mind Willy Loman's first entrance when he staggers through the gloom, bone-weary and defeated, carrying his heavy sample cases. The theater has a marvelous facility for filling our heads with rich visual experiences.

Peter Stein staged *As You Like It* in a movie studio in West Berlin so that he had
ample opportunity for spectacular scenery. The above is only a part of one of two
locales that required the audience to move along with the play.

Throughout history, as we shall see in Chapter Ten on stage design,
theaters have appealed to the eye as well as the ear, whether or not actual
scenery was used. In the production of Greek, Elizabethan, and Japanese
Noh plays virtually no representation of locale was required, except that
supplied by the architecture, and of course, the performers themselves. In
the Greek and Noh theaters, masks and striking costumes and the dancing
of the chorus and actors enriched the spectacle.

During the Renaissance, the proscenium arch was introduced into the
theater, separating audience and performers by placing the acting area behind an architectural framework so that the spectators looked through the
opening to the stage. This innovation was quickly exploited as theatrical

production became dominated by spectacular, changeable scenery, which often ran away with the show. Scenic artists vied with one another in creating lavish settings and spectacular effects. The impulse for display often spilled over into the auditorium and was reflected in theatrical architecture.

The proscenium arch, with its use of pictorial scenery, dominated the theater even to the present day, although its style and function have changed a good deal, as we shall see.

During the nineteenth century, melodrama gained a wide following in the theater; part of its popularity depended on spectacular scenic effects, coupled with vigorous action. As realism and naturalism made their impact on the late nineteenth-century audiences, scenery took on a new importance in production because of the scientifically inspired concern with environment as a conditioning force in determining behavior. Hence, spectacle assumed an organic, psychological role in the performance, as reinforcement of the meaning of the action and as a device relating character to the social milieu.

Tastes have changed considerably in modern times, and although many plays still require a semblance of representational setting, many innovators reject not only scenery but the theater as well. However, even in experimental productions, the visual aspects of drama are important in the environment of the performance and the action. The visual stimuli of lights and color are fundamental in creating states of mind and atmosphere.

The taste for spectacle is not gone; it has merely changed directions, and theater will continue to be a place for show.

PLAYS TO READ AND SEE

F = Film available; V = Videotape available.

F	V	Shaffer, *Amadeus*
F	V	Miller, *Death of a Salesman*
F	V	Ibsen, *A Doll's House, Hedda Gabler*
F	V	Hellman, *The Little Foxes*
		Norman, *'Night Mother*
F	V	Wilder, *Our Town*
F		Hansberry, *Raisin in the Sun*
F	V	Williams, *A Streetcar Named Desire*

BIBLIOGRAPHY

BECKERMAN, BERNARD. *Dynamics of Drama: Theory and Method of Analysis.* New York: Alfred A. Knopf, Inc., 1970.

BENTLEY, ERIC. *The Life of the Drama.* New York: Atheneum Publishers, 1967.

ESSLIN, MARTIN. *An Anatomy of Drama.* New York: Hill & Wang, 1976.

NICOLL, ALLARDYCE. *The Theater and Dramatic Theory.* New York: Barnes & Noble Books, 1962.

STYAN, J. L. *Elements of Drama.* Cambridge, Eng.: Cambridge University Press, 1960.

———. *The Dramatic Experience.* Cambridge, Eng.: Cambridge University Press, 1965.

NOTES

1. Thornton Wilder, *Our Town* (New York: Coward-McCann, 1938).

2. Lanford Wilson, *Talley's Folly* (New York: Hill & Wang, 1979).

3. Peter Shaffer, *Amadeus* (New York: New American Library, 1984).

4. Marsha Norman, *'Night Mother* (New York: Hill and Wang, 1981).

5. Arthur Miller, *Death of a Salesman* (New York: Viking Penguin, Inc., 1949).

6. Lillian Hellman, *The Little Foxes* (New York: Random House, Inc., 1939).

7. Tennessee Williams, *A Streetcar Named Desire* (New York: New Directions Publishing Corporation, 1947).

8. Lorraine Hansberry, *A Raisin in the Sun* (New York: Random House, Inc., 1959).

9. Charles Fuller, *A Soldier's Play* (New York: Hill & Wang, 1981).

10. Shaffer, *Amadeus.*

11. Norman, *'Night Mother.*

12. Henrik Ibsen, *Hedda Gabler,* trans. Edmund Gosse and William Archer (New York: Charles Scribner's Sons, 1907).

13. Eric Bentley, *The Life of the Drama* (New York: Atheneum Publishers, 1967).

14. John Lahr, *Casebook on Pinter's Homecoming* (New York: Grove Press, Inc., 1971).

15. Harold Pinter, *The Birthday Party* (New York: Grove Press, Inc., 1959).

16. Elder Olson, *Tragedy and the Theory of Drama* (Detroit: Wayne State University Press, 1961).

17. Jean-Louis Van Ittalie, *America Hurrah!* (New York: Putnam Publishing Groups, 1965).

3

Tragedy

Tragedy is a strange and mysterious country, despite considerable efforts to fix its boundaries, blaze its trails, and establish its configurations. All who venture here must find their own way through an entangling jungle of conjecture and a luxuriant undergrowth of verbiage surrounding a bewildering, semantic swamp. There is no short cut, no easy, known way, because tragedy is a quality of experience we must all discover for ourselves.

Tragedy is rare. It does not bulk large in the history of the theater, nor does one find it listed in the record of popular attractions on Broadway. Yet tragedy is the most discussed genre, and it was the first kind of drama that the Greeks introduced into the theater. Of the original Greek tragedies we have only seven plays each by Aeschylus and Sophocles and eighteen by Euripides. From the Renaissance, we have the tragedies of the Elizabethans, mostly Shakespeare, and the neoclassic works of Racine and Pierre Corneille. In addition, we have a body of critical theory that is even more diverse and contradictory than the plays themselves.

The first to mark the way was Aristotle, who in the fourth-century B.C. work, the *Poetics,* sought to guide those who followed him. Although he found his direction from limited observation of carefully chosen examples, we may still retrace his steps with profit, so acutely did he designate his landmarks. But we should remember that the *Poetics* is a short analysis of the kind of tragedy that was created a century before, in Athens. His study is, therefore, an investigation of the drama that preceded him, not a set of rules for his contemporaries or followers, even though Renaissance writers misapplied his views as those of a lawgiver. Moreover, there is considerable latitude for misunderstanding Aristotle, partially because of his language, and partially because of the examples he cites as evidence to support his views. Aristotle's *Poetics,* therefore, should be regarded as a lamp in the darkness, not the source of all light.

ARISTOTLE'S DEFINITION OF TRAGEDY

Let us turn our attention to Aristotle's *Poetics,* probably the most discussed piece of criticism in dramatic literature. He begins with this definition of tragedy:

> Tragedy, then is an imitation of an action that is serious, complete, and of a certain magnitude; in language embellished with each kind of artistic ornament, the several kinds being found in separate parts of the play; in the form of action, not of narrative; through pity and fear effecting the proper purgation of these emotions.[1]

The origin of the word *tragedy* is a matter of conjecture. *Tragos* in Greek means "goat"; *oide* means "song." The exact connection of goat-song to drama is not clear, although three hypotheses have been advanced: (1) A goat was sacrificed as part of the original improvised ritual honoring Dionysus; (2) the chorus wore goatskins for costumes; (3) a goat was offered as a prize in the early choral contests. In any case, tragedy was associated with goat-song or goat-singer in its early stages. The terms *tragic* and *tragedy* as we use them in everyday speech have little to do with "tragedy" as a form of drama. A person may speak of the "tragic" death of a small child in an automobile accident. Although tragedy usually involves catastrophe, it is not the calamity itself on which attention is focused in drama. Death may even seem incidental in *Hamlet* or *Romeo and Juliet* when it occurs to such secondary characters as Polonius or Paris or Tybalt. The validity of genuine tragedy is not concerned with the act of violence but with what that act says about life—the struggle of the protagonist, the issues at stake, the effect of his or her suffering.

An "action" refers to the play as a dynamic organized process intended for presentation in the theater—not a narrative for a solitary reader.

Tragedy is *serious* in nature, not trivial or frivolous. It deals with the most profound problems of humanity—identity and destiny, the nature of good and evil, the mysterious forces of the universe, and the consequences

In Shakespeare's *King Lear*, the protagonist experiences terrible suffering when he loses his throne and sees his kingdom torn by strife. It is a play of great magnitude that ends with release and reconciliation. Morris Carnovsky as Lear.

(American Shakespeare Festival in Connecticut.)

of individual responsibilities. Its purpose is not mere diversion or amusement but an investigation of ethical and spiritual values.

Tragedy attains *magnitude* in the heroic stature of its characters, in the use of poetry, in the universality of its meaning, and in the loftiness of its ideas. Tragedies are elevated; they possess scale and scope beyond the petty vicissitudes of daily existence. Magnitude of character is realized through highborn characters, persons of nobility and prominence who occupy "exposed positions"; people who, as Aristotle said, "are better than we are" or those who achieve greatness.

A tragedy is *complete;* it has a beginning, a middle, and an end—and according to Aristotle, each of these parts is a well-articulated structure without extraneous material. The course of action is a "necessary and probable" linking of antecedents and consequents. Such unity and wholeness are fundamental to the Greek aesthetic view of life.

The chief difference between the *dramatic* and *narrative form* is a result of the *manner* of presentation. A narrative may be written or told; drama must be presented with impersonation and action—it is "a thing done."

Pity, fear, and *catharsis* are terms that have perplexed and intrigued generations of scholars and critics. This special effect that tragedy aims to produce will be discussed at length later in the chapter. For now, let us recognize that pity goes beyond mere pathos to include the compassion that accompanies shared grief, and that fear transcends sheer fright to convey a sense of anxious concern and profound reverence. Catharsis suggests purgation and purification—a release of emotional tension that results in tranquility.

The idea of tragedy is man-made. There is no ideal tragedy—only a small collection of plays that (with more or less agreement) we refer to when we talk about it. For the moment, we will confine ourselves to "classic" tragedy, which includes the Greeks, the works of Shakespeare and some of his contemporaries, and the French neoclassicists Racine and Corneille. We will deal with modern attempts at tragedy a bit later.

PLOT

Aristotle lays great stress on plot—the "soul of tragedy." He cites the need for a unified and complete sequence of interlocking action; the proper use of reversal, discovery, and recognition; and the obligation of the playwright to make everything "necessary and probable." Most Greek tragedies follow these precepts. They have a few episodes without subplots or extraneous complications, and they do not mix comic matter with the tragic.

The French neoclassicist Racine had no difficulty in plotting his tragedies in the Greek format, but Shakespeare and his fellow Elizabethans composed their plots with utmost freedom. The unities of time, place, and ac-

Prometheus Bound depicts the conflict between Zeus and Prometheus brought on because the latter had brought light to mankind. The magnitude of the struggle is captured in the setting by Richard L. Hay in this production at Stanford, under the direction of Erik Vos.

tion were of no concern in the flexible playhouses designed to accommodate complex stories that showed all the action. Comic and serious matter were blended together, and highborn characters mixed with lowly ones in complicated plots.

Nevertheless, there are valid generalizations that do apply to the tragic form. Tragedy usually deals with a positive, active protagonist caught in sharp conflict with opposing forces. In the ensuing struggle, he or she suffers greatly and goes from fortune to misfortune. Tragic conflicts are of a particular kind. The issues at stake are not mundane considerations, such as economic or environmental problems. The struggle is ethical, spiritual. Consider the story outlines of two of the best-known tragedies, *Antigone* by Sophocles and *Hamlet* by Shakespeare.

A great battle over the city of Thebes claims the lives of the two sons of Oedipus, Eteocles, the defender, and Polyneices, the invader. The new king, Creon, issues an edict that the body of Polyneices should not be buried

Ismene tries in vain to dissuade her sister, Antigone, from defying the King's edict
not to bury the body of their slain brother. Antigone pays for her decision with her
life.

(Greek National Theater at Epidaurus.)

because he had attacked the city. Funeral rites were a sacred obligation to
the Greeks, and Oedipus' daughter Antigone is determined that her
brother shall be given a decent burial. Her sister, Ismene, fearing the threat
of death to anyone who defies the King's edict, attempts to dissuade Antigone. Creon's son, betrothed to Antigone, pleads for her life, but the King is
adamant. An old prophet, Tiresias, comes to the court, and he too urges
Creon to rescind his decision to put Antigone to death for defying his edict.
The King reconsiders and hastens out to bury Polyneices and to free Antigone, but he finds that she has taken her own life. With her is Haemon,
who also kills himself. As Creon grieves over the body of his dead son, he
learns that his wife, shattered by the death of Haemon, has stabbed herself.
Creon, broken in spirit, laments:

Creon: Lead me away, I pray you; a rash, foolish man; who have slain thee,
        ah my son, unwittingly, and thee, too, my wife—unhappy that I am! I

Hamlet finds himself in conflict with the King and court, and with his own sensibilities. Here, he philosophizes over the skull of Yorick.

(Purdue University production.)

know not which way I should bend my gaze, or where I should seek support; for all is amiss with that which is in my hands,—and yonder, again, a crushing fate hath leapt upon my head.

(*As* CREON *is being conducted into the palace, the* LEADER OF THE CHORUS *speaks the closing verses.*)

Leader: Wisdom is the supreme part of happiness; and reverence towards the gods must be inviolate. Great words of prideful men are ever punished with great blows, and, in old age, teach the chastened to be wise.[2]

Prince Hamlet comes home from Wittenburg to attend the funeral of his father and learns that his mother, Gertrude, has hastily remarried the old King's brother, Claudius, who is now on the throne. The ghost of Hamlet's father reveals that he was poisoned by Claudius. Hamlet is sworn to avenge the murder. To establish the validity of the ghost, Hamlet composes a dramatic scene that resembles his father's murder, to be played before the court by a traveling troupe of players. (See "The Mousetrap" in Chapter One.) Polonius, the King's advisor, thinks Hamlet is mad for the love of his daughter, Ophelia, whom he and the King use as a decoy to discover Hamlet's motivations. Claudius blanches in guilty fear when he sees the simulated poisoning and knows that Hamlet is a dangerous adversary. While Hamlet is berating his mother for her alliance with Claudius, he hears a noise behind the curtain; he stabs through it and slays the eavesdropping Polonius. Ophelia's mind snaps from the tension, and she drowns herself. Her brother, Laertes, determined to avenge the deaths of Ophelia and his father, is persuaded by Claudius to engage Hamlet in a "friendly" duel, with Laertes' foil tipped with poison. To make doubly sure that Hamlet dies, Claudius prepares a poisoned drink for him. As a result of these machinations, which go awry, Laertes, Gertrude, Claudius, and Hamlet all die. The Prince's friend, Horatio, eulogizes,

> Now cracks a noble heart. Goodnight, sweet Prince,
> And flights of angels sing thee to thy rest!

Fortinbras, king of Norway, arrives to restore order to the kingdom.

Antigone and *Hamlet* are sharply contrasting plays in structure. The Greek play has nine characters, plus the chorus, shown in a single place over a short period of time. Hamlet is a complex play, involving more than forty characters, twenty different scenes, and numerous changes of locale. Yet both are tragic plots in that they are serious, complete, and of a certain magnitude; and they have two protagonists who suffer mightily and go to their deaths with their integrities intact. There is no last-minute reprieve, no escape from catastrophe. Neither Sophocles nor Shakespeare exploits the suffering for pathos. The end result is a catharsis, an enlightenment, a feeling of exaltation from seeing the greatness of the human spirit confronted with adversity.

Suzanne K. Langer, in her perceptive book *Feeling and Form*, sees tragedy shaped by a "tragic rhythm"—a pattern transferred from nature, of growth, maturation, and decline. The action of the play shows the hero's "self-realization as, under increasing pressure, he reaches the highest potential in "the vision of life as accomplished . . . a sense of fulfillment that lifts him above defeat."[3] *Antigone* and *Hamlet* follow Langer's pattern of the tragic rhythm.

THE TRAGIC HERO

One of the most discussed aspects of Aristotelian thought is his concept of the tragic hero, who is seen as good but not free from faults—"an intermediate kind of personage," who although not preeminently virtuous, is not depraved. The hero's "flaw" (*hamartia*, which means "missing the mark") is a term that has caused endless argument since it is not uniformly applicable to all tragedies, nor does it appear to be consistent in the variety of characters involved in catastrophes.

How does one equate the suffering of Prometheus with that of Oedipus? Antigone or Hippolytus with Medea? Hamlet with Macbeth, Lear with Romeo and Juliet? The degree of guilt seems to have little or nothing to do with justice. All tragic figures suffer, regardless of their degree of guilt or responsibility. Sometimes their fall seems to be a matter of cause and effect rather than crime and punishment. Pity is not related to vengeance but to "undeserved misfortune." Antigone and Hamlet are not evildoers who are punished for their sins. Our attention as we look at tragic protagonists is not on their guilt or innocence but on the quality of their spirit. How do they respond to those "boundary situations" in which they are tested to the limit? What is the effect on them of evil and injustice? Implicit in the Aristotelian

This photo pictures the denouement of *Romeo and Juliet,* when the lovers are united in death as a result of the conflict between the Montague and Capulet families.

(Scenography by Josef Svoboda at the National Theater, Prague.)

concept of the tragic hero is that he or she must be a character of some magnitude—an elevated figure, one who occupies an important position in society so that the fall is from a high place.

Northrop Frye gives us the image of the tragic hero at the top of the wheel of fortune, above humanity and below something greater in the sky, who acts as a "conductor" of power from above. "Tragic heroes are wrapped in the mystery of their communion with that something beyond which we can see only through them and which is the source of their strength and their fate alike."[4]

DICTION

The elevated style of Greek, neoclassic, and Elizabethan tragedy, with its characters and themes of great magnitude, required poetic language: tragedy is also characterized by the grandeur of the diction. But like all good language for the stage, it is functional, as an appropriate level of speech for the dramatic situation, not as a separate element of the play. In general, tragedy has been written by dramatists with the poetic gifts to combine dignity with clarity, who speak with an eloquence free from bombast or self-conscious display. Their verse lifts the drama through images and rhythms that have the essential quality of being eminently speakable.

Robert F. Goheen, in his *The Imagery of Sophocles' Antigone*,[5] found in Creon's and Antigone's language clues to their opposing views of the world. Because the King has a materialistic focus, he consistently uses imagery associated with measurable fact, whereas Antigone, with her interior motivation that is emotional and intuitive, expresses herself in recurrent sensory language aligned to pain, pleasure, and tears. On the other hand, Sophocles makes a positive statement graphic through imagery of nature in a choral ode in praise of human achievement:

> Wonders are many, and none is more wonderful than man; the power that crosses the white sea, driven by the stormy south-wind, making a path under surges that threaten to engulf him; and Earth, the eldest of the gods, the immortal, the unwearied, doth he wear, turning the soil with the offspring of horses, as the ploughs go to and fro from year to year.
> And the light-hearted race of birds, and the tribes of savage beasts, and the sea-brood of the deep, he snares in the meshes of his woven toils, he leads captive, man excellent in wit. And he masters by his arts the beast whose lair is in the wilds, who roams the hills; he tames the horse of shaggy mane, he puts the yoke upon its necks, he tames the tireless mountain bull.[6]

Caroline Spurgeon's monumental work, *Shakespeare's Imagery and What It Tells Us,* was the first large-scale systematic investigation of imagery. She discovered that Shakespeare used two prominent categories: images of the English countryside and the homely concerns of domestic life. In *Hamlet* Spurgeon identified 279 images; the dominant one was of sickness, decay, and disease; blemishes of nature and of the body; and the idea of an ulcer or tumor as descriptive of the unwholesome condition of Denmark.[7]

Hamlet, bitterly resenting the hasty marriage of his mother and King Claudius, expresses his dark view in this image:

> How weary, stale, flat and unprofitable
> Seem to me all the uses of this world.
> Fie on't! tis an unweeded garden,
> That grows to seed; things rank and gross in nature
> Possess it merely.

AESTHETIC PLEASURE

The pleasure that tragedy affords is not moral but aesthetic. We admire the grandeur of conception, the ability of the dramatists to create significant action around great themes. And we also enjoy "insight experiences," showing us that despite injustice and evil, excessive pride and passion, violence and tyranny, the human spirit has the capacity to endure. The tragic hero's purpose is defeated, his passion is agonizing, but he comes to terms with his fate through perception. And from that imitation we learn—we attain a clearer awareness of the mystery of our own nature. As Langer suggests, there is aesthetic pleasure in seeing the tragic rhythm completed, the expectation fulfilled, and within the tragic rhythm, human dignity retained.

There are those who see the universality of tragedy as a way of connecting us to the latent experiences of myth and ritual, which have absorbed the attention of Carl Jung and his followers, in archetypal patterns of thought and behavior—patterns and experiences that Jung said are "deeply implanted in the memory of the race." Gilbert Murray describes the phenomenon in these terms:

> In plays like *Hamlet* or the *Agamemnon* or the *Electra* we have certainly fine and flexible character-study, a varied and well-wrought story, a full command of the technical instruments of the poet and the dramatist; but we have also, I suspect, an undercurrent of desires and fears and passions, long slumbering yet eternally familiar, which have for thousands of years lain near the root of our most intimate emotions and have been wrought into the fabric of our most magical dreams. How far into the past ages this stream may reach back, I dare not even surmise; but it seems to me as if the power of stirring it or moving with it were one of the last secrets of genius.[8]

CATHARSIS

The most significant element that distinguishes tragedy from other forms of drama is the tragic effect. Just what it is in tragedy that gives pleasure through pain is difficult to determine. August Schlegel felt that the tragic tone was one of "irrepressible melancholy" when the audience is consoled and elevated by witnessing human weakness exposed to the vagaries of fate and natural forces. Arthur Schopenhauer saw the meaning of tragedy as resignation and renunciation in the face of a miserable and desolate existence. On the other hand, Henry Myers saw evidence of a just order in tragedy:

> Since it is positive and affirmative, great tragic poetry satisfies our deepest rational and moral inclinations. As rational beings, we are always looking for patterns, for order, for meaning in experience; as moral beings, we can be satisfied only by discovering in the realm of good and evil the special kind of pattern or order which we call justice. Tragedy reconciles us to evil by showing us that it is not a single, separate phenomenon but one side of change of fortune, and makes us feel that the change of fortune of a representative man is just.[9]

From these opposing statements, it is clear that what constitutes the tragic effect is capable of many interpretations. The effect is complex and highly personalized, arrived at through one's own experiences in life.

In any discussion of the tragic effect, we must keep Aristotle's words "fear" and "pity" before us. What did he mean by them? Pity is not simply pathos, a soft sentiment of sorrow for one who is weak or unworthy, even though it arises from "undeserved misfortune." Pity is not contemptuous nor patronizing. Tragic pity implies a sharing of grief. We enter into the experience of another through our sympathy and our fellow feeling. Our pity for the tragic hero is an act of compassion.

Aristotle's concept of fear extends beyond sheer fright or terror to include anxious concern, solicitude, awe, reverence, and apprehension. In tragedy, fear is not merely a hair-raising, spine-tingling reaction of the nervous system; it is an emotion that warms the heart and illuminates the mind. Fear carries a sense of wonder that may include admiration for an individual whose spirit remains intact despite all that the world can do to it. The purging of fear and pity, then, in tragedy must be universalized into a general concern for others rather than a private and personal identification with disaster.

The catharsis is not the automatic result of following a dramatic formula. We have the capacity for compassion for many kinds of people, good and bad, in many kinds of situations, provided that we have understanding. Our sympathies can go out to foolish and evil characters like Lear and Macbeth. What really counts is our ability to enter into the suffering of the characters as they are tested, and to find within ourselves an echo of their frailty and their flaws.

This emotional response to tragedy is a complex one. It must be broad enough to encompass a variety of experiences and extensive enough to include shades of feeling, such as the heartbreak at the end of *King Lear,*

Euripides' *The Trojan Women* dramatizes the sorrow and suffering that followed after the fall of Troy. The devastation of Queen Hecuba and the other grieving women elicits a feeling of pity and fear. Aleka Katseli as Hecuba, Epidaurus festival.

Phèdre, Romeo and Juliet, and *Oedipus Rex;* the sense of triumph at the end of *Hamlet, The Crucible,* and *Antigone;* and the appalling sense of waste at the end of *The Trojan Women, Ghosts,* and *Othello.* Catharsis is a purging of the spectator's fear and pity, resulting in a sense of release and tranquility. We are cleansed and exhilarated when we are liberated from our own emotional entanglements, our disturbing passions. Fear gives way to certainty, even though that certainty is death. Pity goes beyond feeling and becomes understanding. The spectator leaves the theater "in calm of mind, all passion spent." The end result, as Frye suggests, is that the audience experiences a "kind of buoyancy." Or again, in Edith Hamilton's words, "the great soul in pain and death transforms and exalts pain and death." Myers universalizes the meaning more explicitly:

> These are the main features of the tragic spirit. It lifts us above self-pity and reconciles us to suffering by showing that evil is a necessary part of the intelligible and just order of our experience. It lifts us above the divisive spirit of melodrama by showing that men are neither naturally good nor inherently evil. It saves us all from the pitfalls of utopianism and fatalism. It teaches moderation by showing that the way of the extremist is short, but that at the same time it shows the man of principle that an uncompromising stand is not without its just compensations. And most important, it teaches us that all men are united in the kinship of a common fate, that all are destined to suffer and enjoy, each according to his capacity.[10]

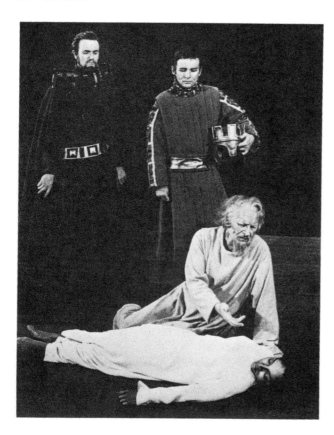

King Lear is a play of self discovery, in which Lear, through suffering, learns of his daughter's genuine affection for him and of the savagery of his other two daughters, Regan and Goneril. Morris Carnovsky as Lear and Ruby Dee as Cordelia.

(American Shakespeare Theater.)

The eminent Shakespearean scholar A. C. Bradley makes an interesting and valid contribution to the idea of tragedy by suggesting that catharsis results when pity and fear unite with a profound sense of mystery and sadness because of the impression of waste.[11] In the catastrophe, something of value is destroyed. Important and worthwhile connections are broken. This is perhaps one of the reasons the layperson speaks of the "tragedy" that occurs through some accident to a person of promise who had a bright future.

A POSITIVE STATEMENT

Although tragedy involves suffering, evil, and death, many critics feel it is a positive statement about life. As Allardyce Nicoll says, "Death never really matters in tragedy. . . . Tragedy assumes that death is inevitable and that its time of coming is of no importance compared with what a man does before his death."[12]

Death may overtake the protagonists, but they are spiritually victo-

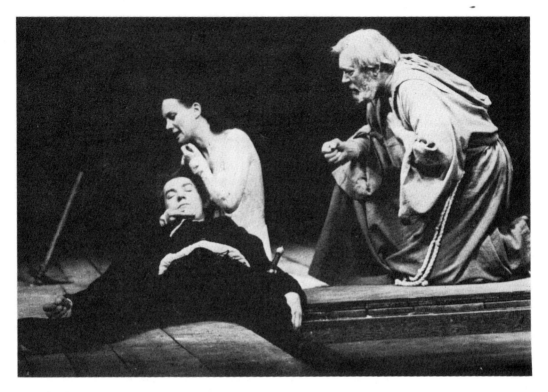

Tragedy often produces a sense of waste as in *Romeo and Juliet* when the young lovers give up their lives. Juliet grieves over the death of Romeo.
(Royal Shakespeare Company.)

rious. They are not abject, craven victims of fate who go cowering to their doom. The principles for which they lived and died survive their passing. The hero dies; heroism lives on. We admire the audacity of those who disregard human frailty, revealing an astonishing capacity for suffering in matters of the spirit. Their action is an affirmation of life. They sustain our faith in humanity.

HONESTY

The writers of tragedy are unflinchingly honest. They show life as it is, not as one wishes it might be. They have the courage to confront the terrors and perplexities of life; they acknowledge human frailty. Their plots are not manipulated to spare the protagonist; the hero or heroine goes relentlessly to catastrophe. Nor does tragedy demonstrate poetic justice in which the virtuous are rewarded and the wicked punished. Instead, the dramatist shows the clash between our desire for justice and what really happens. The evil is presented along with the good. In the treatment of character, the protagonists are not the idealized heroes of romanticism or the unmitigated villains of melodrama. They are a mixture of clay and stardust; they are admirable characters, but they usually possess a flaw, and their imperfection links them to us. Tragedy rests on a solid basis of integrity, making no concessions to the wishes of the audience. In Jean Anouilh's modern version of *Antigone* the chorus makes this cogent statement about tragedy:

> Tragedy is clean, it is firm, it is flawless. It has nothing to do with melodrama—with wicked villains, persecuted maidens, avengers, gleams of hope and eleventh-hour repentances. Death, in melodrama, is really horrible because it is never inevitable. The dear old father might so easily have been saved; the honest young man might so easily have brought in the police five minutes earlier. In a tragedy, nothing is in doubt and everyone's destiny is known. That makes for tranquility. Tragedy is restful; and the reason is that *hope*, that foul, deceitful thing, has no part in it. There isn't any hope. You're trapped. The whole sky has fallen on you, and all you can do about it is to shout. Now don't mistake me: I said "shout": I did not say groan, whimper, complain. *That*, you cannot do. But you can *shout* aloud; you can get all those things said that you never thought you'd be able to say—or never knew you had it in you to say. And you don't say these things because it will do any good to say them; you know better than that. You say them for their own sake; you say them because you learn a lot from them. In melodrama, you argue and struggle in the hope of escape. That is vulgar; it's practical. But in tragedy, where there is no temptation to try to escape, argument is gratuitous: it's kingly.[13]

SIGNIFICANT CONTENT

Tragedy achieves significance because it is concerned with the deep and abiding questions and problems that have perplexed man throughout the ages. As Nicoll says, tragedy puts us in "contact with infinity. If we are religious, we shall say it is in contact with forces divine; if we are aesthetic, we shall say it is in contact with the vast illimitable forces of the universe. Everywhere in tragedy there is this sense of being raised to loftier heights."[14]

Myers asserts that "tragedy best expresses its conceptions of the orderly and absolute nature of values,"[15] and Fergusson observes that tragedy "celebrates the mystery of human nature and destiny with the health of the soul in view."[16] Tragedy confronts suffering and evil with honesty in such a way as to reveal both the weakness and nobility of human beings, their strength of will, and their capacity for suffering without breaking in the face of inevitable doom. Tragedy is not the drama of small souls bedeviled by the minor irritations of humdrum life. It does not concentrate on the physical environment or welfare, with getting and spending, or with collecting things. On the contrary, tragedy lifts our vision beyond petty cares and

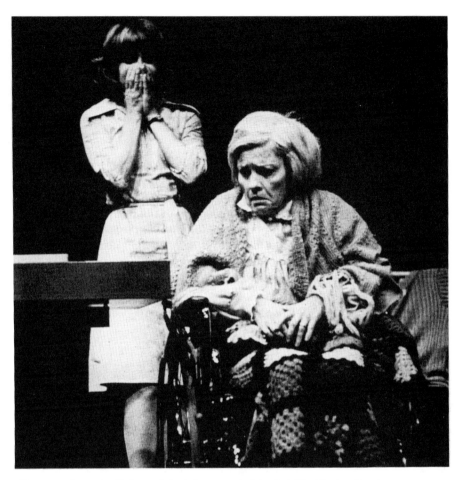

The atmosphere of suffering and death is present in Cristofer's *The Shadow Box*, but there is no sense of magnitude.

(Mark Taper Forum. Gordon Davidson, Artistic Director.)

mundane anxieties by focusing on the great issues that affect our spiritual welfare. Clytemnestra is caught between avenging the death of her daughter and her duty to her husband; Lear, between sympathy and pride; Macbeth, between ambition and conscience. Tragedy deals with matters of great consequence.

The significant content of tragedy gives this form of drama a sense of *universality*. The effect of the play goes beyond the particular characters and the immediate circumstances to achieve an atmosphere of broad application. If even kings may suffer, how vulnerable are we? To the Greeks and Elizabethans the fate of the rulers was connected directly with that of their subjects. There is implicit in genuine tragedy not only an elevation of life but also an acute awareness of our common frailty and humanity. Tragic characters face problems not of a particular group or society but of all people, ones that we all must face. The problems are not temporary, external ones that can be overcome once and for all. Tragedy is rooted in the nature of our humanity, out of the clash between good and evil that confronts all of us. Thus, the suffering and struggles of the tragic hero become a part of the universal experience of those who share the play.

MODERN TRAGEDY

Our modern temper, with its anxieties and doubts, is often regarded as inhospitable ground for the nurture of the tragic spirit. The political practice of raising the common man to a dominant position has changed our fashion in heroes from highborn and romantic characters to ordinary, contemporary individuals, certainly not those of magnitude and grandeur. But even more important, it is alleged, our cultural condition, which results from a

Although Mother Courage is a lowly creature, her grief over the dead body of her son gives a sense of universality to her suffering.

(Munich Kammerspiele.)

GEORGE BARNWELL;
A TRAGEDY, IN FIVE ACTS.—BY GEORGE LILLO.

Act IV.—Scene 2

Generally considered the first domestic tragedy, the hero-apprentice George Barnwell is led astray by a scheming prostitute and is sent to the gallows despite his abject repentance. Lillo's *The London Merchant,* 1731.

shifting sense of values, and our exaggerated concern with the material world have crippled our spiritual vision, and we now find ourselves in a world of despair, anguish, and absurdity. In place of the "eternal verities," we have situational morality, adapting our ethics to the needs of the moment. Without a firm foundation to stand on, the modern playwright shows us the individual's desperate need for illusion—and what happens when illusions disappear.

As a result of the contemporary climate, tragedy is difficult or impossible to write, some critics claim, because the genre depends on characters of a heroic mold who spiritually transcend their sufferings to attain nobility, giving the spectator a sense of exaltation. Joseph Wood Krutch laments the "enfeeblement of the spirit" in our society and indicates why he thinks Ibsen could not write dramas of the heroic stature of Shakespeare:

> The materials out of which the latter created his works—his conception of human dignity, his sense of the importance of human passions, his vision of the amplitude of human life—simply did not and could not exist for Ibsen, as they did not and could not exist for his contemporaries. God and Man and Nature had all somehow dwindled in the course of the intervening centuries, not because the realistic creed of modern art led us to seek out mean people, but because this meanness of human life was somehow thrust upon us.[17]

George Lukacs, another critic, supports Krutch's view:

> The thematic material of bourgeois drama is trivial, because it is all too near us; the natural pathos of its living men is undramatic and its most subtle values are lost when heightened into drama; the fable is wilfully invented and so cannot retain the natural and poetic resonance of an ancient tradition.[18]

On the other hand, it is argued that expecting the modern playwright to imitate antiquity is a mistaken notion. John Gassner voices this point of view:

> A fundamental premise has been the opinion that a great deal of the tragic art of the past, while excellent as far as it went, belongs to the past. The pagan beliefs that served Attic tragedy twenty-five centuries ago are no longer acceptable to modern man. Neither are the beliefs of the Elizabethan period and the age of Louis XIV. There is simply no single time philosophy of tragedy any more than there is a single inviolable tragic form. Tragic art is subject to the evolutionary processes, and tragedy created in modern times must be modern. The fact that it will be different from tragedy written three, five, or twenty-five centuries ago does not mean that it will no longer be tragedy; it will merely be different. . . . We may also arrive at the conclusion that there is really no compelling reason for the modern stage to *strain* toward tragedy. There are other ways of responding to the human condition. . . . The creative spirit of an age should be allowed, and indeed expected, to engender its own dramatic forms or to modify existent ones.[19]

Gassner's point is well taken. After all, great tragedy is rare in theater history and we should not castigate modern dramatists because they do not recapture the ancient grandeur. Since we are so much a product of the conditioning forces of our times, it is legitimate that the theater should express the concerns of our society—the identity crisis, the clash between generations and cultures, the loss of freedom, faith, and security, the disparity between illusion and reality, the cost of integrity, and the difficulty of finding meaning in a world of shifting values.

Two outstanding examples of our modern theater are Ibsen's *Ghosts* (1881) and Miller's *Death of a Salesman* (1949). *Ghosts,* one of the most violently protested plays in the history of the theater, tells the story of Mrs. Alving's unsuccessful attempts to escape from the conventional strictures of a sterile Victorian society. She married Captain Alving because he was regarded as socially acceptable, but she discovers that he is dissolute and has contracted syphillis. She sends her son, Oswald, abroad to study art and to shield him from his father's corruption. When the Captain dies, Mrs. Alving uses his legacy to build an orphanage in his honor, thus concealing her husband's true character and preventing Oswald from inheriting a tainted fortune. As the play opens, Mrs. Alving is confident that she has successfully laid to rest the ghosts of the past. However, Oswald becomes involved with the maid, Regina, who is actually his illegitimate half-sister. Pastor Manders, who at one time rejected Mrs. Alving when she fled to him to escape from her dissolute husband, visits the house to inquire about the efficacy of insuring the new orphanage. Oswald reveals to his mother that he is fatally ill with the venereal disease he inherited from his father. He makes her promise to give him a deadly drug when he loses his mind. Regina refuses to have anything more to do with Oswald and goes off to work in a tavern as the orphanage burns down. Under the strain of learning about his father's degeneracy and of Regina's parentage, Oswald's mind gives way and he begs his mother to give him the drug that will release him from his miserable life. As the curtain comes down, Mrs. Alving stands over her babbling son, the poison in her hand, unable to act.

Death of a Salesman (1949) shows Willy Loman, a traveling salesman, returning to his Brooklyn home after an aborted trip. At sixty-five, Willy has come to the end of his strength. Through flashbacks, we are taken back to earlier, happier times, when he pampered his sons, Biff and Happy, and sold them on his view of popularity and financial success based on a backslapping personality and a snappy appearance. Willy is convinced that Biff, a high school football star, will make a name for himself in the world. But Biff has a crisis with his academic work and visits his father in Boston, where

Arthur Miller, in his *Death of a Salesman,* created a moving portrait of the common man as a tragic protagonist in Willy Loman, who unfortunately "didn't know who he was."

(Wayne State University. Directed by Don Blakely.)

he discovers Willy in a hotel with a woman. Happy has become a self-in-dulgent womanizer. Willy struggles to pull himself together, but his young, callous employer fires him. Linda, the devoted wife and mother, defends Willy against his disrespectful sons. Biff accuses Willy of being a failure and of selling his sons a phony dream. As a final gesture, Willy commits suicide and leaves his paid-up insurance as a legacy. Miller ends with a requiem at Willy's grave, where Biff comments, "He had the wrong dreams. All, all wrong."

Both *Ghosts* and *Death of a Salesman* are serious, complete, and honest. The actions seem necessary and probable. There is a kind of universality in both plays because the characters and their environments were, in their time, common enough to be creditable to their contemporaries. Certainly, the narrow strictures of Victorian conventions were familiar enough to late nineteenth-century society, and Willy's empty, materialistic illusions are close enough to us for recognition and identification; but there is no sense of elevation, no enlightenment, no catharsis. Mrs. Alving and Willy are not positive characters striving to assert ethical values. On the other hand, Ibsen and Miller dramatize characters in scenes of intense suffering, and although the exhilaration of spiritual triumph is missing, we are caught up in the strong and vivid theatrical experiences with which we can identify. The characters may not be enlightened, but the audiences come away with fresh perceptions.

Other playwrights of the last century who have created compelling, serious plays are Strindberg, Chekhov, O'Neill, Pirandello, Sean O'Casey, Shaw, Williams, Anouilh, Beckett, Shepard, Osborne, Pinter, and Peter Shaffer. You will recall Bradley's view of tragedy, which includes the sense of waste. This feeling is aroused by contemporary playwrights, who so often dramatize characters and conditions in which something of great value is lost—a potential not realized, a promising life destroyed, a dream unful-filled. And although the fall is not from a high place, there is a stark urgency and immediacy in our response because these people are familiar and their actions are close to our own experience.

Miller may not be far from the mark when he says;

> The tragic right is a condition of life, a condition in which the human person-ality is able to flower and realize itself. The wrong is the condition which sup-presses man, perverts the flowing out of his love and creative instinct. Tragedy enlightens—and it must, in that it points the heroic finger at the enemy of man's freedom.[20]

The origin of the theater began with tragedy in the sixth century B.C. in Greece. Critical assessment generally regards tragedy as the highest form

Long Day's Journey into Night, by Eugene O'Neill, dramatizes the story of the matinee idol, Tyrone, and his troubled family.

(Wayne State University. Directed by N. Joseph Calarco.)

of dramatic art, and its small collection of plays is considered one of the most important aesthetic achievements of Western culture. However, although tragedy has attracted more critical attention than any other form of drama, it is the least produced.

Tragedy confronts the individual with the most profound issues of life, with the complexities of human nature, with the forces of good and evil. It makes no concession to wish fulfillment, sugary optimism, or happy endings.

PLAYS TO READ AND SEE

F = Film available; V = Videotape available.

		Sophocles, *Antigone, Oedipus Rex*
F	V	Miller, *Death of a Salesman*
		Ibsen, *Ghosts*
F	V	Shakespeare, *Hamlet,* Olivier's *Hamlet,* Olivier's *King Lear, Macbeth, Romeo and Juliet*
F	V	O'Neill, *Long Day's Journey into Night*
F	V	*Shakespearean Tragedy*
F	V	Euripides, *Trojan Women*
F		*What Happens in Hamlet*

BIBLIOGRAPHY

BRADLEY, A. C. *Shakespearean Tragedy.* London: Macmillan, 1957.

FRYE, NORTHROP. *The Anatomy of Criticism.* Princeton, N.J.: Princeton University Press, 1957.

HEILMAN, ROBERT BECHTOLD. *The Iceman, the Arsonist, and the Troubled Agent: Tragedy and Melodrama on the Modern Stage.* Seattle: University of Washington Press, 1973.

KERR, WALTER. *Tragedy and Comedy.* New York: Simon & Schuster, Inc., 1967.

KITTO, H. D. F. *Greek Tragedy.* London: Methuen, 1950.

LANGER, SUZANNE. *Feeling and Form.* New York: Charles Scribner's Sons, 1953.

MULLER, HERBERT. *The Spirit of Tragedy.* New York: Alfred A. Knopf, Inc., 1976.

MYERS, HENRY ALONZO. *Tragedy: A View of Life.* Ithaca, N.Y.: Cornell University Press, 1956.

OLSON, ELDER. *Tragedy and the Theory of Drama.* Detroit: Wayne State University Press, 1961.

NOTES

1. Ingram Bywater, trans., *Aristotle on the Art of Poetry* (Oxford: Clarendon Press, 1920).

2. Sophocles, *Antigone,* trans. R. C. Jebb (Cambridge: Cambridge University Press, 1902).

3. Suzanne K. Langer, *Feeling and Form* (New York: Charles Scribner's & Sons, 1953).

4. Northrop Frye, *The Anatomy of Criticism* (Princeton, N.J.: Princeton University Press, 1957).

5. Robert F. Goheen, *The Imagery of Sophocles' Antigone* (Princeton: Princeton University Press, 1951).

6. Sophocles, *Antigone,* trans. R.C. Jebb (Cambridge: Cambridge University Press, 1902).

7. Caroline Spurgeon, *Shakespeare's Imagery and What It Tells Us* (Cambridge: Cambridge University Press, 1935).

8. Gilbert Murray, "Hamlet and Orestes," in *The Classical Tradition in Poetry* (Cambridge, Mass.: Harvard University Press, 1927).

9. Henry Alonzo Myers, *Tragedy: A View of Life* (Ithaca, N.Y.: Cornell University Press, 1956).

10. Myers, *Tragedy.*

11. A. C. Bradley, *Shakespearean Tragedy* (London: Macmillan, 1957).

12. Allardyce Nicoll, *Theory of Drama* (New York: Thomas Y. Crowell Co., 1931).

13. Jean Anouilh, *Antigone,* trans. Lewis Galantiere (London: Van Loewen, 1946).

14. Nicoll, *The Theory of Drama.*

15. Myers, *Tragedy.*

16. Francis Fergusson, *The Idea of a Theater* (Princeton, N.J.: Princeton University Press, 1949).

17. Joseph Wood Krutch, *"Modernism" in Modern Drama* (Ithaca, N.Y.: Cornell University Press, 1953).

18. George Lukacs, "The Sociology of Modern Drama," trans. Lee Baxandall, *Tulane Drama Review,* 9 (Summer 1965).

19. John Gassner, "The Possibilities and Perils of Modern Tragedy," *Tulane Drama Review,* I, no. 3 (June 1957).

20. Arthur Miller, "Tragedy and the Common Man," *New York Times,* February 27, 1949.

4

Melodrama

Melodrama conjures up images of cliffhangers, in which damsels in distress are rescued by stalwart heroes from the clutches of wicked villains. We associate the term with such bygone hits as *East Lynne, Under the Gaslight, Ten Nights in a Bar Room,* and *The Drunkard.* Although such fare dominated the stage in the nineteenth century, the spirit of melodrama is also very much alive and flourishing now. The external trappings have changed and the exaggerations have been toned down, but the basic melodramatic appeals that brought our forefathers to the theater are the same as those that appear tonight on our television and motion-picture screens.

The reason for the enormous popularity of melodrama is that the audience may be sure that something will happen. People don't just sit around and talk—they act. The characters are not resigned to meek acceptance of their fate, incapacitated by despair or fear—they cope.

Eric Bentley describes melodrama in these words:

> It is the spontaneous, uninhibited way of seeing things. . . . The dramatic sense is the melodramatic sense, as one can see from the play acting of any child. Melodrama is not a special and marginal kind of drama, let alone an eccentric or decadent one, it is drama in its elemental form; it is the quintessence of drama.[1]

Melodrama aims at maximum involvement so that the spectator identifies with the hero and participates vicariously in the action. Bentley suggests that in its response to melodrama the audience may have "a good cry—the poor man's catharsis." Thus, melodrama becomes a way to release frustration and aggression and achieve one's wishes.

Outwardly, melodrama tries to create the illusion of real people in genuine jeopardy, but actually it manipulates the plot toward reprieve, rescue, or reform. It exploits physical and material difficulties; escape from danger is a typical plot line. Melodrama generates excitement, suspense, and thrills for their own sake. Like a game, melodrama builds tension and exhilaration, but it is transitory and without substantial significance. One leaves the theater with a sense of relief at the outcome but untroubled by the conditions that caused the suffering and conflicts.

In the previous chapter we considered tragedy, the loftiest and rarest form of drama. How does it differ from melodrama, which on the surface seems to deal, like tragedy, with characters involved in serious and critical situations? Fundamentally, the distinction lies in the point of view. Tragedy confronts good and evil with unblinking honesty; melodrama escapes from life. Tragedy considers eternal spiritual problems; melodrama deals with the transitory, the material, the physical. Tragedy evokes fear and pity; melodrama arouses suspense, pathos, terror, and sometimes hate. However, melodrama is not mere ineffectual tragedy. As a matter of fact, a well-written melodrama may be superior to an inept tragedy. The point is that the two forms of drama are different. They are similar only in that they both

A recent revival of *The Count of Monte Cristo* at the University of Minnesota.

(Directed by Robert Moulton.)

seem serious, but in melodrama the seriousness is only a pretense for the sake of the theatrical game.

Melodramatic scenes and situations have been a part of the history of the theater almost from the beginning. Euripides, in striving for effect, was sometimes very close to melodrama, and Seneca exploited sensational and horrible material to the hilt. The Elizabethan "tragedies of blood" employed much of the machinery of melodrama, with scenes of horror and violence. Jacobean playwrights delighted in grisly scenes of exciting action. The early eighteenth-century "she-tragedies" of Nicholas Rowe, with their sentimentalism and overwrought emotions, were in the melodramatic vein. Johann Schiller's romantic *The Robbers* (1781) capitalized on the fugitive situation so dear to writers of melodrama.

The term *melodrama* combines two Greek words meaning "music" and "drama." At one time the word was literally synonymous with opera. Melodrama was first allied with music in Italy and France. In Germany the term referred to dialogue passages spoken to orchestral accompaniment.

The modern connotation of the word, however, stems from the late eighteenth-century French theater and its subsequent development, especially in England and America.

Until 1791, the Comédie Française and the Italian Comedians enjoyed monopolistic control over the legitimate theaters of Paris. Ingenious man-

In 1802, Thomas Holcroft gave British audiences a taste for melodrama with his *A Tale of Mystery,* featuring violent action in a gothic atmosphere.

agers circumvented governmental restrictions by contriving a kind of entertainment based on pantomime accompanied by dance, song, and dialogue, which elicited a popular following because of its sensational qualities. When freedom of production was granted to all theaters, the word *melodrama* was attached to the pantomime with dialogue and music.

Frank Rahill, in his study of melodrama, with emphasis on the nineteenth century, defines the genre in these terms:

> Melodrama is a form of dramatic composition in prose partaking of the nature of tragedy, comedy, pantomime and spectacle, and intended for a popular audience. Primarily concerned with situation and plot, it calls upon mimed action extensively and employs a more or less fixed complement of stock characters, the most important of which are a suffering heroine, or hero, a persecuting villain, and a benevolent comic. It is conventionally moral and humanitarian in point of view and sentimental and optimistic in temper, concluding its fable happily with virtue rewarded after many trials and vice punished. Characteristically, it offers elaborate scenic accessories and miscellaneous divertissements and introduces music freely, typically to underscore dramatic effect.[2]

The French playwright Guilbert de Pixérécourt at the beginning of the nineteenth century became the foremost playwright of the new form, which exactly fit the taste of the lower classes. He made a careful study of his audiences until he perfected the machinery that was to dominate melodrama from that time to this and was to make him one of the most popular playwrights who ever lived. He wrote nearly sixty melodramas, which played more than 30,000 performances in France alone. His plots were based on exciting action, surprise, and suspense—the sharp contrasts of vice against virtue, the comic versus the pathetic—and he thrilled his audiences with spectacular scenes such as fires, floods, and collisions. Although he wrote his plays rapidly, he worked with them in the theater personally, taking great pains to have them produced exactly as he intended. The success of his efforts caused him to be known as "the Napoleon of the Boulevard."

Before Thomas Holcroft returned to London from France with his popular melodrama, *A Tale of Mystery* (1802), the taste for its mood and action had already been set by the sentimentalized, long-suffering heroines of gothic novels and by the theater's spectacular scenery. "Monk" Lewis' *Castle Spectre* (1797) employed much of the machinery of melodrama in the dramatization of an orphan girl, Lady Angela, ensnared by the wicked Lord Osmond, who has slain her father and taken over his property. The setting is a castle haunted by the ghost of the girl's mother. Thanks to the efforts of Earl Percy, disguised as a farmer, the villain is foiled and a happy ending ensues. *Castle Spectre* was a smashing success, and its basic ingredients were endlessly copied.

In the late eighteenth century in Germany, August von Kotzebue wrote more than 200 plays combining sensational scenes with heavy sentimentality. He was not only commercially successful but also very influential on playwriting for years to come. In England, Richard Sheridan translated and presented Kotzebue's *The Spaniard in Peru* as *Pizarro* in 1799; and in 1798 William Dunlap adapted Kotzebue's *The Stranger,* one of the first melodramas to be presented in America in the nineteenth century, although most plays were imported from France and England rather than from Germany. Later American playwrights learned to exploit the native scene for plays of big-city life, rural stories with local color, plays about firemen, and dramas of the wild West.

At first melodrama owed its popularity to its story line. Its pattern was a series of strong actions performed by clear-cut characters demonstrating the triumph of simple virtues and the ultimate defeat of villainy. To satisfy the tremendous demand for new material, playwrights ground out new plays as do today's television writers; and like their modern counterparts, most writers followed well-established formulas.

As the nineteenth century progressed, efforts were made to create more realistic melodramas. The easiest way to suggest reality was through the external aspects of production—especially the stage scenery. Toward the end of the century, the theater technician ran away with the show. New and spectacular effects became a primary source of appeal. The stage mechanic was called on not only to represent accurate replicas of familiar landscapes, buildings, and monuments but also to reproduce all manner of sensational effects. Melodrama tended to become simply a scenario for exciting actions. As a result of its elaboration of the visual aspects of production and its demand for strong stories and movements, nineteenth-century melodrama led directly to the development of the motion-picture industry.

By the end of the nineteenth century the old-fashioned melodrama had run its course because of the increasing sophistication of the audience and the changes in the world outside. As drama moved toward realism, the old formulas and characters of melodrama gave way. Even when the theater aimed at the popular audience, it was necessary to make plots more credible, to include more kinds of characters and to give them more depth, and to capture the impression of more normal speech. As for one of the major appeals of melodrama—the sensational scenes—the new film medium offered spectacle far beyond the capacities of the limited stage. Today our films and television plays still use many of the techniques and appeals of old-time melodrama in horse operas and tales of adventure, crime, and warfare, both terrestrial and astral.

PLOT

Melodrama in the nineteenth century relied heavily on stories that had colorful characters, opportunities for strong "sensation" scenes, and outlets for powerful emotions. Audiences preferred dramatic situations that showed characters struggling against fearful odds, trapped or marooned, but holding out until help comes—the last bullet, the last drop of water, the last bite of food, the last cent. The art of playwriting, therefore, became the art of devising scenes of excitement. Melodrama exaggerated climaxes and crises so that the structure of the play was a series of peaks of action rather than a well-knit steady progression of logically related events. A typical scene of climax from Dion Boucicault's great favorite, *The Colleen Bawn* (1860), illustrates not only the kind of situation but also the emphasis on action:

> (*Music, low storm music. . . . Myles sings without, then appears U.E.R. on rock. . . . Swings across stage by rope. Exit U.E.I.H. Music, boat floats on R.H. with Eily and Danny. Eily steps on to Rock C. (Danny) stepping onto the rock the boat floats away unseen. . . . Music. Throws her into water, L.C. She disappears for an instant then reappears clinging to Rock C. . . . Thrusts her down. She disappears. . . . Shot heard U.E.L.H. Danny falls into water behind C. Rock. Myles sings without. . . . Swings across by rope to R.H., fastens it up, then fishes up Double of Eily—lets her fall. Strips, then dives after her. Eily*

appears for an instant in front. Then double for Myles appears at back and dives over drum. Myles and Eily appear in front of Center Rock. Tableau. Curtain.)[3]

This kind of physical action is, of course, the standard material of melodrama, made appealing to nineteenth-century audiences by novel effects. It is interesting to note the use of character "doubles" in order to keep the scene moving. Other elements of special interest in this scene are the music for reinforcing the atmosphere and the tableau at the end of the act. The writer of melodrama depended on all kinds of *coups de théâtre* for releasing strong feelings, often utilizing climactic curtains, such as in this scene, literally as "clap traps."

To create continuity of the narrative, the dramatist tied the scenes together by a variety of techniques. Changes of scenery were covered by music or special lighting effects. Often, the scenes were changed in view of the audience. Sets were devised for the use of simultaneous or parallel action. Still another practice was that of shifting the locale from one place to another while the action continued. The following example from *A Race for Life* indicates this device, which anticipates cinematic practice:

A scene from Boucicault's melodrama *The Colleen Bawn,* when the villain Danny tries to drown the heroine Eily. The scene was staged with every effort to make it as realistic and exciting as possible.

Daumier's famous print showing a sensational moment during a French production of a melodrama. Notice the empathic response of the audience.

(Officers fire. Convicts rush on, struggle with officers. Shots outside; Gaspard seizes Jacques—is thrown off. Officer seizes Jacques, he throws him off when Holmes struggles off with Brady R.H. Men and officers struggle off R. and L. when all clear. Sound Change Bell.

Rocks drawn off R. and L. Prison double set center revolves to old Light House and comes down stage. Jacques and Brady come on in boat. Men work sea cloth. Patty throws rope from light house window. Brady catches it. Picture. Slow curtain.)[4]

Good writers of melodrama were skilled craftspeople with a shrewd sense of pace, rhythm, and a feeling for climactic action. They were adept storytellers and showmen. They not only knew the possibilities of the stage but also understood their audience. Logic did not interest them as long as their plays gave the impression of credibility, which they achieved by keeping the narratives moving and by creating the illusion of actuality through realistic backgrounds, appropriate costumes, and good casting.

CHARACTER

Robert B. Heilman suggests that the contrast between melodrama and tragedy is a matter of character treatment:

> The identifying mark of the melodramatic structure is not the particular out-
> come of the plot, but the conception of character and the alignment of
> forces. . . . In melodrama, man is seen in his strength or in his weakness; in
> tragedy in both his strength and weakness at once. In melodrama, he is vic-
> torious or he is defeated; in tragedy, he experiences defeat in victory, or vic-
> tory in defeat. In melodrama, man is simply innocent; in tragedy, his guilt and
> his innocence coexist. In melodrama, man's will is broken, or it conquers; in
> tragedy, it is tempered in the suffering that comes with, or brings about, new
> knowledge.[5]

Heilman's concept, then, of the melodramatic hero is of a whole character,
not one torn by internal stress, whereas the tragic hero is a divided human
being confronted by basic conflicts, perhaps not soluble, of obligations and
passions.

Nineteenth-century melodrama and our motion-picture and television fare testify to the validity of Heilman's observation. Characters are generally good or bad one-dimensional figures who pursue their objectives in
a straight line. The opposition comes from without rather than from within.
Characters do not think—they act, and as a result they often become involved in entanglements a judicious person might avoid, such as being
caught on a train trestle at midnight without a lantern, lost in a snowstorm
without food or shelter, or duped by the villain's traps and schemes because
of their own gullibility and ignorance. The writer of melodrama was not
concerned with delineating characters as complex individuals who were
conditioned by their backgrounds. They were people who were simple in
heart and mind. As nineteenth-century melodrama developed, however,
some playwrights made efforts to create more credible characters with more
complex motivations. Indeed, the waywardness of the villain might be explained at some length as the result of an unfortunate conditioning experience in early life when he was abused or unjustly treated, and as a result
he might make some claim on the audience's sympathy and understanding.

Most characters in melodrama were types. This was important in performance so that the spectator could readily recognize them, and it was also
essential for the acting company in the distribution of the roles. Owen Davis,
one of the most successful writers of melodrama in the early part of the
twentieth century, used stock characters in such hits as *The Lighthouse by the
Sea* and *The Chinatown Trunk Mystery*. He describes the typical personnel required for his plays:

> There were eight essential characters: the hero, who can be either very poor,
> which is preferable, or else very young and very drunk (if sober and wealthy
> he becomes automatically a villain); the heroine, by preference a working girl
> (cloak model, "typewriter," factory girls, shopgirl, etc.) and practically indes-
> tructible; the comic—Irish, Jewish, or German—played usually by the highest
> paid member of the company; the soubrette, "a working girl with bad manners
> and a good heart," devoted to the heroine; the heavy man, identified by a
> moustache, silk hat, and white gloves; the heavy woman, a haughty society

dame or an "unfortunate"; the light comedy boy; and the second heavy, "just a bum," a tool of the villain; it was usual to kill him along toward the middle of the second act.[6]

The pivotal character of old-time melodrama was the villain, who was the motivating force of much of the plot. Just as it was essential to show the goodness of the hero and the heroine to enlist the sympathy of the audience, it was mandatory to demonstrate the wickedness of the villain to generate the audience's hostility. One of the pleasures of melodrama was loathing the evildoers and seeing them get the punishment they so richly deserved. Hence the playwright was careful to build up the iniquitous villains with their sinful desires, their smoldering grudges and passions, and their inexhaustible supply of devilish schemes.

Melodrama was the entertainment of the masses, and since maximum identification was the playwrights' aim, they often used characters from the ordinary walks of life. Heroes were not the elevated figures of the past; they were firefighters, cowboys, soldiers, sailors, farmhands. Although they were stock types, the bare outlines of the text were fleshed out by the imaginations and personalities of the actors who brought them to life. Leading roles in melodrama provided exceptional opportunities for some actors, who spent most of their careers identified with a single part. James O'Neill played in *Monte Cristo* for 5,817 performances, and Denman Thompson appeared in *The Old Homestead* more than 7,000 times.

The emotional response to melodrama often depends upon the villain, who inspires fear and hatred. Dracula is one of the most popular villains in stage history.

(Pacific Conservatory of Performing Arts, California.)

THOUGHT

Most writers of melodrama were primarily concerned with entertaining an audience rather than delivering a message. But because of the genre's broad appeal, melodrama often reflected a vague humanitarianism in its sympathetic treatment of the downtrodden and its condemnation of arrogant authority, the overprivileged, and the avaricious manipulators in big business. Although there was frequently an implied suggestion to take action and throw off the tormentors so everyone could be free, the implication was not a direct call for rebellion. Instead, melodrama commonly expressed a staunch loyalty to orthodox morality, backed by an optimistic faith in the future. The root of the social evils that oppressed those who suffered was generally lodged in the evil nature of the villains rather than in the political or economic system.

It was customary to end melodramas with arbitrary scenes of poetic justice, in which couples were paired off and rewards and punishments were parceled out according to the actions of the characters. As the final curtain descended, the audience was reassured that virtue will triumph, murder will out, and the wages of sin is death. But melodrama with its sharp conflicts between good and evil did not altogether neglect the opportunity for propaganda. The evil of drink was a favorite target, as were usury, heavy taxes, and the sinful nature of the big city. One of the most popular hits of all time was George L. Aiken's dramatization of Harriet Beecher Stowe's novel *Uncle Tom's Cabin* (1852), which held the stage for eighty years. Its depiction of slavery was one of the strongest pieces of propaganda of the nineteenth century.

Duty and self-sacrifice were pictured as the ennobling virtues of the lower classes. Whatever the misfortunes, the honorable person performed his or her duty, confident that in the end justice would be meted out—in the next world, if not here and now. Dozens of heroines declaimed such sentiments, as seen in the following passage from Augustan Daly's highly successful *Under the Gaslight:*

Laura: Let the woman you look upon be wise or vain, beautiful or homely, rich or poor, she has but one thing she can really give or refuse—her heart! Her beauty, her wit, her accomplishments, she may sell to you— but her love is the treasure without money and without price. She only asks in return, that when you look upon her, your eyes shall speak a mute devotion; that when you address her, your voice shall be gentle, loving, and kind. That you shall not despise her because she cannot understand all at once, your vigorous thoughts, and ambitious designs; for when misfortune and evil have defeated your greatest purposes—her love remains to console you. You look to the trees for strength and grandeur—do not despise the flowers, because their fragrance is all they have to give. Remember—love is all a woman has to give; but it is the only earthly thing which God permits us to carry beyond the grave.[7]

DICTION

The language of melodrama was often singularly undistinguished. Since common characters carried the burden of the plot, playwrights attempted to suggest onstage the everyday idiom. This effort performed some service in undermining the bombast and extravagance of romantic diction, although the writer of melodrama was not entirely immune from flowery language. In moments of strong emotion, characters spouted such purple passages as that cited from *Under the Gaslight*. But by and large, the playwright's emphasis on common characters involved in scenes of violent action led to dialogue that suggested the texture of ordinary speech. As a result of this attempt to imitate the language of life, some playwrights endeavored to copy the dialects and provincialism of specific locales, which was a move toward increased realism.

A climactic moment in *Under the Gaslight* when the heroine escapes from the tool shed in the nick of time to rescue Snorky from the onrushing locomotive.

Writers of melodrama made free use of such technical devices as asides and soliloquies, which not only aided them in the difficult problems of exposition imposed by episodic structure but also gave them the opportunity to reveal character and motivation.

MUSIC

Melodrama, originally linked with music, continued that association. As the excerpt from *The Colleen Bawn* indicated, music was an important accompaniment to the action. When the motion pictures took over melodrama, music was soon found to be extremely useful for eliciting emotional response. Silent films were accompanied by appropriate scores for piano or pipe organ. For more ambitious productions such as *The Birth of a Nation,* a complete orchestral accompaniment was written and played. In our present films and television dramas, music continues to be an indispensable element of production to establish atmosphere, bridge the action, or generate excitement.

Nineteenth-century melodrama made another interesting use of music. The entrances and exits of leading characters were accompanied by special musical themes suitable for their roles. Actors often performed to music that not only helped them establish the emotional atmosphere of the scene but also influenced their timing and movement.

Sound effects were sometimes an important adjunct of productions, especially in climactic scenes—in "turf" dramas, when the horses thundered down the straightaway toward the finish line; or when in *Under the Gaslight* the rumbling, whistling train approached with its headlights picking up Snorky tied to the tracks while the heroine, Laura, frantically attempted to shatter the walls of the toolshed in time to save him; or when, in the fire plays, the firefighters raced to the scene of a spectacular blaze amid the crackle of flames, the cries for help, and the sound of the equipment.

SPECTACLE

In the first half of the century almost all theaters used two-dimensional stock pieces consisting of backdrops and wings on which were painted a variety of backgrounds, such as a kitchen, palace, prison, grotto, or woodland glade. This system possessed two virtues—it was economical and it made shifting rapid and easy. To change to a new setting, the backdrop was raised to reveal another one behind it, while wings slid along the grooves to uncover the new ones for the following scene. Throughout the country, theaters were equipped with stock sets so that a touring company needed to bring only its special effects and costumes. But as the taste for sensational novelties grew, productions became increasingly elaborate and expensive.

Metropolitan stages became more complicated, with bridges, traps, elevators, moving platforms, and paraphernalia for producing fires, floods, explosions, and all manner of astounding displays. The two-dimensional scenery was replaced by built-up solid pieces, making the sets substantial, and difficult to move. Playwrights built their plays around sensational scenic displays. The following scene from *Pauvrette: or Under the Snow* shows the kind of effects required.

> (*The summit of the Alps. Rocks and precipices occupy the stage. A rude hut on one side in front. A bridge formed by a felled tree across the chasm at the back. The stone-clad peaks stretch away in the distance. Night . . . storm, wind. She (Pauvrette) throws her scarf around her, and hastily ascends the rock—utters a long wailing cry—listens. . . . Descends to her hut. Maurice cries for help. Takes her alpenstock and a coil of rope, and reascends the rock. The wind increases—the snow begins to fall. She crosses the bridge and disappears off left. Bernard appears below on the rocks, L. He climbs up the path. . . . Pauvrette appears on the bridge, leading Maurice. . . . They cross the bridge. . . . They descend and enter the hut. . . . Large blocks of hardened snow and masses of rock fall, rolling into the abyss. Pauvrette falls on her knees. . . . Pauvrette enters the hut. The avalanche begins to fall—the bridge is broken and hurled into the abyss—the paths have been filled with snow—and now an immense sheet rushing down from the R. entirely buries the whole scene to the height of twelve or fifteen feet, swallowing up the cabin and leaving above a clear level of snow—the storm passes away—silence and peace return—the figure of the virgin (in window) is unharmed—the light before it still burns.*)[8]

During the third quarter of the nineteenth century, Boucicault was the acknowledged master of melodrama, both in writing and in staging his plays. He catered to the taste of the public with his sensational scenes, to which he gave the utmost care. *The Octaroon* (1859) featured a fire aboard a river boat; in *Arrah-na-Pogue*, Shaun's prison escape begins inside the cell, then turns inside out to reveal him coming out the window and over the wall.

At the turn of the century, "Drury Lane melodramas" were famous for their stage effects. *The Prince of Peace* (1900) presented Parliament in session, a wedding in Westminster Abbey, and a collision at sea in which a yacht is smashed by a steamer. *The Sins of Society* (1907) thrilled the spectators with a huge transport ship that slowly sank beneath the waves on a fog-shrouded stage, while a wireless crackled and sparked and a steam siren sounded the alarm.

David Belasco set a new standard for Broadway with the ultrarealistic staging of his melodramas celebrating the American heritage: *The Heart of Maryland* (1895), *Under Two Flags* (1901), and *The Girl of the Golden West* (1905). He toned down much of the violence and blatant sentimentality and made the plot and dialogue more credible, even though he depended a great deal on startling scenes carefully produced. He also had the advantage

In such plays as Boucicault's *Pauvrette*, the stage effects were often more interesting than the characters. Staging a credible avalanche challenged the theater technician's skill to the utmost.

of working with electricity, which he used with imagination and taste. Typical of Belasco's theatricality was the staging of the prologue to *The Girl of the Golden West*. Rahill describes it in some detail.

> . . . a painted canvas scene, rolled vertically on drums, presented a moving map-like panorama of the whole picturesque area where the action unfolds; first, the heights of cloudy mountain in the moonlight, then the girl's cabin perched aloft and a steep footpath winding down the walls of the canyon to the settlement below; and next, the little camp itself, shown at the foot of the path, the miners' cabins huddled about the Polka Saloon, through the windows of which drifts the muted din of rough revelry—the rattle of poker chips, the strains of banjo, and concertina, and masculine voices raised in a chorus of "Camptown Races." This is erased suddenly in a blackout, and a moment later the lights come on full to reveal the interior of the saloon, where a shindig is in full swing—the music continuing meanwhile and serving to bind the two scenes together.[9]

It should be remembered that although sensational scenery called attention to itself, it was also used for more than pictorial representation. The setting was functional in that it served the actors' needs in a particular scene. A waterfall was not simply shown as an enlarged calendar picture for its visual appeal. It became a factor in the action when the hero struggled to save the heroine from plunging to her death. A railroad trestle was set onstage not merely for the novelty of showing a train but also as a weapon of the villain, who tied the hero to the tracks as the train's light and whistle approached. The setting was an essential part of the action. Hence, a considerable amount of ingenuity was required by the stage mechanic to advise effects that were not only visually credible but also utilitarian enough to be used in chases, fights, and escapes. Incidentally, the actor had to be something of an athlete to dive from burning buildings, scale steep cliffs, and chase or be chased through a canvas jungle—and recite lines. (It is no wonder that doubles were often used to keep the action continuous.)

One device by which melodrama sought to create an illusion of reality was the use of actual and authentic properties. Belasco actually bought pieces of buildings and moved them onstage. Some playwrights and producers cluttered their sets with endless detail to make the stage picture seem real. Often a real property, such as a rowboat, made an incongruous contrast with the obviously painted backdrop of the sea. On the other hand, the use of genuine and homely objects onstage enhanced the realism of the acting by giving the actors an opportunity to create business and pantomime. James A. Herne, a successful writer of melodrama who attempted to emulate the new realism, was very fond of filling his scenes with the everyday objects and actions of life. In some of his plays he brought on dogs, chickens, a horse, geese, and live babies. He showed a shipyard in operation, during which a boat was painted each evening.

As the elaboration of scenery progressed, it became increasingly difficult for a road company to tour since many of the outlying theaters could not accommodate the special scenery because of lack of room or equipment, not to mention the increased cost of the touring production. The solidity and complexity of scenery also affected playwriting. Scenes could not be shifted as rapidly as previously, and the cost of production mounted. The result was to reduce the number of scenes, so that there were fewer locales and episodes. Under these conditions, the dramatist was forced to use less physical action, the narrative lost some of its fluency, and there was a tendency toward fuller development of character and dialogue.

Realism ultimately made its impact on melodrama, although until 1900 most American plays were written for the exploitation of a star or for the spectacular effects of the staging. Early in the twentieth century the circuit theaters that catered to the lower classes lost some of their audiences to the films. Edwin S. Porter's *The Life of an American Fireman* and *The Great Train Robbery* taught moviemakers that their medium was ideally suited for narratives with vigorous action. In popular melodramas they found stories and situations that became the basic ingredients for film. Stage hits like *Oliver Twist, Under Two Flags,* and *Lady of Lyons* were put on the screen, where they attracted large audiences to the new kind of theater.

By and large, melodrama has been taken over by the motion pictures, since they are so well suited to action stories that involve chases, battles, and death-defying stunts. Adventure stories that pit brave and reckless characters against evil and powerful adversaries are the familiar plots of what our film and television catalogs list under the captions of "Adventure," "Western," "Horror," "Science Fiction," and "War." Well-known titles that fit the dramatic mold are such films as *Gunfight at the O.K. Corral, Star Trek, Von Ryan's Express, Goldfinger,* and *Raiders of the Lost Ark.* Modern technology contributes to the illusion of surface reality because of ingenious and imaginative ways of simulating and recording exciting and fantastic action. But essentially the human motivation follows the well-worn wish-fulfillment and escape patterns of melodrama.

In the current theater, melodrama is largely confined to murder mysteries and psychological thrillers such as *Gaslight, Dial "M" for Murder, Angel Street,* and plays about the adventures of Dracula or Sherlock Holmes. Two contemporary thrillers that were Broadway box-office hits are Anthony Shaffer's *Sleuth* (1,222 performances) and Ira Levin's *Deathtrap* (1,793 performances). Both of these melodramas were built on the machinations of

Sherlock Holmes as a melodramatic hero was also featured in *The Crucifer of Blood* by Paul Giovanni. The chief attractions, however, were the sensational stage effects, such as this scene in which two boats emerge out of a dense fog and a gunfight ensues.

(Photo: Martha Swope)

Anthony Shaffer's *Sleuth* is a popular modern melodrama, full of the traditional techniques, depicting a lively struggle between two ingenious adversaries.
(University of Toledo.)

two mystery story writers, who are familiar with the ways of setting diabolical traps that challenge the audience to follow the surprising twistings and turnings of the plots.

Another popular hit was *The Crucifer of Blood,* a throwback to old-fashioned melodrama that capitalized on spectacular scenic effects, especially in a climactic scene in which two boats float out on stage during a terrifying thunderstorm and a lively gun battle ensues.

Although such melodramas are rare on the stage today, their plot patterns have by no means disappeared from the theater. For example, the enormously popular play and film *Amadeus* owed much of its success to Mozart's music, but it also appealed to a wide audience because of its melodramatic conflict between a ruthless and powerful villain and a gifted, but naive, long-suffering victim. Salieri, tortured by his jealousy, systematically destroys his rival by a series of treacherous maneuvers. He stops Mozart's income, sabotages his chances for advancement, and persuades him to reveal the Masonic Lodge mysteries in his opera, thus alienating the source of his support. Finally, Salieri disguises himself as an apparition and stalks Mozart's window night after night. Then there is the emotionally loaded reunion of Mozart and his wife, with his death in her arms as he feebly attempts to beat out the drum measures of his Requiem Mass. The melodramatic touches continue when the guilt-ridden Salieri vainly tries to cut his throat but survives as a madman, bitterly confessing that he killed Mozart. Shaffer's play, of course, rises above the melodramatic formulas because of Mozart's soaring music, because of the emphasis on Salieri's motivation and his suffering, and because the playwright scrupulously avoided any attempt to sentimentalize the action. Nor did he build his plot to a spectacular climax in which the hero defeats the villain. The hero dies, but his music lives on. Salieri is destroyed by his guilt and the stark reality of his mediocrity.

Sweeney Todd is a musical based on the fascinating career of a nineteenth-century character known as "the demon barber of Fleet Street." His objective is to gain vengeance on the judge who sent him to prison. At last Sweeney has the Judge in his barber chair. Despite such sensational scenes, *Sweeney Todd* escapes melodrama by virtue of Stephen Sondheim's music.

(Photo: Martha Swope)

Sweeney Todd, the Demon Barber of Fleet Street, which featured Stephen Sondheim's music, created a sensation in 1979 with its melodramatic story of a man who returns from prison, determined to get revenge on the unscrupulous judge who framed him. The macabre events of the story rise above the blood and thunder, like the libretti of many operas, because of the elevated quality of the music.

In the works of many American writers, there are melodramatic touches in character motivation and climactic action. One thinks of O'Neill's *Anna Christie* and *Desire Under the Elms,* Miller's *All My Sons* and *A View from the Bridge,* Williams' *A Streetcar Named Desire,* and Hellman's *The Little Foxes.*

Most serious plays are neither melodrama nor tragedy. They are rather middle-class plays for a middle-class audience, dealing with contemporary humankind in commonplace circumstances. Plays having the objective of telling the truth about life are remarkably varied in style and content; but they do have a common denominator in attempting to examine values and to create a sense of awareness about the place of the individual in the present society.

DRAME

This vast body of dramatic literature defies definition because of its great diversity, its experimentation in structure and production, and its mixtures of several forms and modes of writing at once, for example, realism with

Chekhov, like other realists, avoided violent action for its own sake and centered his attention on the inner feelings of believable characters who vacillate between comic and serious experiences, as in *The Cherry Orchard.*
(Asolo State Theater, Florida. Directed by Mark Epstein.

Elmer Rice's *Street Scene* won the Pulitzer Prize in 1929. The melodramatic plot
deals with a husband who discovers his wife in the arms of a milkman; he kills
them both. Interest is centered in the characters and their environment rather than
in the action.

(American Conservatory Theater revival.)

expressionism or comedy with tragic material. Some critics simply use the
term *drama,* but I prefer, as a lesser evil, the French term *drame,* by which is
meant those plays of serious intent usually dealing with contemporary life.
Just as realism has been the dominant mode of modern drama, so drame
has been the preponderant form.

Drame is allied to melodrama in that the playwright involves the spectator in the action through identification with familiar characters and the
creation of suspense and tension through conflicts. Drame differs from melodrama in that it is concerned with the realm of ideas, with sociological and
philosophical issues at stake, whereas melodrama deals with escape. In
drame, characters participate in genuinely significant action that provokes
discussion and reflection after the curtain has gone down. Melodrama is
played at the game level. There is no residue of meaning.

Drame is allied to tragedy in its seriousness of purpose, in its relentless
honesty of treatment, in its concern with the meaning of human conduct.

Arthur Miller's *A View from the Bridge* is a mixture of light and heavy material. It avoids melodrama despite violent action because of its seriousness of purpose and depth of characterization.

(Asolo State Theater, Florida. Directed by John Ulmer.)

Drame differs from tragedy in its narrowness of vision—with its emphasis often on material, temporary, or local conditions that deny universality; with its mechanistic or nihilistic sense of values; and with its general lack of elevation. Frequently, the writer of drames is fascinated by the psychological complexities of character. The dramatis personae are not the stock characters of melodrama; they are individuals with subtle and complicated motivations. They are not the tragic heroes of great stature who fall from high places, but ordinary people painfully searching for meaning and security in a baffling world of shifting values.

PLAYS TO SEE

Melodramas available on video cassettes:

Sleuth
Deathtrap
Gaslight
Dial "M" for Murder
Goldfinger

Raiders of the Lost Ark
Star Wars
Sherlock Holmes
Dracula

Drames available on video cassettes:

Cat on a Hot Tin Roof
Mister Roberts
A Streetcar Named Desire
Who's Afraid of Virginia Woolf?
A Soldier's Play
Witness for the Prosecution
A Doll's House
Look Back in Anger
A Man for All Seasons

BIBLIOGRAPHY

BENTLEY, ERIC. *The Life of the Drama.* New York: Atheneum Publishers, 1964.

BOOTH, MICHAEL. *English Melodrama.* London: Herbert Jenkins, 1965.

DISHER, MAURICE. *Blood and Thunder: Mid-Victorian Melodrama and Its Origin.* London: Muller, 1949.

HEILMAN, ROBERT BECHTHOLD. *The Iceman, the Arsonist, and the Troubled Agent: Tragedy and Melodrama on the Modern Stage.* Seattle: University of Washington Press, 1973.

LACEY, ALEXANDER. *Pixérécourt and the French Romantic Drama.* Toronto: University of Toronto Press, 1928.

MOSES, MONTROSE JONES. *American Dramatist.* New York: Benjamin Blom, Inc., 1964.

NICOLL, ALLARDYCE. *A History of the Late Nineteenth Century Drama, 1850–1900.* Cambridge, Eng.: Cambridge University Press, 1946.

RAHILL, FRANK. *The World of Melodrama.* University Park: Pennsylvania State University Press, 1967.

VARDAC, NICHOLAS. *Stage to Screen.* Cambridge, Mass.: Harvard University Press, 1949.

NOTES

1. Eric Bentley, *The Life of the Drama* (New York: Atheneum Publishers, 1964), p. 216.
2. Frank Rahill, *The World of Melodrama* (University Park: Pennsylvania State University Press, 1967).
3. Dion Boucicault, *The Colleen Bawn.*
4. ——, *A Race for Life.*
5. Robert B. Heilman, "Tragedy and Melodrama," *The Texas Quarterly,* Summer 1960.
6. Owen Davis, *I'd Like to Do It Again* (New York, 1931).
7. Augustan Daly, *Under the Gaslight* (New York: Samuel French, Inc., n.d.).
8. Dion Boucicault, *Pauvrette* (New York: Samuel French, Inc., n.d.).
9. Rahill, *The World of Melodrama.*

5

Comedy

One of the most popular pleasures of life is the enjoyment of laughter, and we seek its solace and release in all manner of activities. Not content with laughter arising spontaneously out of personal experience, we are avid customers of comedy in the theater and on the screen. Making people laugh is a big business, and there is an eager audience waiting for the skilled comedian and the hit play or musical.

Comedy's purpose is to delight and entertain an audience through characters in action in the spirit of fun. There is also a form of comedy, sometimes called black or dark comedy, that uses contrast, like rubbing salt on an open sore spot to cause pain. Ridiculous and serious materials are combined to generate harsh laughter that is sardonic or savage. The gravediggers in *Hamlet* crack jokes while they prepare Ophelia's grave. Sir Thomas Moore, too weak to ascend the steps to the gallows where he is about to be hanged, says, "If you'll help me up, I'll see to the coming down." But in general, comedy works best in a light, congenial environment. Tragedy achieves its catharsis through fear and pity; comedy purges through laughter to help us retain our balance and sanity and to remind us of our human frailties.

High comedy, that is, social comedy or comedy of manners, is intellectual in appeal, catering to the tastes of a sophisticated audience with a commonly accepted code of behavior that is a matter of manners, not morals. The Restoration period in the late seventeenth century in England is generally acknowledged to be the apex of high comedy. William Congreve, William Wycherly, Sir George Etherege, and Sir John Vanbrugh ridiculed the gauche, the outsiders, the pretenders whose awkward conduct caused them to lose their sense of control. In other periods of theater history, writers have used the wit of high comedy to direct criticism at more universal targets. Aristophanes scorned the militarists, sophists, and politicians; Molière attacked hypocrisy and pretense; Shaw delighted in exposing the sham behind the sentimental and rigid precepts of Victorian society. High comedy is, therefore, a social weapon armed with critical laughter.

At the other end of the comic scale is farce, or low comedy, whose main purpose is to amuse. The response to farce is immediate and direct. The language barriers are apt to be slight since comedians express themselves in the universal vocabulary of action. Along with melodrama, farce is our most popular kind of theater.

Farce may be presented as a complete play, such as Shakespeare's *The Comedy of Errors* or *No Sex Please, We're British,* or as such film and television fare as that of the Marx Brothers and Monty Python.

In between the extremes of high comedy and low is a vast area, which for want of a better term, can simply be referred to as "comedy" to distinguish plays that rely heavily on neither intellectual appeal nor exaggerated physicality. These plays attend more to character and the significance of the action. Molière's farces, such as *Sganarelle* and *The Doctor in Spite of Himself,* are based on extravagant situations calculated to elicit easy laughter, but

One of the greatest periods of high comedy that exposed the follies and foibles of the upper classes was during The Restoration. In Wycherly's *The Country Wife* a middle-aged husband brings his young bride to London and tries unsuccessfully to protect her from the wolves.

(Wayne State University. Directed by Richard Spear.)

when more concerned with character and ideas, as in *Tartuffe* and *The Miser*, Molière wrote plays in the general area of comedy.

THE COMIC ATTITUDE

The question of pain and pleasure arises in comedy as well as in tragedy, for laughter and ridicule can be dangerous weapons. Molière, who was frequently in hot water for satirizing the law, medicine, and the church, observed that people do not mind being wicked, but "they object to being made ridiculous." As Freud pointed out, comedy becomes aggressive and easily leads to abuse and to the destruction of its essential lightness of spirit. Teasing turns into torment, mischief into vandalism.

In tragedy, there is a good deal of suffering when the integrity of the characters is tested. In comedy, there is apt to be discomfiture. The butts of the jokes, usually the unsympathetic characters who arouse our hostility because of their antisocial behavior or self-ignorance, are put in situations that

O'Neill's *Ah, Wilderness* deals with a New England family and their domestic problems such as the drunken Uncle Sid, who disrupts the 4th of July dinner. The comic atmosphere is warm and gentle.

(South Coast Repertory, Costa Mesa, California.)

release our aggression or sense of superiority. The objects of our derision are embarrassed, rejected, defeated, deflated, unmasked, or deprived of their status or possessions. Even sympathetic characters may be laughed at, especially if they deserve it. In any case, the discomfiture must not become genuinely painful or the comic atmosphere is destroyed.

KINDS OF COMEDY

Comedy wears many masks and appears in many guises—the ill-fitting tattered rags of the drunken hobo, the elegant evening clothes of the most sophisticated aristocrat, the overdressed finery of the fop. Comedy evokes many responses—the belly laugh, warm and sympathetic general laughter, a well-concealed smile, or derisive ridicule. Its armor includes such a variety of weapons as the rapier, the slapstick, the barbed shaft, and the custard pie. Comedy speaks many languages—epigrams, conceits, puns, obscenities,

Program cover from *Noises Off* at the Ahmanson Theater, Los Angeles. The play is obviously a farce.

bon mots, wisecracks, insults, double entendres, hard and ruthless mockery—ranging from high to low.

Most comic playwrights are aware of the need to establish a light atmosphere at the outset. You know you are in for comedy when the program cover of *Noises Off* features Mrs. Clackett, a rattlebrained housekeeper, staring cross-eyed at a sardine. When the curtain rises, Mrs. Clackett appears, carrying a plate of sardines. She is stopped by the voice of the director, Lloyd Dallas, from the rear of the auditorium:

Lloyd: You leave the sardines, and you put the receiver back.
Dotty: Oh, yes, I put the receiver back.

(She puts the receiver back and moves off again with the sardines.)

Lloyd: And you leave the sardines.

Dotty: And I *leave* the sardines?

Lloyd: You *leave* the sardines.

Dotty: I put the receiver back and I leave the sardines.

Lloyd: Right.

Dotty: We've changed that, have we, love?

Lloyd: No, love.

Dotty: That's what I've always been doing?

Lloyd: I shouldn't say that, Dotty, my precious.

Dotty: How about the words, love? Am I getting some of them right?

Lloyd: Some of them have a very familiar ring.

Dotty: Only it's like a fruit machine in there.

Lloyd: I know that, Dotty. .

Dotty: I open my mouth, and I never know if it's going to come out oranges or two lemons and a banana.

Lloyd: Anyway, it's not midnight yet. We don't open till tomorrow.[1]

Playwright Michael Frayn immediately catapults his audience into the daffy atmosphere of *Noises Off.*

In Arthur Kopit's play, the title, *Oh Dad, Poor Dad, Momma's Hung You in the Closet and I'm Feeling So Sad,* indicates the bizarre nature of his comedy, but you are not quite sure of the comic climate when two bellboys enter a hotel room carrying a coffin. The handles come off and the coffin crashes to the floor. You soon learn through other objects and stage business that you are in for an off-beat experience.

Kopit's *Oh Dad, Poor Dad, Mamma's Hung You in the Closet and I'm Feelin' So Sad.* In this off-beat comedy a guileless boy is no match for the flirtatious baby-sitter.

(Cleveland Play House. Directed by Kirk Willis.)

Max Eastman analyzed the conditions essential for the "enjoyment of laughter" in his book of the same title. He observed that humor depends on the existence of a favorable circumstance, and he concludes that "the condition in which joyful laughter most continually occurs is that of play."[2] As part of his evidence, Eastman cites the naive response of a child who may welcome shock and disappointment as a pleasurable experience provided that an atmosphere of play has been established. If the child is teased, however, when tired or hungry, the fun is over; the spirit of play has been destroyed.

In Shakespeare's romantic comedies, in the plays of Sheridan and Oliver Goldsmith in the eighteenth century, and in many of our contemporary works, the spectator is invited to enter into the emotions of the characters. We become concerned about the fortunes of the protagonist; our sympathies and hostilities are aroused by the playwright's treatment of the characters, so that we take pleasure in seeing the hero and heroine achieve their objectives, usually accompanied by the jingle of money and the ringing of wedding bells. The characters may be laughable, may at times appear foolish and weak, but the playwright treats them with tolerance and indulgence. Examples of comedies that involve our sympathies are *As You Like It, The Rivals, She Stoops to Conquer, Born Yesterday, The Odd Couple, My Fair Lady,*

One of the favorite comic characters in English comedy is Tony Lumpkin in Goldsmith's *She Stoops to Conquer.* An irrepressible spirit, Tony delights in practical jokes. Here, he pretends no interest in his girlfriend.
(Syracuse Stage.)

Another favorite comic character from musical comedy is Tevye in *Fiddler on the Roof*.

(Clarke College. Directed by Carol Blitgen.)

One Flew Over the Cuckoo's Nest, Talley's Folly, La Cage Aux Folles, Butterflies Are Free, and *Fiddler on the Roof.* We usually sympathize with the characters in their struggles. For example, in *Fiddler* there is no malice in our laughter when we respond to Tevye, the Jewish dairyman in a small Russian village, when he seeks help from above:

Tevye: Today I am a horse. Dear God, did you have to make my poor old horse lose his shoe just before the Sabbath? That wasn't nice. It's enough you pick on me, Tevye, bless me with five daughters, a life of poverty. What have you got against my horse? Sometimes, I think when things are too quiet up there, You say to Yourself: "Let's see what kind of mischief can I play on my friend Tevye?" . . . As the Good Book says, "Heal us, O Lord, and we shall be healed." In other words, send us the cure, we've got the sickness already. . . . I'm not really complaining—after all, with your help, I'm starving to death. I realize, of course, that it's no shame to be poor, but it's no great honor, either. So what would have been so terrible if I had a small fortune?[3]

Henri Bergson argues that "laughter has no greater foe than emotion. . . . Its appeal is to the intelligence, pure and simple." Alonzo Myers supports Bergson in this view: "Without detachment, we cannot realize the effect of comedy, which transforms the frustrations of reason into laughter." This point of view is well taken, especially at the extremes of the comic scale—low comedy and high. In most farce, enjoyment stems from the action itself, the momentary laugh, the sudden release. We recognize that it is a form of playing; we do not take the characters' sufferings seriously. No one feels genuine pain; the emotions do not penetrate the grease paint. Thus the spectators are detached from reality and are conscious of the artificial world before them.

Dark Comedy

There is, however, a kind of drama sometimes called black or dark comedy in which a "gallows humor" creates an emotional jarring—a harsh contrast.

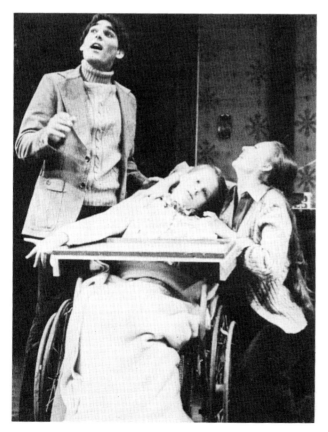

In *A Day in the Death of Joe Egg,* by Peter Nichols, the parents of a handicapped child try to lighten their somber situation by forcing themselves to play games. The resultant laughter has the bitter quality of black comedy.

(Purdue University.)

Comedy and serious matter are combined to generate an uneasy or bitter laughter that is apt to be sardonic or even savage. In the film *M*A*S*H* the characters at a Mobile Surgical Unit in Korea relieved the tension and horror of their situation through laughter that was often harsh and mordant.

The practice of introducing comic relief into a serious situation to heighten the effect by contrast is an old one. We think of the porter in *Macbeth* and the gravediggers in *Hamlet*. With the coming of realism and its emphasis on objective observation, it was apparent to some playwrights that in life the incongruous was often side by side with the beautiful, the comic with the tragic—like grotesque gargoyles on the façade of a beautiful cathedral. Many of the outstanding playwrights of the last century have united the dark and the light. We think of Chekhov, Pirandello, and Shaw and of present-day playwrights Shepard, David Mamet, Edward Albee, Stoppard, Henley, and Lanford Wilson. Even though plays like *Amadeus* and *The Dresser* end in death, they contain considerable comic material, mostly arising from the characters themselves.

Following World War II the absurdists, among them Beckett and Ionesco, expressed their feelings of alienation and spiritual dislocation in

Another black comedy reflects the wild, zany atmosphere of Joe Orton's *What the Butler Saw.*

(Cincinnati Playhouse in the Park.)

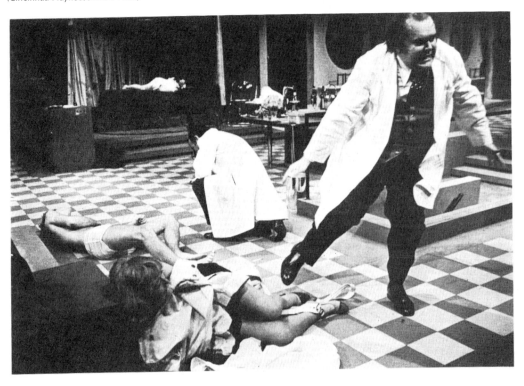

plays filled with bizarre lunacy and bleak humor in *Waiting for Godot* and *Rhinoceros.*

In postwar England black comedy, with its bitterly satiric overtones, made an enormous impact on the theater. Simon Gray in *Butley* mocks the academic world through the protagonist, a university professor who is transformed from a promising scholar into a detestable bureaucrat. Joe Orton's wildly imaginative dark farces, such as *Loot* and *What the Butler Saw,* are scathing satirical assaults on the establishment, particularly the police, the Roman Catholic Church, and psychiatry. Peter Nichols, in *A Day in the Death of Joe Egg,* shows how a couple with a severely retarded child attempt to retain their sanity and preserve their marriage through jocular banter and improvised games.

Sources of Laughter

The sources of comic effect have given scholars, critics, philosophers, and psychologists endless stimulation for speculation, and although their efforts have resulted in no universally accepted conclusions, we may find some substance in their ideas. Let us briefly examine three theories cited by Nicoll in *The Theory of Drama* as the most prominent, realizing that a good deal of their validity depends on personal interpretation and careful selection of examples. The three theories are *derision, incongruity,* and *automatism.* You will recognize immediately the tendency of the theories to overlap because of the mercurial nature of comedy.

Derision

Aristotle's observation that comedy deals with men as "worse than they are" implies a comic theory of derision or degradation. Derision is ordinarily used as a form of criticism to combat pretentiousness or ignorance. Its objective is to keep people humble, balanced, and human. The legitimate targets of derision are stupidity, hypocrisy, and sanctimoniousness. As in life, laughter is used to keep people in line, to insure conformity to a socially acceptable code of behavior. Certainly, Aristophanes was fully aware of the possibilities of derision when he ranged far and wide in his jibes against his contemporaries. Not even the audience was safe from his wit. In Aristophanes' *Peace* (421 B.C.) the protagonist, Trygaeus, rears a huge dung-beetle on which he attempts to fly to Olympus to beg peace from Zeus. As he flies aloft on the back of the beetle, Trygaeus looks down at the spectators and jeers at them:

> Ah! it's a tough job getting to the gods! My legs are as good as broken through it. (*To the audience*) How small you were to be sure, when seen from heaven! You all had the appearance too of being great rascals, but seen close, you look even worse.

Greek comedy ridiculed physical deformities as well as conduct. Comic characters were intentionally distorted and misshapen in appearance through the use of masks, phallic symbols, and padded costumes. A man's attempts to rise above himself were often counteracted by the reminder of his biological needs. Aristophanes delighted in mocking men and gods by exhibiting them in all kinds of embarrassing physical situations. He was ruthless in aiming his shafts of wit at all levels of life. The satirist exploits situations in which characters are debased and reduced to objects of scorn by such formula devices as physical beatings and bodily functions, situations in which an individual is caught off balance, red-handed, under the bed, in the closet, in underwear—in any of the circumstances of life in which people are exposed, their dignity punctured, their flaws revealed, reminding everyone of their kinship with the animal world.

Degradation of character often involves a reversal of status. The deviates from normal social behavior or inflated persons are brought down off their pedestals. Such stock offenders against common sense and decent humanity as fools, fops, hypocrites, bumpkins, louts, misers, philanderers, braggarts, bores, and battleaxes, are ridiculed because of their deformed behavior; lack of wit; or excess of ambition, greed, lust, or stupidity. The satirist uses barbs of derisive laughter to prick the inflated reputation of entrenched authority, often a popular form of comic appeal since the common people find release and enjoyment in the discomfiture of those above them.

Sigmund Freud described this process of degradation:

> The methods that serve to make people comic are: putting them in a comic situation, mimicry, disguise, unmasking, caricature, parody, travesty and so on. It is obvious that these techniques can be used to serve hostile and aggressive purposes. One can make a person comic in order to make him become contemptible, to deprive him of his claim to dignity and authority.[4]

Although physical degradation and insulting language are confined mostly to farce, the satirist bent on attacking ideas also makes use of ridicule. Ben Jonson used his wit as an instrument of mockery against his fellow Elizabethans, as he indicated when he stated the purpose of his comedy: "to strip the ragged follies of the time." Molière likewise brought low those who were guilty of excess, deriding people who were too ambitious in *Le Bourgeois Gentilhomme*, too clever in *Les Precieuses Ridicules*, too exacting in *Le Misanthrope*, and too gullible in *Tartuffe*. As we noted earlier, comedy since World War II has been notable for its vigorous aggression and, in the 1960s, for its radicalization, so that today there is no target immune from the satirists' slings and arrows. Derision is an effective weapon, and it often antagonizes those who are laughed at and may arouse bitter retaliation.

Charles Ludlum's Theater of the Ridiculous has been lampooning cultural and political institutions since 1966 with its clowning style that tends toward kitsch, camp, and parody. *Hamlet* becomes *Stage Blood*, a backstage burlesque of a Shakespearean-style whodunit. The Lady Godiva fable becomes, in the playwright's words, a preposterous, "hysterical adventure of Coventry Convent." *Le Bourgeois Avant-Garde* uses Molière's seventeenth-century comedy as a point of departure for ridiculing the modern penchant for artistic novelty and for the avant-garde.

El Teatro Campesino, founded by Louis Valdez in 1965, uses comedy as a weapon in the battle of the Chicano migrant workers against white growers in California. Its short, dramatic pieces, called *actos,* although filled with burlesque and caricature, had the serious purpose of inspiring the audience to social action.

The San Francisco Mime Troupe in the 1960s began with the improvised commedia dell'arte technique in its productions but later developed its own style of broad comic playing that includes circus techniques. Its comic arsenal has been used to promote its political concerns in mobilising its audiences against war, racism, industrialism, and social conformity.

Such groups as the Ridiculous Theater Company and the San Francisco Mime Troupe use comedy in much the same way as political cartoonists satirize the contemporary scene.

Incongruity

Perhaps because it is the most elastic and extensive theory of comedy, the idea of incongruity has the widest application. Incongruity is the result of

Two inept and unwilling adversaries attempt to avoid bloodshed despite the support of their seconds in *Twelfth Night.*

(University of California, Santa Barbara.)

the tension or dissonance set up by the juxtaposition of two objects or people that creates a laughable contrast, such as a large, fat woman mated with a small, skinny man, or a person out of place in the surroundings—in a bathing suit at the opera or in formal clothes at the beach. The contrast usually depends on the establishment of some kind of norm so that the discrepancy is emphasized. The gap between the expected and the unexpected, between the intention and the realization, between the normal and the abnormal results in comic discord.

Incongruity may take several forms—situation, character, and dialogue. The comic situation based on incongruity presents a contrast between the usual or accepted behavior and the unusual or unacceptable. A typical pattern is to place a character in an environment that reveals that person's social incongruity, such as a country bumpkin in polite society, the socially elite in bucolic surroundings, an intellectual among barbarians, a clown or an inebriate in a dignified gathering, a sailor in a harem, a tramp in the

A classic example of incongruity is this scene from *A Midsummer Night's Dream* in which Titania is enamored of Bottom, the weaver.

(Asolo State Theater. Directed by Gregory Abels.)

mayor's bed. Shaw built *Pygmalion* on the incongruous stunt of transforming Eliza, a cockney flower-seller, into a lady who circulates in high society. In *A Midsummer Night's Dream* the fairy Queen Titania falls in love with Bottom, the weaver, who has been burdened with an ass's head. In the Joseph Papp production of *The Pirates of Penzance,* the swashbuckling Pirate King stabs himself in the foot. Juxtaposition of contrasting characters is the basic comedic idea behind Neil Simon's *The Odd Couple,* when two men, separated from their wives, try to live together; however, one is sloppy and the other is fastidious: The result is comic conflict.

Incongruity of character involves a contrast between expectation and reality. For example, most of us came to *Amadeus* with a preconceived impression that Mozart, because of his elevated music, must have been a man of exemplary social conduct. But in the play, he makes his first entrance in quite an unexpected manner, as already seen on page 34-35.

Incongruity of language occurs when the language has the opposite effect of that intended by the speaker. Mrs. Malaprop, in Sheridan's *The Rivals,* gave her name to this kind of incongruity, such as when she spoke of "the allegories on the banks of the Nile." Another kind of incongruous diction occurs when the language is in sharp contrast to the social or emotional situation. For example, in Henley's Pulitzer Prize play, *Crimes of the Heart,* the three McGarth sisters in Hazlehurst, Mississippi, await the news of their grandfather's fate in the hospital. Here is their incongruous reaction:

Beth Henley's Pulitzer prizewinning comedy involves the daffy outlook of three sisters from Mississippi.

Babe: Ah, Meg—

Meg: What—

Babe: Well, it's just—It's . . .

Lenny: It's about Old Granddaddy—

Meg: Oh, I know; I know. I told him all those stupid lies. Well, I'm gonna go right over there this morning and tell him the truth. I mean every horrible thing. I don't care if he wants to hear it or not. He's just gonna have to take me like I am. And if he can't take it, if it sends him into a coma, that's just too damn bad!

(*Babe and Lenny look at each other. Babe cracks a smile. Lenny cracks a smile.*)

Babe: You're too late—Ha, ha, ha!

(*They both break up laughing.*)

Lenny: Oh, stop! Please! Ha, ha, ha!

Meg: What is it? What's so funny?

Babe: (*Still laughing*) It's not—It's not funny!

Lenny: (*Still laughing*) No, it's not! It's not a bit funny!

Meg: Well, what is it, then? What?

Babe: (*Trying to calm down*) Well, it's just—it's just—

Meg: What?

Babe: Well, Old Granddaddy—he—he's in a coma!

(*Babe and Lenny break up again.*)

Meg: He's what?

Babe: (*Shrieking*) In a coma!

Meg: My God! That's not funny!

Babe: (*Calming down*) I know. I know. For some reason, it just struck us as funny.

Lenny: I'm sorry. It's—it's not funny. It's sad. It's very sad. We've been up all night long.

Babe: We're really tired.

Meg: Well, my God. How is he? Is he gonna live—

(*Babe and Benny look at each other.*)

Babe: They don't think so!

(*They both break up again.*)

Lenny: Oh, I don't know why we're laughing like this. We're just sick! We're just awful!

Babe: We are—we're awful!

Lenny: (*As she collects herself*) Oh, good, now I feel bad. Now I feel like crying. I do; I feel like crying.

Babe: Me, too. Me, too.

Meg: Well, you've gotten me depressed!

Lenny: I'm sorry. I'm sorry. It, ah, happened last night. He had another stroke.

(*They laugh again.*)[5]

Automatism

One of the most imaginative and provocative theories of comedy was that advanced by Henri Bergson in his book *Laughter,* in which he contends that the essence of the laughable is automatism—"something mechanical is encrusted on the living." Automatism of character occurs when individuals lose their human flexibility, and their behavior becomes mechanical in its repetition, or when people become puppets, no longer in control of their actions. The gist of Bergson's thinking is indicated by these representative statements about comedy and character: "We laugh every time a person gives us the impression of being a thing." "Any individual is comic who automatically goes his own way without troubling himself about getting in touch with the rest of his fellow beings." "Rigidity, automatism, absent-mindedness, and unsociability are all inextricably entwined, and all serve as ingredients to the making up of the comic in character." Bergson's point of view on one-sided characters is similar to that of Jonson's comedy of "humours," in which he ridiculed those characters who were guilty of some imbalance, some excess:

> As when some one peculiar quality
> Doth so possess a man, that it doth draw
> All his effects, his spirits, and his powers
> In their confluctions, all to run one way
> This may be truly said to be a humour.

In Jonson's *Epicoene, or the Silent Woman,* old Morose, obsessed with silence, is tricked into marrying Epicoene, the silent woman, who turns out to be a boy. *Volpone, or the Fox* shows a group of characters who have lost their humanity because of their greed. Molière used comic targets who were out of balance because of some fixation—Orgon in *Tartuffe* for his gullibility, Harpagon in *The Miser* for his avarice, and Alceste in *The Misanthrope* for his intolerance of human frailty.

Automatism of situation is often based on repetition. Characters are caught in the grip of circumstances and subjected to mechanical domination. Chaplin used this device in his famous mechanized corn-on-the-cob eating sequence and his hilarious shaving pantomime to the accompaniment of a Brahms' Hungarian Dance. Repeated patterns of behavior have been used very often as the framework for comedy, as in D. L. Coburn's *Gin Game,* in which the central action of the play is a series of gin rummy games played by two senior citizens. Fonsia, an apparently prim woman, is inexperienced in card playing, but she wins every hand against Weller, who considers himself an expert. Coburn skillfully devises ways to use repetition not only for comic effect but also to reveal the meanness of the characters. Simon's *The Last of the Red Hot Lovers* exploits repetition in the story of Barney Cashman, a middle-aged proprietor of a fish restaurant, who makes three unsuccessful attempts at seduction. Vsevolod Meyerhold, in directing his interpretation of Chekhov's farce *The Proposal* found thirty-eight references to fainting, which he exploited as a recurrent leitmotif in production.

Automatism of dialogue takes several forms. For example, Bergson says, "Inadvertently to say or do what we have no intention of saying or doing, as a result of inelasticity or momentum is, as we are aware, one of the sources of the comic." Inelasticity, of course, implies repetition, a standard form of comedy. To mock the monotonous dullness of ordinary social conversation, Ionesco, in *The Bald Soprano,* uses the phrases "that is curious," "how bizarre," "what a coincidence," in various forms more than two dozen times in four pages of dialogue. One of the most successful uses of automatism of language occurs in Molière's *The Imaginary Invalid* when Toinette, a pert maidservant, is pretending to be a physician examining her hypochondriac master, Argan:

Toinette:　Let me feel your pulse. Come, come, beat properly, please. Ah! I will soon make you beat as you should. This pulse is trifling with me. I see that it does not know me yet. Who is your doctor?

Argan:　Mr. Purgon.

Toinette:　That man is not noted in my books among the great doctors. What does he say you are ill of?

Argan:　He says it is the liver, and others say it is the spleen.

Toinette:　They are a pack of ignorant blockheads; you are suffering from the lungs.

Argan:　The lungs?

Toinette:　Yes; what do you feel?

Argan:　From time to time great pains in my head.

Toinette:　Just so, the lungs.

Argan:　At times it seems as if I had a mist before my eyes.

Toinette:　The lungs.

Argan:　I feel sick now and then.

Toinette:　The lungs.

Argan:　And I feel sometimes a weariness in all my limbs.

Toinette:　The lungs.

Moliere's *The Imaginary Invalid,* Texas Christian University.

Argan: And sometimes I have sharp pains in the stomach, as if I had the colic.

Toinette: The lungs. Do you eat your food with appetite?

Argan: Yes, Sir.

Toinette: The lungs. You feel sleepy after your meals, and willingly enjoy a nap?

Argan: Yes, Sir.

Toinette: The lungs, the lungs, I tell you. What does your doctor order you for food?

Argan: He orders me soup.

Toinette: Ignoramus!

Argan: Fowl.

Toinette: Ignoramus!

Argan: Veal.

Toinette: Ignoramus!

Argan: Broth.

Toinette: Ignoramus!
Argan: New-laid eggs.
Toinette: Ignoramus!
Argan: And at night a few prunes to relax the bowels.
Toinette: Ignoramus!
Argan: And, above all, to drink my wine well diluted with water.
Toinette: Ignorantus, ignoranta, ignorantum.[6]

Bergson's theory is, of course, an interesting extension of the idea of incongruity, the jostling together of the human and the mechanical. By his ingenuity and persuasiveness, Bergson makes quite a plausible argument for automatism, especially for the comedies of Molière; but like other comic theories, automatism does not explain all the sources of laughter, nor is it appropriate to all kinds of comic effects.

From the preceding discussion, it is apparent that a case can be made for derision, incongruity, and automatism. It should also be obvious that it is impossible to fix comedy in a single rigid mold, although recurrent patterns and mechanisms show through the diverse forms. This will be increasingly evident as we consider the structure and content of comedy.

PLOT

Comedy requires skillful plotting. A comedy is not simply a loosely knit accumulation of gags. Laughs must be carefully timed and built, in context with the complete structure of the play. The jokes are important as they relate to the total effect, not as isolated laughs. On the other hand, the writer of comedy has more freedom in developing the play's structure than in any other form of drama since the audience cares more about entertainment than it does about logic.

Laughter is the result of the mechanism of tension and release. On the printed page, a joke takes this form:

She: - - - - - - - -
He: - - - - - - - -
She: - - - - - - -
He: - - - - - - -
She: - - (Punch line) - - -!

A comic strip often assumes this pattern:

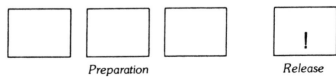

Preparation   Release

The mechanism for inducing laughter has this structure:

The punch line releases the tension. A surprise occurs. Expectancy is tricked. There is a sudden change in direction. The light bulb goes on.

In making or telling a joke, the structure is important. It cannot be too long or wordy; the punch line must be concise and on cue. The preparation must build expectancy: Without this tension, there is no release. Laughter depends on the structure as well as on the idea or the language.

A comedy playscript is a score for playing; just as the composer must be cognizant of the possibilities of the music in the hands of musicians, the writer of comedy must be fully aware of the techniques and resources of the actor that will animate the material.

The comic writer is acutely concerned with the individual in a social environment. Basic patterns of comedy depict a character who deviates from the norm or who is out of place with the surroundings. The implicit contrasts and conflicts require adroit delineation of the social milieu in order to expose the laughable elements of conduct. Tragic writers may concentrate on heroic figures isolated from other characters, from the human scene, from the group situation, and from the interrelationships of characters. Comedy emphasizes the here and now, not the long perspective. The playwright frequently develops timely allusions, local references, and contemporaneous characters. Comic material must have a sense of crispness and spontaneity. It must not smell of the museum or the dead past. Hence, it is difficult for comedy to survive its time and place of origin because many of its most telling referents are gone.

The earliest extant comedies are those of Aristophanes from the fifth century B.C. His typical plots were based on "a happy idea." The women in *Lysistrata* hope to bring about peace by a sex strike; in *The Acharnians* a private citizen negotiates his own personal peace treaty with Sparta. In *The Frogs*, Dionysus decides to take a trip to Hades to visit the tragic poets Aeschylus and Euripides. In each play, the merits of the idea are debated, and despite opposition, the happy idea is put into practice and the results demonstrated. The plays end in revelry.

In the subsequent development of comedy, the original pattern persists. Characters strive for objectives and are thwarted by obstacles and opposition, but their problems are solved when misunderstandings are cleared up and the truth emerges and/or the opponents are reconciled. The play ends happily, often with the lovers united in an embrace, a reminder of the orgiastic celebration of the end of most old comedies.

Georges Feydeau is noted for his complicated farces filled with frantic action
played at breakneck speed. A typical scene from *Hotel Paradiso* directed by Tom
Moore.

(American Conservatory Theater, San Francisco.)

Jan Kott sees the basic comic plot in these terms: "The oldest and most
enduring kind of comic action, from ancient comedy to commedia dell'arte,
from popular farce to Molière, is a clash between two houses."[7] One house
represents authority and appearances; in the second house are bachelors,
easy girls, thieves, and crooks. Kott suggests that the fundamental plot is the
aggression on the house of virtue by the house of ill repute.

Although Kott's theory is not universally applicable, his analysis is basically sound in that the comic plot usually involves an imbalance caused by
the presence of some ridiculous element through error, ignorance, or ambition. The resulting conflicts and contrasts create comic tension, which is
released in laughter.

The plots of most comedies are made up of sharp complications that
require careful craftsmanship in the use of exposition, climaxes, crises, discoveries, and the denouement. The tangled threads of action must remain

clear to the audience, which is tricky business in plays of rapid action, mishaps, and misunderstandings. The climaxes and crises of comedy demand technical mastery because the high points of the action often involve a social situation in which a number of people are caught in the same net, obliging the playwright to deal with complex materials. Frequently, the emotional peaks are those of action and discovery, which require the playwright to have a strong sense of visual humor. Climaxes must be built and sustained without being prolonged beyond the limits of the material. The playwright's touch must be deft and sure to keep the pace rapid and to create the special climate of comedy that will ensure laughter.

The structure of farce is a framework for vigorous, rapid, and exaggerated action in which the characters move, rather than think, and where laughter justifies nearly any means. Once the engine has been cranked up and set in motion, the speed is accelerated; by expected blowouts, backfirings, and explosions, the mechanism careens crazily, gathering momentum, until it finally lurches to an awkward but happy end in a cloud of steam with all the parts still spinning. Although there has been a whirlwind of activity, the machine has not really moved an inch in any direction.

The skill of plotting farce is determined by the dramatist's ingenuity in inventing a variety of entanglements that will give the comedian a chance to play for laughs. The playwright usually exploits a basic situation that is highly improbable and atypical: A woodcutter reluctantly consents to become a court physician to cure the King's daughter of a feigned illness; two long-lost twin brothers, whose servants are another pair of twins, strive for reunion; two young Communists, sharing a one-room apartment, fall in love with each other's newlywed wives; a shy greeting-card writer becomes involved with a gang of racetrack touts because of his skill in predicting winners; a taxicab driver is married to two women, and his secret is disclosed because of an automobile crash.

Low comedy exploits the physical aspects of humanity. The body, its desires and functions, is a primary source of comic material. To a large extent, farcical situations depend on visual humor. Not only sex but also any drive or appetite that causes one to lose one's balance or control is a target for ridicule. Farcical characters move in an active physical world; they are out of place in an intellectual atmosphere.

In the days of the silent motion picture, farce was exceedingly popular in the slapstick comedies created by Mack Sennett, Chaplin, and Buster Keaton. The basic requirement for silent pictures was action; hence it was a medium ideally suited for farce. Comedians tumbled their way through crazy situations, full of violence set off by the slightest provocation and usually ending in a chase that annihilated all the restrictions of time and space. For example, Harold Lloyd, playing a book salesman, approaches a tough customer and is thrown out. He returns a dozen times, accelerating the pace. On another occasion, he serves as a practice tackling-dummy for a football squad. He makes a speech at a dance with a kitten crawling inside his sweater. Keaton chases butterflies in the countryside, completely oblivious to a band of wild Indians who pursue him. In another picture, he sits on a hot stove, then on a cake of ice, which melts rapidly. Ben Turpin, a cross-eyed explorer, surrenders to a stuffed lion.

These familiar farcical patterns are still in use today. Consult the television listings or a movie guide and you will find such farcical situations as these:

> The Jefferson's landlord threatens to terminate their lease unless his niece is selected Miss Jefferson Cleaners.
>
> A woman gains control of a football team in a divorce settlement and must contend with an alcoholic coach and a shady general manager.
>
> Dudley is married to two different women, both of whom are expectant and go to the hospital at the same time.
>
> Woody wakes up in a strange police state in the year 2173.
>
> A man is brainwashed in a psychology experiment into thinking he is from another planet. He gets a face resembling Humphrey Bogart's and sets himself up as a private eye. Suddenly he is besieged with clients, all wanting him to find a priceless pair of matching blue sapphires.

The materials from which comedies are made are venerable ones, as old as the theater itself. The sources of comic effect, which the ancient playwrights Aristophanes, Plautus, and Terence used to delight audiences of Athens and Rome, can still be seen on your television or motion-picture screen tonight.

Similarly, the *devices* of comedy that the playwright uses are well established. Let us consider three representative examples of common mechanisms for evoking laughter.

COMIC MECHANISMS

Teasing

One of the most reliable comic mechanisms is that of teasing, which may take a variety of forms, for example, the delay of news when the Nurse withholds Romeo's message from Juliet. In *Lysistrata*, Myrrhina, having joined the women in a sex strike to make peace, teases her amorous husband, Cinesias, by a series of delaying tactics. Another form of teasing occurs when characters are intentionally placed in embarrassing or awkward situations. Tony Lumpkin, in *She Stoops to Conquer*, teases his mother by driving her around her own garden in a carriage at night, pretending that they are beset by robbers.

In *The Taming of the Shrew* the madcap Petruchio tames his wife through a series of teasings. Dressed like a madman, he arrives late for the wedding, boxes the priest's ears, and drags Kate away before the wedding

A teasing scene from Aristophanes' fifth century B.C. comedy in which the women sue for peace by holding a sex strike. Myrrhina finds ways to keep away from her husband.

(Greek National Theater, Athens.)

feast. Countering her every wish, snatching good food from her mouth because he pretends it is burned, tearing rich gowns into rags, Petruchio bends her toward submission. On the way home, he and Kate pause as the groom tests her once more:

Petruchio: Come on, i' God's name; once more toward our father's—Good
     Lord, how brightly and goodly shines the moon!
Katherine: The moon! the sun; it is not moonlight now.
Petruchio: I say it is the moon that shines so bright.
Katherine: I know it is the sun that shines so bright.
Petruchio: Now, by my mother's son, and that's myself,
     It shall be moon, or star, or what I list
     Or ere I journey to your father's house.
     Go on, and fetch our horses back again.
     Evermore cross'd and cross'd: nothing but cross'd!
Hortensio: Say as he says, or we shall never go.
Katherine: Forward, I pray, since we have come so far,
     And be it moon, or sun, or what you please:
     An if you please to call it a rush-candle,
     Henceforth, I vow it shall be so for me.
Petruchio: I say it is the moon.
Katherine: I know it is the moon.

One of the most famous battles of the sexes in comedy is Shakespeare's *Taming of the Shrew,* which is filled with verbal and physical skirmishes.

(Utah Shakespeare Festival. Directed by Brian Hansen.)

Petruchio: Nay, then you lie: it is the blessed sun.
Katherine: Then, God be blessed, it is the blessed sun:
  But sun it is not, when you say it is not;
  And the moon changes even as your mind.
  What you will have it named, even that it is;
  And so it shall be so for Katherine.

Reversal

Another familiar plot mechanism is reversal, or inversion. The entire play may be based on the turnabout of a downtrodden character who ultimately achieves a dominant position, as in such plays as *The Solid Gold Cadillac,* and *Born Yesterday.* The reversal may be one in which the characters are temporarily thrown out of their usual milieu, only to return to their customary status; for example, in *Jeppe of the Hills,* the drunken ne'er-do-well is placed in the mayor's bed, pampered for a day, and then returned insensible to the gutter where he was found. In Brecht's *Caucasian Chalk Circle,* an outcast suddenly becomes a judge and rules over the district. Nikolai Gogol's *The Government Inspector* tells the story of a disreputable down-and-out clerk, who being mistaken for the Inspector General, makes use of the opportunity; he is wined and dined as if he were an aristocrat, and the Mayor's wife and daughter make a play for him. At the end, the real Inspector arrives and the circle is about to begin again.

Another well-worn comic device that frequently includes inversion is the unfamiliar. A character or group of characters is placed in strange surroundings, or they are engaged in unaccustomed activities. One form this device takes is that of teaching something to an inexperienced and often inept person, such as the English lesson in *Henry V,* the fencing lesson in *Everyman in His Humour,* and the dancing lesson in *Le Bourgeois Gentilhomme.* The humor may be heightened by the additional twist of having the instructor as ignorant as the pupil. The awkward, embarrassed, or shy person, making an adjustment to a new experience or surroundings, is used again and again for comic effect.

One of the favorite reversal devices is the sex switch—men playing female roles. Dustin Hoffman, in the film *Tootsie,* disguises himself as a woman and gets involved in a series of awkward comic situations, such as being the object of his girlfriend's father's romantic advances. This same sex switch was employed by Aristophanes twenty-five centuries ago in *Thesmophoriazusae,* in which a male dons female attire and spies on the women's assembly. Brandon Thomas has delighted theatergoers since 1892 with *Charley's Aunt,* which has the same device of putting a male disguised as a woman in a number of unfamiliar situations, even a marriage proposal. When Lord Fancourt Babbersly is impersonating Charley's aunt, an unexpected suitor, Sir Francis, approaches Lord Fancourt, who is dressed as Donna Lucia, Charley's aunt.

Sir Francis: (*Aside*) Well, I've put myself to it, so I must come to the point. (*Clears throat again.*)

Lord Fancourt: What, again?

Sir Francis: (*Going to R. of table*). Donna Lucia, do you know what a man longs for when he's lonely—desolate—and wretched?

Lord Fancourt: A drink?

Sir Francis: (*Turns away R.—aside*) What a woman—doesn't help one a bit! (*Up to R. of table—aloud*) No, Donna Lucia, this is what he longs for— he longs to plant in his own heart that bright little floweret.

Lord Fancourt: (*Pointing L.*). I know—by the wayside—that one. Does he really?

Sir Francis: Yes, Donna Lucia, yes. And I have come all the way from India to find that little floweret.

Lord Fancourt: You must be tired. (*Indicating chair R. of table*) Take a chair.

Sir Francis: Thank you. (*Sits R. of table C., puts hats on C. table.*) It is a long way, Donna Lucia.

Lord Fancourt: Oh, quite a long walk.

Sir Francis: But I have found it.

Lord Fancourt: Then why don't you wear it in your buttonhole?

Sir Francis: Will you let me or will it be given away to another as you did before?

Charley's Aunt by Brandon Thomas has been delighting audiences for nearly a century with the exploits of Lord Fancourt when he is coerced into disguising himself as a middle-aged aunt.

(Repertory Theater of St. Louis.)

Lord Fancourt: Ah, yes—I remember, I was a naughty girl this morning. (*Putting corner of fichu in mouth, holds the other end, L. hand shaking it to and fro coyly—and putting R. hand unconsciously on table*)

Sir Francis: (*Looking about cautiously*) But dear Lucia—(*Places hand on that of Lord Fancourt's for a second, then removes it and looks off R. again.*)

Lord Fancourt: (*Taking hand off table—aside*) He's getting on!

Sir Francis: The floweret, I mean, must sit at the head of my table, walk by my side, live in my heart for ever. (*Absent-mindedly slightly moves hat. Then looks away R.*)

Lord Fancourt: (*Quickly tilts corner of hat and looks under brim—aside*) He's going to show me a conjuring trick.

Sir Francis: But I'll waste no more words—Donna Lucia, will you be my wife? (*Quick gasp from Lord Fancourt.*) Will you be my little floweret?

Lord Fancourt: (*Hesitatingly*) Well, you see, (*Then suddenly remembering*) "you've taken me so much by surprise."

Sir Francis: Then I may hope?

COMEDY **145**

Lord Fancourt: (*Quickly*) I'm afraid not. (*Firmly*) No, don't hope. (*Looking at Sir Francis humorously out of the corner of his eye*) I wouldn't hope if I were you.
Sir Francis: I beg pardon, Donna Lucia. Do I understand—(*Rises*)
Lord Fancourt: I must refuse you. The fact is, I am another's.[8]

These comic devices—teasing, reversal, and the unfamiliar are three of the venerable mechanisms that have been endlessly repeated ever since the origin of theatrical performances. Other familiar devices are mistaken identity, pretense or deception, jeopardy, violence, and fancy footwork or skillful recovery. This is not an exhaustive list, nor do the devices occur separately; rather they mix freely with one another. It is interesting to note that the mechanism by itself will not create a comic effect. Indeed, many of these patterns also appear in tragedy, for example, the reversal formula: A high-born character in an elevated position at the beginning of the play falls to catastrophe, as in *Hamlet* and *Antigone*. In comedy the reversal often goes in the other direction. The little person, ignored and beaten down, emerges at the end of the play in a dominant position, as in the musical *How to Succeed in Business without Really Trying:* A window washer manipulates his way to becoming the president of a large corporation.

CHARACTER

Comedy wears many guises. Characters may be comical because of their eccentric behavior; their lack of wit or judgment; their delightful facility with language, engaging vivacity, or animal spirits; their charming manners; their buoyant attitude toward life; or their extraordinary appearance, speech, or life-style. Comic characters are often associated with the performer who plays the same role again and again, such as Chaplin, Lucille Ball, Jackie Gleason, Woody Allen, and Bill Cosby.

Comic characters tend to be stock types. Playwrights frequently are more concerned about developing the intricacies of plot than about revealing depth of character. Hence they sketch their figures lightly or resort to readily recognizable types. Comic dramatists may deliberately create one-sided, exaggerated characters who show their inhumanity by their fixations and inflexibility. Or dramatists may purposely create stock figures to prevent excessive emotional attachment that might destroy the light atmosphere of comedy. As character becomes more genuine and complex, drama moves away from comedy. As an example of how a type character may evolve into a sympathetic and complex human being, thus altering the flavor of the play, we may consider the case of the braggart soldier. As Lamachus in Aristophanes' *Acharnians*, Miles Gloriosus in Plautine comedy, and the Capitano in commedia dell'arte, he is an elementary source of comic effect because of the disparity between his pretended bravery and his cowardice in the face of danger. As Shakespeare's Falstaff, the character is vastly enriched as he rollicks his way through *The Merry Wives of Windsor* and then is developed into a complete personality in *Henry IV*.

Characters in high comedies are usually from the upper echelons of society—urbane, sophisticated people who live in a special kind of environment with their own code of behavior. In contrast, farcical characters are from the humble walks of life. Their speech and behavior are simplified as they race through the complicated machinery of the plot.

THOUGHT

Most comedy does not bear a heavy burden of thought. The comic playwright usually is concerned more with the interaction of characters in a social situation than with a serious treatment of emotionally loaded problems.

In the high comedy of Restoration England, the plays demonstrated who won and lost in the social games that everyone played. The winners were witty, self-assured, sophisticated individuals who were always in control. The losers were out-of-place, awkward pretenders, unaware people, flawed in their manners. The comic dramatists wrote plays about this artificial world as part of the game, and there was no genuine concern for humanity under the polished surface.

Goldsmith and Sheridan, in the eighteenth century, used much of the same comic machinery in their sentimental comedies *The Rivals* and *She Stoops to Conquer*, but they stressed the good side of most of their comic characters rather than emphasizing the foibles and frivolities.

Shaw stands virtually alone in the twentieth century as a satirist who attacked conventional ideas of morality and manners with keen intelligence and incisive wit. His comedies of ideas were written to produce what George Meredith called "thoughtful laughter," notably in *Candida, Major Barbara, Pygmalion, Man and Superman,* and *Heartbreak House.*

The modern writer of popular comedy is much more concerned with amusing those who come to the theater—who wish to avoid facing someone else's problems and who have no immediate interest in intellectual stimulation. They want to have a good time—to laugh and to forget themselves. This attitude is evident when one looks at the list of the most popular plays on Broadway. The twenty-five longest running productions have been comedies, mostly musicals. The only serious play over 1,000 performances was *Equus.*

Although such entertainment may imply an accepted code of behavior and a system of values, the emphasis is not on weighing the merits of social conduct except insofar as it serves as a frame of reference for displaying incongruity. The comic playwright does not question values but rather exposes ridiculous behavior or characters. The action is more important than the meaning of the action. As Gary Trudeau said, "True satire—that is, satire guided by a moral purpose—is more difficult to take, and people at this point want comedy that is mindless. . . . Today, the joke's the thing. . . . The gag is more important than any sustained point of view."

Yet, as suggested earlier, recent writers of dark farce frequently use broad comic plots and characters to attack their political and cultural adversaries. Likewise, the protest theater often resorts to a blatant style of low comedy for maximum shock value. An outstanding example was the "tribal love-rock musical" *Hair* of the 1960s, which boasted such show-stopping numbers as a song-and-dance sequence when the flower children break up a high-society party.

Such comedy is not without significance because it releases a good deal of aggression by permitting the gratification of repressed tendencies through laughter. In the darkened auditorium we feel free to laugh at authority and conventional restrictions of speech and behavior. For a moment we are superior to the characters who are ridiculed onstage. In the nineteenth-century French "bedroom farces" of Feydeau and Labiche, there is implicit criticism of society and its mores—particularly of hypocrisy and pretension—but this is a byproduct of the farcical action, not its main reason for existence.

DICTION

Comedy employs a wide variety of language devices for its effect, from cleverly turned conceits and one-liners to crude puns, insults, vulgarisms, and deformed words. We have already observed some of comedy's comic uses in derision, automatism, and incongruity. Most successful comic writers have an excellent ear for dialogue and they take apparent delight in their verbal skill. The Elizabethans were fond of exploiting language for comic effect.

The writer of high comedy, of course, is especially concerned with dialogue since wit and repartee are the drama's chief appeal, the animated language and nimbleness when playing with ideas replacing physical action. The English Restoration playwrights of the late seventeenth century, such as Congreve, Wycherly, Vanbrugh, and Etherege, wrote for a select, sophisticated audience, mostly about amorous adventuring—depicting true wits in contrast to the unconscious incongruities of the inept witwords. The polished dialogue of this comedy of manners appeared again briefly in the late eighteenth century in the dramas of Goldsmith and Sheridan.

Among modern playwrights no one was more skilled in making his characters articulate than Shaw. In *Major Barbara* he contrasts Barbara, who is devoted to the Salvation Army, with her father, Undershaft, a munitions manufacturer who considers poverty the greatest evil.

Shaw's *Major Barbara* presents Undershaft, a wealthy munitions maker, and his daughter in a series of verbal clashes over their differing views on economics and religion.

(Arena stage. Photo: Joan Marcus.)

Undershaft: I save their souls just as I saved yours.

Barbara: (*Revolted*) You saved my soul! What do you mean?

Undershaft: I fed you and clothed you and housed you. I took care that you should have enough to live handsomely—more than enough; so that you could be wasteful, careless, generous. That saved your soul from the seven deadly sins.

Barbara: (*Bewildered*) The seven deadly sins!

Undershaft: Yes, the deadly seven. (*Counting on his fingers*) Food, clothing, firing, rent, taxes, respectability, and children. Nothing can lift those seven millstones from Man's neck but money; and the spirit cannot soar until the millstones are lifted. I lifted them from your spirit. I enabled Barbara to become Major Barbara; and I saved her from the crime of poverty.

Cusins: Do you call poverty a crime?

Undershaft: The worst of crimes. All the other crimes are virtues beside it, all the other dishonors are chivalry itself by comparison. Poverty blights whole cities; spreads horrible pestilences; strikes dead the very souls of all who come within sight, sound or smell of it. What you call crime is nothing; a murder here and a theft there, a blow now and a curse then; what do they matter? They are only the accidents and illnesses of life; there are not fifty genuine professional criminals in London. But there are millions of poor people, abject people, dirty people, ill fed, ill clothed people. They poison us morally and physically; they kill the happiness of society; they force us to do away with our own liberties and to organize unnatural cruelties for fear they should rise against us and drag us down into their abyss. Only fools fear crime: we all fear poverty.[9]

Among present comic playwrights, Stoppard is noted for his flair with comic language. In *Travesties* he shows off his verbal dexterity with parodies, puns, alliterations, double entendres, literary allusions, and music hall patter. In this play, Stoppard brings together in Zurich in 1919 a marvelous assortment of characters—Lenin, James Joyce, Tzara (one of the founders of dadaism), and Carr, a minor official in the English ministry who remembers imperfectly the events that occurred. The odd combination of characters gives Stoppard the chance to play with words and ideas in a dazzling manner. When Joyce enters, he speaks in limericks! Carr and Tzara engage in a delightful verbal exchange.

Carr: Well, let us resume. *Zurich By One Who Was There.* (*Normal light*)
Bennett: (*Entering*) Mr. Tzara.
Carr: How are you, my dear Tristan? What brings you here?
Tzara: Oh, pleasure, pleasure! What else should bring anyone anywhere?

(*Tzara, no less than Carr, is straight out of* The Importance of Being Earnest.)

Carr: I don't know that I approve of these Benthamite ideas, Tristan. I realise they are all the rage in Zurich—even in the most respectable salons, to remark that one was brought there by a sense of duty leads to terrible scenes, but if society is going to ape the fashions of philosophy, the end can only be ruin and decay.
Tzara: Eating and drinking, as usual, I see, Henry? I have often observed that Stoical principles are more easily borne by those of Epicurean habits.
Carr: (*Stiffly*) I believe it is done to drink a glass of hock and seltzer before luncheon, and it is well done to drink it well before luncheon. I took to drinking hock and seltzer for my nerves at a time when nerves were fashionable in good society. This season it is trenchfoot, but I drink it regardless because I feel much better after it.
Tzara: You might have felt much better anyway.
Carr: No, no—post hock, proper hock.
Tzara: But, my dear Henry, causality is no longer fashionable owing to the war.
Carr: How illogical, since the war itself had causes. I forget what they were, but it was all in the papers at the time. Something about brave little Belgium, wasn't it?

David Dukes in the role of Carr in Stoppard's *Travesties* describes his experiences in World War I.

(Mark Taper Forum.)

Tzara: Was it? I thought it was Serbia . . .

Carr: Brave little Serbia . . . ? No, I don't think so. The newspapers would never have risked calling the British public at arms without a proper regard for succinct alliteration.

Tzara: Oh, what nonsense you talk!

Carr: It may be nonsense, but at least it is clever nonsense.

Tzara: I am sick of cleverness. The clever people try to impose a design on the world and when it goes calamitously wrong, they call it fate. In point of fact, everything is Chance, including design.

Carr: That sounds awfully clever. What does it mean? Not that it has to mean anything, of course.

Tzara: It means, my dear Henry, that the causes we know everything about depend on causes we know very little about, which depend on causes we know absolutely nothing about. And it is the duty of the artist to jeer and howl and belch at the delusion that infinite generations of real effects can be inferred from the gross expression of apparent cause.

Carr: It is the duty of the artist to beautify existence.

Tzara: (*Articulately*) Dada dada dada dada dada dada dada dada dada dada dada dada dada dada dada dada dada dada dada dada dada dada dada dada dada dada dada dada dada dada dada dada dada dada dada.

Carr: (*Slight pause*): Oh, what nonsense you talk!

Tzara: It may be nonsense, but at least it's not clever nonsense. Cleverness has been exploded, along with so much else, by the war.

Carr: You forget that I was there, in the mud and blood of a foreign field, unmatched by anything in the whole history of human carnage. Ruined several pairs of trousers. Nobody who has not been in the trenches can have the faintest conception of the horror of it. I had hardly set feet in France before I sank in up to the knees in a pair of twill jodphurs with pigskin straps handstitched by Ramidge and Hawkes. And so it went on—the sixteen ounce serge, the heavy worsteds, the silk flannel mixture—until I was invalidated out with a bullet through the calf of an irreplaceable lambswool dyed khaki in the yarn to my own specification. I tell you, there is nothing in Switzerland to compare with it.[10]

Diction in farce, on the other hand, is not distinguished by literary pretensions. Only in rare instances has a playwright like Wilde combined the framework of farce and the repartee of social comedy because wit depends on an intellectual frame of reference. A critical ear is incompatible with farce. The linguistic devices of low comedy are puns, repetitions, tag lines, wisecracks, insults, vulgarisms, and deformed language. The playwright needs an excellent sense of theater to pace the dialogue, build for laughs, and realize the comic possibilities in the contrast of words and phrases—the incongruities of human speech.

COMEDY IN PERFORMANCE

More than other forms of drama, comedy depends on performance for its full effect. The timing of the actors, their ability to play pieces of business, to project laugh lines, to bring out the ridiculous in situation and character without destroying the light atmosphere—these are special requisites for the complete realization of comedy.

Comedy often makes considerable appeal to the eye so that scenery, properties, and costuming are essential. An interesting case in point is Peter Shaffer's *Black Comedy*, in which the audience is asked to accept the convention that most of the action takes place in the dark, with the resultant mixups in which the performers exploit the visual humor in groping for one another, crawling under rugs, falling down the staircase, and tripping over the furniture.

The Brothers Karamazov perform in a carnival-circus style, as in their zany production of the *Comedy of Errors*.

(Goodman Theater.)

Since disguises, concealments, discoveries, fights, chases, and entrapments are standard comic fare, the physical aspects of production are apt to be very important in devising "sight gags." In high comedy, in which much of the laughter stems from the wit or awkward social behavior, less emphasis is placed on visual humor, but farce is apt to tax the physical facilities of production to the utmost.

PLAYS TO READ AND SEE

F = Film available; V = Videotape available.

F	V	Simon, *Barefoot in the Park*
F	V	*I Ought to Be in Pictures*
F	V	*Odd Couple*
F	V	Gershe, *Butterflies Are Free*
F	V	Orton, *The Entertaining Mr. Sloan*
F	V	Brighouse, *Hobson's Choice*
F	V	Gogol, *Inspector General*

F V Shaw, *Major Barbara, Pygmalion*
F V Shakespeare, *A Midsummer Night's Dream*
F V *Taming of the Shrew*
        Wilson, *Talley's Folly*
        Molière, *Tartuffe*

BIBLIOGRAPHY

BENTLEY, ERIC. *Let's Get a Divorce and Other Plays.* New York: Hill & Wang, 1958.

BERGSON, HENRI. *Laughter.* Trans. Cloudesley Brereton and Frank Rothwell. London: Macmillan, 1917.

EASTMAN, MAX. *Enjoyment of Laughter.* New York: Simon & Schuster, Inc., 1942.

FELHEIM, MARVIN. *Comedy, Plays, Theory and Criticism.* New York: Harcourt Brace Jovanovich, Inc., 1962.

KERR, WALTER. *Tragedy and Comedy.* New York: Simon & Schuster, Inc., 1967.

NICOLL, ALLARDYCE. *The Theory of Drama.* New York: Barnes & Noble, 1962.

LAUTER, PAUL. *Theories of Comedy.* New York: Doubleday & Co., Inc., 1964.

STYAN, J. L. *The Dark Comedy: The Development of Modern Comic Tragedy.* Cambridge, Eng.: Cambridge University Press, 1962.

NOTES

1. Michael Frayn, *Noises Off* (London: Methuen, 1982).

2. Max Eastman, *Enjoyment of Laughter* (New York: Simon & Schuster, Inc., 1942).

3. Joseph Stein, *Fiddler on the Roof* (New York: Crown Publishers, Inc.,).

4. Sigmund Freud, *Jokes and Their Relation to the Unconscious*, trans. James Strachey (New York: W. W. Norton & Co., Inc., 1960).

5. Beth Henley, *Crimes of the Heart* (New York: The Viking Press, 1981).

6. Molière, *The Imaginary Invalid,* in *The Dramatic Works of Molière,* trans. C. H. Wall (London: George Bell & Sons, 1900).

7. Jan Kott, "The Eating of 'The Government Inspector,' " *Theatre Quarterly,* 5, no. 17 (1975).

8. Brandon Thomas, *Charley's Aunt* (New York: Samuel French, 1934).

9. George Bernard Shaw, *Major Barbara* (New York: Dodd, Mead & Company, 1941).

10. Tom Stoppard, *Travesties* (London: Fraser and Dunlop, 1975).

6

Realism and Its Derivatives

The term *realism* in the arts is an arbitrary one. An easel painting on a framed flat piece of canvas may be an aesthetic representation of an actual landscape, but viewers know that they are not looking through a window at genuine trees, water, and sky. Likewise, the spectator in the theater knows that the stage setting is not a real room and that the characters in it are performers. What is meant by realism is the suggestion of actuality—the impression of truth—by the depiction of characters whose speech and actions convey the effect of reality. Realism deals with the here and now; it is "concerned essentially with detail"; it is a "copying of actual facts"; it is "a deliberate choice of the commonplace"; it is "a factual interpretation of life"; it is, in short, *truth*.

You know you are dealing with realism when Henley begins her play *Crimes of the Heart* like this:

(*The lights go up on an empty kitchen. It is late afternoon. Lenny McGrath, a thirty-year-old woman with a round figure and face, enters from the back door, carrying a white suitcase, a saxophone case, and a brown paper sack. She sets the sax case down and takes the brown sack to the kitchen table. After glancing quickly at the door, she gets the cookie jar from the kitchen counter, a box of matches from the stove, and then brings both objects to the kitchen table. Excitedly, she reaches into the brown sack and pulls out a package of birthday candles.*)[1]

Clearly, Henley's intention is to communicate the impression of reality despite the artificial conditions under which she wrote. She was obliged to compress the action to a few hours; she had to create effective entrances and exits, to provide necessary exposition to let the audience know what had happened in the past or what was taking place offstage, and to construct a series of episodes in which characters confronted one another in meaningful actions. Despite the artificial nature of theatrical production, the effect of the play in the theater is realistic.

Realism has been the dominant mode of theater for over a century. By *mode* I mean the temper or spirit that affects the creator's point of view. The mode reflects the cultural climate in which a work of art was created. The classicism of fifth-century B.C. Greece grew out of the ideal of the golden mean and the emphasis on reason, so that classicism is characterized by beauty of form, proportion, balance, symmetry, and control. When the neoclassicists in Renaissance Italy and France sought to create their own society of enlightenment celebrating the age of reason, they attempted to transplant the Greek ideas, with mixed results. In drama, strict application of misinterpretations of Aristotle made it exceedingly difficult to write a playable work and resulted in a rigid theatrical style that emphasized form and rhetoric. It was an elevated drama in its use of verse; highborn characters; and themes of love, honor, and loyalty, testing the will of exemplary individuals.

THE ROMANTIC MOVEMENT

At the end of the eighteenth and nineteenth centuries a new audience made up of the middle classes found its heartfelt desires reflected in Romantic drama. The spirit that animated romanticism was faith in the "natural man"—an individual unfettered by the strictures of organized society, whose conduct was guided by his heart. The major European playwrights were Johann Goethe and Friedrich Schiller in Germany. In France, Victor Hugo led the revolt with his preface to *Cromwell* (1827), in which he rejected the rules of the past and called for a new free spirit in the theater that "will set about doing as nature does, mingling in its creations—but without compounding them—darkness and light, the grotesque and the sublime." Three years later the tumultuous reception of *Hernani* at the Comédie Française signaled the overthrow of neoclassicism. In England, romanticism was more closely associated with poetry and the novel, but its effect was clearly marked in the staging of spectacular melodramas in the nineteenth century.

Romanticism as a literary movement began as a revolt against the strictures of classicism because dramatists insisted on dealing freely with the imaginative aspects of nature and man. The romanticists gave full rein to their emotions, and they discarded the rigid form of the classics. They insisted on freedom for a wide scope of action celebrating the individual as a child of nature, and they combined beauty with the grotesque and the lowly with the elevated. Their heroes were picaresque figures—rebels and outcasts, active protagonists with uncomplicated emotions, such as Schiller's *William Tell* and James Nelson Barkers's *The Indian Princess* or *La Belle Sauvage*. Such plays expressed the sense of wonder and mystery of life; the action was often remote, exotic, and picturesque. In their dialogue, the playwrights attempted to use elevated verse or colorful rhetoric that would suggest their characters' natural exuberance.

Although romanticism was significant for clearing the stage of the austere rigidity of the past, its built-in tendency for excess made it susceptible to such abuses as too much straining for effect and superficiality in character, emotion, and situation. As the basic function of theater became escape, romanticism offered too little contact with the real world and everyday life. Nevertheless, the spirit of romanticism was an appealing one; it easily made its way into popular melodrama. Today, not only do we find echoes of romanticism in motion pictures and television, musical comedies and opera, but also we wistfully compare our present regimented, mechanized, crowded world with the idealized one of the natural man.

Because the intellectual climate of the nineteenth century was profoundly changed by science and technology, a new kind of drama was required—realism. In general, we may say that modern dramatic literature has focused on the form of *drame* and the mode of realism. Although in the last few years it has been under attack, realism has been surprisingly per-

Cyrano de Bergerac is one of the theaters' most romantic, dashing heroes. His grotesque nose prevents him from pursuing his love for Roxane, so he puts his poetic gifts to work for his friend, Christian.

(Asolo State Theater, Florida. Directed by John Ulmer.)

sistent and durable. Since most of the serious plays of the last century follow this mode, and since the current rebellion is antirealistic, we need to understand its background and rationale. In evaluating realism it is important to keep in mind the kind of artificial drama it was rebelling against and the new thought the realist was seeking to express. Those who led the way were serious individuals, genuinely dedicated to presenting the truth. Their dramatic practice, like that of all playwrights, was to seek the most effective means for touching the minds and hearts of their audiences.

THE REALISTIC MOVEMENT

From the change in speculative thought arising from the works of such men as Charles Darwin, Freud, and Karl Marx, three implications are of particular significance to drama and the theater. The first is the dynamic notion of change. In place of the older, static concept of a perfect creation a few thousand years ago, the scientist presented the idea that all life is in a constant process of alteration, and as a creature of nature, humankind, too, is subject to change.

A second implication is that a person is a biochemical entity. Said the biologist: There seems to be nothing about human life or behavior that is not susceptible to explanation according to naturalistic laws and principles. The individual is a product of a callous nature, rather than a child of special providence whose life is subject to divine intervention and revelation. We act mechanistically. Physiology is as important as intellect in determining our conduct. The human being is merely the leading member of the simian group, and for the time being, the dominant species of the animal kingdom on this planet.

A third implication of the new thought is that humanity is subject to scientific inquiry. A person can be a case study, capable of being examined and investigated.

In 1877 Antoine inaugurated the Théâtre Libre to give a chance to realistic playwrights. The natural style of performance is apparent in this old photograph of Metenier's *En Famille*.

These changes in the intellectual climate have been variously interpreted. At one extreme Émile Zola, the nineteenth-century French firebrand, and his fellow naturalists emphasized the sordid and mechanistic aspects of life to the exclusion of all else. Their thinking was shadowed by a somber view of life, which threw a blighting chill of determinism on all human conduct. At the opposite extreme, many realists saw in science a buoyantly optimistic assurance of the ultimate perfectability of humanity. They extended the doctrine of evolution to a view of the entire universe as fulfilling the promise of one glorious purpose—the elevation of humankind.

In between the optimistic realist and the pessimistic naturalist was a variety of interpretations, but each stressed the importance of the individual and the significance of the environment as a formative influence on behavior. In addition, most realists were conscious of the humanitarian implications of the new way of looking at life: The artist plays a part in the elevation of humankind by insisting on the necessity of a congenial social atmosphere. The realist deals with the ugly and untrue because they are forces hostile to personal fulfillment. This point of view did not cause realists to become professed propagandists; their desire to be objective ruled against this possibility. Nevertheless, humanitarian concern colored the selection of dramatic material.

The realistic movement had its origin in nineteenth-century French fiction. Honoré de Balzac, Gustave Flaubert, and the brothers Edmond and Jules Goncourt created conspicuous examples of the new attitude. The nature of that realism and its guiding principles is summed up by Bernard Weinberg:

> Realism aims to attain truth. Now truth is attainable only by the observation (scientific and impersonal) of reality—and hence of contemporary life—and by the unadulterated representation of that reality in the work of art. Therefore, in his observations, the artist must be sincere, unprejudiced, encyclopedic. Whatever is real, whatever exists is a proper subject for art; this means that the beautiful and ugly, the physical and spiritual, are susceptible of artistic treatment; it does not imply that the artist refrains from choosing his subject and his detail, for choice is fundamental in art. The principal object of imitation is always man; description of the material world, construction of plot, are thus subsidiary and contributory to character portrayal.[2]

In French drama, the theory of realism was rooted in the teaching of Denis Diderot, who in the eighteenth century called for "middle-class tragedy." In the early nineteenth century when Pixérécourt popularized romantic melodrama, he required realistic scenery with usable steps, bridges, and boats for the exciting action of his bourgeois plays. Eugene Scribe's technical dexterity in manipulating plots and his portrayal of types found in contemporary society gave his plays an air of superficial probability. His skill as a craftsman resulted in the writing of what became known as "well-made plays," whose techniques were so popular in the theater that his structural pattern was widely imitated.

In a well-made play the author attempts to deal naturally with current society, constructing a play with careful craftsmanship so that all parts are connected together in a plausible way. Climaxes are carefully built up by cause-and-effect progression. The well-crafted play is a controlled environment influencing the characters that inhabit it. Scribe was followed by Émile Augier, an enormously successful playwright whose impartiality of treatment, careful depiction of background based on minute observation of objects and incidents, and competence in characterization took drama a step nearer to realism. Alexandre Dumas *fils* continued the advance by his concern with the decadence of the social scene in such plays as *Le Demi-Monde* (1855) and *La Question d'Argent* (1857). His treatment of men and women who were not heroic, but weak, sensuous, and selfish, added new roles to the theater. Together with Augier, Dumas made a critical assault on the corruption of middle- and upper-class society.

Elsewhere in Europe, the intellectual revolution taking place found expression in the new playwrights—Ibsen, Leo Tolstoi, Chekhov, Strind-

Alexander Dumas fils' *Camille* (1852) was a sentimentalized treatment of the courtesan with a "heart of gold." Because of its theme, it was forbidden production for three years.

(Guthrie Theater. Directed by Garland White.)

berg, and Gerhart Hauptmann. These men were interested in telling the truth about the common person in everyday circumstances, but because their dramas were so outspoken and their subject matter so bold, they found it difficult to get a hearing until the Independent Theater movement, a group of subscription theaters, was organized for the specific purpose of opening up the theater to the new drama. Under the leadership of André Antoine in Paris, Otto Brahm in Berlin, Stanislavski in Moscow, and John Grein in London, this movement broke the shackles of tradition and introduced a new exuberant spirit into the drama, linking the stage once more with literature and life.

Ibsen's *Ghosts* was an especially important play because of its sensational impact wherever it was produced. Because of its bold subject matter *Ghosts* stirred up some of the most vituperative critical abuse in the history of the theater. In Berlin (1889) when the censor banned the play in the public theaters, it played to a subscription audience at the Freie Bühne. English reaction to *Ghosts* (1891) was especially virulent. One London critic, Clement Scott, compared Ibsen's play to "an open drain, a loathsome sore unbandaged, a dirty act done publicly, a lazar house with all its doors and windows open."

In America in the 1890s, Herne and a number of disciples of the new realism in fiction attempted to introduce the new spirit through productions of Herne's *Margaret Fleming* in Boston and New York. This play, the first sociological play in the American theater, recalled Ibsen's boldness in its theme of a wayward husband whose affair with a maid results in her death and the birth of an illegitimate child. But the play ends on an upbeat note because Margaret Fleming forgives her husband and accepts the child as her own. Herne's effort appealed to a limited audience; American theatergoers were not hospitable to such advanced subjects.

In addition to the development of realism as literary theory during the latter part of the nineteenth century, there was also considerable change taking place in the techniques of writing and producing farces and melodramas, which made up most of the popular stage fare. Characters of humble origin became more and more prominent, local color was exploited, native speech and costuming were more accurately reproduced, and the stage scenery and effects became increasingly more substantial and convincing. Although much of the plot and character motivation was artificial, realism made its influence felt, especially in the external aspects of production.

The ultimate result of the revolution in the late nineteenth-century theater was to win the twentieth century over to realism. Although realism as a complete aesthetic theory soon lost its impetus, its techniques and attitudes have nevertheless continued to dominate our modern stage, even in the face of a great deal of experimentation with new forms and despite a rather general dissatisfaction with its restrictive outlook.

Observation and Objectivity

Having received their inspiration from the scientists, the realists turned to science for their techniques as well, attempting to follow basic concepts drawn from the scientific method. The realist, therefore, came to rely on meticulous and precise observation, analysis, and recording of specific details. Minutiae that previous writers passed by were accumulated a bit at a time to build up character or locale in much the same manner that Georges Seurat used to apply his paint in tiny spots of broken color. And like Gustave Courbet and Edouard Manet, who took their easels out of their studio to paint commonplace subjects from direct observation, rather than saints and miracles from their inspiration and imagination, realistic writers looked hard at life at first hand and jotted down in their notebooks the texture of their responses. It was one's mission to see, hear, and report everything. Such an emphasis on observation affected not only the realist's choice of subject but also the method of handling it. The plot must be allowed to develop where an honest treatment of the characters takes it; the environment and its atmosphere must be depicted with scrupulous fidelity; emotion must be employed without artificiality or sentimentalism; the writer must be faithful to the facts as observed.

The realists also maintained an attitude of objectivity toward their work, just as the scientist conducts experiments, examines the data, and draws impersonal conclusions. As the realists avoided idealism and romanticism, they were equally opposed to cynicism and pessimism. As impartial observers they tried to escape personal bias and report on life as it is.

Against this general background of a literary theory stemming from the intellectual revolution of the nineteenth century, let us now consider the application of realism to specific dramatic problems.

Plot

The dramatic structure of the early realists resembles classical drama in its concentration on characters caught in moments of crisis. Thus the realist generally uses a late point of attack, employs a few incidents, and deals with a small group of characters over a short space of time. The result of this dramaturgy is a gain in intensity and dramatic tension because the action is continuous and concentrated, free from the extraneous diversions of constantly changing locales and complicated plots and subplots. The writer of popular nineteenth-century melodrama dramatized simple people in a complicated plot based on a pattern of physical conflicts. The realist reversed this approach by showing complex characters in a simple plot involving psychological action. The result was realistic *drame*.

Realistic plays are not full of arbitrary climaxes, building up to "big scenes" of violent action. Even in moments of great stress, the emotional expression is often deliberately restrained, underplayed, suggested rather than exploited. Playwrights learned that the most telling moments of their plays might be the quiet closing of a door, the distant sound of an axe on a tree. There is an absence of sensational and "stagey" devices, but not an absence of emotional effect.

To secure the semblance of reality, the realists were obligated to make their work seem logical and plausible, with no clanking machinery or whirr of motors. They avoided all manner of contrivances that might destroy illusion. They did not interrupt the action to make explanations, preferring to integrate exposition by gradual revelation throughout the course of the play.

The realist's method of handling plot was responsible for clearing away much of the trickery of popular drama. Plays became much more credible, closer to actual experience and the observed facts of life. Because they based their dramas on problems and ideas, rather than on external action, and because they were concerned with character revelation, the realists achieved an intensity of effect. On the other hand, their method of working narrowed the scope of action, slowed down the pace, and sometimes became downright sedentary. Critics were quick to point out that in their attempts to condense the action and frame it in a logical, tight mold, amid a welter of concrete details, the realists sacrificed the chance to stimulate the imagination and to give free play to fancy. They had trapped themselves in the stuffy atmosphere of a middle-class living room.

As realism has developed in the past half century, the validity of this criticism has been acknowledged, and the contemporary playwright breaks through the conventional realist's methods and has enormous freedom while working within the realistic mode. For example, in Taylor's *And a Nightingale Sang,* Helen Stott serves as narrator and the leading character in the play. In the middle of a dialogue with another character, she pauses to talk directly to the audience. Meanwhile, her father, George, is at the piano, picking out pieces throughout the play that are appropriate to the action. Although most of the play takes place in the Stott's drab home in an interior setting, the downstage area, used as an unlocalized area, becomes a park and a hotel. Fuller begins his Pulitzer Prize-winning *A Soldier's Play* with a flashback showing the murder of a drunk, black soldier. The rest of the play is an investigation of the crime through a series of scenes played in fragmentary set pieces in a horseshoe set of several platforms at varying levels. The staging is open theater in technique, but essentially the play is realistic. For want of a better term to describe this freer use of the theater, *selective realism* can be used, which simply means that complete sets with three walls and a ceiling and a room full of furniture and props have been replaced by a few selected pieces that convey the impression of the environment.

Character

The realists' attempt to achieve objectivity and their reliance on observation brought into the theater an entirely new gallery of characters who were delineated in a new way. In the past, playwrights used lower-class people mostly for minor or comic roles. Now, attention was focused on the humble, downtrodden, and ordinary people. This concern with common people, begun by Ibsen, Hauptmann, and Chekhov, continues today, as indicated by three recent Pulitzer Prize winners.

Norman, in *'Night Mother* (1983), shows the intimate details of two individual, ordinary women, as the daughter moves relentlessly toward suicide in the face of her mother's ineffectual protest. In *Crimes of the Heart* (1981), Henley lights up the stage with her account of three McGrath sisters in Hazelhurst, Mississippi, after the youngest of them shoots her pompous husband in the stomach. Fuller's *A Soldier's Play* involves a dozen segregated enlisted men (one white captain) in the investigation of the death of a black sergeant in Fort Neal, Louisiana. In realism, the common person came onto center stage.

Dramatists became concerned about psychological forces that conditioned behavior, and they brought into the theater characters whose pathology was explained in terms of repression, subconscious desire, and early childhood conditioning. The playwright dramatized these people at critical

Chekhov achieved a new kind of realism with his plays that emphasized the inner life of his characters and their relationships with one another. *The Seagull* at Clarke College.

(Directed by Carol Blitgen.)

Another production of Chekhov's *The Sea Gull,* at the Guthrie Theater, when Nina, an aspiring actress, attempts to impress her friends.
(Directed by Lucian Pintilie; settings by Radu Boruzescu.)

moments of their lives, not those of violent physical action so much as inner crises, thus penetrating the surface and giving insight into their desires, aspirations, and frustrations. Realists seemed especially concerned with presenting women on the stage, and they created such memorable feminine characters as Strindberg's Laura and Julie; Chekhov's Madame Ranevsky and Nina; Shaw's Candida and Eliza; and Ibsen's Nora, Hedda, Rebecca West, and Mrs. Alving.

In shifting the attention to people from the common walks of life, realists lost the elevation and magnitude of classic tragedy with its heroic figures. The naturalists, as we shall see later in the chapter, carried the mechanistic and bestial aspects of people to an extreme in their overemphasis of the sordid and the bizarre. The realists, however, found it possible to show both sides of humankind, and they dealt with many characters who had redeeming qualities—characters who were close to the norm in behavior and outlook.

Significant contributions to drama were made by the realists in the integrity of their characterization, their concern with sound psychological motivation, their cumulative technique of character revelation, and their treatment of protagonists drawn from the common walks of life. Although many playwrights today remain deeply concerned with the problems stressed by early realists, they now have greater flexibility in treating characters. Because of a freer approach to playwriting and staging, characters can be revealed more deeply by more exposure. Flashbacks, monologues, and direct communication with the audience provide for more extensive commentary than the simulated conversation of many parlor-talk plays. A character may now begin a speech as a young person and shift to old age within a few lines simply by modifying the voice. People mix with animals that may be shown as complex creatures with human traits—without destroying theatrical credulity. Although realism gave up much of the grandeur associated with classic drama and the dynamic, imaginative protagonists of romanticism, realists peopled the stage with a remarkable gathering of fascinating creatures, whom we have come to know as authentic human beings.

Thought

The realists dealt boldly with new themes, many of them growing out of their awakened interest in the social sciences—economic conflicts, sex problems, domestic difficulties, and social strife. Emulating the ways of science, playwrights attempted to record life objectively, so they pulled no punches, honored no taboos, found no material too commonplace or sordid for their probing. They became absorbed in the facts of human existence here and now—commonplace facts about contemporary, commonplace people. They tried to discard everything that smacked of the artificial, the contrived, the sentimental. The result was to open the doors of the theater to the dramatization of day-to-day existence. In insisting on complete freedom in the treatment of character, dialogue, and subject matter, the realist brought about a franker, freer stage, so that today there are almost no holds barred.

Diction

The realists' interest in accurate observation and reporting prompted them to suggest the speech of everyday life. Dialogue frequently was ungrammatical, fragmentary, and blatantly frank. Realists abandoned the theatrical devices of unmotivated "purple passages" and the inflated bombast of "paper speeches." Even in scenes of strong emotional climax, the dramatist avoided rhetorical display, having learned the eloquence of a broken phrase, a small gesture, and silence. Stage dialogue became more utilitarian, serving to advance or delineate character rather than to call attention to itself.

As Shaw demonstrated, another benefit that resulted from realism was the opportunity to exploit discussion in drama. Playwrights were concerned with ideas, and they took pains to stimulate the audience's thinking about their ideas by expressing them onstage. Ibsen's and Shaw's characters not only act, they also think—and they discuss their thoughts. Their dialogue becomes action—an investigation, an adventure, a verbal tug-of-war.

Critics of realism lament that the speech of the new drama drove poetry out of the theater. It is true that playwrights turned their ear in another direction and sacrificed poetic speech, but it is also true that much of the embellished dialogue of nineteenth-century romantic writers of melodrama was poor stuff—sentimental and pretentious. Moreover, in the hands of skillful playwrights, realistic speech has a clarity and intensity that goes directly to the heart of the matter. Hamlin Garland found much to admire in Ibsen's dialogue:

> How true and unconventional his style. We hardly realize how false and stilted current stage conversation is, till we hear the real word spoken there. His words come to us at times like the thrusts of the naked fist. They shake the hearer with their weight of real passion. In one sense it is astoundingly direct, and then again it is subtly indirect—as in life.[3]

A good example of the eloquence of small talk is in Wilson's *Talley's Folly,* in which Matt Friedman, a St. Louis accountant, woos Sally, a shy spinster of thirty-one, in a dilapidated boathouse on the river bank in Lebanon, Missouri. He strives to break through her protective shell and wants her to come away with him.

Matt: . . . Oh, my gosh! I do not know how to begin! I am walking into an unfriendly church in my underdrawers here.
Sally: What are you talking about?
Matt: You don't have a dream? I congratulate you. That is a terrible dream. I mean, I am at such a disadvantage here. (*With an energy born from frustration*) None of my skills is appropriate to the situation I find myself in. And I have amazing skills. I could be an attraction in a sideshow. Give me a list of three, six, up to fifteen numbers, five digits each, I'll tell you the sum immediately. In my head, Mr. Adding Machine. Everbody gapes. How does he do that? He's got it all written down. I know the multiplication table up to seventy-five times seventy-five. Truly. It's something I know. What is sixty-seven times sixty-eight? Four thousand five hundred fifty-six. I have amazing skills. Only I feel like Houdini in the iron box under the ice at the bottom of the river. I forgot where I put the key to the handcuffs. Such a frustrating dream.

Sally: One of the boys at the hospital is an artist. He's developed a facility for when a dream starts to go bad. It starts to get scary. He, in the dream, changes it all into a drawing, wads it up, and throws it away.

Matt: Freud wouldn't like it.

Sally: Oh, drive him crazy.

Matt: I am foolish to insinuate myself down here and try to feel like one of the hillbillies. Who ever heard of this Friedman—I don't blame you. I won't be Matt Friedman any more. I'll join the throng. Call myself . . . August Hedgepeth. Sip moonshine over the back of my elbow. Wheat straw in the gap of my teeth. I'm not cleaning my glasses, I'm fishing for crappie. Bass.

Sally: Sun perch.

Matt: Oh, heck yes. Only I'm not. I can't even take off my shoes without feeling absurd.

Sally: People don't walk around with their shoes off here, sipping moonshine. It isn't really the Hatfields and the McCoys. The ones who go barefoot only do it because they can't afford shoes.[4]

Matt persists in his romancing, and in the end Sally goes with him.

Spectacle

Although realistic scenery had been employed in the theater in the past, its appeal was based on novelty and picturesqueness. The realist had quite a different purpose. It became important to show the environment in order to understand the character. Thus, realistic scenery is not a mere accompaniment of the action; it is a causal force of the action. It shapes and molds the characters. In such plays as *American Buffalo, Look Back in Anger,* and *The Effect of Gamma Rays on Man-in-the-Moon Marigolds,* the setting is an obvious source of character motivation, with its sociological implication that to improve the person it is necessary to improve the circumstances.

The early realists' observation of actuality and concern with the commonplace prompted them to locate the action in a setting crammed with the domestic details of everyday life. The stage and action of their plays were filled with properties, but in the hands of the genuine realist these were not mere clutter for verisimilitude; they were selected because of their organic and symbolic relationship to the characters, such as Hedda's pistols, Nora's macaroons, and Oswald's pipe. The use of such props illustrated the notion of the significant trifle. Incidentally, the props were an enormous help to the actors in achieving naturalness in performance.

Just as the realists rejected the cardboard cutout figures of the past, they also discarded the "painty" two-dimensional wing and groove and backdrop setting. The box set (with three continuous walls, often capped with a ceiling), which had been introduced earlier in the nineteenth century, became a standard requirement for realistic drama. Practical doors and windows, appropriate furniture, and genuine props were added to further the illusion of actuality. The actor was now surrounded by scenery and played *within* a locale rather than in front of it. As a logical accompaniment of the new scenery came the convention of the "fourth wall"—a tacit agreement with the audience that the opening framed by the proscenium arch was the fourth wall of the set, thus giving the illusion of a solid room instead of a platform. The fourth wall defined the downstage limit of the acting area and confined the actors to the setting; they pretended not to see or communicate with the audience. Realism is no longer restricted to box sets and rigid time limitations. The playwright is free to move around to suit the needs of the plot. Many productions these days are performed in arena theaters with little or no scenery; locale of the action is established by furniture, props, and dialogue.

Although realism was until recently the predominant mode of drama, it had, and still has, the seeds of revolt within itself. Later we will deal at length with modern experiments, but now we will consider two offshoots of realism in the past—naturalism and expressionism.

NATURALISM

The term *naturalism*, sometimes used interchangeably with *realism*, is historically an independent movement that began in France in the 1870s under the messianic leadership of Zola. It was unlike realism in its concentration on the squalid side of life, its atmosphere of despair, and it was structurally different in avoiding theatrically motivated situations, climaxes, and curtains. Like the realist, the naturalist responded to the influence of science—especially to the notion of environmental conditioning of contemporary humankind. It was Zola who wrote the first naturalistic play and bombarded the senses of his contemporaries as he clamored for a dramatic style that would reflect the method of science:

> I am waiting for them to rid us of fictitious characters, of conventional symbols of vice and virtue which possess no value as human data. I am waiting for the surroundings to determine the characters, and for the characters to act according to the logic of the facts. . . . I am waiting until there is no more jugglery of any kind, no more strokes of the magical wand, changing in one minute persons and things. I am waiting, finally, until this evolution takes place on the stage; until they return the source of science to the study of nature, to the anatomy of man, to the painting of life in an exact reproduction, more original and powerful than anyone has so far dared to place upon the boards.[5]

Zola's play *Thérèse Raquin* (1873) dramatizes the story of Thérèse and her lover, who drown her unwanted husband but are unable to live down their crime under the accusing eyes of the dumb and paralyzed mother of the victim. Zola's play was not a popular success, but his example led to similar attempts by others. Henri Becque, in *The Vultures* (1882), pictures the destruction of a family and its fortune as a result of the sudden demise of the father and the preying activities of the dead man's business associates. Hauptmann, in *Before Sunrise* (1889), a story of misery and death, gave Berlin's independent stage, the Freie Bühne, a graphic view of the degradation of a Silesian coal-mining family suddenly grown rich. His *Weavers* (1892) has a rioting mob as the protagonist in one of the earliest and best plays of social conflict. Tolstoi, in *The Power of Darkness* (1886), tells a grim story of illicit love, drunkenness, and murder, although he tempers the gloom with spiritual overtones. Strindberg's *Miss Julie* (1888) is a story of lust and suicide. Shaw, who wrote two plays in naturalistic style, *Widower's Houses* (1892) and *Mrs. Warren's Profession* (1898), indicates his motivation for writing as he did: "I felt the need for mentioning the forbidden subjects, not only because of their own importance, but for the sake of destroying taboo by giving it the most violent shocks."

The naturalists introduced a new collection of characters to the stage—the dregs of society, the wayward and twisted victims of the lower depths. Their characters are bedeviled by doubts and frustrations, torn by inner conflicts, ridden by passions. As Strindberg says, "They are conglomerates made up of past and present stages of civilization, scraps of humanity, torn-off pieces of Sunday clothing turned into rags—all patched together as is the human soul itself."[6] Naturalists attempted to translate into concrete images what they had gained from changing thought. The hard shell that protected the traditional views of love, authority, duty, honor, and morality was shattered when the playwright probed beneath the surfaces to investigate the innermost desires and passion of individuals in their relations with their mates, their families, and their society.

Although the rigid realism and naturalism of the first part of the twentieth century has given way to much more freedom and experimentation, many playwrights today aim at presenting the illusion of authentic daily life, especially in characterization, dialogue, and thought. The realists' and naturalists' penchant for forbidden or controversial material characterizes the theater of shock and cruelty that has emerged since World War II.

The naturalist's dialogue had a new texture and frankness as it reflected the speech of the lowborn and humble. Themes that had hitherto been considered too controversial or salacious for the theater-going public became the accepted norm. Although the new boldness aroused shocked protest in many places, the naturalists performed an important service in ridding the stage of bombast and sentimentality. They also made painstaking efforts to show the locale of their action as accurately as possible to emphasize how physical conditions may deform character. Sometimes the result was an excess of clutter and an obsession with the solidity and au-

Naturalistic setting and characters in Gorki's *The Lower Depths,* showing life in the slums of Moscow.

(Moscow Art Theater, 1902.)

thenticity of material objects, which at its extreme led Antoine of the Thé-âtre Libre to hang sides of beef on the stage.

As a literary style, naturalism gave way to the more moderate realism, which found ways of relieving the steady diet of misery, crime, and disintegration; but the naturalist did succeed in bringing to the stage new characters and themes with honesty and forthrightness. Although naturalism as a movement lost its impetus, echoes of its quality are seen in the present theater in such plays as Jack Gelber's *The Connection* (1959), a brutal portrait of drug addicts waiting for a fix; Kenneth H. Brown's *The Brig* (1963), an attack on the inhumane conditions in a Marine Corps prison; in LeRoi Jones's plays of racial discrimination, *The Dutchman* and *The Toilet* (1964); Rabe's plays of the Vietnam war, *The Basic Training of Pavlo Hummel* (1972) and *Sticks and Bones* (1972); Mamet's *American Buffalo* (1975), which shows three sleazy characters in a junk shop vainly trying to plan a crime, and his Pulitzer Prize play, *Glengarry Glen Ross* (1984), a scathing depiction of real estate sharks and their vicious way of operating.

Shepard's themes, characters, and dialogue are a form of contemporary naturalism, dealing with people who are at the edges of society. *Buried Child,* Clarke College.

(Directed by Carol Blitgen.)

EXPRESSIONISM

Another mode of modern drama that was a reaction to realism is expressionism. The expressionist is actually a superrealist insisting that reality is not to be judged by external appearance. Truth is within. Beneath the social façade of behavior is a vast jungle of secret and often unconscious desires, aspirations, conflicts, frustrations, and hallucinations. It is this strange and confusing subjective reality that the expressionist explores. Although this perspective never became dominant, it attracted some remarkable talent, and it made an important impact in production techniques, especially in musical comedies and motion pictures.

Strindberg was the first to state the expressionist's approach to drama: "Anything may happen; everything is possible and probable. Time and space do not exist. On an insignificant background of reality, imagination designs and embroiders novel patterns; a medley of memories, experiences, free fantasies, absurdities, and improvisations." A drama, he said, may have the "disconnected but seemingly logical form of a dream." He demonstrated his theory in two remarkable plays, *The Dream Play* (1902) and *The Ghost Sonata* (1907). For a time, Strindberg was an isolated innovator, but from 1912 to 1925 expressionism became an important theatrical style, especially in Germany for those who knew the traumatic experiences of World War I and its aftermath.

Expressionists rejected the ordered structure of the realist, since they

Henry May's design for the office scene in Sophie Treadwell's expressionistic play,
Machinal.

(University of California, Berkeley.)

wished to center their attention on specific instances without being obliged
to provide a chain of causes and effects. They presented the essential action—the high points of an experience—without being bogged down by
small talk or the machinery of plotting. The critical moments of a career
were shown in a jagged series of explosive scenes. In Elmer Rice's *The Adding
Machine* (1923), Mr. Zero's crime and punishment were shown in seven fragmentary scenes; O'Neill's *The Hairy Ape* (1922) dramatized the important
steps in Yank's quest for status; Georg Kaiser's *From Morn to Midnight* (1916)
was a disconnected series of events that showed a bank clerk's theft, spending orgy, and death; in Ernst Toller's *Transfiguration* (1918), a kaleidoscope
of dream pictures illustrated the horrors of war. Miller in *Death of a Salesman*
(1948) effectively used expressionistic scenes combined with realistic ones
to define Willy Loman's mental state. Expressionists flung open the windows of the mind and allowed the spectator to look in on the private, disordered, associative processes of their characters. They rejected the
carefully shaped, logically organized structure of the realist and used a fragmentary system of actions because it created the effect they desired—a view
of the chaotic inner reality.

Characters in expressionistic plays are often depersonalized. They are
not individuals but types who are given such names as the Gentleman in

Black, the Billionaire, the Young Woman in Taffeta, Mr. Zero, the Blues and the Yellows. They are not psychologically complex except perhaps for the protagonist through whose eyes all the action may be seen. To reveal the inner state of the character, playwrights revived the technique of the soliloquy so that the characters could externalize their private thoughts. In witnessing the distortion that characterized the protagonist's subjective point of view, the spectator was often confused by bewildering symbols and actions, especially when the distortion was that of an abnormal psychic condition. Character itself was often handled symbolically and with great freedom, as Strindberg indicates in *The Dream Play:* "The characters split, double, multiply, evaporate, solidify, diffuse, clarify. But one consciousness reigns above them all—that of the dreamer; it knows no secrets, no incongruities, no scruples, no law." Sometimes, the protagonist is the voice of the author, as in Toller's *Transfiguration,* in which the hero, Friedrich, is the playwright protesting against militarism and nationalism. Friedrich is something of an individual with a specific background, but he is also an abstract symbol of humanity, appearing in many guises—soldier, professor, sculptor, judge, priest, and laborer.

Peter Shaffer, who is extraordinarily innovative in his theatricalism, confesses that he struggled for a year to create an effective way of beginning *Amadeus.* He finally hit on an approach that is expressionistic in style.

Act One, Scene 1, Vienna

(Darkness
Savage whispers fill the theater. We can distinguish nothing at first from this snake-like hissing save the word Salieri! repeated here, there and everywhere around the theater. Also, the barely distinguishable word Assassin!

The whispers overlap and increase in volume, slashing the air with wicked intensity. Then the light grows Upstage to reveal the silhouettes of men and women dressed in the top hats and skirts of the nineteenth century—citizens of Vienna, all crowded together in the Light Box, and uttering their scandal.)

Whisperers: Salieri! . . . Salieri! . . . Salieri! (*Upstage, in a wheelchair, with his back to us, sits as old man. We can see, as the light grows a little brighter, the top of his head, encased in an old red cap, and perhaps the shawl wrapped around his shoulders.)*

Salieri! . . . Salieri! . . . Salieri!

(Two middle-aged gentlemen hurry in from either side, also wearing the long cloaks and tall hats of the period. These are the two venticelli: purveyors of fact, rumor and gossip throughout the play. They speak rapidly—in this first appearance extremely rapidly—so that the scene has the air of a fast and dreadful overture. Sometimes they speak to each other, sometimes to us—but always with the urgency of men who have ever been first with the news.)

Venticello 1:   I don't believe it.
Venticello 2:   I don't believe it.
V. 1:   I don't believe it.
V. 2:   I don't believe it.
Whisperers: *Salieri!*[7]

In general, expressionists have had an axe to grind. Their plays have been linked to social causes, for example, in Germany, where the frustrations and yearnings of a people tormented by guilt and despair found in expressionism not merely a theatrical style but also a desperate and agonized plea for some kind of salvation. In Kaiser's *Coral* (1917) the Billionaire's son revolts against the injustice of capitalism: "We are rich, and these others who stifle in torment and misery are men like us." Again in *From Morn to Midnight,* Kaiser directly attacks materialism: "Not with all the money from all the banks of the world can one buy anything of value. . . . Money is the crowning deceit of all."

The expressionists' free use of language anticipated most of the "innovations" of the absurdists and the present workers in the new theater. They also expanded the theatricalism so that playwrights who were writing

In Georg Kaiser's *From Morn to Midnight,* set in Berlin 1923, the protagonist's guilty state of mind is shown in Cesar Klein's scene design when a tree turns into a skeleton.

in another mode used expressionistic techniques, for example, to depict distorted mental images in emotionally loaded situations.

In another Peter Shaffer play, *Equus*, about a seventeen-year-old mental patient, the psychiatrist explores the boy's tortured psyche and finally exposes the jealousy that drove him to blind seven horses with a spike. The technique of revealing an emotionally disturbed character's state of mind through expressionistic techniques is clearly evident in this scene, in which the psychiatrist Dysart confronts the boy with his jealousy:

> (*The boy turns round, hugging himself in pain. From the sides two more horses converge with Nugget on the rails. Their hooves stamp angrily. The Equus noise is heard more terribly.*)

Dysart: The Lord thy God is a Jealous God. He sees you. He sees you forever and ever, Alan. He sees you! . . . *He sees you!*

Alan: (*In terror*) Eyes! . . . White eyes—never closed! Eyes like flames—coming—coming! . . . God seest! God seest! . . . NO! . . .

> (*Pause. He steadies himself. The stage begins to blacken.*)

(*Quieter*) No more. No more, Equus.

> (*He gets up. He goes to the bench. He takes up the invisible pick. He moves slowly upstage towards Nugget, concealing the weapon behind his naked back, in the growing darkness. He stretches out his hand and fondles Nugget's mask.*)
> (*Gently*) Equus . . . Noble Equus . . . Faithful and True . . . Godslave . . . Thou—God—Seest—NOTHING!

> (*He stabs out Nugget's eyes. The horse stamps in agony. A great screaming begins to fill the theatre, growing ever louder. Alan dashes at the other two horses and blinds them too, stabbing over the rails. Their metal hooves join in the stamping.*
> *Relentlessly, as this happens, three more horses appear in cones of light; not naturalistic animals like the first three, but dreadful creatures out of nightmare. Their eyes flare—their nostrils flare—their mouths flare. They are archetypal images—judging, punishing, pitiless. They do not halt at the rail, but invade the square. As they trample at him, the boy leaps desperately at them, jumping high and naked in the dark, slashing at their heads with arms upraised. The screams increase. The other horses follow into the square. The whole place is filled with cannoning, blinded horses—and the boy dodging among them, avoiding their slashing hooves as best he can. Finally they plunge off into darkness and away out of sight. The noise dies abruptly, and all we hear is Alan yelling in hysteria as he collapses on the ground—stabbing at his own eyes with the invisible pick.*)

Alan: Find me! ... Find me! ... Find me! ... KILL ME! ... KILL ME! ...[8]

American expressionists worked over familiar social themes in a much milder vein. O'Neill's *The Hairy Ape* is a criticism of human disorientation in a materialistic society. His *The Emperor Jones* dramatizes man's inability to escape from his primitive past. Rice's *The Adding Machine* is a merciless satire on the plight of the little man trapped in a mechanistic world; and George Kaufman and Marc Connelly's *Beggar on Horseback* (1924) lampoons philistinism in America. The expressionists were not so notable for their advanced thinking as for their theatrical ability to give new shape and expression to familiar ideas.

One of these ways was a theatrical treatment of language to create effects and atmosphere. An interesting device was the use of short, rhythmic bursts of staccato speech with a sharply marked tempo. The effect was to remove the speaker one step from reality, reinforcing the offbeat atmosphere and the dehumanized characterization. A typical example occurs in Kaiser's *Gas* (1918), Part One:

O'Neill's *The Iceman Cometh* at the Circle-in-the-Square Theater in New York. Ming Cho Lee's design using a few simple elements creates a realistic atmosphere for the bar bums who frequent it.

(The door to left is flung open. A Workman—naked—stained by the explosion totters in.)

Workman: Report from Shed Eight—Central—white cat burst—red eyes torn open—yellow mouth gaping—humps up crackling back—grows round—snaps away girders—lifts up roof—bursts—sparks!—sparks! *(Sitting down in the middle of the floor and striking about him)* Chase away the cat—Shoo! Shoo!—smash her jaws—Shoo! Shoo! bury her eyes—they flame—hammer down her back—hammer it down—thousands of fists! It's swelling, swelling—growing fat—fatter—Gas out of every crack—the tube![9]

Where the realists stressed the outward appearance of actuality in solid-looking stage settings, the expressionists used fragmentary, distorted images, skeletal pieces, and odd lighting effects to reveal a disordered world. In so doing, they created a frankly theatrical world. The phantasmagoria of weird landscapes, of the dream world where images and symbols are projected in baffling and exaggerated shapes, colors, and patterns, made expressionism a challenge to the designer's imagination and ingenuity. In Kaiser's *From Morn to Midnight,* a guilty fugitive suddenly sees a tree trunk transformed into a pursuing skeleton; in Strindberg's *A Dream Play,* eerie landscapes appear, merge, and alter like disconnected fragments of a nightmare.

The expressionists' bold theatricalism demonstrated new and effective uses of the medium; it cleared the stage of the rigid three walls and replaced the clutter with a few imaginative fragments, picked out by light on a relatively bare stage, which gave the actors the appropriate psychological setting for their performance. The creative influence of the expressionists was apparent in ballet, musical comedies, motion pictures, and the simple settings of realistic plays. Every experimental venture in the twentieth century is in debt to the expressionists for their innovative theatricalism.

As literary movements, naturalism and expressionism are passé, and the revolt against realism is now going on. Actually, a revolt has gone on within the mode itself, so that present-day realism bears little resemblance to Ibsen's. Our increased technical skills and facilities; the use of light, film, and sound; the arena and thrust stages give the playwright a previously unknown freedom. Moreover, today's audience, in its willingness to participate imaginatively in all kinds of new theatrical practices, has encouraged more creative and flexible playwriting and production.

The case against realism is couched in such terms as *narrow, commonplace, superficial, contrived, passive,* and *illusionary.* It is criticized as being a device for avoiding life rather than facing it—a process of hypnosis and delusion, deficient in spirit. In its selection of character and incident it is said to be too artificial. It is charged with being too narrowly confined to a few unimportant people partitioned off from the real world, too much involved with psychological case studies rather than with the more significant issues of society. It is said to make a fetish of external appearance and factual data and to be theatrically pedestrian and trivial in its restrictions of setting, vocabulary, plot situations, and style of performance.

Supporters of realism and its derivatives point out that historically it accomplished its initial objective of ridding the theater of much that was meretricious and false. Realistic playwrights turned the theater to a serious purpose and dealt with its fundamental theme—the dignity and integrity of the individual and the vital interests of the common man. In their emphasis on the conditioning power of heredity and environment, the realists made the public aware of an important concept of human behavior. They created a respect for the objective observation of facts, but they went beyond them to a concern with humanity's spiritual destiny in a changing and perplexing world.

The realists replaced inflated and artificial rhetoric with new means of communication in speech, action, and setting that encouraged more direct interaction. They were concerned with the problems that engage our foremost experimentalists today—self-realization and freedom from bourgeois conventionality. In their efforts to imitate real people's action, the realists turned the theater in a new direction by their emphasis on the careful observation of human behavior. They sought to give pleasure through learning by means of their fresh perceptions of contemporary people and their world.

PLAYS TO READ AND SEE

F = Film available; V = Videotape available.

Realism

F	V	O'Neill, *Anna Christie* (Garbo)
F	V	Williams, *Cat on a Hot Tin Roof*
		Chekhov, *The Cherry Orchard*
		Henley, *Crimes of the Heart*
F	V	Ibsen, *A Doll's House*
		Strindberg, *The Father*
F		Ibsen, *Hedda Gabler*
F	V	Fuller, *A Soldier's Play (Story)*
F		Rabe, *Streamers*
F	V	Williams, *A Streetcar Named Desire*

Naturalism

Mamet, *American Buffalo*
Shepard, *Buried Child*
Gelber, *The Connection*
Gorki, *The Lower Depths*
Strindberg, *Miss Julie*

Expressionism

Rice, *The Adding Machine*
Kaufman and Connelly, *Beggar on Horseback*
O'Neill, *The Emperor Jones*

F   Miller, *Death of a Salesman*

Film: The Cabinet of Dr. Caligari (1919)

BIBLIOGRAPHY

ANTOINE, ANDRÉ. *Memories of the Théâter-Libre.* Coral Gables, Fla.: University of Miami Press, 1964.

BENTLEY, ERIC. *The Playwright as Thinker.* New York: Meridian Books, 1957.

BIGSBY, C. W. E. *Confrontation and Commitment: A Study of Contemporary American Drama, 1959–1966.* London: MacGibbon & Kee, 1967.

BOGARD, TRAVIS, and WILLIAM I. OLIVER. *Modern Drama: Essays in Criticism.* New York: Oxford University Press, 1965.

BROCKETT, OSCAR G., and ROBERT R. FINDLAY. *Century of Innovation.* Englewood Cliffs, N.J.: Prentice-Hall, Inc., 1973.

BRUSTEIN, ROBERT. *The Cultural Watch: Essays on Theater and Society.* New York: Alfred A. Knopf, Inc., 1975.

———. *The Theater in Revolt.* Boston: Little, Brown & Company, 1962.

CLARK, BARRETT H., and GEORGE FREEDLEY. *A History of Modern Drama.* New York: Appleton-Century-Crofts, 1947.

CLURMAN, HAROLD. *The Fervent Years.* New York: Hill & Wang, 1957.

MILLER, ANNA IRENE. *The Independent Theater in Europe, 1887.* New York: Ray Long and Richard R. Smith, 1931.

SOKEL, WALTER. *The Writer in Extremis: Expressionism in Twentieth-Century German Literature.* Stanford, Calif.: Stanford University Press, 1959.

WAXMAN, S. M. *Antoine and the Théâtre Libre.* Cambridge, Mass.: Harvard University Press, 1926.

WILLIAMS, RAYMOND. *Drama from Ibsen to Brecht.* New York: Oxford University Press, 1969.

NOTES

1. Beth Henley, *Crimes of the Heart* (New York: The Viking Press, 1981).

2. Bernard Weinberg, *French Realism: The Critical Reaction, 1830–1870* (New York: Oxford University Press, 1937).

3. Hamlin Garland, "Ibsen as a Dramatist," *Arena,* 2 (June 1890).

4. Lanford Wilson, *Talley's Folly* (New York: Hill & Wang, 1983).

5. Émile Zola, *The Experimental Novel* (New York: Cassell, 1893).

6. August Strindberg, "Preface to Miss Julie," in *Plays of Strindberg,* Vol. 1, trans. Edith and Warner Oland (New York: Bruce Humphries, 1912).

7. Peter Shaffer, *Amadeus* (New York: New American Library, 1984).

8. Peter Shaffer, *Equus* (New York: Avon Books, 1974).

9. Georg Kaiser, *Gas I* (Cologne: Verlag Kiepenheuer & Witsch, 1918).

7

Theatricalism and the New Theater

The twentieth century has seen a motley parade of rebels, visionaries, and avant garde experimentalists, marching to the beat of varied drummers. They follow an odd assortment of leaders or strike out in broken ranks; some they follow are soon obscure, some frenzied and vulgar, but always defiant and confident that they are the voices of truth. There is a glint in their eyes and a sense of urgent dedication that often belies their incongruous manner. Their destinations may not be clear, but they are on the march—a march of protest, a boisterous, scathing protest: The world must change, and the theater with it. The linking of these two objectives is important, for the avant garde is alienated from the total human condition. Out of this rebellion came a rejection of the traditional, illusionistic dramatic performance and a new interest and stress on theatricalism.

THEATRICALISM

Theatricalism is a catchall term for all types of nonrealistic stylization, free from any effort to create the illusion of actuality. Theatricalism accepts the premise that performer and spectator share an experience that is frankly a *theater piece*. The actor suggests or assumes a role, rather than creating a psychological character. The performer may step in and out of character, go from youth to old age in a single speech, play several roles, go in and out of emotional states, address the audience directly, comment on the action, or simply tell a story. The performers may lead the audience as the high priests of a celebration.

In staging, theatricalism may employ scenery, lighting, costuming, and sound effects for their own sakes, not as accessories for creating atmosphere or eliciting emotional responses appropriate to the play. The total effect of the production may come from a series of signals in spurts, juxtaposed or simultaneous, projected in incongruous ways without obvious continuity or significance. In traditional theater, all elements are synthesized in support of the text; in the new theater, all aspects celebrate a theatrical occasion.

This contemporary age of anxiety had its roots in the scientific and technological revolutions of the nineteenth century. We have already seen how that disruption touched off a rebellion in the theater under the label of realism and its derivatives, as people tried to orient themselves to a materialistic and mechanical world. But this quest for meaning and identity was subverted by the holocaust of World War I. The old faith in political institutions and the beneficence of scientific progress was shaken by the spectacle of toppling regimes, the barbarism of mechanized warfare, and the dehumanization of the individual. Those closest to the flames were infected by a deep sense of frustration, which broke out in the savage distortions of the expressionists and in the dadaist's brash assault on everything. The Great Depression, World War II, the uneasy peace under an ominous

Pablo Picasso's "Guernica," 1937, a powerful combination of distorted shapes of people and animals and objects that project the anguish and terror of senseless warfare. Guernica, an ancient Basque capitol, was bombed during the Spanish Civil War.

bomb, the Vietnam disaster, the exposure of sordid political corruption, and the ruthless struggle for power turned pessimism and doubt into a general malaise instead of a localized infection confined to the defeated or the have-nots. The result has been a universal sense of concern, a gnawing doubt about the ability of the race to survive, and a search for something solid to hold on to.

Beginning with realistic playwrights, questions have been raised about humanity's place in the universe, but drama has not been overly concerned with social and economic conditions. Moreover, theater, a social institution, usually tied by its purse strings to the status quo, has often lagged behind the others in revolutionary fervor. Dissidents have had a difficult time in attracting sympathetic audiences with the ability to pay. To many, the popular function of the commercial theater is to provide relaxation, not friction or serious investigation of the problems of society. Some questions one does not ask in public. The audience might listen to the voice of protest if it were as witty as Shaw's or tolerate political didacticism if it were as theatrical as Brecht's, but the main course of the drama was not marked by militant dispute. As the outside world became more precarious, however, the protest grew louder and the walls could no longer keep out the clamor. Indeed, because those within began to bring their doubts with them, the theater could not remain aloof. The rebels found their way into song, film, and the visual arts; they turned coffeehouses into theaters, found audiences on the sidewalks and in the streets, and staged their own brand of events with such impressive numbers and raucous insistence that their message came through: The world must change and the theater with it.

The rebels opposed both form and content in drama. They would relegate the traditional, carefully structured system of action to the scrapheap, for to them system and order are suspect. Human experience, they said, is not tidily organized into a beginning, middle, and end. Life comes at us in spurts—without clear causes or predictable effects. People are not rational, logical creatures. The protesters find support for this view in such statements as Freud's description of the id: "a chaos, a cauldron of seething excitement with no organization and no unified will, only an impulse to obtain satisfaction for the instinctual needs, in accordance with the pleasure principle." The form of art, the rebels insist, reflects the form of our lives— bewildering, confusing, illogical, incomprehensible.

As for the content of drama, it must deal forthrightly with the larger issues of the human condition. It is not enough to dwell on the petty squabbles of little lives or to probe into the personality problems of insignificant individuals. The visionaries ask for a theater that will rise up against all powers and institutions that belittle the individual, a theater that expands our levels of awareness—that challenges, stimulates, offends, and shocks.

Tom O'Horgan's *Hair,* an entertaining protest musical, was a box-office hit in the 1960s. Its exuberant spirit captured the public's fancy.

(Photo: Martha Swope)

DADAISM

Just as the cultural turbulence following World War II was mirrored by an assault on the conventional forms of the theater, the upheaval of World War I was reflected in the arts. The poet Tristan Tzara led a group of European artists, writers, and thinkers in a nihilistic onslaught against nearly everything, including the standards of conventional aesthetics. During a five-year period, Tzara and the dadaists expressed their disgust with social and artistic traditions as they "spat in the eye of the world." Their attack against the façade of the bourgeois ethic was motivated by a desire to clear the way for a better society. They rejected "art-art" in favor of antiart. Instead of pure painting, they "engineered" new works. The dadaists exploited the "gratuitous act," the spontaneous, chance gesture, which by its rejection of preplanning, could convey the irrational and subconscious. Improvisation was at the center of their activities. Individual words on slips of paper were drawn out of a hat in a random fashion to become poems. Their often chaotic and accidental pranks and displays anticipated the "happenings" of the 1960s and current "performances." (Stoppard's *Travesties*, 1975, deals with Tzara and some of the dadaists' activities in Zurich. See pp 149–151.)

KURT SCHWITTERS AND COLLAGE

In any discussion of theatricalism and the new theater, the term *collage* occurs frequently. The man who pioneered much of the work with collage, around the year 1920, produced over 2,000 pieces in this area as well as experiments in poetry and theater with what he called his "Merz" creations. Kurt Schwitters, one of the most prominent dadaists, disdained traditional painting and the galleries that displayed them. Instead of working like the usual easel painter with oil or watercolors, Schwitters gathered together "found" materials, such as old papers, photographs, worn fabrics, and burlap, which he pasted on a background. He was interested in juxtaposing objects so that they played against one another—a torn piece of a letter next to an old, faded photograph; a column of figures against a label; a fragment of yellowed newspaper against a railroad ticket. Although his compositions are abstract, there are recognizable words, numbers, headlines, and scraps of handwriting or printed papers.

Schwitters describes his approach to art:

> Art is a primordial concept, exalted as the godhead, inexplicable as life, indefinable and without purpose. . . . The medium is unimportant. I take any material whatsoever if the picture demands it. When I adjust materials of different kinds to one another, I have taken a step in advance of mere oil painting, for in addition to playing off color against color, line against line, form against form, etc., I play off material against material.[1]

Kurt Schwitters, a pioneer collage maker, created interesting compositions out of scraps of paper and materials, such as in this *Merz: Santa Claus,* 1922. The collage has become a very influential art form in the twentieth century.

When writing poetry, which Schwitters read publicly, his collage approach to the use of language parallels his work with visual material. His poem "Green Child," written about 1918, deals with a child's nightmare flight from imprisonment.

> [. . .]
> Blood —
> Fear —
> Chase —
> Fly —
> Scream —
> Blood grins yellow-bright-yellow
> Yellow green —
> Brightyellowgreen —
> Brimstoneyellowgreen —
> Brightbrimstoneyellowgreen —
> Blood grimaces brightbrimyellowstoneyellowgreen.
> Could I but wash the green blood![2]

Schwitters' creative work illustrates two important principles that characterize much of the avant garde of the twentieth century: first, the rejection of traditional forms and techniques, and second, the fragmentation of disparate objects and images, instead of a unified design built around a center of interest. A collage is a key symbol of our aesthetic landscape.

Another group of rebels were the surrealists, who like the dadaists, took the view that "man must escape from the control of reason" and that the artist should "surrender to the dark forces of the unconscious." They were interested in exploring the world of dreams and the imagination. They improvised games of automatic writing and drawing—creations entirely free from rational control, made up of strange and distorted images. André Breton, the chief spokesman, said that the surrealist "took pleasure in re-uniting the sewing machine and the umbrella on the dissecting table." Their purpose was to bring about a kind of super or absolute reality—"surrealite."

The works of art growing out of dadaism and surrealism are characterized by incongruous combinations of objects and figures, simultaneous

The influence of the collage on scene design is apparent in Svoboda's setting for *The Last Ones* at the National Theater in Prague. In this case the assemblage includes a live band at an upper level and motion pictures of some of the actors projected on a screen.

action, fragmentation, and the distorted and seemingly irrational atmosphere of a dream. These characteristics of visual art are similar to those of much of avant garde drama, for they are rooted in a rejection of the strictures of conventional theater and an insistence on the need to be liberated and spontaneous.

Following the Russian Revolution (1917), the Soviet theater showed its dissatisfaction with the old regime by its rejection of the Stanislavski realism and illusionistic production. To show their hostility to the old order, the constructivists devised scenery that was deliberately antidecorative, emphasizing instead the stage as a machine, with playing areas of steps, ramps, and platforms to serve the actors' functions.

Two examples from the Russian theater of the 1920s show the nature of the theatricalism espoused by Eugene Vakhtangov and Meyerhold. In 1922, Vakhtangov staged a highly theatricalized production of Carlo Gozzi's *Turandot* in Moscow. He told his cast, "Our work is senseless if there is no holiday mood, if there is nothing to carry the spectators away. Let us carry them away with our youth, laughter, and improvisation." When the spectators came into the theater, the actors were already onstage, wearing street clothes. They talked to the audience about the play and what they would see.

As a waltz played, the actors improvised costumes from pieces of cloth and fabric, turning rags into riches. Stagehands moved furniture and properties into place, while scenery appeared like magic from the flies and wings—window frames, doors, and pillars. It was in this playful atmosphere that the play continued and became one of the notable Russian productions of the decade.

Our second example of theatricalism occurred in 1926 in Meyerhold's last great production—Gogol's nineteenth-century satire on greed and hypocrisy, *The Government Inspector*. The director transferred the locale from the provinces to Moscow and updated the text to make the comedy more relevant and biting. Gogol's plot deals with civic officials who learn of an impending visit of the government inspector. They mistake a ne'er-do-well young man, Kheslakov, and his companion for the inspector and his valet. Kheslakov, an opportunist, exploits the situation to the limit, accepting the officials' bribes and favors and pretending a romantic interest in the Mayor's daughter. Before being exposed as an impostor, Kheslakov manages to escape with the loot, just when the real inspector is about to arrive. Meyerhold's theatricalism in this production made an enormous impression.

In the bribery scene, the setting is made up of fifteen highly polished mahogany doors. Following a public reception, Kheslakov returns to his quarters, where he is besieged by fifteen petty officials who offer him bribes. Two guards stand at attention before the central doorway. Kheslakov staggers in through the wrong door, almost falls but regains his feet with acrobatic dexterity, and drops into a chair. He confides to the audience that

Meyerhold's highly energized theatricalism was enthusiastically received by Moscow audiences in the 1920s as in this celebrated performance of Gogol's *The Government Inspector.*

he is dead drunk. One of the officials hurries in to notify Kheslakov that others are coming to grease his palm. Suddenly, all fifteen doors open at once, and the politicians enter with the mechanical movements of robots, chanting their lines in unison. Kheslakov responds in the same rhythmical manner, accepting each of the proffered gifts with clockwork precision. The image is of an immense bribe machine.

Meyerhold, originally associated with Stanislavski, became dissatisfied with conventional techniques and freely experimented with those borrowed from the oriental theater, carnival, music hall, and circus. He devised an acting style known as "biomechanics," in which actors perform as gymnasts or machines to convey their feelings through physical gestures. For example, to express joy an actor might turn a handspring or slide down a pole. Meyerhold's theory was that behavior is best expressed through theatricalism—not by words but by carefully controlled poses, movements, and gestures. Meyerhold's theories and methods were demonstrated in several remarkable productions, especially *The Magnificent Cuckold,* in which he erected on a bare stage the skeletal suggestion of a hill, reached by stairs and ramps, with a bridge, trapeze, and other mechanical devices. The actors, dressed as workers, gave an acrobatic performance accompanied by a jazz orchestra. In *Earth on Its Hindlegs,* the cast rode bicycles and motorbikes about the stage and dragged on a heavy canvas followed by a regiment of marching soldiers.

Meyerhold's essential contribution was in his attitude toward the theater as a total vehicle to be exploited in all possible ways. By word and especially by example, he was the epitome of the theatricalism of the twentieth century.

BERTOLT BRECHT

Brecht (1898–1956) was one of the most influential playwrights and theoreticians of the twentieth century. Fleeing Germany in 1933, he wrote most of his major plays while living abroad; in 1947 he returned to Berlin, where he founded *The Berliner Ensemble,* which specializes in producing Brecht's plays and is one of the most remarkable acting companies of our time. He was influenced by dadaism and expressionism, as well as his association with Erwin Piscator and Max Reinhardt in Berlin. His first popular success occurred in 1928 with *The Threepenny Opera.*

Brecht links himself with theatricalism through his rejection of the illusionistic stage. "How long," he asked, "are our souls going to have to leave our gross bodies under cover of darkness to penetrate into those dream figures up there on the rostrum in order to share their transports that would otherwise be denied us?" Brecht was a rebellious spirit, who mixed his theatricalism with political propaganda, who explored, with incredible verve and gusto, his "ugly, brutal, dangerous" man in the seamy side of his existence. He was a brilliant inventor and a notorious borrower, whose proclivity for criticism of humankind and all its institutions naturally included overthrow of the conventional theater and led him to create his own imaginative "epic theater."

Traditionally, the epic form was sharply separated from drama, the latter being characterized by compact action that could be presented by living performers; the epic, because of its freedom of time, place, and action, was confined to the written word. But Brecht did not see these two forms as irreconcilable because technical advances enabled the modern theater to exploit the narrative through projections, films, lighting, and machinery for changing scenery more rapidly. Furthermore, Brecht felt that the most important human experiences were no longer personal stories of individuals but rather significant social events and the forces that caused them.

Since he was dealing with social content rather than emotions, Brecht sometimes described his stage as a "tribunal," in which he wanted "to teach the spectators to reach a verdict." The analogy is an apt one. Instead of presenting a tightly knit plot, Brecht used the stage to present evidence piece by piece, as in a trial, to introduce witnesses with conflicting testimony who are interrupted and cross-questioned. They testify by giving facts or by relating events rather than by impersonating characters. Evidence is presented in a variety of exhibits—weapons, drawings or photographs of where the action occurred, documents, letters, tape recordings, slides, models, and films. The intention is to put the event itself on trial. Brecht's plots often startled and shocked the audiences, thus counteracting the tendency toward illusion. He deliberately broke the mood of a scene by interrupting action with music, by playing irony against sentiment and comedy against seriousness, and by the constant use of inversion and reversal.

As a young man coming out of a bitter experience in the military as a medical orderly, and acutely aware of the social and economic calamities of postwar Germany, Brecht wrote savagely from his view that "the meanest thing alive, and the weakest is man." His early plays are filled with depravity and crime and illustrate his cynical theme that virtue brings no reward; indeed, ethical behavior is really a sign of stupidity. He looked at all men with suspicion, for the poor are as cruel as the rich. As for justice—it is a delusion.

After he accepted Marxism, he came to believe that the evils of the world could be cured by revolution, and to that premise he devoted a number of his *Lehrstücke,* or learning pieces. In 1928 Brecht, along with Kurt Weill who wrote the music, staged his most commercially successful work, *The Threepenny Opera.* He borrowed the plot of Gay's *The Beggar's Opera,* a fashionable London hit of 1728. But where the original had been a light-hearted lampoon of the aristocracy, Brecht's play was a scathing satire of the bourgeoisie. He created a vivid collection of depraved characters, thieves, swindlers, prostitutes, and crooks who infest a human jungle—a jungle whose code is summed up in the pawnbroker Peachum's words: "What keeps a man alive—he lives on others by grinding, sweating, defeating, beating, cheating, eating some other man." But Brecht relieved the sting of the characters and situation through his considerable gifts as an entertainer, which he was never quite able to suppress despite his political purpose. He was fond of slapstick, vaudeville, sporting events, clowns, and beer-hall entertainers, and his theatricalism stems in part from the direct and earthy quality of these kinds of performers and performances.

Brecht's mature years are notable for his three "parables," which constitute his major contribution: *The Good Woman of Setzuan, Mother Courage and Her Children,* and *The Caucasian Chalk Circle.*

The good woman of Setzuan is a compassionate young prostitute, who is rewarded for her hospitality to three wandering gods. They set her up in a shop, but because she has no talent for making money, others exploit her

The three gods are flown in during *The Good Woman of Setzuan* in this performance of Brecht's play at the Volksbuhne in Berlin.

generous nature and bring her misery. In desperation, she assumes the role of a heartless male cousin. Only under the disguise of ruthlessness and avarice can she provide for herself and her unborn child. At the end, she is unable to reconcile herself to the evil ways of the world. She says to the gods, "Something must be wrong in your world. Why is there reward for wickedness and why do the good receive such hard punishment?" The gods, whom she has befriended, give no answer.

Mother Courage, which Brecht wrote just before the outbreak of World War II, is a bitter attack on militarism as an aspect of capitalism. To Brecht, heroism invariably comes from human error and brutality. His attention is not focused on the military action, which is narrated with legends and slogans, but on Mother Courage, a camp peddler in Germany during the Thirty Years' War (1618–1648). She is a scheming, salty character, who will use any means to serve her purpose. And her purpose is to survive, by buying and selling life's necessaries, and to protect her children from harm amid the shifting fortunes of princes and their marauding bands of soldiers. Her wagon symbolizes her view that war is "just the same as trading" and "you must get in with people. If you scratch my back, I'll scratch yours. Don't stick your neck out." It is while she is involved in bargaining that each of her children dies. In a magnificently theatrical scene, Courage's good-hearted, mute daughter, Kattrin, climbs up on a rooftop and drums a tattoo to warn the villagers of the invading soldiers, until she is shot down. Like Miller's Willy Loman, Courage's absorption with profits causes her destruction, but she must go on—and at the end, having learned nothing, but with her spirit apparently unquenched, she finds it possible to continue dragging her load of misery behind her.

In his last work, *The Caucasian Chalk Circle,* written in 1944–1945, Brecht's tone mellowed and the political message was incidental. The story concerns a young girl, Grusha, who saves the despotic governor's infant son during a rebellion. She makes her escape with the child, submits to a marriage of convenience, and is brought ultimately to trial; thanks to an eccentric judge, she is allowed to keep the child because she had demonstrated true motherly spirit.

The "epic" qualities of the play are seen in the prologue and epilogue, which frame the main story; the sharp break between Grusha's adventures and the trial scene; the extension of the social environment to include the military uprising and the comic marriage; and the use of song and dance.

As we look at Brecht's plays, we are struck by the contradiction between his theory and practice. He speaks of scientific objectivity, whereas one of the sources of his power is the towering indignation that gives his work such force and texture. His didactic purpose is deadly serious, but his lyrical gifts, his flair for the comic, and his talent for showmanship burst through the seams of his intent. He repudiates realism and the Stanislavski method of acting because they are based on emotional involvement, and he speaks of his wish to keep the audience "cool" and estranged. Ironically, his plays offer some of the most irresistible acting roles in the theater, which time and time again in performance, arouse the emotions of the audiences profoundly. This contradiction brings us back to the playwright's problem of relating action and its effect.

Let us examine two widely quoted statements of Brechtian theory and attempt to reconcile them with his practice. In the following chart, Brecht compares the traditional stage and his own:

The dramatic theater	*The epic theater*
the stage embodies a sequence of events	the stage narrates the sequence
involves the spectator in an action and	makes him an observer but
uses up his energy, his will to action	awakes his energy
plot	narrative
implicates the spectator in a stage situation	turns the spectator into an observer, but
wears down his capacity for action	arouses his capacity for action
provides him with sensations experience	forces him to take decisions picture of the world
the spectator is involved in something	he is made to face something
suggestion	argument
instinctive feelings are preserved	brought to the point of recognition

the spectator is in the thick of it, shares the experience	the spectator stands outside, studies
the human being is taken for granted	the human being is the object of the inquiry
he is unalterable	he is alterable and able to alter
eyes on the finish	eyes on the course
one scene makes another	each scene for itself
growth	montage
linear development	in curves
evolutionary determinism	jumps
man as a fixed point	man as a process
thought determines being	social being determines thought
feeling	reason[3]

A second important statement, which Brecht included in "Little Organum" in 1948 after his plays were written, reads,

> Since the public is not invited to throw itself into the fable as though into a river, in order to let itself be tossed indeterminately back and forth, the individual events must be tied together in such a way that the knots are strikingly noticeable; the events must not follow upon one another imperceptibly, but rather one must be able to pass judgment in the midst of them. . . . The parts of the fable, therefore, are to be carefully set off against one another by giving them their own structure, that of a play within a play.[4]

Brecht is describing here his technique of alienating the audience by breaking up the structure into separate events so that the spectator can "pass judgment in the midst of them"; the knots must be "strikingly noticeable." What is the basis for this theory of structured action? To encourage the spectator to think rather than to feel. But action has a way of speaking stronger than words.

In his major works Brecht selected basic formulas for *stimulating feeling* by using the standardized patterns of melodrama and romanticism. In *The Threepenny Opera* he employed a dashing rebel with a price on his head, the enemy of a corrupt social system—a clichéd romantic hero. Brecht was able to achieve his effect despite his central action by making Mack the Knife a corrupt character in a corrupt world. The atmosphere is mordant, not heroic. There is little humanity, no genuine suffering, and through inverted justice Mack is freed and rewarded at the end. When this work is produced in authentic Brechtian style, as at the Berliner Ensemble or in Richard Foreman's version at Lincoln Center, with an attitude of "serious playfulness," the author's purpose is achieved. On the other hand, being played for its quaint characters and picturesque situations completely distorts the play's impact. In *The Resistible Rise of Arturo Ui* (1941) Brecht again uses a potentially romantic central action—the rise of a little man to power—but the hero's evil ways and his obvious parallel to Hitler throw a chill over the action and keep us at a distance, although we are captivated by the brilliant acting of the Ensemble. But the alienation works.

In Brecht's three parables, *The Good Woman of Setzuan* (1938–1940), *Mother Courage* (1937), and *The Caucasian Chalk Circle* (1944–1945), the action follows the most surefire melodramatic device of all: Women in distress try valiantly to protect their children against overwhelming forces of evil. In spite of Brecht's avowed purpose of interrupting the sequence to avoid empathic response, an audience has a way of holding on to the emotional momentum, just as an exciting football game on television keeps the audience in suspense through the interruptions by commercials. Despite the "noticeable knots" and Brecht's theory of keeping each event separate, his practice suggests that step by step his structure in these three parables intensifies the emotional response. We do care about the outcome. In a tribunal, the evidence and testimony form a structure leading suspensefully to a verdict that completes the action. If you put a woman on stage—even a sharp-tongued, grasping one—show her attachment and devotion to her children, place them in jeopardy, and give the audience concrete signs of her suffering, the effect is to gain sympathy. This engagement is especially true if the dramatist creates generous, well-intentioned characters like Shen Te, Grusha, and Kattrin. Show a woman trying to save a child by crossing an abyss over a rickety bridge pursued by brutal soldiers, and the audience will root for her. Show a mother the bullet-riddled body of her child and force her to conceal her agony for fear of losing her own life, and the audience will be stirred.

Brecht was aware of the emotional consequences of the actions he placed onstage, and he took great pains to divert the normal response in another direction. Furthermore, the plays are not melodramas because at the end reward and punishment are not parceled out according to individual merits. Even in the case of Grusha, the ending is not personal but social. Nor is there an orderly world of good and evil. By showing with abrasive humor the futility of heroism and virtue, Brecht combats sentiment for justice. Instead of conceding to the audience's eagerness for wish fulfillment, he tramples on it. His frankly theatrical way of showing an action is intended to dilute the emotional content. In performance, however, what counts more than the degree of realism is the audience's *willingness to believe.* And an audience is quite capable of believing in actions in all kinds of styles, including the "epic."

Brecht is a significant force in the contemporary theater not only because of his theories of a new kind of theater but also because of the theatricalism of his productions and plays. He gave the experimental theater of this century what it needed most—a first-rate playwright. He gave us a fresh insight into the uses of the theater and enlarged its scope, although the breath of fresh air was tinged with a chill that could cut to the bone.

ANTONIN ARTAUD

One of the most imaginative and influential figures between the great wars was Artaud (1896–1948). A tormented iconoclast, with scant success in actual production, he was, nevertheless, the fountainhead of much of the experimental theatricalism on the contemporary stage. He began working in the theater in Paris in 1921 and opened his Théâtre Alfred Jarry in 1927 (named in honor of another French innovator who wrote *Ubu Roi* in 1896 and is sometimes credited as the first absurdist because of his mockery of traditional values and conventional drama). Artaud spent two seasons with this theater, dedicated to the production of nonrealistic plays. Artaud's importance is not for his practical work in the theater but for his astonishingly prolific imagination and his vision of theatricalism. His book *The Theater and Its Double* (1938) advanced many ideas that are the basis for the contemporary revolt in acting, playwrighting, design, directing, and architecture.

Artaud's criticism springs basically from his dissatisfaction with the shape of the world about him. He said, "I believe that our present social system is iniquitous and should be destroyed."[5] And again, "There are too many signs that everything that used to sustain our lives no longer does so, that we are all mad, desperate and sick."[6] The existing theater outraged Artaud because it failed to deal seriously with man's social and moral systems. The theater had lost its feeling for seriousness and laughter. It had "broken away from the spirit of profound anarchy which is the root of all poetry." He called for a rejection of the idolatry of fixed masterpieces reserved for the self-styled elite and not understood by or appealing to the public. He raged against the falsehood and illusion of popular distractions that serve as an outlet for our worst instincts. These descriptive and narrative distractions provide stories that satisfy only Peeping Toms—a theater to decorate our leisure with intimate scenes from the lives of a few puppets. He repudiated well-made plots, which serve only to exploit the psychological aspects of human interest. He was enraged to see the theater offering stories about money, social careerism, the pangs of love, and sugar-coated sexuality—stories that fail to touch the public interest, stories that leave no scars.

Artaud was not merely an anarchist determined on a course of destruction; he was rather a true revolutionary, dedicated to change. Although his criticism of the modern theater was scathing, he was even more vehement about suggesting a cure. Extraordinarily creative about all aspects of the stage, technical as well as theoretical, he envisioned a radically different kind of drama and production techniques to implement it. Although he was never able to thoroughly realize his ideas in his own Théâtre Alfred Jarry, the audacity and sweep of his imagination can scarcely be ignored by anyone involved in the contemporary theater.

Artaud emphasized the creation of a theater that "stages events, not men," that deals with the metaphysical concerns of ancient rites—"an exorcism to make our demons flow." The theater must give us "crime, love, war, or madness, if it wants to cover its necessity." It must deal with "atrocious crimes" and "superhuman devotions" as the ancient myths do. His notion of a "theater of cruelty" stems from the mystical, magical forces of a "theater in which violent physical images crush and hypnotize the sensibility of the spectator seized by the theater as by a whirlwind of higher forces." His intention was to free the repressed unconscious in dramatic performance, which resembles a plague because "it is the relevation, the bringing forth, the exteriorization of a depth of the latent cruelty by means of which all perverse possibilities of the mind . . . are localized."

The cruelty that Artaud called for is not physical, nor is the violence for its own sake. Rather it is a process of purification, which "causes the mask to fall, reveals the lie, the slackness, baseness, and hypocrisy of our world." The theater is a means of ridding society of its institutionalized violence. For after experiencing the cruelty that he envisioned in the theater, Artaud said, "I defy the spectator to give himself up once outside the theater to ideas of war, riot and blatant murder."

Artaud conceived of theater as total spectacle that must have the "ceremonial quality of a religious rite." Made up of violent and concentrated action "pushed beyond all limits," it is addressed to the senses and to the theatricality of the unconscious.

Artaud rebelled against the conventional use of language in the theater. To understand his attack, one must remember his background: The French, more than any other people, have placed a high value on polished diction, and the tradition of their theater is rich in rhetoric. Artaud found the language of the theater "dead and fixed in forms that no longer respond to the needs of the time." He objected to the "tyranny of the word" and the dictatorship of the writer. Actually, his rebellion was against the conventionalized nature and form of drama, and in his call for a new theatricalism, language was his first target. He wanted to get away from mere words addressed to the mind. He proposed to use language in a "new, exceptional and unaccustomed fashion." He wanted to replace the utilitarian spoken word with an active language "beyond customary feelings and words," to create a "subterranean current of impressions, correspondences and analogies." Communication in his theater was not merely from actors making speeches; rather the stage was to be a place filled with its own language to include sounds used for their "vibratory quality," onomatopoeia, cries, and intonations. He wanted words to have about the same importance "as they have in dreams." Indeed, Artaud urged an extension of theatricalism so that everything that occupied the stage would create an effect on the senses, even to the point of physical shock.

Too much criticism of Artaud has been directed at his vivid rhetoric rather than at the spirit of his ideas. He was not a pessimistic, destructive sensationalist. At the core, his views were serious, humane, and positive. He invited us to take the theater seriously, to cut through the sham and hypocrisy of society, to face ourselves honestly, and to trap our deep, latent powers that will enable us to take a "superior and heroic attitude." The process involves the cruel practice of exposing society and *oneself* with complete honesty. Here is a voice of one who sees ahead and links future to past:

> Either we will be capable of returning by present-day means to this superior idea of poetry and poetry-through-theater which underlies the myths told by the great ancient tragedians, capable once more of entertaining a religious idea of the theater (without meditation, useless contemplation, and vague dreams), capable of attaining awareness and a possession of certain dominant forces, of certain notions that control all others, and (since ideas, when they are effective, carry their energy with them) capable of recovering within ourselves those energies which ultimately create order and increase the value of life, or else we might as well abandon ourselves now, without protest, and recognize that we are no longer good for anything but disorder, famine, flood, war and epidemics.[7]

THE ABSURDISTS

The opening of Beckett's *Waiting for Godot* in 1953 focused attention on a new dramatist and subsequently a new theatrical movement known as "the theater of the absurd." When the curtain opened the first night, the audience saw two bedraggled bums, Estragon and Vladimir, waiting in a deserted place for a mysterious Godot. His identity is not clear and their relationship to him is never made explicit. A master driving a heavily burdened slave appears briefly, and later a boy enters to inform the tramps that Godot will not arrive tonight. The play ends as it began, with the two waiting. While they wait, they talk, and the conversation explores such themes as death and salvation, the need for affection, the perplexed state of humankind, their personal biological problems, and the recurrent motif—waiting for Godot. The dialogue is interlocked with a wealth of seriocomic business, and the lines as well as the action provide an effective vehicle for the performers.

The audience greeted the play with mixed reactions. Some found it bewildering and dull; others, provocative and fascinating. In any case, the play made a remarkable impression throughout the theater world, and *Waiting for Godot* became the prime example of absurdist theater. In addition to Beckett, the most prominent absurdists are Ionesco, Arthur Adamov, Pinter, and Albee. These absurdists are not neatly compartmentalized, and each of them works in a variety of ways. What brings them together is the absurdist point of view, foreshadowed by Albert Camus in his celebrated statement in *The Myth of Sisyphus:*

A world that can be explained by reasoning, however faulty, is a familiar world. But in a universe that is suddenly deprived of illusions and of light, man feels a stranger. His is an irremediable exile, because he is deprived of memories of a lost homeland as much as he lacks the hope of a promised land to come. This divorce between man and his life, the actor and his setting, truly constitutes the feeling of Absurdity.[8]

Earlier writers had foreshadowed the movement in several ways. Pirandello, in his juxtaposition of the serious and the comic, his concern with illusion and reality, and with the difficulties of human communication, was an important forerunner. Franz Kafka's stories and novels, and particularly Jean-Louis Barrault's production of *The Trial* in 1947, with its nightmarish treatment of weird and puzzling actions, set an interesting example. And in the forthright theatricalism of the expressionists and Brecht, the absurdists found encouragement to strike out along new lines.

Waiting for Godot by Samuel Beckett had an enormous influence on modern drama because of its philosophical perspective and the style of writing and performance.

(Directed by Beckett at the Schiller Theater, West Berlin.)

Another dramatist who was spiritually related to the absurdists was Alfred Jarry, whose *Ubu Roi* caused a sensation when first produced in Paris in 1896 because of its blatant presentation of human grossness and sensuality. Jarry's intentions were clear: "When the curtain rose, I wanted the stage to be before the audience like a mirror . . . in which the vicious one would see himself with the horns of a bull and the body of a dragon, according to the exaggeration of his vices; and it is not surprising that the public was stupefied at the sight of its ignoble reflection which had not yet been completely presented to it."[9]

Jarry's play dramatizes the career of King Ubu, whose wife, like Lady Macbeth, drives him to murder the King of Poland in order to gain the crown for himself. His evil ways force him to hide in a cave, where he is haunted by the spectres of his victims. The content of the play is not as important as Jarry's prophetic view of the world and his way of handling theatrical materials. The sacrilegious spirit of his attack, the naive directness of

Alfred Jarry's *Ubu Roi* as performed at the Royal Court Theater in London.

his characters and their speech, his sense of raillery—these are seeds that found root later on.

Jarry used the theater in a new way to produce a new effect. This was precisely the case with the absurdists, who viewed the conventional drama with contempt. They wanted to put it to new uses. To understand their point of view, we must take into account the fact that those who led the movement and gave it stature shared a similar experience: Beckett (born in Ireland), Ionesco (born in Rumania), and Adamov (born in Russia) all lived in Paris during World War II. At first hand they witnessed the military defeat of France and suffered through the occupation by the German forces. The defeat meant the destruction of the political and social fabric and the ruin of civilian morale, and the occupation resulted in an agonizing sense of frustration in the face of overwhelming power. The existentialists—Jean Paul Sartre, Anouilh, and Camus—responded to this experience by using conventional literary forms to probe into such philosophic questions as the role of humankind in the universe and the effect of materialism on the human spirit. Their answers suggested that a human was utterly alone and must create one's own world, one's own set of values. The absurdists, who lived through the same era, asked the same questions but did not arrive at the same answers. They generalized from their experience. They felt that there were no answers—life was absurd. And it was this attitude that they put into action in the theater. They were dramatizing a simple but terrifying idea: Humanity is lost.

Waiting for Godot begins with Estragon's line: "Nothing to be done." And the play ends,

Vladimir: Well, shall we go?
Estragon: Yes, let's go.

(*They do not move. Curtain.*)[10]

Harold Clurman calls our attention to a parallel passage in Pinter's *The Birthday Party:*

Stanley: How would you like to go away with me?
Lulu: Where?
Stanley: Nowhere. Still we could go.
Lulu: But where would we go?
Stanley: Nowhere. There's nowhere to go. So we could just go. It wouldn't matter.
Lulu: We might as well stay here.
Stanley: No. It's no good here.
Lulu: Well, where else is there?
Stanley: Nowhere.[11]

Ionesco in *The Leader* presents the crowd anticipating the Leader. When he arrives, he has no head.

(Buffalo Festival of the Arts.)

One doesn't go, because there is no purpose to going. As Camus said, we have no homeland to return to and no promised land before us. We have lost our identity in a dehumanized world; we have lost our perspective in a world without God or a fixed scale of values, and we have lost our reason for going because there is really no place where we can make a meaningful connection. From bitter experience we are wary of hollow ideas and of each other. We are trapped in the frustrations of an enigmatic universe.

An elderly couple on a lonely island await the arrival of distinguished guests to hear the orator's important message. As the invisible guests arrive, the couple greet them and fill the stage with chairs. When the orator comes, the couple throw themselves out the window and his message is gibberish (Ionesco, *The Chairs*).

A lonely, guilt-ridden pianist seeks sanctuary in a seaside rooming house. It is revealed that in the past he has offended someone with consid-

An elderly couple prepare for the arrival of a distinguished guest and crowd the stage with chairs.

(Studio Theater, Elysee, Paris.)

erable power. Two sinister strangers appear, and the fear-wracked Stanley realizes they are after him. A mock birthday party, staged in his honor, turns out to be a grotesque ritual at which Stanley goes berserk. At the end, the two men take the crushed Stanley away in a long black car (Pinter, *The Birthday Party*).

A family replaces an adopted child with a handsome physical specimen of American manhood, who turns out to be hollow inside (Albee, *The American Dream*).

In such plays as these, the playwright abandons the notion of depicting psychologically complex characters. They are more apt to resemble puppets or marionettes because they are not personally responsible for their actions. They have been set in motion by an outside force. They cannot act rationally because there is no longer such a thing as logical behavior. They have no means for creating a complete identity, and since communication is virtually impossible, they are not able to relate to one another with understanding and affection.

In a world devoid of meaning, language loses its value, Ionesco wrote his first play, *The Bald Soprano,* as the result of his efforts to learn a foreign language by memorizing standardized phrases. The play parodies the spoken word by exposing its banal vacuity. Here is its opening:

> (*Scene: A middle class English interior, with English armchairs. Mr. Smith, an Englishman seated in his English armchair and wearing English slippers, is smoking his English pipe and reading an English newspaper, near an English fire. He is wearing English spectacles and a small gray English mustache. Beside him, in another English armchair, Mrs. Smith, an Englishwoman, is darning some English socks. A long moment of English silence. The English clock strikes seventeen English strokes.*)

Mrs. Smith: There it's nine o'clock. We've drunk the soup and eaten the fish and chips and the English salad. The children have drunk English water. We've eaten well this evening. That's because we live in the suburbs

Ionesco's *Rhinoceros* is an absurdist play based on the transformation of human beings into rhinoceroses. Berenger is aghast when his friend Jean begins to change before his eyes.

(University of California, Santa Barbara. Directed by the author.)

of London and because our name is Smith. (*Mr. Smith reads and clicks his tongue.*)

Mrs. Smith: Potatoes are very good fried in fat, the salad oil was not rancid. The oil from the grocer at the corner is better quality than the oil from the grocer across the street. It is even better than the oil from the grocer at the bottom of the street. However, I prefer not to tell them that their oil is bad.

(*Mr. Smith continues to read, clicks his tongue.*)

Mrs. Smith: However, the oil from the grocer at the corner is still the best.[12]

Ionesco has a special flair for satirizing language with gibberish, nonsense words, and broken speech. On the other hand, Beckett and Pinter have a gift for common language that in its diction and rhythm has almost the evocative power of poetry in its ability to suggest meanings beneath the surface. Albee has a good ear for the flavor of the American idiom plus an aptitude for parodying our colloquial speech. The dialogue in an absurdist's play is open to many interpretations and is remarkable for what it leaves to the imagination.

In an attempt to produce their desired effects, the absurdists have created their own arsenal of weapons: the use of shock effects by inverting behavior, by contemptuous mockery of sacrosanct ideas and institutions, by their candor and sometimes their bold frankness. Their comedy, often used ironically, crops out in unexpected places. They present the bizarre, the grotesque, and the unusual. They startle and astonish the audience by their wild flights of fancy and their sometimes incredible inventions. They keep an audience off balance by concealing their hands, making sudden shifts in direction. They bewilder the spectators, and then lead them to a startling discovery. They use the theatrical tricks of the circus clown, the slapstick comedian, and the music hall entertainer, as this comic routine from *Waiting for Godot* indicates:

(*Lucky has left his hat behind. Vladimir finds it.*)

Vladimir: Must have been a very fine hat. (*He puts it on his head. Estragon puts on Vladimir's hat in place of his own which he hands to Vladimir. Vladimir takes Estragon's hat. Estragon adjusts Vladimir's hat on his head. Vladimir puts on Estragon's hat in place of Lucky's which he hands to Estragon. Estragon takes Lucky's hat. Vladimir adjusts Estragon's hat on his head. Estragon puts on Lucky's hat in place of Vladimir's which he hands to Vladimir. Vladimir takes his hat. Estragon adjusts Lucky's hat on his head. Vladimir puts on his hat in place of Estragon's which he hands to Estragon. Estragon takes his hat. Vladimir adjusts his hat on his head. Estragon puts his hat in place of Lucky's* *which he hands to Vladimir. Vladimir takes Lucky's hat. Estragon adjusts his hat on his head. Vladimir puts on Lucky's hat in place of his own which he hands to Estragon. Estragon takes Vladimir's hat. Vladimir adjusts Lucky's hat on his head. Estragon hands Vladimir's hat back to Vladimir who takes it and hands it back to Estragon who takes it and hands it back to Vladimir who takes it and throws it down.)* How does it fit?

Estragon: How would I know?

Vladimir: No, but how do I look in it?

(He turns his head coquettishly to and fro, minces like a mannequin.)

Estragon: Hideous.

Vladimir: Yes, but not more so than usual?

Estragon: Neither more nor less.

Vladimir: Then I can keep it. Mine irked me. *(Pause)* How shall I say? *(Pause)* It itched me.[13]

The absurdist, antitheater in the approach to plot, makes no pretense of interesting the audience in story or character. The difference in the outcome from the traditional play is that the ending does not answer the questions raised, or else the ending is contrary to the expectations of the characters or the audience. The great leader has no head, the orator can only babble, the gorgeous young man is a hollow shell, the intellectual is really a barbarian, and Godot never comes. The playwright gives you a set of figures to add up, but your total is zero. An absurd play is characterized by an absurd ending because that is how the playwright feels about the world. In some plays the playwright doesn't give us an answer at all but brings the action back to the beginning of the circle, which is another way of saying that life is absurd because there are no answers.

Absurdists do not offer a neatly organized, carefully selected set of signs, nor do they lead you by the hand so that you will know where you are all the time. You may get lost and return to your starting place. You may be the victim of a sudden ambush or a strange trap; you will be baffled by directional signs pointing every which way or straight down. You may find yourself in a completely foreign place among strangers speaking in unknown tongues, behaving in odd ways. But the playwrights have a map of the territory and they know what they are about, although their method may baffle you. They may ask you to look at the stars and then pour a bucket of water over your head; they may invite you to climb a tree to find your way and then chop it down from under you. Absurdists offer an absurd experience because they want you to be aware that the world is absurd.

If the absurdists reject a carefully organized chain of action, have no interest in story values, make little effort to reveal the psychological aspects of characters, are uninterested in emotional involvement, refrain from specific identification of locale or character, what effects do their works achieve as theater?

A recent Beckett play *Ohio Impromptu* in which the action consists of one elderly man reading to another one.

(Goodman Theater. Directed by Alan Schneider.)

Some spectators are bewildered and irritated because the action in an absurdist play seems nonsensical. Others enjoy it as a kind of intellectual game by trying to piece together the bits of experience offered to them. Their critical faculties are involved, and they enjoy the learning process of seeking a fresh perception imaginatively presented. They may delight in the playwright's skill of execution or in that of the performers. At a more profound level, the theatergoer becomes acutely aware of the universality suggested by the specific stimulus of the play, and from this awareness may come a strong sense of personal involvement in the playwright's statement.

JEAN GENÊT

A direct spiritual descendant of Artaud is another Frenchman, Jean Genêt (1910–1986), who conceives of the theater in terms of symbol and ritual. Just as the existentialists found it nesessary to reorient themselves philosophically to a shattered world by creating their individual sets of values, so Genêt shaped his own existential view of the world from his strange, tormented childhood and early adult life. An illegitimate child, an unwanted orphan, he found out at age ten that he had no connection with the world, and from that discovery he developed his own inverted hierarchy of values. "I rejected a world which rejected me." A homosexual who had no identity and no status, he turned to a life of crime. He attempted to find his life by losing it. While serving a prison sentence, he began to write and showed so much artistic promise that some leading French intellectuals secured his release. In his plays *The Balcony, The Blacks, The Maids,* and *The Screens,* he has gained recognition as one of the most provocative playwrights of our day, and in his works some of Artaud's ideas of a theater of cruelty have been most successfully realized.

Out of his personal anguish, he visualized dramatic works of myth and ceremony, but in a world of reversed values. Instead of climbing the heights and seeking salvation, humanity finds its spiritual identity by plunging into the depths of darkness and evil. The soul is redeemed only by death, and only the criminal with the dedication of a saint can attain grace. Murder is the highest crime, and the act of betrayal is a sacrament.

A metaphor that Genêt finds appropriate to his purpose is a series of mirrors, some of them placed at odd angles, some that invert or distort the image, and some that, like Alice's looking glass, allow us to see into an oddly perverted wonderland. His metaphor suits his purpose well, for Genêt is concerned with the varied facets and layers of reality: the discrepancy between the genuine and the illusionary, and the loss or disguise of identity through assumed appearances and roles. In his plays, the spectators are often bewildered by the dazzling surfaces and the strange perspectives, so that they are not sure if they are seeing an actual character in a genuine event or a pretender in a masquerade.

Like Artaud, Genêt admires primitive rituals and the oriental theater. He is enamored of the masks, the rich use of spectacle, and the communal act of participation in an event of primary significance enacted in mystery and symbols. He sees the playwright's purpose fulfilled as, in Artaud's phrase, "a master of sacred ceremonies." Ritual provides the opportunity for gaining status by assuming roles and participating in significant acts. In Genêt, these become reflections of the dark areas of the unconscious, where primitive rites and sadomasochistic fantasies hold their strange spell—a many-faceted view through the myths of cruelty whose cathartic powers celebrate a collective ecstasy.

PETER BROOK

Brook (b. 1925) has earned a reputation as one of the most daring and innovative directors in the last two decades. He came out of the traditional theater, serving as an associate director at the Royal Shakespeare Company at Stratford and the Aldwych, where he staged several notable Shakespearean productions, such as *King Lear* (1962) with Paul Scofield. He achieved international fame because of his bold theatricalism. Although he was not at first associated with experimental groups, he prepared the way for much of the avant garde. He introduced Jerzy Grotowski to London, and in 1964, his production of *Marat/Sade* was based on Artaud and his concept of the theater of cruelty. Indeed, the staging of the play grew out of an experimental workshop that explored Artaudian principles.

In 1969, Brook published his influential book *The Empty Space,* which attacks current theater practice and points the way to the theatricalism that Brook envisions for the future.

He categorizes four kinds of theater:

1. The *deadly theater* is the sterile, conventional one that acts as a museum for the "classics," particularly Shakespeare, Molière, and opera.
2. The *rough theater* is close to the people; down-to-earth; natural and joyous; without style; antiauthority; and filled with noise, vulgarity, and boisterous action. Examples are the Elizabethans and Meyerhold's productions.
3. The *holy theater* is one of revelation and ceremony. Its rituals are the genuine ones that affect people's lives, not the pseudorituals injected in much of the contemporary theater. Artaud is the prophet of the holy theater and Grotowski its chief disciple for such productions as *The Constant Prince.*
4. The *immediate theater* is an eclectic one, vigorous, restless, full of joy—a combination of the rough and the holy. It is dynamic, not rigid. Brook's productions demonstrate his commitment to the immediate theater.[14]

JERZY GROTOWSKI

One of the most vital forces in the contemporary theater was the Polish Laboratory Theater and its moving spirit, Grotowski (b. 1933), whose seriousness of purpose and ability to create dramatic experiences with the authenticity of myth linked him with Artaud and Genêt. His emphasis was on the actors, who are called on to use all their mental and physical powers—mime, gesture, intonation, association of ideas—to bring about a fusion of movement and meaning. Rejecting the "wealth" of the traditional theater with its technical facilities, Grotowski called for a "poor theater," stripped of nonessentials, in order to concentrate on the performer. Grotowski's book *Towards a Poor Theater* and his wide-ranging tours to England, Europe, and America made him one of the most influential theatrical forces in the 1970s.

Two of his best-known works, *The Constant Prince* and *Apocalypsis cum Figuris,* conveyed the quality of an authentic ritual. *The Constant Prince* was a free adaptation of Pedro Calderón's seventeenth-century Spanish play, in which five characters acted out the hypocrisy and corruption of the world and caused the humiliation, anguish, and death of the Prince in an emotionally charged atmosphere that suggested the crucifixion. The *Apocalypsis cum Figuris* was a work assembled out of the experiments of the actors and directors, in which the verbal aspects were improvised in rehearsal as needed. When the production took shape, quotations were substituted from well-known sources: Feodor Dostoevski, the Book of Job, the New Testament, T. S. Eliot, and the Song of Solomon. Although the Bible was often a verbal source, and the characters were named after biblical characters, the work did not make a precise religious statement; however, the impact of the production is described as an exploration of the sources of myth—a fusion of religion and drama. The effect that Grotowski's theater achieved was chiefly the result of the shattering quality of the acting. His performers were remarkably trained in all aspects of their craft—speech, mime, and gesture—but in addition they conveyed the impression of a monastic zeal, as if the body were the outward manifestation of the secrets of the soul.

THE NEW THEATER

In the United States, the social upheaval stemming from the cold war and the disastrous entanglement in Vietnam were reflected in a "new theater" movement through which protesters vociferously expressed their discontent with nearly every facet of the establishment—including the theater itself. Just as many European artists and writers were dissatisfied with the political and social conditions that followed World War I, the American dissidents of the 1960s regarded the conventional commercial theater as a shallow and outdated institution. They were antitext, antiillusionistic production, and antitheater as a place for performing. On the creative side, they were for new kinds of theatrical material—a mixture of action, words, sound, music, and theatrical effects. The new theater was not an organized, widespread, sharply defined movement but the result of the efforts of several highly visible groups and individuals who demonstrated their talent for theatricalism.

These efforts came mostly from outside the commercial theater, from coffeehouses and off-off-Broadway groups or from actors' and dancers' workshops, such as Ellen Stewart's La Mama Experimental Theater Club and Joe Cino's Café Cino, which provided opportunities for an enormous outpouring of theatrical energy. In the early years, most of the participants received no pay, and productions were put together on shoestring budgets. The productions were notable for their forthright theatricalism, which put onstage many of the ideas offered by innovative predecessors, such as Meyerhold, Artaud, Brecht, and contemporary theater practicioners—Grotowski, Brook, and the absurdists.

THE LIVING THEATER

One of the most visible groups in the new theater was the Living Theater, founded by Judith Malina and Julian Beck. The company first attracted attention with its performance of Jack Gelber's *The Connection* in 1959. As a metaphor for everybody's compulsion or obsession, the plot deals with a number of drug addicts awaiting the arrival of Cowboy and his supply of drugs. The performance was two-edged, so that the audience was not quite sure what was real and what was pretense, even to the cast members who circulated among the audience during the intermission demanding a hand-out. The next production to achieve notoriety was Kenneth Brown's *The Brig* (1963). This is a violent, brutal depiction of the rigors of existence in a marine camp. The play was performed with searing directness, underscoring the naked brutality of the situation.

Following the loss of its theater because of the failure to pay taxes, the Living Theater went to Europe, where it developed its own brand of theatricalism. The company returned from abroad and gained national attention, chiefly with its productions of *Frankenstein* (1965) and *Paradise Now* (1968). The Living Theater used its plays for Marxist political persuasion, played with frenetic fervor. It was the aim of the actors to tear down the wall that separated them from the spectators. Beck told his company that its mission was "to help the audience to learn to take action."[15] Performers moved aggressively to reach the spectators and, through insults and obscenities, attempted to goad the audience into responding not just to the performance but also to the corruption of the capitalistic, bourgeois society, which the Living Theater projected as the enemy.

When asked, "Why do we go to the theater?" Beck replied, "To crack your head open and let in oxygen . . ."[16]

The Living Theater captured the Artaudian "theater of cruelty" spirit in its aggressive and often abrasive approach to theater in such productions as a modern version of *Antigone.*

Jean-Claude van Itallie was the leading playwright of Chaikin's Open Theater. His play *The Serpent* was presented at the Zellerbach Theater in the University of California, Berkeley. Note the audience surrounding the acting area.

THE OPEN THEATER

The Open Theater began in 1963 as a workshop primarily interested in exploring acting skills. Joseph Chaikin, the leader of the seventeen performers and four writers who made up the group, was formerly with the Living Theater, but he broke away because his central interest was in investigating acting. Chaikin indicates the purpose of the Workshop: "My intention is to make images into theater events, beginning simply with those which have meaning for myself and my collaberators; and at the same time renouncing the theater of critics, box office, real estate, and the conditioned public."[17]

The Open Theater was rooted in a series of exercises aimed at developing a nonrealistic style of acting that emphasized ensemble play. Originally committed to private exploration of acting skills, using improvisational material, the group gradually felt the need to work before an audience and finally staged productions of one-act plays, then Megan Terry's *Viet Rock* at the Sheridan Square and La Mama theaters. The Open Theater's leading writer, Jean-Claude van Itallie, wrote *America Hurrah!,* which was one of the most provocative plays of the 1966–1967 season. When Chaikin declared the Open Theater closed, he could look back on one of the most interesting experimental ensembles of the new theater.

THE PERFORMANCE GROUP

The Performance Group in New York City was spawned by Richard Schechner's contact with Grotowski's Workshop. The Group's aim was to purge the sentimentalism of the traditional American theatrical experience by shattering the boundary between audience and performer and by involving all elements in a communal celebration. Working with exercises derived from Grotowski that subsequently became a part of the performance, Schechner's Group produced *Dionyus in 69.* It was partially based on *The Bacchae* of Euripides and partially on rituals that grew out of exercises and rehearsals. At the center of the performance was the chorus, which intended to create "a

The Performance Group fashioned a theater out of a garage and placed the spectators on scaffolding. The workshop quality of their performances is evident in this shot from *Commune,* a collective creation.

dance of ecstasy." Language was distorted, fragmented, and amplified, and the chorus chanted and wailed in projecting the impression of ritualistic fervor. Schechner's vociferous theatricalism, which exploited sound, movement and nudity, made an impact, although his aesthetic objectives were not clearly apparent from the performance.

The Group's production of *Makbeth* was another effort to achieve a blatant theatricalism, which joined Shakespeare's text to excerpts from other classics as well as contemporary allusions to the Manson murders and the massacre in Vietnam. It was a collective venture, growing out of Grotowski-like exercises and improvisations.

In a third production, *Commune,* Schechner again went back to the Manson case and the Vietnamese massacre. It was an effort to engage the audience in a communal experience that the director felt should arise from confrontation with acts of violence, although actions that occur simultaneously are not necessarily linked to one another causally. Again the Group achieved moments of striking theatricality by its assault on the senses.

In lamenting the passing of the Performance Group, Schechner said, "One of the truly fine things to come out of the period now ended is the recognition that theatricality is a primary human activity."

OTHER NEW THEATER GROUPS

Another innovative group that has demonstrated its staying power is Charles Ludlam's Ridiculous Theatrical Company, founded in 1967. Ludlam borrows freely from the commedia dell'arte and anything else that suits his slam-bang, comic-strip style for ridiculing everything in sight. One of the company's recent productions was its freewheeling *Le Bourgeois Avant-Garde* (1983), a scathing satire on various "isms" to champion a new one, "Repressed Expressionism," a form of art so esoteric that no one can understand it. Ludlam's company continues to stay in business, thanks to his comedic gifts and the Company's beguiling ability to achieve a sense of immediacy with the audience.

Peter Schumann's Bread and Puppet Theater is a unique kind of folk theater that plays in streets and open public places. Its brand of theatricalism stems from the use of puppets, some as tall as eighteen feet. Schumann's background as a sculptor and choreographer is evident in the remarkable puppets and their actions. The Theater seems to be motivated by a strong Christian drive, aimed at spiritual renewal. It uses simple fairy stories or tales from the Bible, sometimes treated ironically. The puppets go through the movements; their dialogue is taped or narrated. A blend of "poor" and "total theater," Schumann's Bread and Puppet Theater has established a solid reputation for its humanistic concerns and its extraordinary manner of expression in gestures and ceremony.

The San Francisco Mime Troupe plays anywhere, often under improvised
conditions. The Troupe's informal, intimate style was useful in its plays of protest.
False Promises.

The San Francisco Mime Troupe

The politically activist San Francisco Mime Troupe began performing out-
doors in 1962—playing in parks, in marketplaces, and on the streets. Using
the broad comic techniques of improvised Italian comedy and working under the motto "Engagement, Commitment, and Fresh Air," the Troupe sat-
irizes the establishment. With its Marxist orientation ("a small theater
collective, dedicated to the principle that all art is political"), the company
regards spectators not as passive onlookers but as a human resource to ac-
tivate and mobilize in its attack on war, racism, industrialism, and conformity. In recent years, the Troupe has moved away from the commedia
dell'arte style to play melodrama, which is a more satisfactory means of encouraging people to face important questions. The San Francisco Mime
Troupe, always in precarious straits financially, has survived because of the
comic skills and imagination of dedicated performers.

El Teatro Campesino

Louis Valdez began his theatrical career with the San Francisco Mime Troupe, but he became involved in supporting a strike of the migrant field workers in California. Taking his talent from field hands, Valdez formed El Teatro Campesino to play agit-prop *actos* before Chicano audiences as a way of inspiring political action. These sketches satirized those who exploited them in an entertaining way, which was very effective propaganda. Their theatricalism was characterized by an exuberant spirit and broad comic action. Valdez became interested in broadening the base of El Teatro Campesino, moving away from political action to a concern with the spiritual and literal spirit of the Chicano culture. In 1978, he produced a full-scale drama, *Zoot Suit,* which played successfully at the Mark Taper in Los Angeles, although it failed to attract a wide audience on Broadway. El Teatro Campesino continues as a virile cultural force, pursuing Valdez's call for "a teatro of ritual, of music, of beauty, and spiritual sensitivity. A teatro of legends and myths. A teatro of religious strength."

THE THEATER OF IMAGES

Despite the avowed protest against "the tyranny of the word," most theater productions revolve around a written script. There are, however, notable innovators who are interested in the presentation of images. Most prominent among these are Robert Wilson, Richard Foreman, and Lee Breuer's Mabou Mines Company.

Robert Wilson

Robert Wilson is a highly regarded experimentalist whose theatricalism appeals primarily to the eye. He has been called a "seer genius" and a "feeler genius" because of his imaginative productions of striking visual displays in *The Life and Times of Sigmund Freud, Deafman Glance* (1971), *A Letter for Queen Victoria* (1975), *The Life and Times of Joseph Stalin, Einstein on the Beach* (1976), *I Was Sitting on My Patio This Guy Appeared I Thought I Was Hallucinating* (1977), and *Death, Destruction and Detroit* (1979). *Einstein on the Beach,* which was performed at the Metropolitan Opera House after highly successful productions in major European cities, combined all aspects of the theater, but the emphasis was on the sensual imagery loosely tied to musical motifs. Wilson's background as a painter explains his visual approach to theatrical production.

> I am always concerned with how the total stage picture looks at any given moment. The placement and content of film, paths and gestures of performers, and lighting were all major considerations, no less important than the dialogue or music.[18]

In *A Letter for Queen Victoria*, Wilson presented what one reviewer called a "phantasmagoric enigma" of striking and beautiful images. There is talk, some of it articulate, some gibberish, but with little apparent meaning. One sequence shows a group of masked aviators huddled up against a wall in fear. There are smoke and crocodiles and living monuments formed by the aviators watching crashing airplanes outside the window. In another scene, a fragment of a café is set against a backcloth on which a repeated pattern of the words *Chitter* and *Chatter* appear. People in gray sit at tables with pink tulips, chattering away, at times interrupted by gunfire. One of the characters seems to be shot and slowly dies, only to revive nimbly and resume chattering. And so Wilson leads the spectator from one beguiling moment to the next in a stunning collage of all elements of the theater.

In *Death, Destruction, and Detroit*, which premiered in West Berlin (1979), Wilson makes more extensive use of language than in his previous works. Some of it is fragmentary, oblique, precise, and lyrical, but there is an ordered verbal sequence. Like the other elements—music, dance, and spectacle—the language is a way of stirring the imagination and expanding the awareness rather than a means of conveying factual information.

Death, Destruction and Detroit concerns the Nazi leader Rudolf Hess, confined since 1945 in a prison in Berlin. One scene, particularly striking because of the evocative images that Wilson fashions, suggests Hess's prison cell. Dale Harris describes the action:

> . . . Hess, now an old man dressed in white tie and tails, dances by himself to the sound of a Keith Jarrett piano solo. He is preoccupied, self-absorbed, utterly content. Even when the stage begins to fill up—first with couples in evening dress, then with waiters carrying huge salvers and domed lids, all of them dancing with the same self-absorption and fixity of purpose—he stays in his own world, weaving in and out of the crowd as if they didn't exist. At the front of the stage, in the center, stands a little boy (who may or may not be Hess's son), wearing scarlet diplomat's dress, gleaming with gold frogging—a colorful note among the pervading shades of grey and black.
>
> Meanwhile, from one side of the stage a woman (who may or may not be Hess's wife) stares out at the audience during the course of the scene being transformed from a shabby looking *Hausfrau* with a cotton scarf knotted under chin to a *grande dame* in magnificent black evening dress, her head crowned with feathers, her wrists and neck encircled with diamonds. It is hard to imagine a more telling comment on the economic rise and gradual historical amnesia of West Germany between 1945 and the present.[19]

In 1983, Wilson was slated to prepare a production for the Olympic Games Arts Festival in Los Angeles. Dubbed a "planetary opera," it was to consist of scenes and acts produced in six different countries, to be brought together in its final form in California. This *CIVIL warS* (1983) was an avant garde panorama about war and peace. The American segment was to consist of "knee plays," fourteen vignettes intended to link together the five larger segments prepared by Holland, Germany, France, Italy, and Japan.

Robert Wilson has an uncanny capacity for creating beguiling images such as this one in "the knee plays," intended to be a part of the mammoth production *Civil Wars*. The knee plays were performed at the Walker Art Center, Minneapolis, 1984.

Unfortunately, the project had to be abandoned because of lack of financial support. Nevertheless, the plans for *CIVIL warS* indicate the audacious range of Wilson's imagination.

His work is difficult to assess because it is so unique in conception and so lacking in ordinary theatrical referents. Of recent innovators who have rejected traditional dramatic production and achieved a highly personal and provocative theatricalism, Robert Wilson stands at the forefront, both here and abroad.

Richard Foreman

Richard Foreman is another experimentalist who has received considerable attention through his Ontological-Hysteric Theater productions of *Dr. Selavy's Magic Circus, Elephant Steps, Angel Face, Hotel for Criminals, Penguin Touquet,* and *Cafe Amerique.* Like Wilson, his interest is in the presentation of a series of theatrical, provocative images, without a story line or continuity. He delights in the "act of making the thing we are looking at," which he regards as constantly changing directions. When asked what he would like an audience to experience from his productions, Foreman replied, "I would like them to feel refreshed, you know, energized."

Again like Wilson, Foreman as an experimentalist has earned recognition in the conventional theater for his striking production of Brecht's *Threepenny Opera* (1975) at the Vivian Beaumont Theater, Lincoln Center, New York City. In this revival, Foreman announced that he intended to "restore the original anguish to a piece meant to disturb, confound, and thereby excite." Brecht's work has a definite story line and several clearly delineated characters, so Foreman was not able to fragmentize the play as he does with his own creations. Nevertheless, his actors achieved a cold, brittle "serious playfulness" that made the production a memorable one and enhanced Foreman's reputation for imaginative theatricalism.

Foreman's own plays are a collection of tableaux joined to disruptive dialogue and arbitrary visual images and sound effects. Seeking to destroy the stage through delicate maneuvers, he deliberately distorts his materials to avoid linear and logical patterns. His plays are intended to reject the tyranny of meaning, although Foreman in his *Manifesto* and other writings explains at length his rejection of a clear rationale. In dealing with the unimaginable, he has created his own version of the absurd.

The Mabou Mines Company

Linked with Wilson and Foreman in its visual approach to theater is the Mabou Mines Company, an ensemble that since the early 1960s, writes and produces its own plays. The group toured Europe for three years before becoming the resident company first at Le Mama and then at the New York Festival Theater.

The company works as a collective, under the guidance of Lee Breuer, who serves as director, writer, and actor. His early plays feature animals as their main characters, in what he calls "Animations": *The Red Horse* (1970), *B. Beaver* (1974), and *Shaggy Dog* (1978). They are satirical, highly imaginative fables that attack contemporary culture through pop music, films, television, and the high gloss of Madison Avenue commercialization. They aim at stripping away the veils that conceal romanticism and sentimentality. The *Shaggy Dog* animation presents the life and loves of a dog named Rose, who develops a fixation for her master and longs to take on human characteristics. Rose is played by a puppet about two-thirds human size, manipulated by from one to four of the actors. The dog's past and her thoughts and feelings are projected over a sound track and accompanied by strange and evocative actions and images.

Beckett's *Come and Go* was a highly imaginative Mabou Mines production in which the three actors sat on a balcony behind the audience. They were made visible by a large mirror on stage. This play featured spectacular visual and sound effects—a bomb falling, splitting the stage floor and disintegrating the room amid fireworks, explosions, and vivid lighting.

Even plays written to be performed in a proscenium arch theater are now conceived of in terms of their theatricality. In *Amadeus*, a single unit set serves for thirty-one scenes over a span of forty-two years. In one scene, Salieri begins as an old man in a wheelchair and ends transforming himself before the audience into a young man in the prime of life. Throughout the play, he confides to the audience, discusses his motives and feelings of guilt, and provides necessary exposition.

One of the chief targets of the new theater was the tyranny of the word—the sanctity of the text. Traditionally, the play was the core of the production, and those who brought it to life onstage attempted to be faithful to the playwright's words and purpose. Now the play is often regarded as one element of the performance, no more important than the acting or setting or music. Fragments of several plays may be pieced together in nearly haphazard fashion, or the language and images may be probed for a subtext to make the meaning relevant to the contemporary world.

The Living Theater began its production of *Frankenstein* with a scene in which fifteen actors attempted to levitate a girl; however, their efforts failed, and she was caught in a net and placed in a coffin, which was carried off in a procession. This interpolated action was a personal statement by the company about its faith being overcome by frustration. In a production of *Oedipus the King* at the Kammerspiele Schauspielhaus in Munich, director Ernst Wendt updated Sophocles' play to demonstrate that tragedy is the lack of communal rapport with the action of the individual. Wendt's modernized version replaced the original actions with contemporary ones. In the classic version of the play, the prologue shows a band of suppliants, suffering from the plague, coming to Oedipus for help. Wendt showed the miserable condition of the citizens by individual actions. One character pounded on an electronic piano; a girl did a frenzied tap dance on top of a billiard table; a wandering man, mumbling incoherently, shuffled through the debris that littered the stage; and a woman stabbed herself again and again, screaming at the top of her voice. Later in the play, when Jocasta learns of her incestuous relationship to Oedipus, she goes silently into the house and hangs herself. Director Wendt updated this action by having Jocasta run up a moving escalator, collapse, and die.

Sophocles' *Oedipus at Colonus* is a Greek classic that depicts the ancient, blinded Oedipus wandering about with his daughter seeking sanctuary. The original play ends with his death and transfiguration offstage, narrated by a Messenger. In Breuer's modern adaptation, the Messenger is a preacher who has been an eyewitness to the miracle, which he ecstatically describes onstage with the help of a gospel-style choir that performs with the ardor of a black Baptist Church revival meeting.

More recently Breuer created *A Prelude to Venice*, which shows a single character with a giant puppet stashed between two public telephone booths. The scenario dramatizes the disintegration and fragmentation of humanity, caught in the tensions and anxieties of the modern world. Breuer's skill in creating imaginative and entertaining theatricalism while making social comment accounts for his company's longevity.

PERFORMANCE ART

For a time, a good deal of experimentation came under the catchall term *happenings*. More recently, *performances* is the key word, with such ramifications as *auto-performances, activities,* and *performance workshops*. Sally Barnes describes performance art as "an anti-theatrical forum that displaces illusion with real time, character with personality, skill with spontaneity, artifice with the banal. It values idea over execution. . . . It is a kind of throw-away art."[20] As Barnes says, "performance art" is actually antitheater in concept in that it reverses or negates traditional theater values.

You will recall Aristotle's hierarchy of plot, character, thought, diction, music, and spectacle. Performance art reverses the importance of these elements by placing top priority on spectacle and music. Plot, a sequential orderly structure of elements, organized on the basis of the "necessary and probable," is replaced by broken fragments that avoid complications and resolutions and are replaced by abstracted images without beginning, middle, and end.

The performers are not characters but agents of the action, without psychological complexity. Their humanity may be delimited by the use of masks or the substitution of puppets. Their speech and actions are flat and abstracted.

There is no clear thought element, no didactic purpose. The meaning is the act itself, which is deliberately opaque or ambiguous, as if to warn the spectator against the danger of seeking a clear rationale.

Performance art is geared toward private responses; it is self-oriented. The diction is not dialogue to reveal character or to advance the plot. It takes the form of exposition or description, often lyric in feeling. The verbal material uses diaries and biographies, sometimes taped or shared by several performers.

The sound element may include all kinds of music, generally electronically performed. Jazz and rock music and a variety of sound effects are played from tapes.

The spectacle depends on the projection of images—slides and home movies arranged in conflicting or ambiguous patterns. And through it all, the performer remains remote, austere, and depersonalized.

Performance art is more at home in a gallery or studio than it is on-stage because in many ways it is an extension of the painters' or printmakers' art than it is of the theater. Stuart Sherman sets up a TV tray on a street corner or on a Staten Island ferry, opens a battered suitcase, and manipulates a variety of commonplace objects in a rapid series of brief "routines" that comprise his "spectacles." He makes no effort to involve the audience, except to invite them to watch his actions. In a more ambitious undertaking, Sherman produced a *Classical Trilogy* that included *Hamlet, Oedipus Rex,* and *Faust.* Shakespeare's play ran twenty-five minutes and involved eight actors; Sophocles' play had four actors and ran thirty minutes; and *Faust* was simply a five-minute bit with Sherman seated under a desk lamp, reading the play. The lines were not spoken by any of the performers; there were taped patches of dialogue to accompany the actors' deadpan performance of the essential actions.

Allan Kaprow gathered together a group of interested people, paired them off, and sent them out into the streets of Naples to find suitable doorways where each couple performed a "routine" consisting of a short passage of dialogue made up of simple phrases, such as "after you," "excuse me," and "thank you." Their dialogue was to be accompanied by appropriate action. Each couple repeated the routine in four different doorways. There was no attempt to attract an audience—the pleasure was in the doing.

The intended effect of such experiments is generally "perceptional enhancement." In our "mind-blowing" world we have become acutely aware of the rich lode of our inner resources and experiences. As Marshall McLuhan says, "Once more reality is concerned as being *within* one, and the search of truth has become an inward trip." Hence, the efforts to break through the established patterns of fixed language and action to a fresh experience of intuitive perception and heightened sensitivity not tied to specific meanings.

Like so many other innovations in the arts, performances emphasize the creative process rather than the final product, and often technical skill yields to improvised inspiration. The act is its own excuse for being.

The future of the new theater will no doubt depend on the social climate of the times. The valid gains it has made in promoting a varied brand of theatricalism will be reflected in the main current of the theater, while fresh attempts will be made to express the human experience. The door is wide open since there has never before been such a wide range of styles, technical facilities, or tastes. As always, with every form of theater, the future will depend mostly on the talent and imagination that is attracted to its service.

The new theater is no longer a strident voice of protest, but it continues in many forms to be a theater of experimentation that emphasizes theatricalism. However, the shock has worn off and many of the freedoms that the experimentalists fought for have been won. The theatricalism that so short a time ago seemed novel has merged into the mainstream of the theater. Playwrights immediately exploited the new permissiveness in language, behavior, nudity, and subject matter. Writers now find far more latitude in shaping their material or in using the technical facilities of production. In short, those who boldly struck out to find new territory have broadened the horizons of us all.

PLAYS TO READ AND SEE

F = Film available; V = Videotape available.

F	V	Shaffer, *Amadeus, Equus*
F		Lorca, *Blood Wedding*
		Brecht, *Caucasian Chalk Circle*
F	V	Ragni, Rad, *Hair*
F		Weiss, *Marat/Sade*
F	V	Kopit, *Oh Dad, Poor Dad*
F	V	Wilder, *Our Town, Skin of Our Teeth*
F	V	Ionesco, *Rhinoceros*
F		Duerrenmatt, *The Visit*

BIBLIOGRAPHY

ARTAUD, ANTONIN. *The Theater and Its Double.* Trans. Mary C. Richards. New York: Grove Press, Inc., 1958.

BECK, JULIAN. *The Life of the Theater.* New York: 1972.

BRAUN, EDWARD. *The Theater of Meyerhold: Revolution of the Modern Stage.* London: 1979.

BROCKETT, OSCAR G., and ROBERT R. FINDLAY. *Century of Innovation.* Englewood Cliffs, N.J.: Prentice-Hall, Inc., 1973.

BROOK, PETER. *The Empty Space.* London: MacGibbon and Tree, 1968.

BRUSTEIN, ROBERT. *The Third Theater.* New York: Alfred A. Knopf, Inc., 1961.

CHAIKIN, JOSEPH. *The Presence of the Actor.* New York: 1972.

DAVY, KATE, ed. *Richard Foreman and Manifestos.* New York: 1976.

ESSLIN, MARTIN. *The Theater of the Absurd.* New York: Doubleday & Co., Inc., 1961.

EVANS-ROOSE, JAMES. *The Experimental Theater.* New York: Universe Books, 1970.

GROWTOWSKI, JERZY. *Towards a Poor Theater.* New York: Simon & Schuster, Inc., 1968.

KIRBY, MICHAEL. *The New Theater Performance Documentation.* New York: New York University Press, 1978.

MARRANCA, BONNIE. *The Theater of Images.* New York: Drama Book Specialists, 1977.

SCHECHNER, RICHARD. *Public Domain: Essays on the Contemporary Theater.* Indianapolis: The Bobbs-Merrill Co., Inc., 1969.

SHANK, THEODORE. *American Alternative Theater.* New York: Grove Press, Inc., 1982.

WELLWARTH, GEORGE. *The Theater of Protest and Paradox.* New York: New York University Press, 1967.

NOTES

1. Kurt Schwitters, quoted in Robert Motherwell, *The Dada Painters and Poets* (New York: Wittenborn, Schultz, 1951).

2. Quoted in John Elderfield, *Kurt Schwitters* (London: Thames & Hudson, Ltd., 1985).

3. Bertolt Brecht, *Brecht on Theatre*, trans. John Willett (London: Methuen, 1964).

4. Bertolt Brecht, "Little Organum for the Theater," trans. Beatrice Gottlieb. *Accent,* 11 (1951).

5. Antonin Artaud, *The Theater and Its Double*, trans. Mary C. Richards (New York: Grove Press, Inc.. 1958).

6. Artaud, *Theater and Its Double.*

7. Artaud, *Theater and Its Double.*

8. Albert Camus, *The Myth of Sisyphus* (New York: Alfred A. Knopf, Inc., 1955).

9. Alfred Jarry, cited in Leonard Cabell Pronko, *Avant-Garde: The Experimental Theater in France* (Berkeley: University of California Press, 1962).

10. Samuel Beckett, *Waiting for Godot* (New York: Grove Press, Inc., 1954).

11. Harold Pinter, *The Birthday Party* (New York: Grove Press, Inc., 1959).

12. Eugene Ionesco, *The Bald Soprano,* from *Four Plays* by Eugene Ionesco, trans. Donald M. Allen (New York: Grove Press, Inc., 1958).

13. Beckett, *Waiting for Godot.*

14. Peter Brook, "Introduction to *Marat/Sade*" by Peter Weiss (New York: Atheneum Publishers, 1965). From the introduction by Peter Brook to the play *The Persecution and Assassination of Jean-Paul Marat as Performed by the Inmates of the Asylum of Charenton Under the Direction of the Marquis de Sade*, by Peter Weiss. Copyright 1965 by John Calder Ltd. Reprinted by permission of Atheneum Publishers.

15. Toby Cole and Helen Krich Chinoy, eds., *Actors on Acting* (New York: Crown Publishers, Inc., 1970.

16. Cole and Chinoy, eds., *Actors on Acting.*

17. Joseph Chaikin, "Closing the Open Theater," *Theater Quarterly,* XVI (November 1974–January 1975).

18. Robert Wilson, "I Thought I Was Hallucinating," *Drama Review,* T76 (December 1977).

19. Dale Harris, "Berlin Report," *Performing Arts,* June 1979.

20. Sally Barnes, *Village Voice,* December 30, 1981.

8

The Director

The Suppliants (c. 492 B.C.) is generally regarded as the oldest extant play in Western European literature. When the author, Aeschylus, won the right to present his play at the Festival of Dionysus, like other Greek dramatists, he was obliged to direct his own work. He must have learned that directing a play is a complex and tricky business. Since he was the author, he did not have the usual problem of interpreting the meaning of his text, but like all directors, he went through the intriguing and sometimes frustrating process of putting the words into action. Aeschylus had to make sure his lines were spoken or sung correctly; he had to work out all the movement and choreography of the actors and chorus members; and he supervised all aspects of production—costumes, casting, music, and dance.

Even a cursory glance at *The Suppliants* indicates the need for painstaking planning and rehearsal. Aeschylus dramatizes the story of the fifty daughters of Danaus who flee to Argos, seeking sanctuary from the pursuing sons of Aegyptus. At the climax of the play, Herald and his attendants attempt to carry off the maidens by force, but they are saved by the King, who refuses to release them.

Perhaps the most difficult task Aeschylus faced in producing his play was that of training the chorus of fifty maidens, who recite and chant more than 600 lines of poetry, sometimes combining words with dance and sometimes engaging in vigorous action, as when they cling to the altar in terror, pleading for asylum. In addition to the careful preparation of speech and choreography of the chorus, it was necessary to provide them with appropriate costumes—striking Egyptian robes and linen veils fastened to their heads with gold bands. In the action of the other performers, two entrances required special care. In the first, the King and his retinue make a dramatic entrance, probably with horses and chariots. The second complicated entrance occurs when the Herald and his coterie appear and threaten to tear the suppliant maidens away from the altar. Although this play has a simple plot, its implicit demands for the movement of a large group of performers must have required arduous rehearsal. We may be sure that Aeschylus was grateful for his military experience when he prepared *The Suppliants* for performance.

Throughout the history of the theater, the manifold tasks of production have been handled in a variety of ways. The assigned officials and Greek playwrights were in charge of the presentation of tragedies. In the medieval cycle plays, with their fragmentized episodes, many of them requiring realistic staging, an enormous amount of organization was necessary, much of which was parceled out to various participating groups. In the Elizabethan theater, with its permanent professional companies of actors and playwrights, the theater manager selected the plays and assigned the casts. Undoubtedly, the playwrights took considerable interest in seeing that their works were performed as they intended them to be. And just as Hamlet found it expedient to advise the players about their style of acting in the

Directing an ancient play in a Greek theater was no simple task, especially in a play like *The Suppliants* by Aeschylus. The director had to organize the singing, dancing, action, and the arrangement of actors and a chorus of fifty in an enormous acting area.

(Modern revival directed by A. Solomos at the theater in Epidaurus.)

play within the play, it requires little stretch of the imagination to believe that Shakespeare made a similar effort in the performance of his dramas at the Globe. Molière, in the seventeenth-century French theater, labored for twelve years with his troupe in the provinces, polishing and perfecting the performance of his plays before returning to Paris. That Molière not only set an example for his company but also took care to improve the quality of his productions is suggested by his wry comment that "actors are strange creatures to drive."

In the eighteenth and nineteenth centuries, such stars as David Garrick and William Macready attempted to make play production less haphazard, but in general many of the responsibilities of organization were delegated to underlings or ignored altogether. Often, plays were patched together with "typed" characters assigned to roles with little or no genuine rehearsal and almost no concern for ensemble acting. Stock sets were refurbished on a makeshift basis, and little attention was paid to lighting. Costuming was mostly a matter of individual taste, and apparently no one worried about the resulting incongruities. There were, of course, a few notable exceptions to these practices. Charles Kean staged remarkable productions of Shakespeare in the 1850s, for which special scenery was

Henry Irving, the English actor-producer, was noted for his sensational staging,
such as in this scene showing the storming of the Bastille in *The Dead Heart,* 1889.

*(Lyceum Theater, London, 1889. Note the wealth of detail and the use of crowds, anticipating
cinematic treatment.)*

designed and painted with accurate geological and botanical detail. In his
productions of *A Midsummer Night's Dream* and *Henry VIII*, Kean was praised
for the harmony of effect that resulted from music, scenery, and choreography especially created for the occasion. A decade later, Squire Bancroft
and Marie Wilton Bancroft introduced rehearsal reforms that were in the
direction of greater unity.

THE MODERN DIRECTOR APPEARS

The Duke of Saxe-Meiningen in Germany performed an invaluable service
for the theater through his exemplary staging of Shakespeare, Ibsen, and
Schiller. All aspects of production were integrated into an artistic whole—
acting, scenery, and costumes. His troupe emphasized ensemble playing,
paying special attention to the use of crowds. The Duke's company tour of
the major theatrical centers of Europe (1874–1890) inspired theater work-

ers elsewhere to emulate his synthesis of production and helped to establish the position of the director as the dominant force.

With the coming of naturalism and realism in the latter part of the nineteenth century, directors and actors became increasingly concerned with unifying all elements of the performance. The new plays, representing authentic views of daily life and based on firsthand observation, demanded a new kind of scenery and acting. Since the conventional commercial theaters were not hospitable to innovation, it became necessary to set up "independent theaters"—places where a subscription audience could see the new kind of drama appropriately played. Antoine led the way with his Théâtre Libre in Paris (1887), in which he directed all phases of production. He made a hall into an improvised theater, selected the plays and the casts, set the style of acting by directing and performing himself, and devised the scenery. He even went out and rounded up an audience through hand-delivered letters and personal contacts. His efforts resulted in a unique integration of performance based on his ideal of achieving an honest representation of reality. In Berlin (1889), Brahm followed Antoine's example at the Freie Bühne, another subscription theater that demonstrated realism, especially in the plays of Ibsen and Hauptmann. In Russia, the Moscow Art Theater (1898) did similar work with the plays of Chekhov under the direction of Stanislavski. The independent theater idea was also influential in England at the Independent Stage Society under J. T. Grein, and in America, Herne directed a production of his own *Margaret Fleming* (1890) in Boston. These efforts to achieve a style appropriate to the new playwriting were

At the Moscow Art Theater, Stanislavski attempted to develop a natural style of performance especially for Chekhov's plays. This old photograph of *Uncle Vanya* in 1899 shows the genuine quality of playing.

instrumental in defining the role of the director as the one responsible for aesthetic unity and the dominant one in the production hierarchy.

In addition to the independent theater pioneers, two visionaries championed the concept of unity in play production in a series of notable stage designs, as well as in their writings. These men were Gordon Craig and Adolphe Appia, whose contributions are discussed in Chapter Ten. Several forces were at work in the late nineteenth-century theater that led to the guiding principle that all aspects of play production should grow from a central interpretation. The corollary of this idea was that to secure such unity, a single creative intelligence must be responsible for designing the whole production—namely, the director. This idea is widely accepted in the twentieth-century theater, and this dominating role has been assumed notably by Reinhardt, Alexander Tairov, Jacques Copeau, Stanislavski, Meyerhold, Leopold Jessner, Guthrie, Piscator, Kazan, Barrault, Brook, Peter Stein, and Victor Garcia.

Directors work under rehearsal conditions that vary, depending on the type of theater they serve. A Broadway director may find it necessary to throw a play together in three weeks; in Russia, some plays have taken two years of rehearsal. Meyerhold, after two months of rehearsal, had not

In America at the turn of the century, David Belasco set the standard for his spectacular productions. He was famous for the authenticity of his sets, costumes, and lighting. This shot shows the protagonist on the way to the guillotine in *Du Barry.*

(Criterion Theater, New York, 1901.)

settled on the casting on any one of the three characters for a one-act play! Reinhardt preplanned his performances to the last detail so that the rehearsal period was one of teaching the actors what he wished them to do; Arthur Hopkins simply turned his actors loose with occasional stimulation and encouragement, his idea of direction being to "put on a play without anyone realizing how it was done." Some directors find that the law of diminishing returns sets in for rehearsals lasting longer than three hours; Belasco was known to rehearse for twenty hours at a stretch. Meyerhold gave his actors every piece of business and read every line for them; Brecht sat and waited for his actors to show him the meaning of his own plays; Vakhtangov conducted round-table discussions with his casts, trying to arrive at a common interpretation; and Stein, through seminars and directed reading, leads his company in researching the period of the play to comprehend its cultural roots.

THE FUNCTIONS OF THE DIRECTOR

As the unifying force in the production of a play, directors have a number of specific assignments. From the time that the script is placed in their hands until the curtain rises on opening night, it is the director who initiates and controls all aspects of the presentation. Directors analyze the script; audition actors; cast the roles; set the basic floor plan for the sets; supervise the design of costumes, scenery, and lighting; instruct the cast in the meaning of the play; conduct rehearsals during which they block out the action; assist the actors with interpretation of character and the reading of lines; and finally polish, time, and unify the play into a cohesive whole. Everything about the interpretation and performance of the play is the director's business.

The director's function may be indicated by quoting representative statements by four outstanding men of the theater. John Mason Brown said that the "director is a critic in action." Guthrie, well known for his highly personalized productions, said, "The director, then, is partly an artist presiding over a group of other artists, excitable, unruly, childlike and intermittently 'inspired.' He is also the foreman of a factory, the abbot of a monastery, and a superintendent of an analytic laboratory. It will do no harm, if in addition to other weapons, he arms himself with the patience of a good nurse, together with the voice and vocabulary of an old-time sergeant-major."[1] Meyerhold describes his purpose in these terms: "A director builds a bridge from the spectator to the actor. Following the dictates of the author, and introducing on the stage friends, enemies, or lovers, the director with movements and postures must present a certain image which will aid the spectator not only to hear the words, but to guess the inner, concealed feelings." The eminent French director Louis Jouvet described his task as follows: "He must organize that area where the active players on the stage and the passive players in the auditorium meet each other, where the spectators penetrate and identify themselves with the action on stage."

THE DIRECTOR AT WORK

The director is a skilled craftsperson, capable of revealing the full meaning of the play to an audience in tangible theatrical terms.

Although this text is not a manual of play production, nor is it our intent to discuss in detail every phase of the director's function, it may be helpful in understanding the director's contribution if we indicate the use of stage movement.

A play in the theater is dynamic. It is in a continual process of ebb and flow, action and reaction, adjustment and readjustment. Through its characters, changes take place: The frustrated boy finally gets the girl; a woman comes to understand herself through suffering; a hero falls from a high place to catastrophe; the downtrodden little man achieves status.

When Aristotle described the playwright's approach to writing a play, he suggested that the first step was to frame the central action. The director follows a similar process by searching first for the *main action* of the play, sometimes referred to by theater people as the "spine" or the "superobjective." In Clurman's analysis of *The Member of the Wedding*, he found that the main action was to get "connected." Franco Zefferelli, in speaking of a production of *Hamlet*, saw the hero as "living in a hard world—with no elasticity about it—a closed world, with high walls, no windows, lots of storms. Like a prisoner in a tower." Brook found his approach to *Romeo and Juliet* in a single line: "These hot days is the mad blood stirring." Thus, the director works through the play, line by line and scene by scene, finding the most effective means of forming the action.

Sometimes, the director envisions almost all the action and gives it to the cast. Other directors set a general framework and then encourage the actor to work creatively within it. Joan Littlewood, the colorful English director, approaches the play through the actor, as she did in Brendan Behan's *The Quare Fellow*, through improvisation to capture the feel of the play before tackling the script. The play is laid in a Dublin prison, so she had her cast begin by simulating aspects of prison life such as the dull marches in the "yard" and the bleak confinement of cell living.

The director often concentrates a good deal of attention on blocking out movement, inventing business, and grouping the characters. The playwright may provide directions for such essential plot actions as entrances and exits, duels, love scenes, death scenes, and so on, and the context of the lines may provide clues for movement. For instance, it is clear in Act I, Scene

1 of *Hamlet* that Horatio joins the soldiers in their vigil, that the ghost enters, and that the three watchers attempt unsuccessfully to restrain him. But the director must go far beyond this bare framework of action to devise movement and groupings that will bring out the full dramatic content of the scene. The director is concerned not only with *what* happens but also with *how* an action is performed. How does the ghost make his appearance? How does Horatio's expression of fear differ from that of the soldiers? How does Horatio attempt to stay the ghost?

Since a play is dynamic, the attention of the audience must be shifted constantly from one character to another. Unlike the motion-picture director who can concentrate the camera on a specific person or object at will, eliminating from the screen all extraneous matter, the stage director must find other means to evoke and sustain a steady flow of attention. One of the most important means for this purpose is the use of movement. For example, the opening scene of *Hamlet* is a rather simple one since it is short, relatively uncomplicated, and requires only five characters; yet the movement and grouping need careful planning. The director's primary consideration probably will be to establish the audience's acceptance of the ghost. Most likely it will be kept remote from the audience, played in dim light and deep shadow, and perhaps elevated in position. The actor must be able to move freely and without noise so that entrances and exits create the illusion of an apparition in space. The attempts of Horatio and the soldiers to strike at the ghost must not destroy the feeling of majesty and dignity of the dead king. In the grouping of the three watchers, Horatio must be given the dominant position since the others look to him for counsel. Moreover, he carries the burden of the dialogue and has several long speeches, so that he must be placed in an advantageous position to project his lines to the audience.

The director uses blocking to create the appropriate emotional climate for the action. As we have seen with the opening of *Hamlet* the director may have to search the dialogue for clues. On the other hand, many modern dramatists provide very specific directions. As an example, Osborne's *Look Back in Anger*, which started the "new wave" of British drama, begins with a detailed description of a flat in a Victorian house followed by these stage directions:

(*At rise of curtain: Jimmy and Cliff are seated in the two armchairs R and L, respectively. All that we can see of either of them is two pairs of legs, sprawled way out beyond the newspapers which hide the rest of them from sight. They are both reading. Beside them, and between them, is a jungle of newspapers and weeklies. When we do eventually see them, we find that Jimmy is a tall, thin young man about twenty-five, wearing a very worn tweed jacket and flannels. Clouds of smoke fill the room from the pipe he is smoking. He is a disconcerting mixture of sincerity and cheerful malice, of tenderness and freebooting cruelty; restless, importunate, full of pride, a combination which alienates the sensitive and insensitive alike. Blistering honesty, or apparent honesty, like his, makes few friends. To many he may seem sensitive to the point of vulgarity. To others, he is simply a loudmouth. To be as vehement as he is, is to be almost non-committal. Cliff is the same age, short, dark, big-boned, wearing a pullover and gray, new, but very creased trousers. He is easy and relaxed, almost to lethargy, with the rather sad, natural intelligence of the self-taught. If Jimmy alienates love, Cliff seems to exact it—demonstrations of it, at least, even from the cautious. He is a soothing, natural counterpart to Jimmy. Standing L, below the food cupboard, is Alison. She is leaning over an ironing board. Beside her is a pile of clothes. Hers is the most elusive personality to catch in the uneasy polyphony of these three people. She is tuned in a different key, a key of well-bred malaise that is often drowned in the robust orchestration of the other two. Hanging over the grubby, but expensive, skirt she is wearing, is a cherry red shirt of Jimmy's, but she manages somehow to look quite elegant in it. She is roughly the same age as the men. Somehow, their combined physical oddity makes her beauty more striking than it really is. She is tall, slim, dark. The bones of her face are long and delicate. There is a surprising reservation about her eyes, which are so large and deep they should make equivocation impossible. The room is still, smoke-filled. The only sound is the occasional thud of Alison's iron on the board. It is one of those chilly spring evenings, all cloud and shadows. Presently, Jimmy throws his paper down.)*[2]

Few playwrights give such detailed assistance to the director and actor in establishing mood. Usually the directors, with the assistance of the actors, must rely on their own ingenuity to create atmosphere.

One of the functions of the director is to place the audience's attention where it belongs in order to show character relationships and to tell the story. Congenial people draw together; enemies keep their distance, until there is a showdown, when they are brought face to face in open conflict. The blocking of the action shows the moment-by-moment interaction of the characters in physical terms. Performers must act out the playwright's scenario. Orgon must hide under the table while his wife, Elmire, baits the impostor, Tartuffe. At the end of the play, Nora must walk out on her husband. In *Amadeus*, Mozart must die in his wife's arms. These obligatory actions must be staged by the director to convey the playwright's meaning—and the staging requires the director to decide precisely how and where they are to take place. A dominating figure may be given an elevated position, facing front, emphasized by a bright light, a striking costume, visual focus, and movement; a subservient character may grovel on the floor in dim light in a drab costume, turned away from the audience. The director composes a constantly changing pictorial arrangement in accordance with the emotional states of the characters. The director is concerned with all aspects of movement—extent, speed, direction, length, style, position of the mover, manner of moving, and the relationship of the performer's action to other characters, scenery, and important props.

The first scene in *Hamlet* suggests that Bernardo, Marcellus, and Horatio are closely allied; they are friendly men, sharing a common objective. The cold night and the atmosphere of foreboding draws them together.

The ghost enters and they recoil in fear from the dreadful sight. Horatio recovers himself, bravely assumes command, and advances on the ghost, pursuing him until he disappears in the darkness. Then the watchers join together again, trying to find answers to the questions that the ghost's appearance has raised. This opening scene with its homogeneity of grouping makes an interesting contrast to the one that follows, in which Claudius and Gertrude are holding court. They make overtures to soothe the troubled and alienated Hamlet, but he spurns their efforts and isolates himself from them and from those who seek royal favors.

Another function of the director, closely allied to the blocking of movement, is that of inventing and assisting the actor in creating "stage business," that is, the detailed actions of the individual characters, such as using a cane, opening a letter, pouring tea, smoking a pipe, and so on. Stage business is similar to movement in its uses. In general, it is the director's and actor's way of giving life and verisimilitude to the play. Again, like movement, business may be inherent in the playwright's script, such as Hedda burning Lövberg's manuscript, Juliet drinking the potion, and Captain Boyle cooking his "sassige." However, much of the business that is not essential to the plot, but is necessary for enriching the performance, is imposed on the presentation by the inventiveness of the director and actor. This is especially true in comedy, where one of the marks of the skilled performer is ingenuity in creating original business.

The following example records Stanislavski's preparation for a performance of *Othello* at the Moscow Art Theatre in 1929. This excerpt shows Stanislavski's interpretation of the first few lines of the scene in Act III, in which Othello, his suspicions aroused, comes to Desdemona's bedchamber. The first line is spoken by Emilia, Desdemona's nurse.

Emilia: Look, where he comes.

> (*In the last pause Emilia hears steps below. She rushes to the stairs, sees Othello coming and then hurries to Desdemona so as not to be compelled to call out. Her movement shows alarm and excitement.*)

Emilia thinks differently from Desdemona. She did not like Othello's behavior during the day. It does not seem the way to spend one's time during the first days of one's marriage.

Hearing that he is coming and thinking of last night's wonders, Desdemona wants to meet him suitably. She runs to the mirror to touch up her hair.

Emilia waits respectfully at the stairs to disappear at the first opportune moment and not to disturb the husband and wife.

Desdemona: I will not leave him now till Cassio Be call'd to him.

She speaks these word while smartening herself up. Her hair done, she runs to the banisters to meet Othello.

(*Enter Othello*)

Pause. Othello's entry should be delayed to underline its significance. He enters trying to seem cheerful and cordial at all costs and not make Desdemona see how he feels inside.

How is't with you, my lord?

She speaks, leaning over the banisters. Thus their meeting takes place as follows: flirting lightly, Desdemona at the banisters, looking at him questioningly and trying to find out how he is, while Othello stops on the stairs, having had not time to come up yet. Their heads are on a level.

Othello: Well, my good lady. O, hardness to dissemble! (*Aside*)

He tries to sound cheerful. Desdemona suddenly puts her arms around him over the banisters, leaving his head uncovered. His face is turned to the audience, she is showing the back of her head.

How do you, Desdemona?

Desdemona stops dead still in the embrace. He starts at it. The embrace is intolerable, but he restrains himself. One can see by his arms how he would like to, but he cannot make himself, put them around her. His face shows suffering. The embrace over, however, he will try again to seem, if not gay, at least calm.

By the way—it would be better were the actor to make it his task to be cheerful; should he not succeed in being sincere about it, even better: this failure will accentuate the artificiality which Othello requires at the moment.

Pause. This scene of meeting and embrace must be played right through to the end; do not be afraid of prolonging the pause.[3]

Many directors today do not work out the blocking and business in advance; these aspects are developed in the rehearsal process as a joint effort. The blocking may not be set until the final rehearsals, or it might even be changed after opening night. In any case, it is the director who ultimately must decide exactly what the audience will see.

THE DIRECTOR AS AN INTERPRETER

The most important function of the director is to interpret the play.

When such playwrights as Aeschylus, Shakespeare, and Molière produced their plays, they worked directly with the actors; the shape and meaning of the performance was undoubtedly determined by the dramatist. But when the playwright was not experienced in the practical aspects of the theater or not available, individual actors were left to their own devices. This usually meant that the leading actors were concerned only with being seen in a favorable light and considered their colleagues only when they affected their performance. Only a century ago it was customary for star actors to join a local stock company to play the lead in a Shakespearean play without a single rehearsal. Supporting actors adjusted their traditional business and movements to accommodate the leading actors, which pretty much meant leaving the downstage center area open and keeping clear of the stars so that they had ample room to gesture. With the development of the contemporary theater, the director took over the responsibility for integrating the production—and the most important task of deciding on the interpretation of the play.

This goes far beyond a mere acquaintance with the story line or even an intimate knowledge of the play's structure. Drama shows people in action—making decisions, reaching for objectives, attacking, withdrawing, resisting, yielding—and in the course of the action there is talk—argument, pleading, persuasion, discussion. All this action and talk is about something; that is, there is a residue of meaning beneath the surface—the subtext. Directors search the play for the essential core of meaning they choose to convey.

Norris Houghton in *Moscow Rehearsals,* a fascinating account of his visit to Russia in the 1930s, describes Meyerhold's approach to directing. He read the play through a single time, trying to grasp the meaning of the author, noting his first impression of the script. When he produced a play, Meyerhold often changed the text to suit the interpretation he gained from his first reading. Once he determined the motivating idea, he visualized a tentative plan for the scenery and lighting. He came to the first rehearsal without any notes or promptbook but apparently with his head swarming with ideas, which he released spontaneously as he worked with the actors on their interpretation of the lines and their invention of movement and business. A staff of eight to twelve assistants recorded in detail every aspect of each rehearsal, so that by the time the play reached production there was a vast accumulation of material about the play and its performance.

Houghton describes Meyerhold's interpretation of Chekhov's *The Proposal,* which he gave to the actors at the first rehearsal: "Two things are essential for a play's production, as I have often told you," Meyerhold began.

First, we must find the thought of the author: then we must reveal that thought in a theatrical form. This form I call a *jeu de theatre*, and around it I shall build the performance. Molière was a master of *jeu de theatre*: a central idea and the use of incidents, comments, mockery, jokes—anything to put it over. In this production I am going to use the technique of the traditional vaudeville as the *jeu*. Let me explain what it is to be. In these three plays of Chekhov I have found that there are thirty-eight times when characters either faint, say they are going to faint, turn pale, clutch their hearts, or call for a glass of water; so I am going to take this idea of fainting and use it as a sort of leit-motif for the performance. Everything will contribute to this *jeu*.[4]

After this introduction, Meyerhold read the script to the cast and dismissed the rehearsal.

The noted German director Reinhardt, famous for his theatricalism, like Meyerhold, dictated every detail of the production. However, he did not depend on the inspiration of the moment. Reinhardt's presentations were the result of months of careful preparation, during which time he developed a complete annotated account of the play. The purpose of his rehearsals was to teach his interpretation line by line to the actor. Raikin Ben-Ari, who worked with Reinhardt, describes his methods in this fashion:

Reinhardt comes to work with his secretaries and his assistant directors all laden with books. They are volumes with interpretations and explanations, with various data, drawings and symbols relating to the production—the evidence of colossal artistic and technical work which was done in preparing the manuscript for the stage. In these books the working out of every scene, every phrase, is recorded exactly and in detail—precisely when this or that player, when this or that group has to move to another part of the stage; how many musical intervals they have before they move; how much space they have to move in; the exact moment when the light is to go on. All this put together gives birth to the Reinhardt production. Reinhardt, himself a wonderful actor, influences his actors in such a way that they are compelled to do everything that he shows them. Reinhardt's personality dominates one to such an extent that one must copy all his intonations, all his emphases. These are wonderful in themselves, and of the deepest and most convincing sort, but they come to life through Reinhardt and not through the actor.[5]

Two American directors who owe a good deal to Stanislavski in their approach are Harold Clurman and Elia Kazan. Both worked with the Group Theater, one of the most influential production companies of the 30's that was associated with method acting.

Clurman and Kazan make a careful study of the script, searching for a basic interpretation, their interest centering on the psychological backgrounds of the characters. They make detailed notes to guide their thinking during rehearsals. These personal notes reveal the ways Clurman and Kazan worked.

Here are sample notes from Clurman made when he was preparing for a production of *Long Day's Journey Into Night* by Eugene O'Neill, considered one of the most important plays of the American theater.

The director made this breakdown of his "First Impressions":

Guilt—a keynote
Apprehension—suspense   The characters are
More guilt   sustained by no
Self-accusation   faith
The eyes of each character are on the other.
Foghorn—a desolate sound of aloneness.
Loneliness—everyone is alone with his or her own secret and guilt.
The spine of the play: to probe within oneself for the "lost something."[6]

Chekhov's plays are noted for their rich characterization of frustrated individuals. When Clurman prepared to direct *Uncle Vanya*, these are some of his notations on the motivating forces of the leading roles:

Vanya: "*Spine:* to find some way—some positive way—to live through the suffocation of his life."

Astrov: "*Spine:* to do what he has to—despite everything."

Yelena: "Spine: to obey and to justify her obedience—as the only thing she can do."[7]

George Bernard Shaw's plays are sometimes criticized as lacking characterization; they are simply the varied viewpoints of the same individual, the playwright. But when Clurman directed *Heartbreak House,* he found interesting views of the characters. In his preliminary analysis, Clurman says:

Everyone in the play wants somehow to escape his or her condition. All are dissatisfied with it . . . it's a crazy house, driving them crazy. All in a sense are "crazy," not true to themselves, not what they seem or pretend to be. So everyone is somehow odd, a *clown*—disguised, masked.

"In this house," says Hector, "everybody poses. The trick is to find the man under the pose."[8]

In a similar fashion, Elia Kazan, who also came from the Group Theater, analyzes the theme and characters for his famous production of *A Streetcar Named Desire.* Kazan describes the theme as "a bit of light" that "is snuffed out by the crude forces of violence, insensibility, and vulgarity . . ." He views the spine of the character Blanche as "to find *protection.*"[9]

Clurman and Kazan worked from a close analysis of the text, probing into the psychological roots of the action. Their approach is a standard one for many directors working with modern plays written in a realistic vein or centered on revealing complex character motivation.

When director Robert L. Benedetti was invited to direct *Hamlet* at the Oregon Shakespeare Festival, he made it an interesting project by keeping

The conflict between Blanche and Stanley was at the root of *A Streetcar Named Desire* and challenged performers and directors to realize its full expression. Jon Voight as Stanley; Faye Dunaway as Blanche.

(Ahmanson Theater. Directed by James Bridges.)

a production log which describes the step-by-step progress of a production in rehearsal. Benedetti describes the steps of preparation: "Research," "Understanding the action," "The shape of drama," "Understanding character," and "Forming a production concept." His approach is broader than that used by Clurman and Kazan, because he gives considerable thought to the social and political environment of the action and the structure of the play. Benedetti also works on "Focusing on a theme" of *Hamlet* which he summarizes in this way:

1. The complex relationship which binds sons and mothers (the so-called Oedipal theme);
2. The way in which unchecked evil breeds ever more evil (as we see in the poison which flows from Claudius, both literally and figuratively, until it infects the entire court);
3. The conflict between the absolute ethic of the feudal world and the relative ethic of the humanist world, which tears Hamlet between his sense of duty to the Ghost's demand for vengeance and his "university" sense that "two wrongs do not necessarily make a right";
4. The need for the balancing of Will and Understanding ("Thus conscience doth make cowards of us all.")[10]

Another interesting and informative approach to directing was Benedetti's "Mapping Relationships in *Hamlet*." Mapping relationship provides a visual means of understanding the network of character relationship. The main characters are placed at the center, and minor ones at the outside. Lines indicate the connections between characters. Here is Benedetti's chart on *Hamlet:*

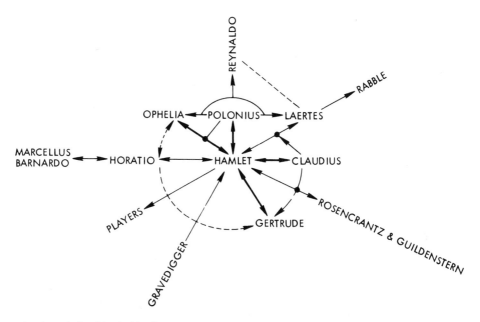

Mapping relationships in *Hamlet.*

Other directors have turned away from the Stanislavski type of production. Guthrie, for example, who left the British theater to establish outstanding companies, first in Ontario, Canada, and then in Minneapolis at the theater that bears his name, was often criticized for "fooling around with Shakespeare." He explained his motives in these terms:

> . . . I should like to discuss what to me is the most interesting part of the job, the blending of intuition with technique. If I may elaborate those terms, by intuition, I mean the expression of a creative idea that comes straight from the subconscious, that is not arrived at by a process of ratiocination at all. It is my experience that all the best ideas in art just arrive, and it is absolutely no good concentrating on them hoping for the best. The great thing is to relax and just trust that the Holy Ghost will arrive and the idea will appear.[11]

Guthrie's view of an intuitive approach to directing is shared by many of the foremost directors today, who regard the text as a launching pad for their flights of fancy. These directors view established plays as complex, many-layered, wide-open works whose meanings vary from generation to generation. They are not content to accept the classics as immutable works, set in cement. They regard a play as an invitation to explore new ground, a challenge to find a fresh impact. The theater, for them, is a medium for understanding and taming the world. A glance at several contemporary directors indicates the scope of their creative vision.

They feel free to cut lines or even whole scenes, to change the sequence of action, to eliminate characters, to use the same actor for multiple roles, or to play the single role with several actors. They do not hesitate to shift the locale from Illyria to India, from the moors of Scotland to a tropical island, from ancient Greece to Nazi Germany.

This freewheeling attitude is partly the result of the avant garde protest against the sanctity of the text and the tyranny of the word, and partly it stems from the desire to make dramatic production more theatrical, more intense, more exciting.

It is quite easy to understand how the English and European theaters would be open to experimentation since their classic repertoires have been played so frequently that they are worn out unless someone breathes new life into them. Moreover, state-supported resident companies, with whom

Peter Brook's production of Shakespeare's *The Tempest* at the Roundhouse Theater in London made use of a multi-layered scaffolding setting that recalled the bio-mechanical staging of Meyerhold.

the box-office appeal need not be the primary consideration, can afford to take risks that are impossible on the American commercial stage. In addition, we do not have a classic repertoire of native plays. It is also to be noted that when directors choose vehicles for innovative interpretations, they generally avoid contemporary, realistic plays in favor of those that give them a broader scope—Shakespeare, Carlo Goldoni, Gogol, Molière, and Beaumarchais. Among the contemporary writers, Chekhov is a favorite because of the challenge to the director to externalize the subtext. In any case, much of today's theater is a "director's theater."

Peter Brook

Brook, one of the most influential modern directors, worked for years at the Royal Shakespeare Company before establishing his own Center International de Creations Theatrales in Paris. Although schooled in the traditional theater, Brook is acutely aware of the drawbacks of what he calls the "deadly theater." He is responsive to and challenged by the new forces at work on the stage, and by word and example he points the way to the future. His approach is geared to answer his own question: "The whole problem of the theater today is just this: how can we make plays dense in experience?" As a partial answer, he seeks a theater that has the same freedom and "density" as that of Shakespeare:

> Shakespeare seems better in performance than anyone else because he gives us more, moment for moment, for our money. This is due to his genius, but also to his technique; the possibilities of free verse on an open stage enabled him to cut the inessential detail and the irrelevant realistic action. In their place he could cram sounds and ideas, thoughts and images which make each instant into a stunning mobile.[12]

In his controversial production of Weiss's *Marat/Sade,* Brook fashioned a "total theater" out of a welter of sensory stimuli, which resulted in the "density" he was talking about and which links him to Artaud. His production offered an emotional impact that recalls primitive ritual in its use of incantation, ensemble miming, discordant music, and the force of the acting, which seemed to be on several levels at once. The action of the play is set in a madhouse, where the inmates act out their fantasies, giving the director unique opportunities for theatricality and macabre business—such as the mass guillotining to the accompaniment of raucous sound effects, and the pouring of red paint down the drains as some of the inmates jump into a cavity so that only their heads show next to the guillotine.

Weiss uses the asylum metaphorically to suggest the state of the world outside. The play was influential not only for the devices of the "theater of cruelty" in production but also for the combination of social and political arguments with stunning theatricalism. Brook found much to admire in its theatrical richness.

> . . . It is above all in the jangle produced by the clash of styles. Everything is put in its place by its neighbor—the serious by the comic, the noble by the popular, the literary by the crude, the intellectual by the physical; the abstraction is vivified by the stage image, the violence illuminated by the cool flow of thought. The strands of meaning of the play pass to and fro through its structure and the result is a very complex form: as in Genet, it is a hall of mirrors or a corridor of echoes—and one must keep looking front and back all the time to reach the author's sense.[13]

Before the production of *Marat/Sade*, Brook and Charles Marowitz set up an acting workshop affiliated with the Royal Shakespeare Company. Its purpose was to experiment with new kinds of acting—not the Stanislavski approach, with its search for inner authenticity, but toward Artaud's vision of shaping the image of communication from a sequence of movements and gestures.

One of the most celebrated theater offerings in the last two decades was Brook's *A Midsummer Night's Dream* (1970) by the Royal Shakespeare Company. The production became a famous one, playing for a total of 535 performances in thirty-six cities in England, Europe, Japan, Australia, and the United States. Although some critical ink was spilled because of Brook's "impertinent travesty" of Shakespeare, in general audiences were enraptured by the magical world invoked. Clive Barnes, the drama critic of the *New York Times*, commented;

> It is a magnificent production, the most important work yet of the world's most imaginative and inventive director. . . . Brook has approached the play with a radiant innocence. He has treated the script as if it had just been written and sent to him through the mail. He has staged it with no reference to the past, no reverence for tradition. He has stripped the play down, asked exactly what it is about. . . . He sees the play for what it is—an allegory of sensual love, and magic playground of lost innocence and hidden fears.[14]

David Selbourne, an English dramatist, was invited to make an "eyewitness" account of Brook's production over the eight-week rehearsal period at Stratford in the summer of 1970. His observations, *The Making of A Midsummer Night's Dream*, are a fascinating account of the rehearsal process, from the initial meeting of the company to opening night. They reveal the immense sensitivities and skills of an imaginative director, leading the cast in an exploration of the play. At the outset, Brook decided to double the roles of the four leading actors; to use a white-walled set that looked like a squash court or exercise room; and to use circus techniques in the playing, such as swinging from trapezes and ladders, tumbling, juggling, walking on stilts, and spinning metal discs at the ends of rods.

Brook's *A Midsummer Night's Dream* is one of the most interesting and controversial productions since World War II. Brook stripped the play of non-essentials and created an entirely fresh and stimulating interpretation.

(Royal Shakespeare Company.)

Brook began his rehearsal period by inviting the seventeen performers from the Royal Shakespeare Company to investigate and experiment with a "wide range of acting styles" in order to achieve "different kinds of illusion and presentation, and to discover which illusion is the most effective." At the first rehearsal, "the mechanicals," the low comedy characters of a *Dream* began with exercises accompanied by a drum beat, and the actors were told to "search for the experienced physical gesture of the experienced craftsman." Brook explained to the cast that "your task is to bring *A Midsummer Night's Dream* to life through your rehearsal of 'Pyramus and Thisby.' " This is a comic interlude to be performed by the artisans before the court. The plot resembles the fatal love affair of Romeo and Juliet with its tragic deaths.

As a part of the process of exploring the play, Brook conducted discussions about ways of discovering hidden meanings in the text, of finding rhythms deeper than words. The nonverbal area of performance is one of special interest to Brook, and in working the cast he often used exercises based solely on sounds, rhythms, and fragments of lines and words. Sometimes the actors were directed to repeat words and lines freely, speaking simultaneously and adding improvised sounds like a jazz combo.

The cast also began experiments and exercises to acquire new skills—spinning discs, swinging on ropes, and walking on stilts. At one rehearsal, the actors were invited to "walk like water." They experimented with gliding, wading, making rippling movements, and simulating a waterfall. A favorite rehearsal technique was for the cast to sit on the floor in a tight circle, while they recited lines from their parts and improvised language, rhythms, and dances.

Brook's rehearsals were intense sessions of exploration and are evidence of his astounding creativity in finding ways to, as he says, "create the circumstances for performers to do interesting work"; "work can only be done with a sense of the magical word. Then the whole world opens." It is the process of opening this world that Brook sees as his particular function.

Selbourne's rehearsal log is valuable in showing how one of the most creative directors of this generation works with his actors. He is not the dictator who has planned everything in advance, but rather he considers himself the leader of an exploration party who can find his destination only with the help of his companions. "I can know what is right, but I cannot discover the experiences for you," he said.

What is surprising to the outsider in Selbourne's account is to learn of the doubts and anxieties that bedeviled the actors and Brook in putting the play together—especially in the first public performances before audiences of children and invited guests. It was not until a tryout performance at the Midland Art Center in Birmingham that the production finally reached the level Brook was striving for.

Selbourne's book provides remarkable insights into the ways that an outstanding director works with his cast, especially in investigating acting techniques rather than direct confrontation with the text.

Liviu Ciulei

Three Romanian-born directors came to this country and immediately gained a great deal of attention because of their extravagant and imaginative theatricalism.

In 1972, Liviu Ciulei was artistic director of the leading playhouse in Bucharest. He set out to "retheatricalize" the Romanian stage, which was bogged down in traditional, staid productions of creaky Russian-influenced drama. Ciulei was influenced by the inventive works of European directors, and he was also indebted to American avant garde experimenters, such as Chaikin, Richard Wilson, and the Bread and Puppet Theater.

Because of his bold productions of the classics in Bucharest, Ciulei alienated his audiences and the authorities, lost his job, and came to the United States. His first important directorial assignment was at the Guthrie, where he again aroused a good deal of controversy by his daring version of Shakespeare's *The Tempest*. Mike Steele, drama critic of the *Minneapolis Star*, describes the set, which gives us some clue to the fertility of Ciulei's imagination:

> The Guthrie's expansive thrust stage had become an island surrounded by a moat of gelatinous blood. Floating in the moat were some of the most familiar artifacts of western culture: a Mona Lisa, clocks without hands, a gleaming suit of arms. Amid the litter on shore was a Venetian horse head, ripped from San Marco, next to a stuffed chicken wrenched from a Robert Rauschenburg collage. Surprisingly beautiful scientific equipment from Galileo's time rested atop a legless piano propped up by stacks of huge books. Double sets of stairs rose to a makeshift Captain's bridge in what looked like a large, mirrored industrial warehouse. A faceless factory window to the rear opened onto constantly changing Magritte landscapes.[15]

Romanian born director Liviu Ciulei, for his first production as artistic director at the Guthrie Theater, staged an exciting version of *The Tempest* using magic as a metaphor, which Prospero uses in an effort to reform his enemies and to provide a suitor for his daughter, Miranda.

In this environment, Prospero appears, dressed in a casual cardigan sweater—an artist-philosopher wandering away from his native shores to an alien land, where he is forced to contend with the Caliban-like primal drives—a man searching for a better world.

Now the artistic director at the Guthrie, Ciulei tests his audiences to the limits, especially those who have a preference for American versions of the British theater. By his forthright theatricalism, Ciulei has made the Guthrie one of the most volatile and controversial theaters in the country.

Andrei Serban

A second Romanian director to achieve considerable prominence is Andrei Serban, who worked with Brook in Paris and then came to America, where he first directed three Greek plays at La Mama. Serban prefers to work with established texts. (Many contemporary playwrights consider him to be too idiosyncratic to deal with their plays.) Serban's association with Brook is evident in his concern with sounds in an attempt to catch the rhythms and emotions behind spoken language. When he directed the Greek plays, Serban experimented with his cast in finding the sounds and rhythms, not only in Greek and Elizabethan English, but in two esoteric African languages as well.

Serban's version of *The Cherry Orchard* at Lincoln Center was a departure from the usually sad, bittersweet interpretations of Chekhov. Instead, the director treated much of the action as broad farce, with such business as falls, chases, and adults playing at children's games. Serban also used choreographed groupings of peasants to create vivid images, creating a multilayered reading of the text. In his production of *Agamemnon*, again at Lincoln Center, Serban rejected the notion of treating the play in a traditional way. He set the action in a wire cage inside of a pit at the front of the auditorium, and his performers were more concerned with evoking feelings by strong aural and visual signs of the subtext rather than a faithful rendition of an ancient drama. Serban's interpretation of his role as a creative artist was not to show the audience a play but to involve the spectators in an experience that happened to be theatrical.

Innovators like Serban risk stepping on the toes of someone who resents anyone taking liberties with the original play. Brendan Gill, drama critic of the *New Yorker*, voices his complaint in reviewing Serban's production of *The Marriage of Figaro:*

> Andrei Serban is master of an art that Niccolo Tucci has defined as "the defoliation of the classics." One takes a play that has given satisfaction for decades, and perhaps for centuries, and mutilates it almost beyond recognition, for a purpose never openly expressed, but seemingly related to the notion that a classic will be refreshed from one generation to the next by being trashed—will gain a factitious illumination by dint of being pitched headlong into some scruffy, dehumanizing, contemporary gutter. . . . The latest Serban victim is

Pierre Augustin Beaumarchais, whose comedy "The Marriage of Figaro" has just opened at the Circle in the Square, adapted and translated by Richard Nelson. Beaumarchais has been in his grave for a hundred and eighty-six years, and is, one assumes, past being troubled by the idiotic disembowelments that have been practiced upon his play in the present production. Still, I would feel delinquent if I failed to raise a cry of protest on the author's behalf. A play that ever since it was first performed, in Paris in 1784, has proved itself capable of being performed successfully all over the world has been reduced by Serban and Nelson to the level of rubbishy farce, fit only for backward schoolchildren to guffaw at. Why? For that matter, why should Beaumarchais's dialogue, as lively and insouciant as the day it was written, be obliged to give way to visual gags employing roller skates, chain saws, skateboards, and other specimens of twentieth-century domestic debris?[16]

Lucian Pintilie

The third Romanian director is Lucian Pintilie, whose extraordinary productions have gained wide attention. In 1972 in Bucharest, Pintilie directed Gogol's comedy *The Inspector General.* He cut the second act and replaced it with material from Gogol's novel *Dead Souls.* He shifted the emphasis of the text from the pseudo-inspector to the mayor to sharpen the satirical bite toward political corruption. But the authorities found Pintilie's efforts "too contemporary"; officials worried about the Moscow reaction, and Pintilie was out of a job.

In Paris, he created another sensation with his direction of Carlo Gozzi's *Turandot,* having a cast of almost all dwarfs.

Pintilie's first notable directing assignment in America was Chekhov's *The Seagull* at the Guthrie in 1983. He revised the order of events by shifting the shooting sequence from the end of the play to the beginning. He pointedly rejected the Stanislavski style of playing Chekhov with subdued voices and gestures. Instead, Pintilie found ways to present metaphors in physical, overt terms. When characters became angry or frustrated, they flung books at one another or threw themselves on the floor.

Another startling Pintilie production was Molière's *Tartuffe,* first at the Guthrie and then at the Arena Stage in Washington, D.C. The director chose to set the play in a white tiled room that suggested an asylum or a laboratory rather than a home. The production was full of sight gags, such as spilling a basket of red apples onto the white floor. Orgon's treasures were kept in a vault beneath the floor so that entrances to this area were highly theatricalized.

Pintilie went to great lengths to stage the arrival of the King's officer at the end of the play. Molière's text simply indicates that the officer makes an entrance through the door, presents the King's edict that revokes Tartuffe's claim to Orgon's estate, and takes the impostor off to prison. In Pintilie's Guthrie Theater version, the officer arrived by smashing through a brick wall in a Dusenburg.

Director Lucian Pintilie staged highly theatricalized versions of Tartuffe at the Guthrie and Arena Theaters. In the Minneapolis version, the King's messenger, who rescues the gullible Orgon from the clutches of Tartuffe, makes a spectacular entrance by driving a Dusenberg through the tiled wall. In the Arena version, he entered in a space ship.

In the Arena production, the Messenger and his Mafialike thugs descended from the grid in a whirling helicopter. Tartuffe is captured in a tumultuous scene in which the tiled floor of the stage splits asunder, leaving a great yawning, smoking hole. The production is replete with Pintilie's inventions: pratfalls, sexual innuendo, and physical comedy, played with enormous energy. The effect was an exuberant and stimulating theatrical experience, but at the expense of the basic values of Molière's play—such as credible characters and their relationships and much of the original comic spirit.

Pintilie's offbeat interpretations of traditional plays arrive only after long and painstaking study of the text. He says,

> . . . Even when I express an ostensibly radically different point of view about a play, I believe I remain faithful to it. The worst thing is to kneel before a lot of sacrosanct prejudices. It is best when the obsessions of a modern artist collide with a great work. The miracle of great works of art is that they can be looked at in new ways every seven years and remain strong and new and surprising.[17]

Ariane Mnouchkine

Ariane Mnouchkine's Théâtre du Soleil in France has gained an outstanding reputation for her productions. The company began in 1964 as a workers' collective and attracted attention with compelling performances of Maxim Gorki's *The Courageous One* and Arnold Wesker's *The Kitchen*. But the ensemble wanted to dramatize historical events from a popular point of view

Ariane Mnouchkine of the Théâtre du Soleil has earned a reputation for forthright theatricalism as in this production of *1789* in a theater that was formerly a cartridge factory. The company is noted for its excellent and imaginative ensemble performance.

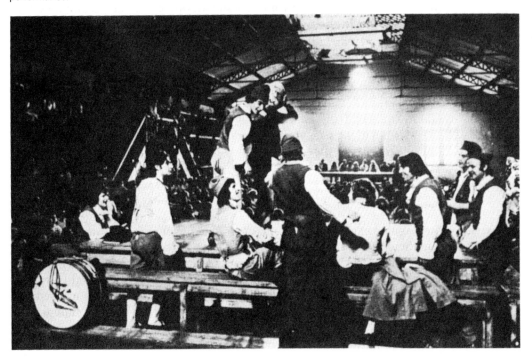

to show how "people might imagine, feel, live, and suffer during the Revolution." Its goal was achieved through a striking performance of *1789,* a collective creation, growing out of months of workshops and rehearsals. The actors' performances were improvised to the extent that no one knew precisely what anyone would do or say, but they worked from a general outline that encouraged individual adaptation. As part of its training, the Théâtre du Soleil visited small villages, where it experimented freely with material before unsophisticated audiences. Mnouchkine's company achieved a highly theatrical style of acting that in *1789* was consciously coarse and free from psychological nuances.

Mnouchkine's ensemble was invited to perform at the Olympic Arts Festival in Los Angeles in the summer of 1984. It made two remarkable contributions to the festival with performances of *Richard II* and *Twelfth Night.* They were played in a large, bare television studio in Hollywood, on a fourteen-meter-square platform before temporary bleachers.

The director chose to place the action of *Twelfth Night* in an illusory India, suggested by sumptuous costumes, properties, and decorative backdrops in vivid colors, and with harem pants, veils, masks, turbans, and huge parasols. Guy-Claude Francous' set design conveyed the feeling of a Japanese Noh stage because it was covered with hemp and marked off by seven thick black lines like a tatami mat. Four horizontal entrance ramps led to decorative paneled pavilions with oversized umbrellas. The exotic visual atmosphere was enhanced by music from an orchestra that accompanied the action with strange and interesting sounds from flutes, whistles, drums, gongs, and stringed instruments.

The acting style was likewise extremely stylized, sometimes suggesting commedia dell'arte, sometimes marionettes, and sometimes the dance movements of India. For example, Sir Toby Belch and Maria walked with a mincing, tipsy gait as they precariously avoided the black stripes or tried (vainly) to keep from falling off the edge of the stage.

Mnouchkine's *Twelfth Night* was a far cry from the Elizabethan stage, but Shakespeare's play served as a framework for a charming and exceptional theatrical experience.

Peter Stein

Stein is another ingenious director, who has brought to the stage at the Hallenschen Schaubühne in West Berlin extraordinary productions of well-known plays. Perhaps his most famous offering was Ibsen's *Peer Gynt.* Stein's interpretation of the play was that human beings are subverted from realizing their potential by overreaching themselves. The director insisted on a long rehearsal period so that the company would have ample time for discussions of Ibsen's life, literature, and brand of realism. The ensemble investigated the roots of ninteenth-century bourgeoisie life through a study of the arts and cultural milieu of the period. Ibsen's text was freely translated and interpreted to emphasize the theme of Peer's inability to find fulfillment.

Instead of producing *Peer Gynt* in a theater, Stein elected to stage it in a large exhibition hall at the fairgrounds. Spectators sat in rows of seats at the side of a long rectangular playing area covered with a canvas and shaped so that there was a hill at one end and a depression at the other. During the performance, which lasted nearly seven hours over two consecutive evenings, props and set pieces were brought in for the eight phases of Peer's career. The leading role was divided among six actors, who played variations of a basic type—a bourgeois dreamer.

Stein's production rejected illusionary scenery and acting, avoided psychological involvement, focused on ideas rather than entertainment, and created excitement by its frank and imaginative theatricalism in a space outside the conventional playhouse. In this instance, because the Schaubühne was concerned with its social message as a people's theater, Stein's interpretation was a group effort.

Bertolt Brecht

When playwrights direct their own productions, they are not concerned with a new reading of their texts, but rather, with finding the most telling ways to project their words and actions to the audience.

Brecht, in directing his own plays at the Berliner Ensemble, was dedicated to finding a *new interpretation of the theater*. As we have seen, Brecht's epic theater was an effort to find a new way of writing, acting, and staging plays.

When Brecht worked with actors on the production of his own plays, he constantly struggled against the old tendencies of empathic identification as he tried to establish the alienation effect. His purpose was to induce the spectators to evaluate critically the onstage events and to relate them to the social and economic conditions of the real world, so that they might work for change. One of his favorite ways of explaining to his casts the quality of playing he wanted was to cite the example of a witness describing a traffic accident. The acting was "not to cast a spell over anyone, but to repeat something which had already occurred"; that is, "the incident *has* taken place, the repetition is taking place."

In the notes that he prepared for the production of *Mother Courage*, Brecht described the business in detail for each of the characters involved. In Kattrin's drumming scene he provided a complete scenario of action for the soldiers, peasants, and Kattrin, including the kind of actions and the attitudes of the participants.

Kattrin's action must "steer free of heroic cliché," Brecht said, and the scene must avoid "wild excitement." To counteract the temptation toward emotional involvement, he suggested that the soldiers should appear apathetic, Kattrin's drumming should be interrupted, and the peasants' dialogue should be spoken as though secondhand. For example, one peasant says, "The watchman will give us warning." Brecht was attempting to avoid the immediate impression of "unique, actual horror" to give the effect of repeated misfortune: "Fear must show through the ceremony in this scene." But despite these efforts to achieve objectivity, Brecht had to admit, "Spectators may identify themselves with Dumb Kattrin in this scene; they may project their personality into this creature; and may happily feel that such forces are present in them, too."

At the end of the play, when Mother Courage, completely alone in an unfriendly universe, drags her wagon into the gathering darkness, Brecht intended the audience to see her as an object lesson of one whose life and energies have been wasted in the traffic of war, of which she is a willing part. But the solitary image was so loaded that at the premiere in Zurich, it created a strong empathic response of compassion. Brecht is reported to have rewritten the part in an effort to make Courage less sympathetic.

Despite the fact that he was never able to reconcile completely his theories with the effects his plays created in the theater, Brecht gave the modern director a new and provocative way of using the actors and the stage.

Others in the New Theater

Sam Shepard, one of the most imaginative of the contemporary American playwrights, worked with an ensemble in San Francisco on *INACOMA*, a play depicting the struggle for survival of a young woman who has been seriously injured in an accident. Shepard, in a program note, describes his open approach in shaping the production:

> I've tried to make use of every influence that has moved me. From vaudeville, circuses, the living theater, the open theater, and the whole world of jazz music, trance dances, faith healing ceremonies, musical comedy, Greek tragedy, medicine show, etc. Our approach has been to include as much information as possible, coming from the material on every level we could find. To try to remain open to any new possibilities and at the same time discard what was unnecessary.[18]

Shepard's views echo the experimental theater's purpose of investigating the outer reaches of an expanding universe, searching for the new and unexpected beyond the prosaic formulas of "tasteless parlor drama."

Grotowski's creative work as director of the Polish Laboratory Theater was unique, since its orientation was spiritual rather than theatrical, and he served not merely as a stage director but also as a secular priest, providing a means of individual self-development directed toward "a search for the truth about himself and his mission in life." His actors underwent a demanding discipline and a rigorous program of training, which made their performances before small, selected audiences an impressive exploration of the uses of theater. The heavy demands on the actor and the limited availability of Grotowski's theater to the public restricted his influence, and few will attain his degree of commitment, but he has given us an authentic example of the dramatic potential of ritual and myth.

Directors in the new theater work with a free hand. In the past, the director aimed at bringing the text to life by giving the lines a careful reading; searching the text for meaning; selecting and training the actors for accurate, credible characterization; and using the technical resources of production to present a dramatic work as a cohesive whole.

The new director is more interested in the performance than in the play; the text has no validity of its own. Unity and coherence give way to the moment-by-moment sporadic sensations that come partially from the actors and partially from sound, light, scenery, and costume. The emphasis is on images, on creating a dynamic montage, often with multiple focus and simultaneous action.

The vehicle for performance may be a truncated or fragmented classic. Stephen Willems eliminated all but the love story of *A Midsummer Night's Dream,* and of the mechanicals, only Bottom was retained. Michael Grüber cut *Faust I* to one hour and a half and used four actors instead of fifty. At the Berkeley Shakespeare Festival, the director reduced the cast from forty odd roles to eleven and changed the witches to street punks, who joined Macduff and Banquo in disposing of Macbeth at the end of the play.

One of the striking features of many contemporary directors is the manner in which they work with actors. In addition to rehearsals of the script, workshops that include exercises, improvisations, and experiments with sound, movement, and style are a part of the preparation process. Sometimes the workshops contribute materially to the play and its interpretation, as in the case of Chaikin's Open Theater production of *Vietnam* and Mnouchkine's *1789.*

Some critics resent the authority that directors now wield over the production of a play, but the temper of our times suggests that the strong-minded individual with original ideas will continue to have a free hand. Innovations of recent years, particularly those in which directors emphasize performance over fidelity to the text, point toward even more emphasis on theatricalism—ritual, total theater, environmental theater, epic theater, open theater, and even antitheater. Although the traditionalist may be wary of some of the chances the daring director takes, it is from the inspiration of such leaders that much of the most exciting theater has come.

PLAYS TO READ AND SEE

F = Film available; V = Videotape available.

F	V	Osborne, *Look Back in Anger*
F		Weiss, *Marat/Sade*
F		McCullers, *Member of the Wedding*
F	V	Shakespeare, *A Midsummer Night's Dream*
F	V	Williams, *A Streetcar Named Desire*

FILMS AND VIDEOTAPES ON DIRECTING AVAILABLE

F	V	Directing a Film: Ionesco's *The New Tenant*
F	V	*Drama: play, performance and perception* (series)
F	V	*Houseman Directs Lear*
F	V	*Ingmar Bergman*

BIBLIOGRAPHY

BENEDETTI, ROBERT L. *The Director at Work.* Englewood Cliffs, N.J.: Prentice-Hall, Inc., 1985. (This is a log of *Hamlet,* directed by Benedetti at Oregon Shakespeare Festival.)

BRAUN, EDWARD. *The Director and the Stage: From Naturalism to Grotowski.* New York: Holmes and Meier, 1982.

COLE, TOBY and H. K. CHINOY, eds. *Directors on Directing.* Indianapolis: The Bobbs-Merrill Co., Inc., 1964.

FERGUSSON, FRANCES. *The Idea of Theater.* Princeton, N.J.: Princeton University Press, 1949.

GUTHRIE, TYRONE. *In Various Directions.* New York: Macmillan, Inc., 1965.

HOUGHTON, NORRIS. *Moscow Rehearsals.* New York: Harcourt Brace Jovanovich, Inc., 1936.

———. *Return Engagement.* New York: Holt, Rinehart and Winston, 1962.

JACOBS, SUSAN. *On Stage: The Making of a Broadway Play.* New York: Alfred A. Knopf, Inc., 1972.

KOTT, JAN. *Theater Notebook.* New York: Doubleday & Co., Inc., 1968.

MORRISON, HUGH. *Directing in the Theater.* New York: Theater Arts Books, 1973.

SAYLER, OLIVER M. *Max Reinhardt and His Theater.* New York: Brentano's, 1924.

SELBOURNE, DAVID. *The Making of* A Midsummer Night's Dream. London: Methuen, 1982.

STANISLAVSKI, CONSTANTIN. *My Life in Art.* New York: Theater Arts Books, 1924.

TAIROV, ALEXANDER. *Notes of a Director.* Coral Gables, Fla.: University of Miami Press, 1969.

WILLS, J. ROBERT, ed. *The Director in a Changing Theater.* Palo Alto, Calif.: Mayfield, 1976.

NOTES

1. Tyrone Guthrie, *In Various Directions* (New York: Macmillan, Inc., 1965).

2. John Osborne, *Look Back in Anger* (Chicago: The Dramatic Publishing Company, 1959).

3. Konstantin Sergeevich Alekseev, *Stanislavski Produces Othello,* trans. Helen Nowak (London: Bles, 1948).

    4. Norris Houghton, *Moscow Rehearsals* (New York: Harcourt Brace Jovanovich, Inc., 1936).

    5. R. Ben-Ari, "Four Directors and the Actor," *Theater Workshop,* January–March 1937.

    6. Harold Clurman, *On Directing,* (New York: The Macmillan Co., 1972) p. 254.

    7. Clurman, *On Directing,* p. 261–2.

    8. Clurman, *On Directing,* p. 230.

    9. Toby Cole and Helen Krich Chinoy, *Directing the Play* (New York: Macmillan Co., 1972).

    10. Robert L. Benedetti, *The Director at Work* (Prentice-Hall, Englewood Cliffs, N.J., 1985.)

    11. Tyrone Guthrie, "An Audience of One," in Toby Cole and Helen Krich Chinoy, eds., *Directors on Directing* (Indianapolis: The Bobbs-Merrill Co., Inc., 1964).

    12. Peter Brook, Introduction to Peter Weiss's *Marat/Sade* (New York: Atheneum Publishers, 1965).

    13. Brook, Weiss's *Marat/Sade.*

    14. Clive Barnes, *The New York Times,* August 28, 1970, 15:1.

    15. Mike Steele, *Minneapolis Star,* 1981.

    16. Brendan Gill, *The New Yorker,* October 28, 1985.

    17. Lucian Pintilie, quoted in Mike Steele's "TK", *American Theater,* July–August, 1985.

    18. Sam Shepard, program note, *INACOMA,* 1977.

9

The Actor

THE ACTOR'S CONTRIBUTION

The life force of the theater is the actor's living presence before an audience. Barnes, when drama critic of the *New York Times,* made this point in his review of George C. Scott in *Death of a Salesman:*

> There is nothing on earth like the magic of great acting. An actor takes off— his words fly up, image and reality become one, the actor creates a patch of humanity on the quietly empty stage, a rustle runs through the theater, a breeze of awareness, a special alertness. One of the world's few renewing miracles flickers into life. Great acting. The kind you can never forget. The kind you tell your grandchildren about. The kind that leaves you in a state of grace, enables you to jump beyond yourself, to see something that perhaps even the playwright himself only dimly perceived.[1]

Our technically adept age may find ways to record actors' voices and movement on film or on tape and ship their likenesses from here to there in a can or cassette, and their images may be projected in enormous colored enlargements on wide screens in immense drive-in lots, or their range of action may be reduced to a twenty-one-inch frame in our living rooms, but genuine theater begins and ends with the actors' living presence. Their creations and interpretations give the theater its special quality. More than the stage settings or the director's skill in organization, sometimes more than the drama itself, the actors give to the theater its reason for existence. It is their histrionic sensibility that induces the audience to live imaginatively in the characters and drama before them. It is the actors who ignite the spark and fan the flame that warms and illuminates the audience.

As we have seen earlier, the impulse to imitate, to impersonate, to act is a very old one in the race and a very early one in our own lives. Because of the peculiarly subjective and intimate nature of acting, the creative processes of the actor are difficult to define and describe. Since acting is a private creation, actors may work through intuition and the unconscious, by means which they do not fully comprehend themselves. Actors, like other artists, vary widely in their methods of approach. Some actors insist that they must have complete emotional identification with the characters they are playing; others are equally adamant that acting is a matter of technique. Interestingly enough, exponents of both extremes can cite examples of brilliant actors in defense of their position.

Not only do approaches to roles vary with individuals, but also actors are prisoners of their times, and especially of the kind of drama in which they appear. Although a modern actor like Sir Laurence Olivier may play in many styles of drama, from Sophocles to Shakespeare to Wilde, an Elizabethan actor like Richard Burbage was obliged to play according to the style of his own period. And no one approach serves all actors in all styles. An Athenian actor in the fifth century B.C. might have been called on to play several roles in three different plays in a single day, speaking, dancing, and singing before an outdoor audience of thousands. Compare the Greek actor's task with that of a performer in Japanese Noh drama, who plays in an intimate theater, seating several hundred people at the most. He performs in an elaborate costume; speaking the archaic language of the old aristocracy; chanting, singing, and dancing within a six-meter-square stage, his every sound and gesture based on tradition; striving to give a performance worthy of his ancestors who played the same role six or seven generations before him.

Consider the difference in demands on contemporary performers when they move from the stage to the screen. In a hit show on Broadway, their chief problem may be how to keep their performances as spontaneous and credible on the three hundredth night as on the first. The same actors working in motion pictures may satisfy the director if they can give a series of satisfactory performances of a few seconds' duration in two to six takes over a period of two weeks. There is no one approach that can be applied to all acting roles, from Oedipus to Willy Loman, Scapin to Salieri, Lady Macbeth to Blanche, Medea to Liza Doolittle, Mrs. Malaprop to Lady Bracknell. There is no one acting style suitable for the naturalism of Gorki, the stylized Kabuki drama of Japan, the neoclassicism of Racine, the romantic comedy of Shakespeare, the sophisticated comedy of Congreve, the expressionism of Strindberg, the epic parables of Brecht, the open theater of Chaikin, the sensual, frenetic style of a rock musical, or the impersonal puppets who become part of the scenery in Wilson's visual displays. The actors' performances vary with the conditions under which they work; and although no rigid formula can be applied, especially for the new theater that has evolved since World War II, certain traditional elements pertain. We will begin with conventional factors and deal with the new ones later.

REQUISITES OF THE ACTOR

The first requisite concerns the actor's physical equipment. With the wide variety of roles available in drama, actors may be almost any size and shape; but whatever their physical endowments, they must control their bodies as precisely as violinists control their fingers and instruments. Actors should move and gesture easily and in a variety of ways to fit the demands of different kinds of characters and plays. They should be as comfortable playing on a bare stage picked out in a cone of light as they are in a modern living room with chairs, cocktails, and cigarettes. They must have a feeling for movement that is expressive and meaningful, not only in their overt gestures, but also in a constant stream of subtle, nearly hidden images that reveal character and motivation to the audience. Their movements must not

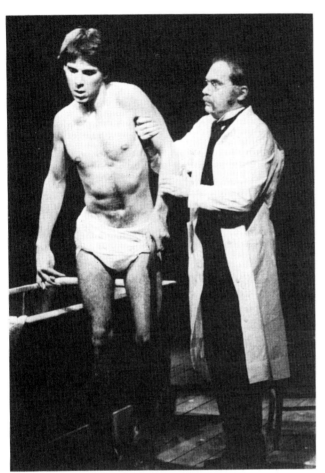

In Bernard Pomerance's *The Elephant Man,* enormous physical demands are placed upon the actor who must convey the impression of a grotesquely deformed character without the use of makeup. Phillip Anglim as John Merrick; Kevin Conway as Dr. Frederick Treves.

be mere posturing: The first law of stage deportment is that every movement should have a meaning and purpose. Actors should be imaginative in the invention of business by which they enrich the characters, indicate the mood, create atmosphere, or reveal emotions. They should be able to handle their props and costumes not only in authentic ways but also in reinforcement of the meaning of their lines and characters. Stanislavski, who is generally thought of in terms of character motivation, insisted that the actors train their bodies so that they would be supple and expressive instruments. In a class session with his students, he demonstrated his skill with a fan to convince them of the need for control over the "language of objects." Nikolai Gorchakov, a visiting director in Moscow, describes Stanislavski's demonstration:

Then he showed us how one should talk with a fan. The fan quivered in his hand like the wings of a wounded bird, revealing his excitement. Stanislavski's figure, face, and half-closed eyes were seemingly calm. Only the movement of his hand and a slight trembling of the closed fan showed his inner excitement. Then the fan opened with a sharp impulsive movement, flying up and hiding his face for an instant, and just as suddenly it lowered and closed. We understood that in this brief moment the face hidden by the fan had time to give vent to feeling and time for a deep sigh or a short laugh. And it was possible that the hand lightly brushed away a tear with the aid of the fan. Then the fan, with scarcely a noticeable movement, ordered someone supposedly nearby to come closer and sit next to him. The fan stopped trembling. It opened calmly and began to sway softly in his hand as though listening attentively to the person sitting next to him. Then the fan smiled and even laughed. "We swore to him later that that's exactly what we heard." The fan closed again for a second and lightly struck the hand of the person next to him as though saying, "Oh, you are mean!"—and then suddenly covered the blushing face. Now his eyes entered the conversation. First they sparkled under the lace-edged fan; then they looked over the fan and half hid behind it.[2]

A second requisite of the actor is clear and flexible speech. The performer's voice should be free from tension, monotony, and unpleasantness, and it should carry easily to all parts of the theater. Actors must be able to read a range of materials, from the verses of Shakespeare and Sophocles to the terse colloquialism of Pinter. They must communicate the full intellectual and emotional content of each line as it relates to their characters and the play as a whole. They must sustain long narrative passages and soliloquies or engage in the rapid repartee of smart comedy with precise timing that maintains the pace without stepping on laughs. They must be part of an ensemble, reading their lines in context with other players in the appropriate action and reaction.

The importance of disciplined control of the voice and speech is evidenced by Ekkehard Schall, the leading actor of the Berliner Ensemble and the foremost Brechtian actor in the world. He spends four to five hours on vocal exercises and script work every day, even when he performs a full play in the evening.

The speaking skill of an excellent performer is apparent from critic Eliot Norton's description of Zoe Caldwell's performance as Cleopatra at the Ontario Stratford Festival production of Shakespeare's *Antony and Cleopatra*.

Miss Caldwell has an astonishing voice. She can purr like a lioness, hiss like an adder or, when anger shakes her Cleopatra, bellow out words with the power of a boat whistle. . . . She did many remarkable things. Her Cleopatra, for example, spoke most of the time quite rapidly, which is fair and reasonable, for the woman's mind works rapidly and her eloquence is unlimited. Yet she was at all times easily and clearly audible. Whether brooding or bellowing, her Cleopatra made her points with exquisite clarity and with the kind of music which is present in the verse.[3]

In *Children of a Lesser God,* the actors must learn to communicate by sign language as well as to convey the emotional content by the usual vocabulary of the theater.
(Asolo State Theater, Florida. Directed by Lucy Martin.)

Finally, the actor must possess a quality difficult to define, which the great French actor François-Joseph Talma referred to as an "excess of sensibility." He meant by this a vivid imagination and an acute awareness, which is indicated by the actor's insight into the role, an understanding of what the play and the character are all about, and in performance, a keen sense of the effect on the audience and the other members of the cast. One of the deadliest defects of actors is the inability to assess the effect of their performance, especially in comedy; in striving too hard to "milk" laughs, insensitive actors unconsciously destroy themselves. The actors' sensibility enables them to perceive the response they are receiving and to communicate the playwright's full meaning in performances that are highly personal and unique, yet fitting and compelling.

Beyond these attributes, the actor must have the ability to adapt to a variety of styles and playing conditions. In a repertory company, it is com-

Zoë Caldwell and Hume Cronyn are two of the most versatile and accomplished performers today. From Moliere's *The Miser.*

(Guthrie Theater. Directed by Douglas Campbell.)

mon for the performer to appear in a leading role one night and a supporting role the next, and to move freely from Greek drama to Elizabethan to Restoration to modern—each requiring a special style of playing. In today's theater, the performers must be open to learning because the playwright may have them perform on trapezes, roller skates, skateboards, motorcycles, swings, and other gymnastic equipment. They may have to dance in a variety of ways, tumble, and play instruments.

In addition, many people would suggest that the actor needs a spark, a magnetism, a personality that projects out to the audience and wins it. Many of our popular stars, especially in television and motion pictures, have this spark as their basic talent.

EVOLUTION OF MODERN ACTING

Until modern times, actors learned their trade mostly by observation and experience. In the past, stage-struck youths watched the stars in action, became apprentices, and worked their way up from spear carriers or servants to speaking parts, assimilating what they could by contact with the veterans. The beginner might be taken under the wing of an experienced actor or a sympathetic manager and be given pointers about acting. But in general, newcomers were left pretty much to their own inspiration, imagination, and powers of observation. A number of published works appeared from time to time on elocution, oratory, rhetoric, and stage deportment, chiefly emphasizing oral interpretation and the use of the voice; and there were occasional attempts to define characteristic emotional states and to relate them to specific postures, gestures, vocal qualities, and facial expressions, but these were entirely subjective and mechanical. The great teacher was the theater itself, where through trial and error, actors groped for interpretation and perfected their techniques. Those who struck the public's fancy at their first attempt in the major theatrical centers were fortunate. Others, like Molière and Mrs. Siddons, two of the greatest performers of all time, met with initial failure and had to spend years in the outlying provincial theaters, mastering their craft before making triumphant returns to Paris and London.

In the latter half of the nineteenth century, as a part of the scientific revolution, in which nearly everything was examined, classified, and catalogued, the Frenchman François Delsarte devised an elaborate system of acting based on purely mechanical techniques. He found in each person a trinity, consisting of the torso, the "vital zone"; the head, the "intellectual zone"; and the face, the "moral zone." Each zone and every part of the mechanisms were in turn divided into trinities, each producing its own specific expression. The student of Delsarte learned to act by memorizing and utilizing the appropriate gestures, vocal qualities, and inflections.

This artificial and external school of acting was opposed by another approach, based on the inner life of the character being portrayed. In part, this new method resulted from the contemporary interest in psychology; but the strongest impulse came from the new drama of realism and naturalism, in which playwrights took their cues from the scientist, attempting to record with strict fidelity the observed facts of human existence, even though they showed an individual in commonplace or sordid surroundings. Because the new science taught that a person was conditioned by environment, naturalistic playwrights depicted the physical surroundings in accurate detail as a causal force on their characters' motivation and behavior.

In 1877, Henri Becque, responding to the new influence, wrote a naturalistic play called *The Vultures,* a somber study of what happens to domestic life when the forces of the economic jungle prey on helpless and unsuspecting victims. In 1882, the Comédie Française was persuaded to give the play a production; but unfortunately it was played in the traditional style of acting, in which the performers declaimed with exaggerated gestures and inflections, rising from their chairs for their speeches and directing much of their dialogue to the audience, thus destroying the atmosphere of Becque's play. It was not until 1887, when Antoine gave *The Vultures* a sympathetic and effective performance at the Théâtre Libre, that the full impact of the drama was realized. Antoine recognized the need for a new way of acting in the new plays, and he demonstrated his ideas in performances in which he and his casts attempted to become completely absorbed in their roles, using such unconventional stage behavior as turning their backs on the audiences and speaking in a conversational manner with the fragmentary gestures of real life.

Antoine's ideas took root, and a revolution occurred in the theater, driving out the old inflated bombastic acting with its pyrotechnic displays of the stars. The ground was ready for the modern style of acting, but it was not a one-sided victory. Although the old exhibitionist school of acting had its faults in its wallowing emotionalism, it was also true that traditional actors could make verse sing, and they knew how to win and hold an audience in the palm of their hands. The virtue that Antoine brought to modern acting

The acting style in the 19th century was often florid and bombastic, especially in Shakespeare and melodrama. Edwin Forrest, one of our first stars, stirred the audience by his vigorous and electrifying playing. His favorite role was Macbeth.

With the coming of realism in the plays of Ibsen and Chekhov, actors were compelled to develop a more natural style in keeping with the commonplace dialogue and environment. It was Stanislavski who led the way in developing credible characterization. Chekhov's *Three Sisters* at the American Conservatory Theater, San Francisco.

was a style that was simple, restrained, and uncluttered with mannerisms and posturing. But in relinquishing the old traditions, many contemporary actors lost much of their unique flair and flavor. John Mason Brown aptly referred to the new style as the "transom school of acting," in which there are "teacup comedians and gas-jet tragedians."

The playwrights who wrote in a naturalistic or realistic manner introduced a new type of character to the audience. The protagonists were no longer picaresque heroes, romantic adventurers, or highbrow ladies and gentlemen in evening clothes. They might be middle- or lower-class protagonists—often the victims of their environments or their passions. Many of these characters were psychologically complex because the primary purpose of the new dramatists might be the revelation of conflicting desires that resulted in aberrant conduct. Strindberg indicates the complex motivation of his protagonist in *Miss Julie:*

> And what will offend simple brains is that my action cannot be traced back to a single motive, that the viewpoint is not always the same. An event in real life—and this discovery is quite recent—springs generally from a whole series of more or less deep-lying motives, but of these the spectator chooses as a rule the one his reason can master most easily. A suicide is committed. Bad business, says the merchant. Unrequited love, say the ladies. Sickness, says the invalid. Crushed hopes, say the shipwrecked. Now it may be that the motive lay in all or none of these directions.[4]

THE STANISLAVSKI METHOD OF ACTING

With the demands of this new kind of characterization, it was inevitable, as Antoine insisted, that new methods of acting should be devised. The most famous and most important innovator was Stanislavski, who not only wrote at length about his method of acting but also demonstrated his ideas through his teaching, his directing, and his own acting. The great Russian actor-director worked out his sytem at the Moscow Art Theater, of which he was one of the founders. As the result of years of experience in the theater, and of his self-analysis and the observation of others, he formulated his method of acting during the first decade of the twentieth century. His ideas were made known in his three books, *My Life in Art, An Actor Prepares,* and *Building the Character,* and through his work with his students and actors, a number of whom became teachers, spreading his gospel throughout the theatrical world.

The Stanislavski "method" is not an eccentric style of acting for psyched-up performers who are off on an emotional jag. It is not based on sheer raw feeling without consideration of the techniques and skills of movement and speech. These common misconceptions about the method are the result of the notoriety of some of the actors who have misunderstood, misapplied, or distorted the basic tenets that Stanislavski formulated.

Stanislavski's purpose was to devise an objective, regularized technique by which the actors could gain control of their bodies and emotions for the appropriate interpretation of the characters and the play. Instead of depending on haphazard inspiration, Stanislavski searched for a system with basic principles by which the actors could discipline their art. Much of his emphasis was in *preparing to act* by means of a conscious technique for causing inspiration as a conditioned response. His books are full of examples through which he sought the practical application of his techniques as he worked with students and actors.

In the following excerpt, Stanislavski is explaining his method to Gorchakov:

Now what are these basic principles of my method? First, my method gives no recipes for becoming a great actor or for playing a part. My method is the way to the actor's correct state of being on the stage. The correct state is the normal state of a human being in life. But it's very difficult for an actor to create this state on the stage. He must be physically free, must control his muscles, and must have limitless attention. He must be able to hear and see on the stage the same as he does in life. He must be able to communicate with his partner and to accept the given circumstances of the play completely.

I suggest a series of exercises to develop these qualities. You must do these every day, just as a singer or pianist does his scales and arpeggios.

My second principle concerns the correct state of being on stage. This calls for the correct actions in the progressive unfolding of the play: inner psychological actions and outer physical actions. I separate the actions in this manner intentionally. It makes it easier for us to understand each other during rehearsal. As a matter of fact, every physical action has an inner psychological action which gives rise to it. And in every psychological inner action there is always a physical action which expresses its psychic nature; the unity between these two is organic on the stage. It is defined by the theme of the play, its idea, its characters, and the given circumstances. In order to make it easier for himself, an actor must put *himself* into the given circumstances. You must say to yourself, "What would I do *if* all that happens to this character happened to me?" I believe this *if* (I call it jokingly the magic *if*) helps an actor to begin to *do* on the stage. After you have learned to act from yourself, define the differences between your behavior and that of the character. Find all the reasons and justifications for the character's actions, and then go on from there without thinking where your personal actions end and the character's begin. His actions and yours will fuse automatically, if you have done the preceding work as I suggested.

The third principle of the method—the correct organic (inner plus outer)—will necessarily give rise to the correct feeling, especially if an actor finds a good basis for it. The sum of these three principles—correct state of being, actions and feelings—will give to your characters an organic life on the stage. This is the road which will bring you closest to what we call metamorphosis. Of course this takes for granted that you have understood the play correctly—its idea and its theme—and that you have analyzed the character accurately. And beyond all this, the actor must have a good appearance, clear and energetic diction, plastic movement, a sense of rhythm, temperament, taste, and the infectious quality we often call charm.[5]

To develop the ability to control the state of being, Stanislavski prescribed a rigorous program of training, which in addition to dance, fencing, movement, and voice and diction, included a series of exercises on concentration, observation, imagination, and improvisation. Considerable emphasis was also given to the analysis of plays and characters, seeking out the basic meanings and objectives as the so-called spine of interpretation.

A factor contributing to the misinterpretation of the Stanislavski method was that his *An Actor Prepares* appeared in English translation thirteen years before *Building the Character* was available. The earlier book emphasizes an internal approach to acting, and it was this aspect to which many actors and teachers gave their attention. Although *Building the Character* stresses much more the technique and training of the voice and body, it was not as widely read and followed as the earlier volume; therefore, the method was often incomplete or distorted in practice.

Stanislavski in his early work developed the technique of "emotional memory," by which the actor is supposed to be able to draw on personal experience to re-create its emotional content for a performance. It is an intriguing idea, but the technique has its drawbacks—the actor's recall lacks spontaneity, or the memory of the emotion may be faulty. Stanislavski himself abandoned the technique, but it is remarkably persistent and has its advocates to this day; they find in it a valid rehearsal technique for character analysis and sometimes for therapy. Another way to attack character motivation and emotional states that was popularized by Stanislavski is the use of improvisations as a rehearsal procedure. Actors spontaneously create actions and conditions similar to those in the play under rehearsal. It was Stanislavski's way of extending the actors' background and understanding of the conditions in the play's environment.

Although the central idea of the Stanislavski system is control, an admirable objective for any actor, the use of the method for all kinds of drama and all styles of production is doubtful. His approach to the production of realistic plays, which permit long periods of rehearsal and experimentation, may be eminently successful, but the method is quite inappropriate for the training of a Japanese Kabuki actor, whose objectives at times may be to simulate the movement and gestures of a puppet. Nor is his system applicable to Meyerhold's acrobatic style of performance, nor does it seem suitable for farce or high comedy. Moreover, in the new theater of the twentieth century, emphasis on character identification is often replaced by a performance that is frankly theatrical or presentational in style.

Jean-Louis Barrault was an innovative theater force whose concept of "total theater" production gave the director a free hand in interpreting the text. Barrault is seen here in *Thus Spake Zarrathrustra* at the Theatre d'Orsay, Paris.

The value of Stanislavski's ideas has been discussed widely. Most of the criticism of the method centers on its abuse. Too many disciples and performers have exaggerated feeling and inspiration and paid too little attention to the originator's insistence on the importance of technique. Those who emphasize technical training point out that the actors must have complete mastery of their voices and bodies so that they are free to move and speak in an expressive, projectile, and appropriate way. It is not enough for Romeo to feel like fighting a duel; he must know how to fence. In reading a comic line, it is not enough to think that the dialogue is funny; the delivery requires skillful timing. Long before Stanislavski, generations of outstanding actors gave compelling performances, based on their own intuitive approaches. All actors must find their own procedures. The value of the Stanislavski system is that it has helped many actors to regularize their way of working.

After Stanislavski, other avenues to realistic acting have focused on the action that accompanies the emotion rather than the emotion itself. Barrault suggested that actors cannot really play emotional states but only the actions

In his "epic theater" Brecht attempted to develop an alienation style of acting—cool, distanced, and free from emotional identification. This style is seen in the playing of two characters from the *Caucasian Chalk Circle* at the Berliner Ensemble.

that accompany them, and it is through their behavior that they express their feelings. Robert L. Benedetti echoes the James-Lange theory that emotions tend to follow the action—we are afraid because we run rather than the reverse. This approach recognizes the *gestalt* concept of the individual as a whole person, whose mind and body are integrated. Feelings are, therefore, a part of a total configuration, not separate entities. So the actor focuses on the actions and the feelings will follow.

One of the most provocative innovators of the new approach to acting, Brecht flatly rejected the Stanislavski system and its identification of character. Brecht wanted onstage the objectivity of a scientist giving a lecture and pointing out the evidence. Hence, Brechtian acting is cool, detached, objective. Brecht's opposition to Stanislavski's brand of acting was based on his rejection of realistic and naturalistic dramas; he regarded them as highly personalized accounts of individuals rather than important documents of social and economic reform.

GAMES THEORY

An interesting and potentially profitable new approach to acting comes from Eric Berne, a Canadian psychiatrist who developed from his clinical research the technique of *transactional analysis*. His ideas were set forth in two books, *Transactions in Psychotherapy* (1961) and the widely read *Games People Play* (1964). His root idea is that because of each individual's basic need to interact with other human beings, we develop systems of handling these transactions. In infancy, the child needs attention and communication, some of it through touch. As adults, we continue to need contact with others, for which we develop rather complex techniques. Berne identifies five kinds of transactions:

1. Rituals—stereotyped, repetitious social patterns
2. Pastimes—interrelationships in which characters have no ulterior motives
3. Activities—work, performing tasks
4. Intimacies—interactions for genuine exploration of feelings and attitudes
5. Games—an ongoing series of complementary, ulterior transactions that may be played on two levels at once. A salesman, on the social level, may take a client to lunch; on the psychological level, he is preparing the customer for a sale.

Berne defines three ego states of each individual—the Parent, the Adult, and the Child—and five levels of gain. Arthur Wagner, in an informative article, relates Berne's theories to drama and to his own work with actors.[6] An interesting use of this method of analysis is its application to the

King Lear opens with a scene in which the three daughters are invited to compete with one another in professing their love to their father. Cordelia's failure to join in the competition leads to tragic consequences.

(Royal Shakespeare Theater.)

first scene of *King Lear,* in which Lear sets up the game of "benevolent father and loving children" by asking his three daughters, "Which of you shall we say doth love us most?" Goneril and Regan play the game with flattering answers to gain the reward, but Cordelia refuses to copy her sisters and her answer causes the King to break out into a fit of childish rage.

Another use of this approach can be seen in Michael Langham's production of *Antony and Cleopatra* at the Canadian Stratford Shakespeare Festival. Langham's prerehearsal notes indicate this perspective:

> The play is full of games, of "putting on a scene," almost as if the author were saying that life, especially public life, were no more than an acted performance. Cleopatra has successfully wooed Antony by the scene she "puts on" in her barge on the river of Cydhus; the episode of the salted fish was "staged" like a charade; and early in the play she taunts Antony to "act" for her his outraged sense of Roman honour. It is all a game. Antony is continually conscious of the performance he is giving—privately and publicly; he "performs" in the Senate, ever mindful of the effect he is making, he "directs" the Bacchanalia, he "acts" to make his followers cry. . . .
>
> Finally, of course, there is the crowning "performance" of Cleopatra staging her death scene.[7]

In examining the conflicts that occur so often in drama, the actor may see them as products of crossed transactions or games. Berne's method is useful in clarifying interactions and making them more concrete than through the conventional Freudian analyses.

Directors and actors have learned that the use of games is one of the most effective ways of combatting repressions and inhibitions that have been built up by early conditioning. They also serve to unmask and free performers and to stimulate their imaginations. Games have been used in the training of actors in the workshops at the Royal Shakespeare Company, the Berliner Ensemble, the Group Theater, the Open Theater, Copeau's Company at the Vieux-Colombier, and the Théâtre du Soleil.

A major influence on the use of games and improvisations in this country stems from the examples and writings of Viola Spolin. She indicates her concept of games by describing their value as a way to liberate the student-actor:

> Growth will occur without difficulty in the student-actor, because the very game he plays will aid him. The objective upon which the player must constantly focus and towards which every action must be directed provokes spontaneity. In this spontaneity personal freedom is released, and the total person, physically, intellectually, and intuitively is awakened. This causes enough excitation for the student to transcend himself—he is freed to go out into the environment to explore, adventure, and face all dangers he meets unafraid.[8]

Her book is a valuable step-by-step manual for training the actor in methods that have found wide acceptance.

THE ACTOR'S WAYS OF WORKING

Actors' ways of working are highly personal since they are the result of their imagination, talent, and physical attributes; but whatever their procedure, they face intriguing tasks. Says Peter Brook:

> Acting is in many ways so unique in its difficulties, because the artist has to use the treacherous, changeable and mysterious material of himself as his medium. He is called upon to be completely involved while distanced—detached without detachment. He must be sincere, he must be insincere; he must practice how to be insincere with sincerity and how to lie truthfully.[9]

The way an actor approaches a new play and builds a character has been the subject of endless conjecture and controversy. Actors themselves freely acknowledge their inability to describe what actually happens to them in performance. The literature of the art of acting is filled with conflicting statements, indicating that the process is too personal for clear-cut intellectual analysis. To quote Brook again:

Outstanding actors like all real artists have some mysterious psychic chemistry, half conscious, yet three-quarters hidden, that they themselves may only define as "instinct," "hunch," "my voices," that enables them to develop their vision and their art.[10]

The actor places faith in feelings. This point is made again and again in a series of interviews that Lillian Ross conducted with outstanding stage and motion-picture performers for *The New Yorker,* in which are found such statements as these:

It's when you start to rehearse, with other people, that things begin to happen. What it is exactly I don't know, and even don't want to know. I'm all for mystery there. Most of what happens as you develop your part is unconscious. Most of it is underwater. [Kim Stanley]

Once you set things you do and make them mean certain things, you then respond to the stimuli you yourself set up. Then you *feel.* [Maureen Stapleton]

When I'm building a role, I start with a series of mental pictures and feel. [Hume Cronyn]

Every actor has, as a gift from God, his own method. My particular method is to go first by the sense of taste. I actually have a physical taste for every part. Then I go to the other senses—hearing, seeing, touching. Thinking comes much later. [Vladimir Sokoloff][11]

Raisin in the Sun demands convincing characterization and emotional involvement in its story of domestic conflict.

(Hartford Stage Company. Directed by Irene Lewis.)

Sir Laurence Olivier describes his approach:

> Some people start from the inside, some people start from the periphery. I would say, at a guess, that Alec Guinness is what we would call a peripheral actor. I think I'm the same. The actor who starts from the inside is more likely to find himself in the parts he plays, than to the parts in himself, but simply to find the parts, go out to them and get them and *be* somebody else.[12]

The veteran British stage and screen actor Michael Redgrave when asked in an interview "How do you control emotion?" responded,

> I think the best description of how that is controlled is the one by Joseph Jefferson, the American actor of many years ago, who, when asked his opinion about the so called Coquelin contoversy (Coquelin believing that an actor shouldn't feel anything at all, and Irving believing that the actor should appear to be the very things he's talking about), said very meekly, "As for me, I find that I act best when my heart is warm and my head is cool."[13]

In working on a new play, many actors testify to an initial period of trial and error before the image becomes clear. Geraldine Page, an outstanding American actress, sees her role developing like a jigsaw puzzle, a small piece at a time. Apparently many actors go through a similar experience until all at once "a bell rings" or "there is a spark" or "suddenly there is a click."

Page makes an interesting observation concerning character identification:

> When you take the character over and use the character, you wreck the fabric of the play, but you can be in control of the character without taking the character over. When the character uses *you*, that's when you're really cooking. You know you're in complete control, yet you get the feeling you didn't do it. You have the beautiful feeling that you can't ruin it. You feel as if you were tagging along on an exciting journey. You don't completely understand it, and you don't have to. You're just grateful and curious.[14]

This statement suggests the interesting dichotomy of the actor who, although assuming the role of another character, still remains in complete control. Whether the actor's approach is emotional or sheerly technical, it must be recognized as a very personal and highly individualized process that defies complete definition or understanding. Nevertheless, there are certain general steps that may be followed.

Like the director, the actor's initial approach to a play is that of analysis—the search for the core idea, the spine. What does the play mean? What is the effect supposed to be on the audience? How is each role related to the complete play? Under the guidance and stimulation of the director, each performer analyzes the play to establish its basic interpretation.

The actor will want to know the style of the play and the production. By style is meant the *manner* of production, the *quality* of the actions and images. For example, it is obvious from the opening lines of *Hamlet* that the play is elevated in style, the language dignified and poetic, the action controlled. There is nothing trivial or folksy about the guards and Horatio when they confront the ghost. Contrast *Hamlet* with the opening lines of *Death of a Salesman*—its ordinary characters and colloquial language. Its style suggests a domestic environment with a husband and wife in a commonplace situation.

The style of the particular production is usually determined by the director, who may elect to stage the play in a manner other than the original one; for example, *The Taming of the Shrew* might be set in the wild West in the nineteenth century, or a Molière comedy may be done in a style that suggests the commedia dell'arte. Even when a play is done "straight," the author may see the characters playing at different levels simultaneously in order to convey both text and subtext.

Rabe's *Sticks and Bones* (1970) is a searing account of the return of a disabled Vietnam veteran whose family finds it impossible to adjust its lifestyle to reality. In an author's note to the published play, Rabe describes the acting style in these terms:

> In any society there is an image of how the perfectly happy family should appear. It is this image that the people in this play wish to preserve above all else. Mom and Dad are not concerned that terrible events have occurred in the world, but rather that David has come home to behave in a manner that makes him no longer lovable. Thus he is keeping them from being the happy family they know they must be. He attacks those aspects of their self-image in which reside all their sense of value and sanity. But, curiously, one of the requisites of their self-image is that everything is fine, and, consequently, for a long time they must not even admit that David is attacking.
>
> Yet everything is being communicated. Often a full, long speech is used in this play where in another, more "realistic" play there would be only a silence during which something was communicated between two people. Here the communication is obvious because it is directly spoken. Consequently the ignoring of that which is communicated must be equally obvious. David throws a yelling, screaming tantrum over his feelings of isolation and Harriet confidently, cheerfully offers Ezy Sleep sleeping pills in full faith that they will solve his problem. The actors must try to look at what they are ignoring. They must not physically ignore things—turn their backs, avert their eyes, be busy with something else. The point is not that they do not physically see or hear, but that they psychologically ignore. Though they look right at things, though they listen closely, they do not see or hear. The harder they physically focus and concentrate on an event, the clearer their psychological state and the point and nature of the play will be, when in their next moments and speeches they verbally and emotionally ignore or miss what they have clearly looked at. In addition, the actors should try not to take the play overly seriously. The characters (except David) do not take things seriously until they are forced to, and then they do it for as short a time as they can manage. Let the audience take seriously the jolly way the people go about the curious business of their lives.

David Rabe's *Sticks and Bones* demands a multi-layered performance over surface realism.

(Miami University, Ohio. Directed by Bonny Wittham.)

Stylization, then, is the main production problem. The forms referred to during the time of writing *Sticks and Bones* were farce, horror movie, TV situation comedy. These should have their effect, though it must be remembered that they are where form was thought, not content. What is poetic in the writing must not be reinforced by deep feeling on the part of the actors, or the writing will hollow into pretension. In a more "realistic" play, where language is thinner, subtext must be supplied or there is no weight. Such deep support of *Sticks and Bones* will make the play ponderous. As a general rule, I think it is true that when an actor's first impulse (the impulse of all his training) is to make a heavy or serious adjustment in a scene, he should reverse himself and head for a light-headed adjustment. If his first impulse is toward light-heartedness, perhaps he should turn toward a serious tack. A major premise of the play is that stubbing your own big toe is a more disturbing event than hearing of a stranger's suicide.

At the start, the family is happy and orderly, and then David comes home and he is unhappy. As the play progresses, he becomes happier and they become unhappier. Then, at the end, they are happy.[15]

Another interesting view of acting style was suggested by Roger Planchon, the outstanding French director of Le Théâtre de la Cité in the suburbs of Lyons. He is primarily interested in bringing the experience of the theater to the common people. When asked by Planchon what kind of stories they would like to see, the factory workers suggested *The Three Muske-*

teers. A dramatization of Alexander Dumas' historical romance was made and proved to be an enormous hit. The play became a joyful vehicle for "demythologizing" a rigid view of French history. Played with great élan, the swashbuckling intrigue included movie techniques of westerns and slap-stick comedies—incongruous homely touches, such as Richelieu frying real eggs on stage and menials interrupting a royal ceremony to change the candles in the chandeliers. Planchon described the acting style he was seeking in these terms:

> I am trying to define a certain style, but it's very fine, very French, if you like, very . . . humorous to play the kind of theater I want. I need, as Brook has also said he needs for his kind of theater, *very intelligent actors.* The more intelligent they are, the more they can play what I want them to play. And another thing: my style is absolutely stripped bare of pathos. I think the Living Theater and others like them are fatally tempted by pathos. Not me, absolutely not. I've no taste for it at all, excess repels me. When I see an actor plunging into pathos, I always feel he is lying. In this I'm very Brechtian. I want someone to tell me a story I can watch smoking my pipe, and I don't want to have to ask myself questions about *feelings.* . . . I love relaxed performances.[16]

The analysis of the play should lead the actor to an understanding of the pervading atmosphere of the play. Does it suggest the hot, sensual quality of *A Streetcar Named Desire?* Is the mood one of menace, as if some alien force were trying to break in, as in many of Pinter's plays? Does the environment require the tempo and flavor of big-city corruption, as in some of Brecht's works? The dominating atmosphere of the play gives the actor clues to interpretation and the method of playing—the tempo, use of props, and business. From a study of the total play, the actor not only sees the relationship of one character to the action as a whole, as a part of a larger metaphor, but also finds many sources of inspiration for the interpretation of the spirit and quality of the playwright's creation.

After a performer has a clear comprehension of the play's structure, atmosphere, style, and basic interpretation, he or she studies the individual character, perhaps approaching the character from the outside—making an inventory of age, occupation, appearance, manner of speaking and moving, physical condition, posture, movement, carriage, and dress. Observations may be directly from life; if it is a period play, it will be profitable to study historical pictures showing the costume, architecture, and manners of the time. Stein, working with his excellent ensemble at the Hallenschen Schau-bühne in West Berlin, has found it worthwhile to spend considerable time getting acquainted with the cultural background of the play and the play-wright through readings, seminars, and discussions.

The actor will find in the script four main sources of information about character. The modern playwright frequently provides a character description, which includes some of the details just listed. Some playwrights,

A group of nervous suiters await the decision of the prospective bride in Gogol's nineteenth-century comedy, *Marriage*. The body language of the actors portrays their anxiety.

(Guthrie Theater. Directed by Anatoly Efros.)

like Shaw, provide very complete portraits, down to the color of the nostrils. Some contemporary playwrights may simply give the actor the barest hint, such as "a waiter," "a young man of twenty-four," or "a tramp." In period plays, the dramatist usually gives no character description at all.

A second source of information comes from the lines the actor speaks. The playwright has usually taken great pains to write dialogue that represents and delineates the character. Lines, of course, are susceptible to a variety of interpretations, and it is obvious that two actors playing the same role may reveal marked differences in the reading of the dialogue. Indeed, the same actor may give a variety of interpretations of the same lines in different performances. The skillful playwright goes beyond the literal meaning of the words, using dialogue as a means of revealing character as well as advancing the plot. The actor, therefore, must search the lines for their essential meaning, not only in reference to the immediate context, but also to the revelation of the total character.

The character of Puck in *A Midsummer Night's Dream* is caught in costume and action by William Rhys.

(Cleveland Playhouse. Photo: Michael Edwards.)

A third clue in the analysis of acting roles is the characters' actions. Are the individuals active agents or are they acted upon? What change do they undergo during the course of the play? What emotions are aroused? What are their primary objectives and how do they go about reaching them? How much of the inner life is revealed by what the performers do? To what extent do they understand their own motives? What choices and decisions do they make and how do these affect their fortunes? Do their actions make them sympathetic characters? Playwrights must convey the inner lives of their characters in clear and concise ways, and very often the actions are more revealing than their words. The essential actions are usually created by the dramatist, but the director and performers also invent stage business that is significant in interpreting the roles. In any case, all the action in a performance should be relevant and essential to the meaning of the play. A pertinent example occurs in *Sly Fox,* a modern revision of Ben Jonson's *Volpone;* it is based on the deceptive actions of Sly, who pretends to be dying in order to elicit gifts from his greedy acquaintances, who are hoping to become his beneficiary. The play opens with an action that is repeated throughout—Sly's feigned illness. He is heard groaning offstage; then he enters, supported by his valet, Able, and three servants. Sly appears to be at death's door, but when the servants leave, he is miraculously "cured."

Sly: (*Standing up on the bed*) No one's better! No one's more fit! (*Getting out of bed*) I've got enough health to start another man!

George C. Scott romped through the role of Sly, alternating his dying act with a vigorous contrast of ebullient life. His actions revealed his true character to the audience.

The actor's *way of acting* reveals character—not just what is done but *how* it is done. Many accomplished performers bring to their roles a wealth of detailed actions—pieces of business that give dimension and sharpness to the portraits they create. A case in point occurred in a production of Rabe's *The Basic Training of Pavlo Hummel*, a play about a misfit who hopes to find his manhood in Vietnam. (This is another part of Rabe's Vietnamese war trilogy.) Using the metaphor of basic training and military service, Rabe builds up a vivid picture of a character who symbolizes all of life's unnoticed young men. Critic Jack Kroll describes Al Pacino's way of playing the part:

> Like Ted Williams waiting for a pitch, Pacino builds potential energy out of a thousand jittery movements. He's one actor you want to film in slow motion. What you'd see would be a flow of behavioral hieroglyphics—jounce the pelvis, touch the hip, rub the face, swing the head, purse the mouth, shift the foot, paw the hair. Even the words come out reshaped by inner tension—the vowels mauled and flattened, the phrases syncopated with savage sensitivity.[17]

A deliberately theatricalized style of playing is evident in this shot from Ghelderode's *Pantagleize* when the protagonist pays a visit on General Macboom to steal the national treasury.

(Guthrie Theater. Directed by Stephen Kanee and sets by Jack Barla.)

Finally, the actor learns a good deal about the role from the reactions of others. The actor must understand the character's dramatic purpose in the action, which is often revealed by the lines of another character. Shakespeare sometimes delineates characters sharply in this way: "Yon, Cassius, hath a lean and hungry look." Coriolanus was captured in one sentence: "When he walks, he moves like an engine, and the ground shrinks before his treading; he is able to pierce a corselet with his eyes, talks like a knell, and his hum is a battery." But it is mostly in the interactions of characters that the playwright indicates their motivations.

The actor does not work in isolation; most preparation takes place in rehearsal with other members of the cast under the guidance of the director. It is in the rehearsal period that actors test their preliminary analysis of the role. By putting the characters on their feet in action the actors find the valid basis for performance. Rehearsal is a time of learning and exploration. Many directors augment the work on the text by exercises and improvisations designed to open the text and explore the actors' potential. Selbourne's account of Brook's *A Midsummer Night's Dream* rehearsals show how important experiments on sound, rhythm, and style were in shaping the production.

ACTING IN THE NEW THEATER

Since the new theater rejected traditional drama and theater practices, it had to find new ways of acting. Sometimes it made this search by working on individual plays; in other instances, workshops were formed to find fresh ways of looking at theater, which meant either making up their own material or revising established plays to suit their needs.

At the Royal Shakespeare Company, Brook began by conducting an actors' workshop with Charles Marowitz to investigate the potential of the "theater of cruelty" and to expose the actors to Artaudian techniques essential for Weiss' play. Similarly, Brook experimented freely with styles of performance in his famous production of *A Midsummer Night's Dream* (pp. 244–246). His rehearsals became a laboratory for investigating sounds, rhythms, and images to suit his vision of the drama's magical world. Rehearsals also became training periods for acquiring the circus skills that Brook imposed on the actions.

Most of the innovative work in the theater came out of groups that were dedicated to experimental acting techniques or politically motivated companies whose productions demanded unconventional methods.

Chaikin's Open Theater began in 1963 in New York as a workshop to explore the art of acting. It was intended to be a private studio with no interest in public performance. Its aims were quite different from the professionally slanted school, in that the members were not primarily concerned with developing themselves for Broadway consumption. They rejected the psychoanalytical orientation to drama and to method acting.

They were dedicated to ensemble play, to the interaction of one performer with another, and to the group as a whole. Said Chaikin, "The actor has to be willing to wake himself up out of this mesmerized state of being where he is unable to distinguish between a person and a picture of a person."

At the center of Chaikin's work was the actors' need to establish "presence"—an awareness of their own body; a sensitivity to the presence of others; and an acute consciousness of the meeting of lives at a specific moment and space, "a visceral confrontation." The actors must go beyond their "prepared responses" in order to *open up*. As Chaikin said, "We must open up to our deepest despair, to coldness around the heart, to the secret wishes about God." C. W. E. Bigsby described Chaikin's efforts in this way:

> In exploring the full potential of the actor, he was seeking simultaneously to assert the infinite capacities of man; in stressing not only the physical accomplishments of the actors and their ability to communicate across a wide range of emotions and through a wide variety of channels, but also their intellectual involvement in the creation of the drama which they perform, he was also offering a model of the integrated sensibility, a self restored to its own lost unity.[18]

The actors in the Open Theater soon realized that as performers it was essential to test themselves before an audience. In December 1963, they presented their first public performance at the Sheridan Theater. The program consisted of some improvisations, sound and movement exercises, and two short plays by writers from the group. Chaikin's program note articulates the perspective of the group:

> What you will see tonight is a phase of work of the Open Theater. This group of actors, musicians, playwrights, and director has come together out of a dissatisfaction with the established trend of the contemporary theater. It is seeking a theater for today. It is now exploring certain specifics of the stage, not as a production group, but as a group trying to find its own voice. Statable tenets of this workshop: (1) to create a situation in which the actors can play together with a sensitivity to one another required of an ensemble, (2) to explore the specific powers that only the live theater possesses, (3) to concentrate on a theater of abstraction and illusion (as opposed to a theater of behavioral or psychological motivation), (4) to discover ways in which the artist can find his expression without money as the determining factor.

Because of the unique approach of the Open Theater to acting, it became essential to find new kinds of material that would give them opportunities for ensemble play. So they invented their own. *Viet Rock*, for example, grew out of their exercises and improvisations, and was finally shaped for public performance by Megan Terry.

Jean-Claude van Itallie became an important writer for the Open Theater with *America Hurrah!* He began by providing structures for the actors to improvise within, such as *The Hunter and the Bird,* whose story line shows a bird wounded by a hunter, who in turn is shot by the bird. The script was primarily a framework for stimulating the actors to develop their skills and to explore their potential rather than a fixed text for public view. A three segment production, *America Hurrah!* gave the actors opportunities to use techniques such as transformations, in which the actors moved rapidly from one situation or character to another in an attempt to break down consistent psychological motivation. In another segment the actors collaborated in forming the parts of a machine, such as a bulldozer or steam engine, to emphasize the antihuman modern world.

In the third segment, *Motel,* the characters are three huge dolls. The Motel-keeper, who represents the motel room as well, is played by a performer with a head three times the size of her body. She can only move her arms and legs, and her voice comes over an amplifier. A couple enters, also in huge doll disguises. As loud rock music batters the eardrums, the two strangers destroy the room and the Motel-keeper. The author is attacking the brutalism of the environment and the mechanistic drive in our society.

Van Itallie's *The Serpent* was an effort to bring audience and actors together in a ceremony they shared because of its roots in popular myths. The plot deals with the Fall of Man and Cain's murder of Abel and the assassination of President Kennedy. Before the actual play begins, the performers engage in their warm-up exercises, so the audience sees them as individuals first, not as actors. A procession follows that resembles medieval mummers. The assassination is played in twelve segments, like film sequences, in slow and reverse order. The serpent is played by five actors, Eve's lines are spoken by a chorus, and the voice of God comes from those who invoke Him.

From these excerpts of van Itallie's plays we see how the Open Theater broke fresh ground in exploring acting techniques. The power of these plays is due to ensemble acting and to the impact of fresh ways of communicating—by stressing physical movement and elemental sounds and emphasizing ritualized performance. In short, the Open Theater's exploration of the actor's potential gives audiences a fresh perception of theater.

Grotowski's "poor theater," the Polish Laboratory Theater, was an actor-oriented workshop whose methods won a worldwide reputation in the late 1960s and 1970s. Grotowski's actors had little interest in communication. Their emphasis was on developing descipline through acting techniques that free the body and mind. Avoiding the customary supporting production elements of scenery, lighting, and costuming, the actors sought to transform themselves before a small audience, selected for their seriousness of interest. By mastering a rigid control of all their faculties, and thereby eliminating the traditional blocks, the actors achieved a new awareness. Grotowski's kind of theater did not generate a wide following, but

In Grotowski's Polish Laboratory Theater, the actors made a profound impression
on the audiences because of their intensity and dedication. Drama returns to ritual
in *The Constant Prince*.

many young actors experimented with his exercises and found them useful
in achieving ensemble integration and discipline.

Brook invited Grotowski and his company to visit London in 1967, and
the impact on the workshops of the Royal Shakespeare Company was considerable. The Laboratory Theater also visited the United States in 1969,
where it attracted a great deal of attention.

Perhaps Grotowski's most direct influence in this country was in the
Performance Group of Schechner, who had worked briefly with the Laboratory abroad.

Capitalizing on his experience with Grotowski, Schechner set up a series of exercises aimed at exploring personal potential, which was in a way
a kind of group therapy, by exchanging "touches, places, ideas, anxieties,
words, gestures, hostilities, rages, smells, glances, sounds, loves." When the
group began rehearsing its version of Euripides' *The Bacchae*, intended to

be "a dance, an ecstasy," in which the audience would participate, it was also an attempt to be an encounter with oneself.

Performances began with exercises derived from Grotowski, which were incorporated into a production. The text of the play was shortened, and words were sometimes split into syllables or prolonged as wails and elemental sounds. Actions became rituals, such as one based on a New Guinea tribal ceremony of rebirth. The performers enacted the roles in an ancient Greek play, but they also played themselves in an attempt to go beyond the mask to a kind of psychotherapy. Schechner challenged his actors to include the audience in a communal event—not just to tell a story but to search "for themes and gestures, for sounds and dances *vis-à-vis* audience and with ourselves."

In the Performance Group's production of *Commune* in 1970, the material came out of the players' personal backgrounds, their experiments in acting, and a study of American history, joined together in a collage arranged to investigate their roots.

> The performers begin with improvised singing and talking; they tell in overlapping speeches of their personal background in relation to the Performance Group; then the evening erupts into a rapid pattern of transformations that defies time and demands the spectator's engagement. As the performers reenact their personal beginnings, they discover archetypal beginnings; out of animal sounds and undefined movements, they become a boat and its inhabitants, as water is scooped and dripped from the tub; they sing revival songs, play cops and robbers, feed and become monkeys, act out scenes from *Lear, Richard III, The Tempest,* and *Moby Dick.* All of these are discovered as part of their matrices; they are not cute memorabilia, but metaphors for finding meaning, performed by a people digging out their own roots.[19]

This work reminds us of Mnouchkine's Théâtre du Soleil's experiments in developing styles for *1789,* which showed both the "rough" kind of performing of the common people, in contrast to the highly artificial genteel style of the aristocracy; we also think of their productions of Shakespeare's *Twelfth Night* and *Richard II,* which featured an assortment of techniques from Japanese Noh, Kabuki, and Bunraku; Indian dancing; and suggestions of the commedia dell'arte.

Similar experiments with exotic styles were used by Ludlow's Theater of the Ridiculous, the San Francisco Mime Troupe, and the Mabou Mines Company, ranging from spoofs of romanticized cinematic acting, puppetry, soul and rock performances, Italian comedy, circus and carnival shows, and nineteenth-century flamboyant melodrama to the burlesquing of high styles of French neoclassicism and Elizabethan and Greek theater.

Although many experimental groups have come and gone, the impact of their work has not been lost. Today there is a much freer, eclectic attitude toward actors and their training, and inevitably, their influence has been felt not only in offbeat plays but also in productions of drama in the mainstream.

As a case in point, note the description of the current eclectic performance of Linda Hunt in the Boston Shakespeare Festival's staging of Brecht's
Mother Courage and Her Children, as described by Arthur Holmberg:

> Her performance—an easy mix of presentational and representational
> modes—shows what a healthy distance the young breed of American actor has
> come from the baneful influence of Lee Strasberg's method. Her eclectic style
> ranges from the broad gestures of music hall in expansive moments to a quiet
> naturalism in Mother Courage's rare spots of introspection.
>
> Hunt's portrayal builds slowly. As the evening advances, she grows into the
> part. Unlike Ann Bancroft, she doesn't use charm to con us. Linda Hunt has
> no charm and that's her greatest asset. Her spell takes time to work. First, she
> gains respect by an unusually disciplined body. Her short, hesitation steps; the
> broad circles she spins across the stage while greed and mother love fight it
> out and Schweizerkäs's life hangs in the balance; the swerve of her body as she
> bends over and raises the rafters with her own version of Weigel's scream, her
> face whorled in the *rigor mortis* of pain and guilt—these are gestures of an ac-
> tress whose muscles have been trained to an athlete's pitch of perfection. She
> turns her body into visual language, silent signs that indicate more deeply than
> words Mother Courage's invisible soul . . . who could forget the tenderness she
> wraps around Kattrin in her winding sheet, still refusing to face up to the con-
> sequences of her acts, even though she holds the proof in her arms? As she
> sings her dead daughter a farewell lullabye, she pounds out, with bare hand
> on bare floor, an angry rhythm.[20]

The freer, more flexible style of acting has also influenced playwriting.
However, some playwrights have been ahead of their time in challenging
actors to enlarge the scope of their performances. Shepard has been espe-

Sam Shepard's plays demand an earthy, vigorous performance
of sharply defined individuals. *Buried Child,* the Pulitzer Prize
winning play of 1979 at the Repertory Theater of St. Louis.

cially demanding because his plays are such mixtures of vivid and often incongruous images, intuitive creations, reflecting a wide spectrum of influences—"car culture" of the young, science fiction, westerns, television in its pop or junk aspects, circuses, ceremonials, medicine shows, hallucinatory experiences, magic, graphic arts, and popular music of various kinds. Somehow, Shepard manages to integrate this welter of pop and countercultures. Though not an absurdist, his parallel to Beckett, Pinter, and Ionesco is apparent in his rejection of linear construction, logically developed sequences, diction with precise meanings, and unified or consistent characterization.

In his preface to *Angel City* in 1976, Shepard made this revealing statement:

> The term "character" could be thought of in a different way when working on this play. Instead of the idea of a "whole character" with logical motives behind his behavior which the victor submerges himself into, he should consider instead a fractured whole with bits and pieces of character flying off the central theme. In other words, more in terms of collage construction or jazz improvisation.[21]

Such an explanation from the playwright brings with it a new perspective to the actor.

Shepard's contribution to the new theater is that he is in time with the revolutionary and experimental fervor of those searching for fresh ways of using the stage. He is a catalytic force in breaking down the boundaries of the established patterns of playwriting. In his efforts he has, of course, taken risks. His spontaneous, volatile, and often unorganized methods make his work seem fragmented and incomplete, but the compensation is in the vigorous and vivid spirit that animates all his plays. His plays are collages of powerful images for performance, and this is why he is the most important American playwright in the new theater.

As performers in the new theater reject many of the practices of the past, they search for a style based on theatricalism. Actors often become agents of the action, with the meaning residing in the performance, not in the person who performs it. For example, in watching a double play in a baseball game, the fan's interest is in how the shortstop fields the ball and tosses it to the second baseman, who in turn fires it to first. There is little or no thought about the psychological significance behind the actions. Likewise, during a concert, the listener's attention is engaged by the pianist or vocalist as a performer, not as a complex character whose playing reveals his or her psyche. Similarly, in the current theater, the actor may simply play the action, not the role. The style may be cool, detached, or even flat—without emotional content.

The acting style may be frankly theatrical, like a storyteller in front of children. Or actors may engage in transformations, like a person assuming several roles while telling a joke. Actors may suggest several parts simultaneously, exchange roles with one another, go through warm-up exercises before the play begins, change costumes and makeup before the audience, and set the stage and move the furniture. Although *Amadeus* is not a play for the new theater (it has a clear narrative and a beginning, middle, and end, and the characterization is coherently developed), it nevertheless exhibits the new theatricalism; for example Salieri, who talks directly to the audience throughout the play, begins Act I, Scene 2, as a man of seventy in a wheelchair and a few minutes later rises, takes off his dressing gown, and becomes a young man in the prime of life—a handsomely dressed, successful composer of the 1780s.

Actors in the new theater may improvise their dialogue and actions, speak a synthetic language, use gibberish or animal sounds, speak simultaneously or mouth tape recorded dialogue, or create a cacophony of unintelligible sounds. They may stress mime and dance, simulate puppets, begin actions that are never completed, avoid moving altogether, or make changes without transitions. They may play deadpan, play behind clown faces or masks, or appear as ciphers without motivation or meaning. In an attempt to go beyond the literal word, performers may present a welter of sensory signals that many traditional theatergoers cannot or will not follow. But despite the disparity between the old style of acting and the new, one essential binds them together: the living presence of the performers; only they can make theater.

PLAYS TO READ AND SEE

F = Film Available; V = Videotape available

F	V	Rostand, *Cyrano de Bergerac*
F	V	Shakespeare, *Hamlet, Henry V, Othello*
		Rabe, *Sticks and Bones*
		(Two interesting films about theater are *The Dresser* and *The Producers*.)
F	V	*Approaches to Hamlet*
F	V	*Exploring a Character* (Shakespeare)
F	V	*Preparing to Perform Shakespeare*
F	V	*Rehearsing the Text*
		(Royal Shakespeare Company on Film for the Humanities.)

BIBLIOGRAPHY

BENEDETTI, ROBERT L. *The Actor at Work*, 3rd ed. Englewood Cliffs, N.J.: Prentice-Hall, Inc., 1981.

BOLESLAVSKY, RICHARD. *Acting: The First Six Lessons.* New York: Theater Arts Books, 1933.

BRECHT, BERTOLT. *The Messingkauf Dialogues.* London: Methuen, 1971.

BURTON, HAL. *Great Acting.* New York: Hill & Wang, 1967.

CARNOVSKY, MORRIS. *The Actor's Eye.* New York: Performing Arts Journal Publications, 1984.

CHAIKIN, JOSEPH. *The Presence of the Actor: Notes on the Open Theater.* New York: Atheneum Publishers, 1972.

COLE, TOBY, and HELEN KRICH CHINOY. *Actors on Acting.* New York: Crown Publishers, 1980.

FRANKLIN, MIRIAM A., and JAMES G. DIXON III. *Rehearsal: The Principles and Practices of Acting for the Stage.* Englewood Cliffs, N.J.: Prentice-Hall, Inc., 1983.

FUNKE, GEORGE, and JOHN E. BOOTH, eds. *Actors Talk About Acting.* New York: Random House, Inc., 1961.

GLENN, STANLEY. *The Complete Actor.* Boston: Allyn & Bacon, Inc., 1977.

HETHMON, ROBERT, ed. *Strasberg at the Actor's Studio.* New York: The Viking Press, 1965.

KURITZ, PAUL. *Playing: An Introduction to Acting.* Englewood Cliffs, N.J.: Prentice-Hall, Inc., 1982.

SAINT-DENIS, MICHAEL. *Training for the Theater, Promises and Promises.* New York: Theater Arts Books, 1982.

SPOLIN, VIOLA. *Improvisation in the Theater.* Evanston, Ill.: Northwestern University Press, 1963.

STANISLAVSKI, CONSTANTIN. *An Actor Prepares.* New York: Theater Arts Books, 1963.

——. *Creating a Role,* trans. E. R. Hapgood. New York: Theater Arts Books, 1961.

NOTES

1. Clive Barnes, *New York Times,* June 27, 1975.

2. Nikolai M. Gorchakov, *Stanislavki Directs,* trans. Miriam Goldina (New York: Funk & Wagnalls, Inc., 1958).

3. Eliot Norton, quoted in *The Stratford Scene, 1959–1968,* ed. Peter Raby (Toronto: Clarke, Irwin & Co.), 1968.

4. August Strindberg, "Preface to *Miss Julie,*" in *Plays of Strindberg,* Vol. 1, trans. Edith and Warner Oland (New York: Bruce Humphries, 1912).

5. Gorchakov, *Stanislavski Directs.*

6. Arthur Wagner, "Transactional Analysis and Acting," *Tulane Drama Review,* 11, no. 4 (Summer 1967).

7. Michael Langham, quoted in *The Stratford Scene, 1958–1968,* ed. Peter Raby (Toronto: Clarke, Irwin & Co., 1968).

8. Viola Spolin, *Improvisation for the Theater* (Evanston, Ill.: Northwestern University Press, 1963).

9. Peter Brook, *The Empty Space* (New York: Atheneum Publishers, 1969).

10. Brook, *The Empty Space.*

11. Lillian Ross, "Profiles: The Player," *The New Yorker,* October 21, 1961; October 28, 1961; and November 4, 1961. Reprinted by permission. Copyright ©1961 The New Yorker Magazine, Inc., October 28, 1961.

12. Laurence Olivier, quoted in *Great Acting,* ed. Hal Burton (New York: Hill & Wang, 1967).

13. Michael Redgrave, interviewed by Richard Findlater in *Great Acting,* ed. by Hal Burton, (New York: Hill & Wang, 1967).

14. Ross, "Profiles."

15. David Rabe, *The Basic Training of Pavlo Hummel* and *Sticks and Bones* (New York: The Viking Press, 1973).

16. Roger Planchon, interviewed by Michael Kustow, "Creating a Theater of Real Life," *Theater Quarterly,* 2, no. 5 (January-March 1972).

17. Jack Kroll, *Newsweek,* May 9, 1977.

18. C. W. E. Bigsby, *Twentieth-Century American Drama,* Vol. 3 (Cambridge, Eng.: Cambridge University Press, 1985).

19. William L. Trilby, "Commune," *Educational Theater Journal,* May 1971.

20. *Mother Courage and Her Children,* Bertolt Brecht, Boston Shakespeare Co., February 1984, reviewed by Arthur Holmberg, Harvard University in *Theater Journal,* December 1984.

21. Sam Shepard, *Angel City, Curse of the Starving Class, and Other Plays* (London: 1978).

10

Scene Design

We go to the theater to *see* a play; it is a show, and the visual appeal is strong. Radio was a good medium for entertainment and communication, but television is far more satisfactory because we like to see what is occurring for ourselves and vicariously participate in the action.

Although most plays begin as words, written texts, a large part of the appeal of the theater comes from the visual aspects: the performers in action, scenery, lighting, and costumes. Greek and Elizabethan dramatic productions made little use of stage scenery as we know it, but they were filled with eye-catching costumes, dances, movement, and pageantry. During the Italian Renaissance, the scenery ran away with the show; and in the eighteenth and nineteenth centuries, striking stage settings were often such a feature of the productions that admission prices were raised because of their sensational appeal.

Although film has taken over the main burden of satisfying the public's craving for the spectacular in such efforts as *Star Wars, Raiders of the Lost Ark,* and *Gunfight at the O.K. Corral,* the live theater does not neglect visual appeal, as almost any musical comedy demonstrates—for example, *Cats, My Fair Lady, Sweeney Todd,* and *Camelot.* A recent Broadway musical that placed unusual emphasis on visual appeal was *Sunday in the Park with George,* whose action revolved around the pointillist painter Georges Seurat. During the course of the first act, the audience saw Seurat's famous *A Sunday Afternoon on the Island of La Grande Jatte* begin as an outline and end as a complete pointillage masterpiece. Trees and characters that were two-dimensional cutouts came alive onstage. The visual effects were the main event of the performance.

THE PICTORIAL TRADITION

The convention of pictorial representation of the dramatic environment is only a few centuries old. Medieval drama, with its manifold stations, often was staged with elaborate attention to realistic detail to secure the maximum amount of identification from the spectator, especially in the scenes from Paradise and Hell-mouth. Essentially, however, our scenic tradition stems from the Renaissance innovation of the proscenium arch at the Farnese Theatre in Parma, Italy (1618). This theater exerted an enormous influence on playwriting and on all phases of production, especially on stage design, which continues to affect our practice today.

Two factors were especially influential in the kinds of sets that appeared in the new proscenium arch theaters. First, the Italian painters were intrigued by the potential of design with linear perspective, by which they could produce the illusion of depth on a flat surface. This development led to the construction and painting of scenery built of wood and canvas, in direct imitation of architecture and natural phenomena. Verisimilitude and

Stagehands at work on an Italian-style perspective setting, showing the wings at the sides, the flies above, and the traps below. A backcloth is being flown at the rear.

solidity were given to the settings by making those units nearest to the audience three dimensional and gradually reducing the space between set pieces until the upstage area was completely two dimensional. As time went on, perspective settings became more and more elaborate, until they became astonishing mazes of corridors, fountains, pillars, and buildings so huge and spectacular that the actor was completely dwarfed onstage. The Bibiena family inaugurated the use of several vistas by running their perspective scenery at divergent angles, thus making possible overwhelming visual displays.

The second factor influencing stage decoration was the custom of creating extravagant "effects"—floats and arches for court pageants and festivals. This taste for ostentatious display and the novelty of perspective scenery were combined in the theaters when designers swamped the stage not only with eye-filling scenery but also with all manner of sensational mechanical stunts, such as great floating clouds and chariots, dazzling practical fountains, and enormous fires that were frighteningly real. Although at first the perspective set served as a neutral background for the production of many plays, under royal and aristocratic patronage the practice was to create specific scenery and effects for specific plays and occasions. Thus, the tradition was established of illusional picture settings—a tradition from which the theater has not entirely escaped to this day.

As the public stage grew and professional companies were forced to make their own way financially, it was impossible for many theaters to af-

An example of Renaissance perspective setting by Giuseppe Bibiena, showing the ornate style of decoration that nearly dwarfed the performers. He was one of a family of designers that dominated the stage all over Europe during the seventeenth and eighteenth centuries.

ford the expense of extravagant scenery. Furthermore, the action of many plays demanded scenery that could be shifted rapidly. A mechanical system was developed, consisting of backdrops and wing-pieces on which were painted a variety of scenes. Wings were portable screens of wood and canvas that could be slid in and out of grooves at the sides of the stage. Rows of these wings, set parallel to the footlights, lined the acting area. Entrances and exits were made by simply walking between the wings. A series of backdrops was flown at the rear of the stage, completing the vista of the setting. Overhead, borders of canvas masked the flies from the spectator. Although these stock pieces were obviously two-dimensional, painted contrivances, they satisfied the audience's taste for reality. Not only were individual pieces of scenery standardized, but every theater owned a series of stock sets, such as an Italian garden, a prison, a mountain pass, a drawing room, a woodland glade, a kitchen, and a palace. These stock sets were used again and again as the various plays demanded. Occasionally, extra care and money were expended to design and construct scenery for specific productions, at which time this fact became a special point of publicity.

In England, Charles Kean, at the Princess Theater (1850–1859), set a new standard for staging plays that were carefully rehearsed and lavishly mounted and costumed. Often called the "illustrator" of Shakespeare's plays, Kean used every opportunity to achieve spectacular effects with scenery, properties, and costumes that were historically correct. His example was influential, especially in the Shakespearean productions of Henry Irving. But by and large, most drama in the eighteenth and nineteenth centuries was performed in stock sets of standardized units of wings and backdrops.

In the chapter on realism we noted the effort in the nineteenth century to achieve authentic environment, not only for visual appeal, but also as a conditioning force on character. The naturalists, in particular, went to great lengths to make their settings as credible as possible. In Paris, Antoine went so far as to hang raw meat onstage for a scene in a butcher shop. The naturalists' excessive concern with imitating the surface aspects of life led to clutter when they attempted to implement the idea of the "significant trifle."

The realists were more moderate, emphasizing simplification and selectivity. In their production of Robertson's plays (1870s), the Bancrofts marked a new approach to realism on the English stage with stage settings that gave the appearance of the appropriate environments, coupled with an acting style that emphasized character and accurate stage business. Their productions won approval for the box set and for the convention of the "fourth wall"—the performers created the illusion that there was an invisible wall across the stage frame, and there was no direct communication with the audience.

A box set consists of three walls of framed canvas and usually a ceiling to enclose the playing area, inside of which the performance takes place. It is usually set with furniture to create the effect of a room, and it is provided with practical doors for exits and entrances.

An example of a box set comes from Ibsen's *An Enemy of the People* (Miller's version):

(It is evening. Dr. Stockmann's living-room is simply but cheerfully furnished. A doorway U.R. leads into the entrance hall, which extends from the front door to the dining-room. Only a small part of the hallway is seen U.R., but there is a passageway extending back-stage from the front door to the dining-room. This dining-room will be described below. The point is that the passage-way is practical for actors, but unseen by the audience. There is a doorway or archway U.L. which leads into the dining-room. Just inside this doorway we see the R. end of a dining-room table. There is one dining-room chair downstage, one at R. of the table and two just above. A short distance up-stage of the end of the table that is visible to the audience is a sideboard or table with one chair on each side of it. The R. end of the dining-room table, the one visible to the audience, stands about half between R. and L. side of the sideboard or table. Down L., about two-thirds of the way to the curtain-line, is another door which leads into Stockmann's study and

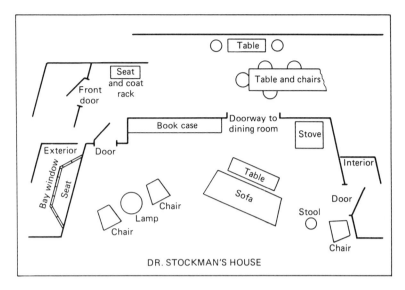

DR. STOCKMAN'S HOUSE

Ground plan for the set of Miller's version of Ibsen's *An Enemy of the People*. This
is a box set with walls surrounding the playing area.

*other rooms of the house. U.L., fitting into the corner of the room, is a tiled stove. Some-
what below this and to R., is a sofa with a table behind it. D.L. below door is an armchair,
and near it another small chair. In R. foreground, somewhat to R. of C., are two chairs,
a small table between them, on which stand a lamp and a bowl of apples. A bay window
is in R. wall about halfway down-stage, and immediately below this is a bench or window
seat.)*[1]

In America, Belasco (1854–1931) achieved a reputation for his realistic staging by such ventures as reproducing onstage a Child's restaurant,
which was daily stocked by the firm with food, and by buying and bringing
onstage, for *The Easiest Way,* the contents of a boarding house, including the
wallpaper. Belasco was also an innovator in new lighting effects, and his
handling of crowd scenes was outstanding.

The effect of wiping out the tradition of painted perspective scenery
brought a new sense of the material rightness of things, and the stage was
filled with casual objects of daily living. Most important, the idea was accepted that scenery should serve as the specific and appropriate environment for the action of the play.

However, with all arts, there is a constant ebb and flow, an action and
a reaction. Realism was no sooner the accepted way of staging drama than
it was challenged by the appearance of plays written in defiance of realistic
practices, as in the works of Maeterlinck, Claudel, Yeats, and Hauptmann.
But even more significant was the appearance of two pioneering spirits, en-
dowed with poetic fervor and imagination, who led the way toward new
stagecraft.

GORDON CRAIG

Although Craig was trained and experienced in the English legitimate theater, his contribution does not lie in the practical aspects of scene painting and construction but rather in his point of view, which was that of a visionary who crusaded for an ideal art of the theater. He castigated the contemporary stage for its shabbiness, for its exaggeration of realistic detail, and most of all, for its lack of artistic purpose and direction. Craig conceived of the theater as an aesthetic unity in which all aspects of production would be harmonized. Toward this end, he called for a director who would achieve this unified concept. Impatient with actors, Craig even suggested replacing them with supermarionettes. His concept of design was based on the selection of a few simple, symbolic set pieces and properties, as his description of a designer illustrates:

> And remember he does not merely sit down and draw a pretty or historically accurate design, with enough doors and windows in picturesque places, but he first of all chooses certain colors which seem to him to be in harmony with the spirit of the play, rejecting other colors as out of tune. He then weaves into a pattern certain objects—an arch, a fountain, a balcony, a bed—using the chosen objects which are mentioned in the play, and which are necessary to be seen.[2]

Craig sought to replace imitation with suggestion, elaboration with simplicity. He insisted on the spiritual relationship between setting and action. He pointed out the emotional potential of figures moving in design, of shifting light and shadow, of the dramatic values of color. He emphasized that the theater was above all "a place for seeing." Craig illustrated his ideas with a series of provocative designs, and he sought to demonstrate his theories in production; sometimes these were doomed to failure because of impracticability, but sometimes they were brilliantly successful. Craig's contribution was not, however, in the utilitarian aspects of the theater; his real significance was in his dream, which he persuaded others to see by the compelling force of his enthusiasm and argument.

ADOLPHE APPIA

The other pioneer of modern staging was the Swiss Adolphe Appia, who in 1899 published his seminal work *Die Musik und die Inscenierung,* in which he called for reforms in the theater. Appia began with the actor and insisted that the design must be in harmony with the living presence of the performer. When a forest was required onstage, for example, it was not necessary to give an accurate representation but only to create the atmosphere of a person amidst the trees. The attention of the audience should be fo-

Drawing by Appia for Wagner's *Die Walkure,* 1892. Atmosphere is created by
skillful use of light and the plastic quality of the setting.

cused on the character, not distracted by detailed branches and leaves.
Painted stage settings are incompatible with the actor because of the contrast
between the actor's plasticity and the flatness of the scenic surroundings:
"The human body does not seek to produce the illusion of reality *since it is
in itself reality!* What it demands of the *decor* is simply to set in relief this reality. . . . We must free staging of everything that is in contradistinction with
the actor's presence. . . . Scenic illusion is the living presence of the actor."

Appia suggested two tenets of good design: The lighting should emphasize the plasticity of the human form, rather than destroy it, and a plastic
scene should give the actor's movements all their value. Implicit in Appia's
theories is the fundamental unity of all phases of production, the major emphasis being on the actor. Appia enforced his arguments by applying them
to a series of designs for the production of Richard Wagner's operas, fash-
ioning uncluttered settings of simple forms in which skillful lighting created
a remarkably appropriate and effective atmosphere. Appia's theories were
well timed since they coincided with the invention of the electric light
(1879), which gave theatrical production a marvelous dimension in design.
Until that time, stage lighting was an awkward and dangerous aspect of production, in which almost all effort went into merely getting enough light on
the stage so that the audience could see. With electricity, lighting could be

used for its evocative potential in creating and enhancing the mood of the play. Appia was the first to demonstrate this new force aesthetically.

The sparks kindled by Craig and Appia ignited, and the "new stage-craft" made its appearance, based on the generally accepted point of view that scenery should augment and reinforce the atmosphere and meaning of the play and that it should give the actor a serviceable environment. This point of view is apparent from the following representative statements: John Gassner regards the function of the setting as a "psychological frame of reference"; Marc Blitzstein says that scenery "should be used to pull the play along its intended course"; and Harold Clurman stresses its practica-

Our Town, 1938, a production that pioneered presentational staging. The environment was suggested by a few pieces of furniture, properties, costuming, and lighting. This is the setting for George's funeral.

bility—"A set is a utensil which cannot be judged until its worth is proved in practice by the whole course of the play's development onstage."

In discussing modern staging, it is important to distinguish between two points of view. First, *representationalism* endeavors to create the illusion of actuality. The characters and events onstage for the moment are intended to convey real life. The second attitude, *presentationalism*, frankly admits that the theater is make-believe and that the actors are only pretending. Although less familiar to Western audiences, presentational staging has a long tradition, notably in the oriental theater, where symbolic conventions are readily accepted. Two coolies, carrying banners on which are painted wheels, become a carriage; a stick becomes a horse when an actor mounts it; a table may be a bridge, a bed, or a mountaintop.

Wilder was the first to successfully introduce presentationalism to the Broadway stage with *Our Town* (1937); he blended the theatricalist elements of absence of scenery and a combined stage manager, narrator, and bit player with a foundation of realistic characterization. Williams followed with *The Glass Menagerie* (1945), in which Tom sets the perspective of the "memory play" as the drama begins by talking directly to the audience and then moving back and forth between playing the role of the brother in the action and stepping outside the fourth wall as narrator and commentator.

Realistic, representational staging is appropriate only to those plays, beginning with Ibsen, written in the realistic mode and intended by the playwright for performance on the picture-frame stage. Drama written outside the realistic mode are presentational by virtue of their creation for such conventions as the masked male actors of the Greek theater and the poetry, soliloquies, and open, flexible platform stage of the Elizabethans. These conventionalized forms of theater created a unified illusion without self-conscious deception. The spectators were aware that they were in a theater and that what was taking place before them was an arbitrary, aesthetic invention, but nevertheless, one powerful enough to arouse deep feelings.

The impact of an action in the theater does not depend on its accuracy so much as on the quality of the performance. An obviously artificial and stylized piece of business can be enormously affecting, for example, in *Equus* when the boy stabs out the eyes of the horses, which are actors wearing sculptured wire heads.

MEYERHOLD AND CONSTRUCTIVISM

One of the most important innovators in the modern theater was the Russian Meyerhold (pp. 188–90, 237–38). Although he was not a designer, he was known for his bold theatricalism—using a presentational approach to staging, especially his *constructivism*. Inspired by the machine and reacting against the ostentatious décor of the czarist regime, the constructivist created stage settings of skeletonized ramps, staircases, bridges, and similar structural forms. The spectator saw the bare bones of the setting against the backstage brick wall, unrelieved by any decorative or aesthetic intention. The set was based entirely on its practicability as a tool for action. Its advantages were that it was frankly theatrical, it gave the performer extraordinary opportunities for movement and the use of space, and it invited fluent and uninterrupted action. Meyerhold made full use of these advantages, even to developing a style of acting, "biomechanics," suited to the machine age, a style that included training in acrobatics, circus movement, and ballet.

EPIC THEATER

One of the most interesting efforts in experimental drama was the "epic theater," which began in the 1920s as a result of the work of Piscator and Brecht. As we have seen, Brecht, in addition to being a director, was also a playwright who put his theories into practice, even to inventing a new approach to acting, like Meyerhold. Epic theater workers revolted against the tradition of Ibsenian realism. They were not concerned with the domestic problems of a husband and wife in a home; epic drama called for a larger arena of action, showing the dynamics of social forces at work. Hence, the epic theater playwright and designer demanded a stage that would serve for many fragments of action, some of them occurring simultaneously.

In 1928, Piscator's production of *The Good Soldier Schweik* offered a brilliant and stimulating example of the new style. A dramatization of a novel, the play concerns the life of a private soldier ground down by the stupidity and brutality of war. His story is told in a kaleidoscopic arrangement of scenes, recitations, songs, and explanations. In addition to the usual facilities of the stage, Piscator used slides, posters, charts, maps, graphs, a treadmill for moving scenery and actors, and a motion-picture screen on which were projected cartoons, captions, and film sequences—all joined together in a welter of sights and sounds.

Gorelik describes the nature of Piscator's production:

> "I'll do my duty for the Emperor to the end," adds Schweik. On the screen a Russian soldier is swimming in a pond. A bush rolls on with the Russian's uniform hanging on it. "A souvenir," thinks Schweik. He puts it on. A shot rings out, and a Hungarian patrol rushes on and seizes him in loud Hungarian tones. "What do you mean, prisoner?" Schweik demands. "I'm on your side . . ." A shell bursts. Schweik falls. From the upper corner of the screen a procession of crosses starts toward the audience. As the crosses, growing nearer in perspective, reach the lower edge of the screen, a muslin drop, lowered downstage, catches them once more, bringing them still closer to the spectators. A rain of crosses falls upon this wry comedy as the lights begin to go up.[3]

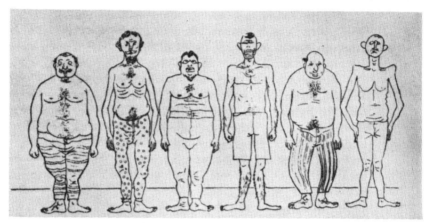

Erwin Piscator's ''epic'' staging of *The Good Soldier Schweik,* Berlin, 1927. All elements of the staging were used in a presentational style.

Brecht's *The Private Life of the Master Race,* another epic play, dramatizes the experiences of a German Panzer crew, moving across Europe from the early stages of World War II until it is defeated by the Russians. The play is really a series of one acts, depicting the effects of Nazism and warfare on the crew. The various threads are knit together by lyrical passages. The play begins with this stage direction:

> (*A band plays a barbaric march. Out of the darkness appears a big signpost:* To Poland *and near it a Panzer truck. Its wheels are turning. On it sit twelve to sixteen soldiers, steel helmeted, their faces white as chalk, their guns between their knees. They could be puppets. The soldiers sing to the tune of the Horst Wessel Song.*)

There follows a series of scenes such as "The Betrayal," "The Jewish Wife," and "The Informer," dramatizing various phases of Nazi terrorism until the Panzer is bogged down in Russia. The sequences are bridged by voices out of the darkness and the roar of the armored car.

Brecht's presentational style rejected the realistic theater of illusion and the notion of ornamentation and display. Scenery was spare and skeletal; the lighting was used to illuminate the stage so that everything was clear, not to create atmosphere through suggestive colors and shadows. No attempt was made to conceal light sources; instruments were mounted in galleries, boxes, or pipe battens, in full view of the audience. Since attending the theater was educational, Brecht used visual aids such as projected slides, maps, charts, and diagrams. Working in the Berliner Ensemble (1947–1956), Brecht demonstrated in his own plays, as well as in a dozen others, his approach to the theater in such a compelling way that he is regarded as one of the most influential forces in the modern theater.

THE SCENE DESIGNER AT WORK

The scene designer today is neither an interior decorator nor merely a skilled craftsperson who is obliged to follow the producer's orders in the construction and arrangement of set pieces on the stage. Like the directors and actors, the scenographers these days are members of a team that shares the challenge of bringing the script to life. Not only do they locate the place of the action, but above all, they reveal the significance of the play.

René Allio, an outstanding European designer who is associated with Planchon's notable Théâtre de la Cité in Lyons, describes his function in the theater:

> To invent a sort of visual language for each play, that, within a chosen expressive style, underscores its various meanings, extending and echoing them, sometimes in a precise and almost critical way, sometimes more diffusely and subtly in the manner of a poetic image where fortuitous meanings are no less important than those that are sought.[4]

Scene from a "Living Newspaper" production of *One Third of a Nation,* 1938. This highly theatricalized setting suggested the quality of "epic" theater staging.
(Set design by Howard Bay.)

The scenographer begins work on a specific play by studying the script, perhaps recording initial impressions during or after a first reading. Ben Edwards, one of the foremost American scenographers, tells how he begins:

I try not to think about the scenery too much when I read the play. I try to think of the play itself and what it is saying, and somehow, have the scenery evolve from the play. If you don't get a lot from the script, it's a very difficult job to design it.[5]

Oliver Smith, who has gained an enviable reputation for his designs, especially for such musicals as *West Side Story, Camelot, Sound of Music,* and *My Fair Lady,* describes his initial steps:

What I do is read the material, listen to the score, and if it's present, read the script. And then I do a lot of thinking. I don't draw a line, I just brood—concentrate. I might make tiny sketches on envelopes or pieces of paper, just as idea sketches, but not anything I plan to use particularly. If it is a project that requires research, I do a thorough research and collect a large body of it, which I study carefully. Then when I start to work, I put all the research away, forget it. I mean, it has to be absorbed subconsciously. . . .[6]

During this early preparation, the scenographer is not primarily concerned with the problems of construction, painting, and lighting, though of course the fact that the set must be capable of being built and used cannot be ignored. In the early planning, the questions are likely to be these: What images dominate the action? What is the atmosphere of the environment? What are the important scenes, and what kinds of performance areas are needed?

When Boris Aronson was asked about his approach to the scenery for *Fiddler on the Roof,* he said,

Fiddler on the Roof is the title of a very famous painting by Marc Chagall. Both the director and producer felt that the lightness, the playfulness of mood found in Chagall's work should be incorporated into the design. This contribution was to the atmosphere, but was not the solution to the design itself. I reread the Sholom Aleichem stories. . . . Tevye's house was described as a circle within a circle. I designed it as two revolving stages . . . one large, and one small. *Fiddler* was an attempt to show the beauty of nature, growing even within poverty.[7]

Mordecai Gorelik searches for the "poetic image of the scene" by making numerous small sketches. He pays no attention to the practicalities of the staging. For example, in his designs for *Golden Boy,* Gorelik began with the concept of a prize ring, even though the playwright, Clifford Odets, did not call for such a scene in his play; however, the basic image influenced the designs of all the scenes. An illuminating example of Gorelik's thinking is indicated in his approach to Chekhov's *The Three Sisters:*

It is the *dramatic metaphor,* probably, which sums up, for each setting, all the thoughts which the designer may have. Thus, the attic bedroom of *The Three Sisters* is not only an attic, not only a bedroom, not only a girl's room, not only a European room, not only a room of the period of 1901, not only a room belonging to the gentlefolk whom Chekhov wrote about. On top of all that, and including all that, it may be for the designer, the scene of a raging fever.[8]

Still another example shows how Donald Oenslager captured the atmosphere of *Hamlet:*

> Hamlet dwells in a dual world, the everyday world of external events which is the life of Court, and the haunted, brooding world of the imagination which is the inner world of an avenging Prince, who drifts down endless corridors of dark, fir-bordered streams. . . . It is the conflict of these two worlds that unbalances his mind and goads him on to indecisive action and helpless frustration.
>
> The way he distorts the external world through the eyes of his own inner world of the imagination must determine the nature and appearance of the scenes. Just as he sees the events of the Court in the curving mirror of his own brooding conjectures, so the scenes which he inhabits must appear as indefinite embodiments of his own inner preoccupations. The members of the Court must seem to be resolved into dewy shadows of this "too, too solid flesh" and cloaked in veiled fragments of reality. . . . For all the Castle scenes bare, chalky walls are pierced with tall tragic doors—always three, whose depth beyond is as black as Hamlet's sable suit. They must be high, very high, to admit his anguish and his spirit. Only flashes of red, the red of blood, livens the scenes—washed over walls, or splotched on characters' clothing.[9]

When Oliver Smith designed *West Side Story,* his overall conception came from the dominant image of the rumble.

Sometimes a designer is faced with a particular difficulty because of the playwright's handling of his or her materials. Miller uses more than forty scenes in *Death of a Salesman,* but he wanted them played without interruption and flowing freely from the present to the past and to the present again. The scenographer, Jo Mielziner, describes how he approached Miller's play by trying to visualize the action as if he were a member of the audience. Then he made a "breakdown" of the scenes and determined where each one could be played. He arrived at this basic concept:

> One thought came to me: In the scene where the Salesman mentally goes back to the early years of his marriage, when his boys were young and the house was surrounded by trees and open country, I had to create something visually that would make these constant transitions in time immediately clear to the audience. My next thought was that, even if we ended up with a big stage, with plenty of stagehands, and I was able to design some mechanism for handling the large number of individual scenes, the most important visual symbol in the play—the real background of the story—was the Salesman's house. Therefore, why should that house not be the main set, with all the other scenes—the corner of a graveyard, a hotel room in Boston, the corner of a business office, a lawyer's consultation room, and so on—played on the forestage? If I designed these little scenes in segments and fragments, with easily moved props and fluid lighting effects, I might be able, without ever lowering the curtain, to achieve the easy flow that the author clearly wanted.[10]

Jo Mielziner's design for *Death of a Salesman*. Note the various acting areas within the framework of the home. The downstage level was used for flashback scenes.

Mielziner went on to design one of the most remarkable sets of the modern American theater.

Although most designers begin with sketches, some prefer working with models, scaled replicas constructed in three dimensions. Many directors prefer the models because the plasticity gives them a clearer idea of the shapes and spaces they will be using. The model is also helpful in planning the shifting of scenery as well as the lighting.

Robert Randolph, who designed such hits as *Bye, Bye, Birdie, The King and I,* and *Gypsy,* comments, "You'll never know what it looks like until it is in a model." Viennese designer Rouben Ter-Arutunian adds,

> I always make models and I do not always make a painted sketch in terms of a pretty picture. . . . The spatial relationships are far more important to present to a director and technical departments than a picture.[11]

The next step in design is the preparation of working drawings through which the sketch and model are translated into actual scenery by the carpenters and painters. The working drawings usually include a scaled and dimensioned floor plan, elevations of the walls, a hanging chart of flying pieces, and detail drawings of special set pieces and properties. Complete specifications are a part of the drawings. In the professional theater, the designer may make only the sketches and the model, turning the preparation of the working drawings over to a draftsman, and the construction over to the professional scene builders and painters. In the educational and community theater, the scene designer often works through all steps of the design, from the preliminary sketches to the actual construction, painting, and mounting of the set.

Perhaps one of the most interesting ways of showing designers at work is to consider their efforts on the same play. The following are descriptive passages of three designers' approaches to *Macbeth*. The first is a celebrated statement by Craig, which illustrates his intuitive and aesthetic feeling for design:

> Come now, we take *Macbeth*. We know the play well. In what kind of place is that play laid? How does it look, first of all to our mind's eye? Secondly to our eye?
>
> I see two things. I see a lofty and steep rock, and I see the moist cloud which envelops the head of this rock. That is to say, a place for fierce and warlike men to inhabit—a place for phantoms to nest in. Ultimately this moisture will destroy the men. Now then, you are quick in your question as to what actually to create for the eye. I answer as swiftly—place there a rock! Let it mount up high. Swiftly I tell you, convey the idea of a mist which hugs the head of this rock. Now, have I departed at all for one-eighth of an inch from the vision which I saw in the mind's eye?
>
> But you ask me what form this rock shall take and what color? What are the lines which are the lofty lines, and which are to be seen in any lofty cliff? Go to them, glance but a moment at them; now quickly set them down on your paper; the *lines and their directions*, never mind the cliff. Do not be afraid to let them go high; they cannot go high enough; and remember that on a sheet of paper which is but two inches square you can make a line which seems to tower miles in the air, and you can do the same on your stage, for it is all a matter of proportion and nothing to do with actuality.
>
> You ask about the colors? What are the colors that Shakespeare has indicated for us? Do not first look at Nature, but look in the play of the poet. Two: one for the rock, the man; one for the mist, the spirit.[12]

The second description is of the banquet scene as it appeared in Reinhardt's production of *Macbeth*, designed by Ernest Stern. Ludwig Lewisohn's account of the production emphasizes the overall severity:

> Take the scene of the banquet in *Macbeth*. Every line is a straight line, every angle a right angle. All form is reduced to a barbaric severity. But the two rectangular windows in the background through which the cold Northern stars glitter are narrow and tall—so unimaginably tall that they seem to touch that sky of doom. The torches turn the rough brown of the primitive walls to a tarnished bronze. Only on the rude table lie splashes of menacing yellow. There is something barren and gigantic about the scene—a sinister quiet, a dull presage.[13]

The eminent theater critic Stark Young described the celebrated designs of Robert Edmond Jones:

Gordon Craig's design for *Macbeth*.

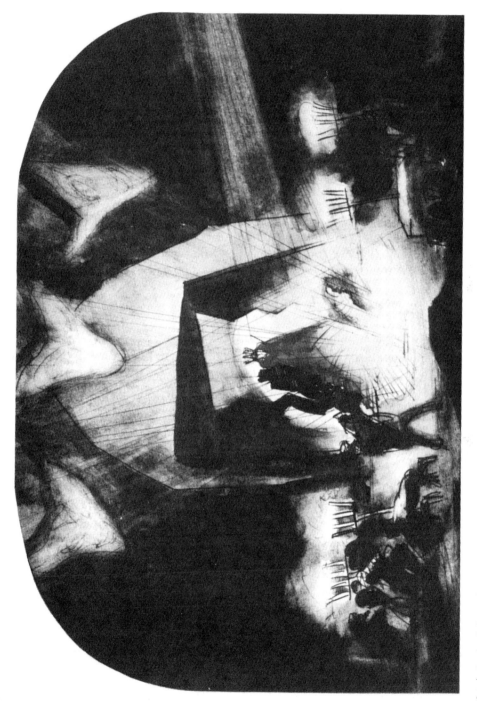

Set design by Robert Edmund Jones for the banquet scene in *Macbeth*.

This design for *Macbeth* was the most profoundly creative decor that I have ever seen in the theater. There was a stage enclosed with a background of black, flat so that no light was caught to break the complete darkness of it. Drawings or photographs can give at least a suggestion, and only a suggestion of the gold frames, or sharp gold lines, or the forms like Gothic abstractions, or however we may define them, which, standing alone against the black, defined the scenes. Three great tragic masks were hung to the front, high above the action, and from them vast daggers of light poured down, crossed, pierced, flooded the action below, as in the witches' scene or the banquet. The banquet hall with its gold and light figures moving, and above all else, Lady Macbeth's robe, in which a hidden combination of many shades, an unheard-of-intensity of red was discovered, defied any conveyance in words.[14]

Each of these designs is valid in its own right. We see the designer's efforts to evoke the appropriate atmosphere of the play; to intensify its emotional content through judicious use of line, color, lighting, and texture; and to create the environment for the action. Each represents the approach of the designer in helping to interpret the play.

SELECTIVE REALISM

The bulk of modern drama up to World War II was written in the realistic mode. It dealt with the problems and frustrations of contemporary human beings against an authentic environment of daily life. Hence, its style was representational—performers simulated real people, often shaped or trapped by their immediate environments. The stage designer was obliged to capture the atmosphere and meaning of the play with scenery that served the needs of the performers. As time wore on, a strictly realistic attitude toward the theater lost its hold; then designers produced stage settings that were increasingly selective and imaginative and less dependent on overwhelming detail.

Robert Edmond Jones, a moving force in American scenography, struck a note that echoes to this day in the theater:

Stage designing should be addressed to this eye of the mind. There is an outer eye that observes, and there is an inner eye that sees. . . . The designer must always be on guard against being too explicit. A good scene, I repeat, is not a picture. It is something seen, but it is something conveyed as well; a feeling, an evocation. Plato says somewhere: It is beauty I seek, not beautiful things. That is what I mean. A setting is not just a beautiful thing, a collection of beautiful things. It is a presence, a mood, a symphonic accompaniment to the drama, a great wind fanning the drama to flame. It echoes, it enhances, it animates. It is an expectancy, a foreboding, a tension. It says nothing, but it gives everything.[15]

The result was *selective realism,* by which is meant that the scenery conveys the impression of reality without reproducing it. Designers take artistic license in asking the spectator to join in the imaginative process of production by working from simplified settings and properties chosen for their evocative power.

Selective realism often uses "space staging" (see pp. 343–44). Working either within the proscenium arch or on a thrust platform, the designer no longer defines the environment of the action by a box set or scenic enclosure; instead the playing area, scene after scene, is picked out of darkness by a pool of light, with either portable furniture and properties, or by moving from one space to another in a permanent set that offers a variety of places and levels. All the properties and furniture, as well as the fragments of scenery, are chosen for their power to locate the action and to create the appropriate atmosphere.

Jocelyn Herbert's design for Brecht's *Saint Joan of the Stockyards* 1964, Court Theater. A few simple elements on a relatively bare stage against a theatricalized background.

(Directed by Tony Richardson.)

Fuller's *A Soldier's Play* is written in a realistic style, with a unit set designed to serve as various areas in the Army camp at Fort Neal. This is the playwright's description of the set:

(Scene: *The inner shell of the stage is black. On the stage, in a horseshoe-like half circle, are several platforms at varying levels.*

On the left side of this horseshoe is a military office arrangement with a small desk (a nameplate on the desk reads: CAPTAIN CHARLES TAYLOR), *two office-type chairs, one straight-backed, a regimental, and an American flag. A picture of F.D.R. is on the wall.*

On the right side of the horseshoe, and curved toward the rear, is a barracks arrangement, with three bunk beds and footlockers set in typical military fashion. The exit to this barracks is a free-standing doorway on the far right. (This barracks should be changeable—these bunks with little movement can look like a different place.) On the edge of this barracks is a poster, semi-blown up, of Joe Louis in an army uniform, helmet, rifle, and bayonet. It reads: PVT. JOE LOUIS SAYS, "WE'RE GOING TO DO OUR PART— AND WE'LL WIN BECAUSE WE'RE ON GOD'S SIDE."

On the rear of the horseshoe, upstage center, is a bare platform, raised several feet above everything else. It can be anything we want it to be—a limbo if you will.

The entire set should resemble a courtroom. The sets, barracks and office, will both be elevated, so that from anywhere on the horseshoe one may look down onto a space at center stage that is on the stage floor. The levels should have easy access by either stairs or ramps, and the entire set should be raked ever so slightly so that one does not perceive much difference between floor and set, and the bottom edges of the horseshoe. There must also be enough area on both sides of the horseshoe to see exits and entrances.[16]

The experimentalists have left their mark on the theater. Staging is increasingly presentational, both in writing and in design. The traditional conventions of the representational style have been changed to accommodate a more frankly theatrical perspective; today, even in box set commercial hits, characters may address the audience in monologues or asides, time sequences may be altered by flashbacks, and scenery may be shifted in full view of the audience by the crew or even the performers.

It is interesting to see what has happened to realism as it has become more and more selective during this century. In the early Moscow Art Theater productions of Chekhov, for example, the interiors were usually box sets, filled with the properties of daily living. Under selective realism, directors and designers have searched for imagery to underscore Chekhov's meaning. In Andrei Serban's production of *The Three Sisters* at the American Repertory Theater, Cambridge (1982), the setting of the Prozorov home was defined by suspended dark red curtains against the gray cinder-block walls of the backstage. As the family disintegrated and lost control, the curtains became separated and crushed until finally, in the fourth act, they disappeared entirely, leaving a mass of fallen autumnal leaves on the floor, leading to the shadowed gray wall.

In a recent Moscow production of the same play, when during the fourth act the military band was heard in the distance, signaling its depar-

A production of Dostoievski's *The Idiot,* designed by Josef Svoboda for a production at the Old Vic, London. The atmosphere is established by projections instead of painted scenery.

(Directed by Anthony Quayle.)

ture, the band was brought onstage and then moved to the brick wall at the back of the stage. The giant loading doors opened to the night. The band marched out into the darkness, the music fading, until at the end the audience was left with an image of a black, silent void.

During the 1985 season, one of the highlights of the London theater was the premiere of *Wild Honey,* a play based on an old manuscript by Chekhov that was found in a Moscow bank after his death. Michael Frayn cut and revised the lengthy manuscript, and it was produced at the National Theater. Although Chekhov's reputation rests on his skillful delineation of sympathetic but frustrated people, usually in Russian drawing rooms, *Wild Honey's* theatrical debut owed a great deal to its sensational staging. The dialogue, situations, and characters have the quality of Chekhovian drama, but the stage effects, which feature a train, made a powerful impact in the theater. Here is the sequence leading up to the stunning climax:

In Act One, Scene Two, which is set in a garden, a distant train whistle is heard, and then another a little closer, with the faint sound of a locomotive. The second act begins with the sound of a freight train clanking and whistling as it passes by, its red tail light receding in the distance. At the end of Scene One, Act Two, Osip, the local ne'er-do-well, crazed by jealousy, tries to commit suicide by lying across the level crossing just as the headlight of an approaching train appears. He is dragged clear of the track just as the train whistle screams to a crescendo. At the end of the play, Platnovov, a philanderer, is caught in the arms of another woman by two of his former conquests. When they threaten to shoot him, Platnovov jumps out of the window. The stage directions read,

> (*In the instant while they automatically look around for four rubles, Platonov jumps out of the window.*
>
> *Sofya and the others rush to the window after him. As they do so there is the sound of an approaching train whistle, and they all turn, struck by the same thought. They run out of the door; and the world falls apart. Amidst the gathering roar of the train the rear wall of the house moves aside and the lights go down. The forest and the railway line of the previous scene are revealed beyond. Stumbling towards us between the rails is Platonov. He stops, blinded by the brilliant headlight of a train approaching from behind the heads of the audience, its whistle screaming. He staggers back a step or two, trying to wave the train away like the flies. Then sudden blackness, and the great roar of the train, its note falling as it passes us. The red tail light of the train appears at the front of the stage and dwindles rapidly into the smoke left by the locomotive. There is a smell of sulphur in the air. Blackout.)*[17]

Modern technology provides scenography with a broad spectrum of new materials. Lightweight metal pipes and tubing enable the designer to erect scaffolding high above the floor, spanning twenty-five to thirty feet, and with the addition of wooden platforms, it makes possible a variety of stairways and ramps. Pressed decorative metal plates are used for ceiling and walls. Other useful metal materials are expanded mesh wire, sheeting, and corrugated iron. Sheets of Mylar allow highly reflective surfaces on walls, floors, or frameworks. Sculptured props and surface decorations are made by using latex and silicone molds and fast-setting plaster bandages. Carved and shaped ornaments are constructed from polyurethane foam.

In his design for *Jacob's Ladder*, Neil Peter Jampolis was obliged to provide the illusion of a vast space through which the "souls" could float. His solution was to fashion silvery clouds out of lucite and silverleaf, making translucent surfaces that could be lighted through and projected on to vary the size and shape of the stage space.

Boris Aronson writes, "*Company* was based upon a series of vignettes about married life in New York . . . people living in glass cages. I designed *Company* using no paint—Plexiglas, steel and projection. New York is a paced city . . . you don't stroll, you dodge. I created obstacles for the actors to relate to . . . forcing them to move certain ways . . . push buttons . . . elevators going up and down. . . . The city moving the man."[18]

Stephen Hendrickson's assignment for *Waiting for Godot* was to provide an endless, open, neutral landscape from which the characters could

Setting for *K2* at the Arena Stage, Washington, D.C. The quality of the frozen mountain is suggested by the plastic foam.

not readily escape. He designed a steeply raked floor that offered no satisfactory footholds. The surface was covered with rusted tin-roofing sheets recovered from a scrapheap.

In Chapter Seven, *Theatricalism and the New Theater,* I pointed out that the dadaists and surrealists made their creations out of incongruous combinations of objects and figures, simultaneous action, fragmentation, and distortion. More than sixty years later, we see this tendency at work in contemporary scene design.

When John Bury became scene designer for Joan Littlewood's East End Theater Workshop in 1954, he was obliged to work on an austere budget, so he designed from the available materials he found in the shop or elsewhere rather than from the drawing board. Hence, he resorted to "real" materials like rusted corrugated iron and used lumber. Later, when Bury worked as a designer with Peter Hall at the Stratford-upon-Avon Theater,

Eugene Lee's enormous setting for *Sweeney Todd* suggests the interior of a
nineteenth-century foundry with its complex mechanical equipment that includes
movable catwalks, platforms, staircases, and set pieces including a large oven. The
demon barber wields his lethal razor in his second level shop equipped with a trick
chair and trap door that dispatches his victims to his confederate in the bakery
below.

he continued to use interesting and "found" materials. A notable example was the set he prepared for Shakespeare's history plays, known as the *War of Roses,* for which he employed expanded metal, textured by acids and copper solutions and lighted directionally to enhance the quality of the material. His central image, the steel of war, created the impression of a hard and dangerous world. On a floor of sheet steel, tables became daggers, staircases axeheads, and doors the traps of the gallows. Everything contributed to the creation of a steel-clad, enclosing prison. Even the trees in the background were harsh with iron foliage.

Another designer, famous for the "poor theater" quality of his settings, in which he uses "found" natural materials, is Edward Stepanovich Kochergin at the Gorki Theater in Leningrad. From visits to the countryside, he gathers rocks, branches, mosses, and old wood to inspire his use of color and texture in his designs. The set for Aleksandr Pushkin's *Boris Godunov* (1973) was a framework made of tree limbs stripped of their bark.

Karl-Emst Hemann's set for Labiche's *The Pot* at the Schaubühne in West Berlin. Note the varied scenic elements and surfaces and the interesting use of textures and shapes.

(Directed by Peter Stein.)

Over the frame, Kochergin stretched tattered burlap in patches that suggested leaves. The raked floor was made of worn wood planking, and the set was "decorated" by old church bells. For Tolstoi's *Tale of a Horse* (1976), the designer fashioned a courtyard where horses are kept. Again, he covered the walls with burlap, with bulges that opened like festered wounds, showing red fabric in the gaps from which tiny blossoms fell. During the climactic moments, red lights flashed with a pulselike beat to suggest the suffering of the horses. Kochergin is fond of breaking through walls to let light pour in. His design for *Hamlet* was constructed of bleached wood that enclosed the acting area except for the audience's side. Cracks and fissures in the wooden shell allowed light to spill on the rough floor. His set for *Monologue for Marriage* depicted the playwright's view of matrimony as a precarious institution by surrounding the action with paper walls, which through the play are torn away, so that at the end the stage is a shambles.

One of the most creative designers is the Czechoslovakian Josef Svoboda, whose combination of aesthetic and technical talents has enabled him

Scenography by Josef Svoboda for *Oedipus Rex* at the National Theater, Prague. *(Directed by M. Machacek. Photo: Dr. Jaromir Svoboda.)*

to provide stunning examples of the new uses of the stage. He sees the theater as providing "a vivid sense of separate elements imaginatively combined to express new insights into reality." He considers that his purpose as a designer is not to provide substitutes for décor or delineation of locale but to create new stage space. His designs exploit the theatrical possibilities of kinetic scenery and multiple images, which can react to or against the live performer on stage.

For his production of *Hamlet* in Brussels (1965), director Ottomar Krejca based his interpretation on the idea that the ghost is a fiction of Hamlet—his alter ego—and that the play is concerned with this dual role. Svoboda's technical solution was to use a mirror whose reflections he could control to reveal not only the protagonist's state of mind but the disparity of his surrounding world as well. For a production of the Capek brothers' *The Insect Comedy,* he used two mirrors, twenty-five feet square, placed at an angle to reflect the decorated area of the stage floor, which contained a turntable. No regular scenery was used, and only the stage floor was lighted. Svoboda's set design for *Romeo and Juliet* at the National Theater in Prague (1963) was made up of architectural components that moved in a variety of ways—rising, sinking, and sliding laterally or forward and back to accommodate the action.

It is particularly in the use of projections that Svoboda has made such interesting contributions, for he is at once an artist and an engineer. One of his devices, the *diapolyekran,* is a complex screen on which simultaneous and synchronous slides and films can be shown and controlled to exploit the interplay between the images. His Laterna Magika is a multiscreen device designed for use onstage with the live actor. It enables the director to work with a visual collage of background or supporting material in a new way—as director Jan Grossman put it, to show "the multiplicity and contrariety of the world in which we live." Svoboda describes the use of projections in his designs for Gorki's *The Last Ones:*

> We stacked things, people, scenes behind each other; for example, action around the wheelchair downstage, above that a girl in a tub being stroked by twigs, "in front" of her a boy being flogged on the screen; then suddenly, a drape covering part of the screen opens and we see a small, live orchestra playing a waltz, with pomp—an image of the regime. A space collage using a triptych principle, truly a dramatic poem—what I wanted to do. A clear spatial aesthetic is formed by the contrast of stage action, flat projection, and live orchestra behind the screen on which the images are projected. It's all structured like music, and a law is present. Break it and a new one is set up. This is what attracts me—leitmotifs and repetitions, then sudden contrast; plus tempo indications. Themes disappear only to crop up again later.[19]

For Luigi Nono's *Intolerance,* Svoboda employed five large screens on which were projected images of intolerance, such as piles of bones and bodies in a concentration camp; a frozen, bloody corpse; a chained black, tied to a tree while being whipped; an angry mob. The effect was to create a montage like a nightmare, shifting from one brutal reality to another.

As we have seen, one of the interesting developments of theatrical staging comes from a fresh interpretation of an established play: Stein's *Peer Gynt*, Svoboda's *Hamlet* and *Romeo and Juliet*, or Brook's *A Midsummer Night's Dream*. One of the striking features of the last was the use of trapezes. Sally Jacobs, the designer, explains that it was decided to delimit a small-sized acting area to a neutral place, where the various elements of the play could be introduced. She describes the solution to the problem of placing performers:

> There are points, for instance, where people are "sleeping" while action is taking place. At first, we wanted the actors stuck on the walls, but didn't know how to do it. Then I suddenly realized that we already had a marvelous mechanism—the flies—for lifting people up and down, and so the trapezes came in. They also accentuated the floating and dreaming aspect of the play. We could use the stage vertically as well as horizontally.[20]

Stage designers explore the new theater in a variety of ways. They respond to the revolution and experimentation in the visual arts by expanding the areas of perception, relating the external image to the unconscious, juxtaposing disparate objects and experiences through simultaneous viewing and the combination of media, and showing the dynamic nature of creation through mobile forms and kinetic objects.

John Napier, one of the most successful British designers (*Nicholas Nickleby*, *Equus*, and *Cats*) views himself not as a maker of pictures for scenic background but as a creator of spaces for the performers and spectators. He says:

> I want to wrap and involve people in the experience that's going on. I want to break down the usual distance between audience, stage, performers, and public, partly because I'm not pictorial, not a painting person.[21]

Napier demonstrated what he meant in his designs for *Cats*. For the London production, he revamped an old theater by transforming the arena into a three-sided audience area, which enclosed a huge, circular stage—a cluttered junkyard that could revolve 180 degrees. The set became a vast assemblage, which he described as

> . . . the accumulation and proliferation of tangible, recognizable materials and artifacts of a given time and place, a highly littered environment which, along with the complex activity of the performers, creates a specific, fictive world and atmosphere.[22]

Ter-Arutunian often uses a collage for the background of his sets, which consists of the juxtaposition of enlarged photographs of conflicting

Design by Sally Jacobs for Peter Brook's famous production of *A Midsummer Night's Dream*. Note the facilities the performers used for flying.

scenes. Likewise, Svoboda sometimes projects a collection of disparate images to create the environment for the action.

In the revolt against the theater in the last two decades, some experimentalists rejected the architecture as well and began playing in garages, lofts, round houses, stores, or the street—environments in which no traditional scenery could be used. Other avant garde innovators created productions that emphasized images as entities in themselves rather than as support for the verbal text. Rock concerts began capturing the eye as well as the ear with light, color, and costumes. In Poland, Jerzy Gurawski designed the audience and acting areas as a single unit for Growtowski's Laboratory productions. In France, R. Moscoso revamped the interior of a munitions factory for Mnouchkine's experimental plays. On tour at the Olympics in 1984, the Théâtre du Soleil took over a Hollywood television studio and installed a large square simulated Noh stage, with enormous decorative silk backdrops that were changed for each scene, in an orientalized version of *Twelfth Night*. The scenographer is moving toward complete responsibility for all visual aspects of theater.

John Napier's design for the English staging of Webber and Eliot's musical *Cats*. The center of the theater was cleared out for the playing area and it was mechanized so that it could revolve part way. The oversize junkyard properties suggest the cat's eye-view. The setting is virtually an assemblage.

(Directed by Trevor Nunn. Photo: J. Burian.)

The revolt in the theater since World War II has resulted in a much freer approach to all aspects of staging, although representationalism remains remarkably persistent, especially on the commercial stage. Two factors influence this preference. Most theaters are proscenium arch, picture-frame playhouses, which were designed for productions using scenic background, and many nineteenth- and twentieth-century dramatists have written their plays in a realistic mode.

It is apparent that the trend toward a more theatrical theater will encourage the elimination of the gaps between performer and spectator, playing space and auditorium. With a more open climate for playwriting, designers will be increasingly concerned with the total environment. With the availability of new materials and facilities, the only limitation will be the designer's imagination.

Peter Stein staged *As You Like It* in a movie studio so he could use huge settings with the audience moving from the Court to the countryside. This view shows the Court, where the actors played above the audience.

The countryside set was very large and filled with realistic set pieces to create a realistic atmosphere which changed when the courtiers approached.

Henry May's setting for *As You Like It* at the University of California, Berkeley.

FILMS TO SEE FOR OUTSTANDING DESIGN

F = Film Available; V = Videotape Available.

F		*An Andalusian Dog*
F	V	*Amadeus*
F	V	*Cyrano de Bergerac*
F	V	*Equus*
F	V	*Henry V*
F	V	*Jesus Christ, Superstar*
F	V	*The Pawnbroker*
F		*The Seventh Seal*
F	V	*Sweeney Todd*
F	V	*West Side Story*
F	V	*Wild Strawberries*

BIBLIOGRAPHY

APPIA, ADOLPHE. *The Work of Living Art,* trans. H. D. Albright. Coral Gables, Fla.: University of Miami Press, 1961.

BABLET, DENIS. *The Revolutions of Stage Design in the 20th Century.* Paris: Leon Amiel, 1977.

BURDICK, ELIZABETH B., PEGGY C. HANSEN, and BRENDA ZANGER. *Contemporary Stage Design, U.S.A.* Englewood Cliffs, N.J.: Prentice-Hall, Inc., 1974.

BURIAN, JARKA. *The Scenography of Josef Svoboda.* Middletown, Conn.: Wesleyan University Press, 1971.

CRAIG, EDWARD GORDON. *Theater Advancing.* Boston: Little, Brown & Company, 1963.

GILLETTE, A. A. *Stage Scenery.* New York: Harper & Row, Publishers, Inc., 1972.

GORELIK, MORDECAI. *New Theaters for Old.* New York: Samuel French, 1940.

HAINAUX, RENÉ, ed. *Stage Design Throughout the World, 1970–1975.* New York: Theater Arts Books, 1976.

JONES, ROBERT EDMOND. *The Dramatic Imagination.* Middletown, Conn.: Wesleyan University Press, 1941.

OENSLAGER, DONALD. *The Theater of Donald Oenslager.* Middletown, Conn.: Wesleyan University Press, 1978.

PARKER, OREN W. *Scene Design and Stage Lighting.* New York: Holt, Rinehart and Winston, 1980.

PECKTAL, LYNN. *Designing and Painting for the Theater.* New York: Holt, Rinehart and Winston, 1975.

SIMONSON, LEE. *The Stage Is Set.* New York: Theater Arts Books, 1963.

NOTES

1. Arthur Miller's adaptation of *An Enemy of the People*, by Henrik Ibsen (New York: The Viking Press, 1950).

2. Gordon Craig, *On the Art of the Theatre* (London: Heinemann, 1905).

3. Mordecai Gorelik, *New Theaters for Old* (New York: Samuel French, 1940).

4. René Allio, quoted in Denis Bablet, *The Revolutions of Stage Design in the 20th Century* (Paris: Leon Amiel, Publisher, 1977).

5. Ben Edwards, quoted in Lynn Pecktal, *Designing and Painting for the Theater* (New York: Holt, Rinehart, & Winston, 1975).

6. Oliver Smith, quoted in Lynn Pecktal, *Designing and Painting for the Theater,* (New York: Holt, Rinehart and Winston, 1975).

7. Boris Aronson, quoted in *Designing and Painting for the Theater.*

8. Mordecai Gorelik, quoted in John Gassner, ed., *Producing the Play* (New York: Holt, Rinehart & Winston, 1953).

9. Donald Oenslager, *Scenery Then and Now* (New York: W. W. Norton & Co., Inc., 1936).

10. Jo Mielziner, *Designing for the Theater* (New York: Bramhall House, 1965).

11. Rouben Ter-Arutuniam, quoted in *Designing and Painting for the Theater.*

12. Craig, *On the Art of the Theater.*

13. Ludwig Lewisohn, *The Drama and the Stage* (New York: Harcourt Brace Jovanovich, Inc., 1922).

14. Ralph Pendleton, ed., *The Theater of Robert Edmond Jones* (Middleton, Conn.: Wesleyan University Press, 1958).

15. Robert Edmond Jones, *The Dramatic Imagination,* (New York: Duell, Sloan and Pierce, 1941).

16. Charles Fuller, *A Soldier's Play* (New York: Hill & Wang, 1981).

17. Anton Chekhov and Michael Frayn, *Wild Honey* (London and New York: Methuen, 1984).

18. Boris Aronson, quoted in *Designing and Painting for the Theater.*

19. Jarka Burian, "Joseph Svoboda: Artist in an Age of Science," *Educational Theater Journal,* 22, no. 2 (May 1970).

20. Sally Jacobs, quoted in René Hainaux, ed., *Stage Design Throughout the World, 1970–1975* (New York: Theater Arts Books, 1976).

21. John Napier in Jarka M. Burian, "Contemporary British Scene Design: Three Representative Scenographers," *Theater Journal,* May 1983.

22. John Napier, "Contemporary British Scene."

11

Theater Architecture

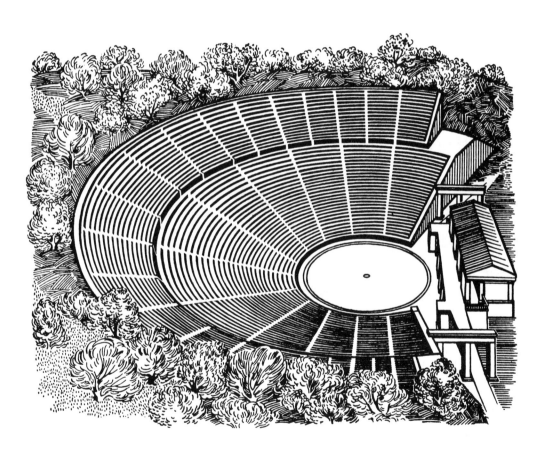

The basic requisites for a theater are that the performers must have a place to play and the audience must be able to see and hear. Two of the outstanding dramatic periods in theater history, the golden ages of fifth-century Greece and Elizabethan England, began by using improvised surroundings, such as marketplaces, threshing floors, inn yards, and banquet halls. However, as drama became more mature and complex, it was necessary to design and construct theaters specifically suited to dramatic production. In both instances the forms that evolved were extraordinarily successful in serving the drama written for them.

THE GREEK THEATER

The first Greek theater was built on the slopes of the Acropolis in Athens at the beginning of the fifth century B.C. It consisted of three parts: (1) the *theatron* for the audience; (2) the *orchestra,* or dancing circle, for the performer; and (3) the *skene,* or stagehouse, for the background of the action. The theatron, first with wooden seats, later replaced by stone, seated about

A view of the theater at Epidaurus during a summer festival performance. Note the variety of blocking and the flexibility of the playing areas.

16,000 spectators and had eighty rows of seats arranged in a semicircular pattern around the orchestra. Although the theatron was large, the absence of barriers between players and spectators gave the effect of a close relationship. Most authorities agree that all the performers—actors as well as chorus—played in the orchestra, a large, earthen circle about twenty meters across with an altar in the center. Passageways at either side of the orchestra, called *paradoi,* made possible spectacular and lively entrances and exits. Actors could also enter from three openings in the skene. There was no stage, as such, although the actors would have been well served by a platform with steps in front of the skene as a place for speeches, debates, and entrances and exits. In the orchestra circle were three acoustical centers, at which the actors could most easily be heard. One center was at the very middle, where an altar was placed, and the other two were about five meters at either side. In festival productions at Epidarus, these centers affected the blocking of the action because directors and actors learned to capitalize on them during many of the most telling moments of the play. The style of acting in the Greek theater demanded broad gestures because of its immense size, but because of the excellent acoustics, voices did not require extensive volume. As a result, the acting style was probably neither stagey nor bombastic.

Although the Greeks used some scenery, it is a mistake to think of elaborate settings that enclosed the action. Since the audience wrapped around the playing area, it was impossible to surround the actors with scenery. There was probably simple iconographic suggestion of locale mounted on the back wall, but as in present-day revivals in Athens and Epidarus, much of the performance was played well out in the orchestra, often in close contact with the chorus. The huge orchestra provided one of the best solutions for an acting area in theater history because it allowed striking entrances and exits and gave the chorus and actors a very large and flexible playing space for movement, dance, and ensemble groupings. Despite the minimal use of scenery, the Greek theater was a spectacular one, with striking masks and costumes, and the movement and dancing of the performers took place in a handsome structure in a picturesque setting.

THE ELIZABETHAN STAGE

The lack of primary evidence about the Elizabethan theater has caused an endless amount of conjecture and controversy. It is enough for our purposes to know that the playhouses used by Shakespeare and his contemporaries were covered, wood-framed, three-storied buildings; round, octagonal, or square in shape; enclosing an open yard or pit. The galleries in the enclosure were provided with benches. A large (about twelve to fourteen meters wide) raised platform projected into the pit; this stage was par-

A visitor to London during Shakespeare's time, Johannes de Witt made this sketch of the interior of the Swan Theater. The accuracy of de Witt's drawing has been endlessly debated.

tially covered by "the heavens" as protection against inclement weather for stage machinery, mostly for flying objects or people, and it also housed musicians and equipment for sound effects. Usually the roof was supported by large pillars, although in some cases it was cantilevered from the structure behind the stage.

The area behind the stage is the subject of most argument; although all agree that it had at least a two-storied façade, some authorities suggest that the spectator galleries completely surrounded the yard, including the backstage. There were two large doors at either side, at the stage level; some scholars argue for a curtained alcove in between that would be useful for storing properties or even for staging some action. In another version a pavilion projected out from the center area, whereas others insist that there was only a blank wall between the doors.

There are also conflicting theories about the "inner above," an alcove at the second-story level, which could have been used for scenes requiring

The second Globe Theater, 1614, as reconstructed by Richard Leacroft. This view shows the large platform stage projecting into the yard, providing a versatile theater so necessary for Shakespearean production.

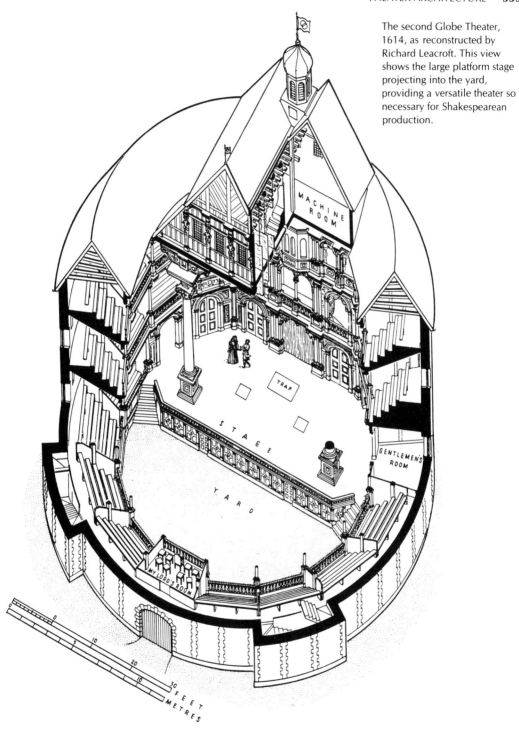

elevation, such as those with a balcony. Some authorities contend that all the action could be accommodated on the large stage and that there was no need for an elevated alcove. Actually, Elizabethan practice may have been as diverse as scholarly conjecture. Given the sightlines of the Elizabethan theater, there was no possibility of backing the performers with illusionistic scenery.

The Elizabethan theater was a highly successful architectural solution for the plays it housed. Working with a playhouse that held as many as 2,000 spectators in close proximity to the performers, dramatists were able to exploit the possibilities of the language to the full, and the unlocalized stage allowed enormous flexibility for the lively action of a complicated plot that moved from scene to scene without interruption.

The architecture of the Greeks and Elizabethans makes the point that a theater must be suitable for the drama it serves. We have had to learn this lesson through trial and error. Efforts to produce Shakespeare for over three centuries in the pictorial tradition of the proscenium arch theater have demonstrated the inevitable loss of fluency so essential to Elizabethan staging. Likewise, the performance of Greek tragedy in the cramped area of our end stage modern playhouses is awkward, not only because our taste for illusion is at odds with the conventions of the ancient theater, but also because the limitations of sightlines and space make it difficult to accommodate the chorus. A part of the difficulty in designing a playhouse today is

One of the most successful Shakespearean festivals in this country, the Elizabethan Theater at Ashland, Oregon, during a performance of *Hamlet.*

that it is expected to accommodate all kinds of plays. In an attempt to achieve flexibility, we risk the danger of constructing a theater that does not serve any drama very well.

Most contemporary drama is written for production in theaters that follow the pictorial tradition of the Renaissance. It is important that we understand how that tradition began and what its implications are today.

THE RENAISSANCE PROSCENIUM ARCH STAGE

In Italy during the latter part of the fifteenth century, interest in the revival of classical drama led academies and wealthy nobles to the performance of ancient plays. Part of the interest in the revival of drama came from the Roman architect Vitruvius (first century B.C.), whose *De Architectura* was discovered in 1414 and published in 1486. Vitruvius' description of the Roman

Le Petit-Bourbon, the first court theater in France, 1577. Moliere's troupe shared this theater with another company. This view shows Louis XIII and Cardinal Richelieu during a performance behind the arch on a raised stage.

stage included settings for three kinds of plays: tragedy, comedy, and pastoral. Interest in Vitruvius was coupled with the Italian fascination for perspective painting, especially as demonstrated in the work of Filippo Brunelleschi (1377–1446). This Florentine architect showed how it was possible to suggest spatial relationships on a flat surface from a fixed point of view. Efforts were made to capitalize on perspective scenery, but it was not until Sebastiano Serlio (1475–1554) that the idea gained popular attention. His *Architectura* (1545) included three celebrated drawings of the settings described by Vitruvius. Serlio's settings for tragedy, comedy, and pastoral were perspective scenery with a central vanishing point. They were made up of four sets of wings at the sides, slightly raked except for the rear ones. Behind the wings, the scene was completed with a painted backdrop. The settings were fixed in place on a temporary stage at the end of a great hall. The front of the stage was used by the performers, whereas the back half was sloped to add an illusion of depth.

Two important Renaissance theaters were constructed in "antique" style to satisfy the vogue of classical revivals. The oldest of these extant theaters is the Olympic Theater at Vicenza, built by the Olympic Academy,

One of the most important Renaissance theaters was the Olympic at Vicenza, Italy, whose most interesting feature was the long, shallow stage, backed by a decorative façade in the Roman tradition with a very large central arch. Permanent perspective street scenes create the illusion of great depth.

which was founded in the mid-sixteenth century to foster interest in classical literature. It was designed by Andrea Palladio (1508–1580), who attempted to follow Vitruvius' plans. However, the Olympic Theater has semielliptical tiered-up seating, constructed around an orchestra, also a semiellipse. It is a roofed-over theater, seating about 3,000, with a colonnade at the rear. The most interesting feature is the stage—a long, narrow platform, backed by a decorative façade in the Roman tradition of pillars, niches, arches, and statuary. The central arch is at least five meters high. There are four other openings in the façade in which Vicenzo Scamozzi (1552–1616), after the untimely death of Palladio, placed permanent perspective scenes, creating the illusion that the stage is a city square from which five streets disappear into the distance. The Olympic Theater opened in 1585 with Sophocles' *Oedipus Rex*, which was sung before a gala crowd.

The Farnese Theater at Parma was designed by Aleotti and completed in 1618, but it was not used for performances until a decade later. The Farnese is important because it is the oldest extant theater with a proscenium arch. There is considerable dispute over this feature since some scholars believe the framing arch to have evolved from the visual arts; others, from triumphal arches; still others, as an expansion of the center doorway of the ancient Roman theater as anticipated at the Olympic Theater. In any case, the proscenium arch served an important function: The frame made it possible to use changeable scenery. During the seventeenth century, the proscenium arch became a standard theatrical feature that continues to this day, and with it the tradition of pictorial scenery. The Farnese Theater is the forerunner of the stage with a proscenium arch, but the development of the auditorium came from the opera house.

In the early part of the seventeenth century, Italian opera's enormous popularity profoundly affected architecture; many of the theaters erected on the continent for the next century and a half were intended for the production of elaborate musical spectacles. These were often public structures, so the auditoriums were large, usually accommodating from two to three thousand spectators. The auditorium assumed a narrow horseshoe shape so that spectators could see the stage area behind the arch. Architects soon learned that tiers of galleries along the walls of the auditorium would enlarge the seating capacity. From three to seven galleries were built, supported by posts that separated the galleries into boxes. Until this time, in court celebrations, members of the royalty occupied seats on the floor level, directly in front of the stage but several meters back. No one could sit in front of these seats for fear of obstructing the view. In the new auditorium of the Renaissance, a royal box was placed in the center of the first gallery, allowing a clear view of the stage and making it possible to increase the capacity of the auditorium by adding seats to the floor level, which was sloped to improve the angle of vision.

The stagehouse became gigantic in size and complex in organization because scene designers and playwrights required increasingly spectacular

The eighteenth-century opera house design by Giuseppe Galli-Bibiena, a member of a famous family of scene designers. Typical Renaissance taste for ornamentation and display. Note the orchestra enveloped by tiers of private boxes.

sets and effects. For example, the Salle des Machines, erected in Paris in 1660, had a stage more than forty meters deep. Ingenious equipment was devised for producing all manner of sensational visual displays. The basic settings were made up of side wings, backdrops or shutters, and overhead borders.

At first, scenery was changed manually, but Giacomo Torelli (1608–1678) developed the "chariot-and-pole" system in Venice in the 1640s. At the stage level, scenery was attached to poles that were inserted in slots cut in the stage floor. Underneath the stage, the poles were fastened to pulleys on tracks. When the chariots were rolled toward the center, the scenery moved onstage. The scenery was removed from view by moving the chariot toward offstage. The chariots and poles were rigged by a series of ropes and pulleys to a single winch, enabling a stagehand to change all of scenery simultaneously. Torelli's system became the standard method of handling scenery in the major theaters until well into the nineteenth century. Another mechanical innovation was flying machinery, used to create all kinds of spectacular effects, especially the magnificent entrances of performers or patrons on clouds, chariots, or other fantastic elements. The perspective of the single vanishing point gave way to multiple vistas, especially in the lavish scenery of the Bibiena family. All kinds of visual displays were created in an attempt to satisfy the audience's craving for novelties—fires, earthquakes, storms, and disasters. By the end of the eighteenth century, Italian-style theaters and scenery extended over the continent and England.

The audience that was attracted to these public theaters was made up of the upper and middle classes. Their taste in theater fare was not so much for spoken drama as it was for opera, ballet, and spectacular exhibitions. Moreover, the play was not always the thing since the theater was considered a social center. Boxes became private drawing rooms for gossip and entertainment, flirtation, and ostentatious show. In attempting to make the theater décor as impressive as possible, extravagant ornamentation was used. Walls were covered with baroque contortions of entablatures, wreaths, cornucopias, statues of nymphs and cupids, and fat rolls of swirling and gilded plaster.

When the public theaters of the late eighteenth century became too crowded with irksome hoi polloi, there was a resurgence of smaller private theaters, more suitable for tasteful performances given to the genteel people of quality. However, the general characteristics of the European theater through the nineteenth century followed the pattern of the Italian Renaissance opera house.

The general effect of the picture-frame Renaissance theater was to encourage spectacle and music. The dramatist was compelled to create plays in which there was ample opportunity for lavish pageantry and show. Drama was often grandiose in style. As a consequence of the huge size of the auditorium and the competition of the scenery, actors faced a difficult task in making themselves seen and heard. Such a theater was not conducive to the development of spoken drama. It was the smaller, private court theaters that gave the playwright a more congenial atmosphere in which to work.

THE DEVELOPMENT OF MODERN THEATER

Architects in the nineteenth century protested against the traditionalism that dominated the theater. Gottfried Semper (1803–1879) and his associates made a major breakthrough in the design for Wagner's Bayreuth Festival Theater (1876). Most of the innovations were in the auditorium, in which Wagner wanted to have a "classless" audience. So there were no side boxes and no gallery. Instead, there was a single bank of thirty rows of seats arranged like a fan to enable every spectator to get a good view of the stage. The rows of seats were widely spaced in what has since become known as "continental seating." This arrangement eliminated the need for a center aisle because spectators could reach their seats without disturbing those already seated. Another feature of this theater was an orchestra pit partially under the apron and deep enough to conceal the musicians. A double proscenium arch framed the illusionary scenery and created a "mystic gulf" between the audience and performer.

The deep, straight slant of the seats did not completely solve the sight-line problem, so other innovations were tried—the most successful being a "dished" floor, which greatly improved the visibility.

During the nineteenth century the impact of science was felt on architecture as well as on dramatic material. A most important technical advance growing out of the scientific revolution was made possible by the use of steel. Architects could design large cantilevered balconies extending at the rear and sides and over the lower level amphitheater like half-opened drawers. Because of the strength of the material, the balconies needed few or no supporting pillars. Thus, it became possible to pack a great many people into a limited area—a fundamental consideration in New York and Lon-

One of the major improvements in theatrical production was electric lighting. From the stage of the Olivier Theater in London, one sees banks of flexible lighting instruments that are controlled by a computerized board.

don, where the cost of real estate dominated the size and shape of the theater.

Another major technical advance was made in lighting. For centuries theaters were inadequately (and dangerously) lit by oil lamps, mostly from chandeliers over the stage and the auditorium. In 1817, gas was used for the first time in the Drury Lane Theater in England; it was quickly installed in most theaters not only because it gave better illumination but also because it could be controlled from a central position, often by the prompter, who could run a series of valves and stopcocks. Such gas systems became quite complicated. In a French opera house in 1880, there were no fewer than twenty-eight miles of gas piping with eighty-eight valves controlling 960 gas jets.

The major breakthrough in lighting came with Edison's invention of the incandescent lamp in 1879. That same year, the California Theater in San Francisco became the first to use electricity for stage lighting. Within a decade, electricity was installed in most theaters throughout the world.

Appia (see pp. 298–300) was the first to envision the possibilities of electric lighting, and his ideas and designs have been the basis for most lighting design since. His aesthetic theory reflected his view that since the actor was a three-dimensional agent, it was incongruous for him to play before flat, painted scenery. Artistic use of lighting could achieve the plasticity desired. Not only was Appia a theoretical visionary, but he was also a practitioner who showed how stage lighting could enhance the performance by creating atmosphere, emphasizing the actor, and following the shifting patterns of meaning. He demonstrated the means for breaking up the light and diversifying its direction, intensity, and color. During the twentieth century, vast improvements have been made in the quality and control of stage lighting, and it is universally recognized as a most important element of theatrical design.

Many of the changes in theater design during the first part of this century were made possible by the availability of electric power. For generations, scenery consisted mostly of two-dimensional painted drops and wings that could be readily shifted. A system of ropes and pulleys enabled stagehands to raise and lower the units, most of which were lightweight in construction because the emphasis was on illusionistic painting. But when scenery became three dimensional and solid, some other means had to be devised for moving sets quickly, noiselessly, and economically. Steele MacKaye demonstrated his elevator stage at the Madison Square Theater in New York in 1880. He developed a large double-deck elevator about seven meters by ten meters. While one deck was being used for performance in view of the audience, the other platform could be set at the basement level. The entire elevator was counterbalanced and moved by electricity, permitting a change of scenery within forty seconds.

MacKaye's ingenuity was widely admired, but its cost was prohibitive for most theaters. The use of mechanical facilities was more prevalent in Europe, especially where government support enabled many cities to build permanent plants for residential companies with generous work and rehearsal spaces as well as bars, restaurants, and lobbies for the public. In Germany especially, theaters were equipped with hydraulic lifts, turntables, winches, and lighting equipment—all electrically controlled so that the scene technician nearly needed to be a trained engineer.

There were some theater practitioners who opposed the proscenium arch. In 1893, William Poel constructed his version of the Fortune Theater on the stage of the Royalty Theater in London and produced *Hamlet* with no interruptions and no scenery. He continued with other Shakespearean plays at Gray's Inn and the Middle Temple, proving his point that a bare, unlocalized stage was more satisfactory for the production of Elizabethan drama than the proscenium arch playhouse with its changeable scenery.

Jacques Copeau, at the Vieux-Colombier in Paris, eliminated the arch from an old hall so that the stage and auditorium were an organic whole. There were no footlights and no barrier between performer and audience. On the stage, at several levels, Copeau placed screens, props, and backings to suggest the environment for each play. In this theater, he produced an extensive range of drama with exemplary simplicity and clarity that made Copeau one of the greatest forces in the French theater during the first half of the twentieth century.

In Berlin in 1919, Reinhardt also proved it was theatrically sound for the players and the audience to share the same space. His circus style structure featured a vast horseshoe-shaped auditorium around a large, projecting forestage, backed by a revolving stage with a plaster dome. It seated 3,500 spectators. Although Reinhardt was working on a large scale, his efforts to put the action close to the audience, as in the Greek theater, gave his productions a sense of participation and immediacy.

BRECHT'S EPIC THEATER

Brecht (1898–1956), in addition to creating new kinds of plays for his epic theater, was also an influential innovator in the use of the stage. Working in a traditional Italianate proscenium arch theater, the Theater-am-Schiffbauerdamm, Brecht gave his staging a new look by emphasizing theatricality rather than illusion, which he despised. In keeping with his principle that "the anatomy of the action should be stripped to the bone," scenery was simplified to a few skeletal pieces. There was no interest in ornamentation or display.

Brecht was opposed to atmospheric lighting; he had no use for intense colors or romantic chiaroscuro. Lighting instruments were exposed to view and gave off a cold, even, clear illumination so that everything on stage was recognizable. Stage action was combined in a presentational way with film clips, slides, maps, banners, diagrams, and soundtracks. Brecht's purpose was not to involve the audience in emotionally loaded fictions of romantic individuals but rather to depict frankly the social behavior of people. Toward that end, Brecht rejected the architectural tradition of the very building in which he worked. Although Brecht did not change theater architecture, he profoundly affected our way of looking at it.

THE SPACE STAGE

During much of the twentieth century, commercial theaters in New York and London produced plays in inadequate buildings, crammed into parcels of expensive land, whose cost usually dictated the size and arrangement of the structure. Since playhouses are frequently rented for single productions, and there is limited work space, scenery is very often built elsewhere and trucked in, and many rehearsals are held outside the theater. These theaters are usually proscenium arch buildings with the traditional separation of performer and spectator. Instead of building new theaters, the practice has been, especially in New York, to revise the old ones by moving the acting area forward and installing new equipment for sound and light as well as for changing scenery.

Progress in lighting has given designers and directors an enormous amount of flexibility, both within the arch and on platforms projecting into the auditorium. Now the acting areas can be defined by light, which is known as the "space stage." A front curtain is no longer needed because to begin a scene, the performance space is picked out of the darkness, and it is ended with a fade-out or blackout.

The size and shape of the playing area is readily controlled, and one scene can follow another virtually without interruption because it is possible to use skeletal settings and a minimal amount of properties and furniture. Sometimes a play is mounted in a large sculpturesque, permanent setting with a variety of spaces and levels, and the action proceeds from one scene to another by illumination of the area needed. For example, a setting suggesting the castle at Elsinore can be designed and lighted to accommodate the scenes of *Hamlet*—a platform, a churchyard, a plain in Denmark, the Queen's closet, and various rooms and halls.

Another advantage of the space stage is its suitability for the use of projections on the cyclorama, on free-standing screens, on pieces of material hung from the flies, or on the performers themselves. Such imagery can accompany the action, expand the environment, make a comment on it, or serve as counterpoint.

Space staging is eminently suitable for multiple-scene plays because no bulky scenery needs to be changed. Hence, the action continues without interruption. Period plays, such as Restoration comedies and those of Molière, can be set with a few pieces of furniture and perhaps a few screens, with the acting area established by the lighting. Although the space may seem bare, well-chosen properties and colorful costumes, supported by an orchestrated light plot that follows the action and constantly changes to fit the play's atmosphere, provide an entirely satisfactory visual experience.

As for realistic plays originally intended to be played in authentic-looking rooms with complete walls and ceiling and with a full complement of furniture as well as practical doors and windows, experience has demonstrated the efficacy of staging with almost no scenic support except for a few pieces of furniture, the minimal suggestion of locale, and most important, the light. The space stage has the great virtue of focusing the audience's attention where it usually belongs—on the actors.

A good example of the flexibility of the space stage can be seen in *Amadeus*, which opened in the National Theater in London in 1979. Act One contains twelve scenes; the second act, nineteen. It spans a period from 1781 to 1823. Peter Shaffer wanted continuous action from one scene to another. Partially, this was accomplished by having Salieri act as a narrator as well as the leading character, so he bridges the gaps and provides the necessary exposition. In part, the continuity was assured by the use of space staging.

The set consisted of a large rectangle that represented interiors: Salieri's salon, Mozart's last apartment, reception halls, and opera houses. At the rear, an imposing decorative arch supported curtains that parted to reveal an inner alcove with varied backdrops on which were projected theater boxes, walls of mirrors, landscapes, figures and silhouettes of Viennese citizens and courtiers, and a huge fireplace.

Scene and time changes were indicated by changes in the lighting. The continuity of the action was enhanced by liveried servants who changed the props and furniture between scenes.

THE THRUST STAGE

Since World War II, there has been a persistent attack against the proscenium arch in favor of the thrust stage—a bare platform, projecting into the audience area, which encloses it on three sides.

Guthrie designed a thrust stage theater that proved to be such a successful arrangement for staging Shakespeare and other playwrights that it has been widely influential. The stage, which often has steps leading to the audience level, is reached by entrances from the sides, the rear, and below, allowing great variety in movement. Because of the sightline problems, scenery is often fragmented or eliminated altogether, so the actor is no longer

The thrust stage of the Guthrie Theater during a modern dress version of *Hamlet*.
Note the blocking of the foreground characters, who are placed at lower levels for
the sake of good sightlines.

confined by canvas wall. A good example is the Crucible Theater thrust
stage at Sheffield, England, which has the same dimensions as the Shakespeare Festival Theater at Stratford, Ontario. It is eighteen feet wide,
twenty-eight feet deep, two feet six inches above the moat, and two feet nine
inches below the audience's eyeline. The latter dimension is critical, because
at the Mark Taper Forum in Los Angeles the eyeline is too high. As a result,
no armchairs can be used onstage because they would block the audience's
view of part of the acting area. As it is, a seated actor's knee may block out
his face.

The Mark Taper has other limitations because it was designed not for
theatrical production so much as for chamber music and lectures; however,
the auditorium and thrust stage have proven to be exemplary for an intimate style of production, so directors and designers have learned to live
with the limited backstage space. One of the directors with considerable experience at the Mark Taper, Edward Parone, described the use of the stage:

> The most difficult plays to stage are realistic, naturalistic, etc. . . . Chekhov can
> and has worked on this stage, but it is not easy, particularly with scene changes.
> We have severely limited backstage space and almost no storage space for one

thing. Then too, sets must be changed in full view of the audience. . . . In a production of *Major Barbara* which I directed, I changed time periods as part of the production concept, and I staged the changing of the sets. It worked. And with Shaw, all the talk works very well on the thrust stage; it is rather like a platform for debate, discussion, speeches, and pronouncements. The problem then is to get everybody else out of the way.

The Greeks and Shakespeare of course are a minimum of trouble.

The truly exciting challenge of the thrust stage is that it *looks its best with nothing on it*. Nothing, that is, except the actor and the words of the play. Whatever looks sculptural, simple and three-dimensional acquires a richness and purity that, with the right play, can be breathtaking.[1]

Another director with extensive experience with the thrust stage is Michael Langham at the Stratford Theater, Ontario:

I am convinced that one can achieve a greater imaginative bond between actor and audience with a thrust stage theater. In a picture-frame theater, I think

Plan of the Festival Theater, Ontario, Canada, built under the direction of Tyrone Guthrie. This design has been very influential in leading to similar structures.

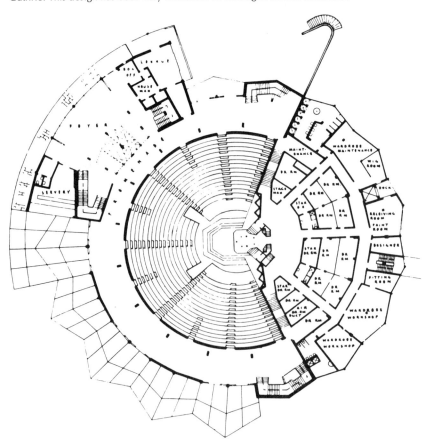

the tendency is for the actor to pretend to play to his colleagues where in fact he is playing to the audience. This is an impossibility on a thrust stage—the actor is forced to play to the actor and consequently the relationships that develop between characters are deeper and draw the audience more fully into the experience.[2]

THEATER-IN-THE-ROUND

A widespread form of theater architecture, particularly among campus and civic organizations, is the arena stage, also referred to as "theater-in-the-round" or "central staging." Glenn Hughes, at the University of Washington, led the way in this venture with his Penthouse Theater. He simply placed a few rows of seats around an acting area in a large room. Locale was defined by props, furniture, and costumes; and the only separation between performer and spectator was an attempt to keep the latter in the dark, although it was difficult to keep the light from spilling onto the audience from the playing area. The advantages of arena staging were immediately apparent—it was more economical, it gave the audience a fresh kind of theatrical experience, and it was excellent training for the actor in concentration and ensemble play.

At first, central staging was considered suitable only for drawing-room plays, but Margo Jones, in her Dallas theater in the 1950s, demonstrated that many other kinds of drama could be performed successfully—except

Arena Stage, Washington, D.C. The rectangular playing area is surrounded by tiers of seats for 752 spectators. Part of the seating is movable for flexibility. A cat-walk lighting grid overhead and a trapped floor give added versatility.

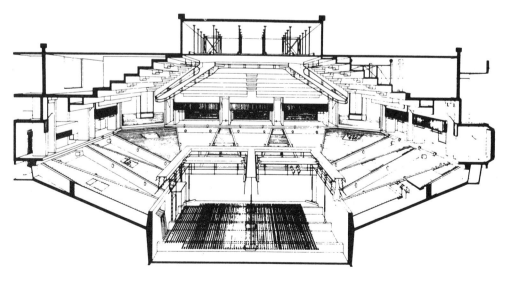

for those with too much violent action. The original Arena Stage in Washington, D.C. demonstrated that theater-in-the-round could be used for professional productions in a theater that seated 750 people and that nearly any kind of play was possible. The idea spread, especially to tent and music theaters. Now most college and university campuses have some version of arena staging; various arrangements have been tried, such as placing the audience on two or three sides and including a considerable amount of scenery.

COLLEGE AND UNIVERSITY THEATERS

In the United States, a unique development in the twentieth century was the rise of college and university theaters. Since these buildings generally grew out of the needs of dramatic arts or theater arts departments and were designed as an extension of the academic program, a distinctive kind of architecture emerged. Freed from the pressure to make box-office appeal the primary target, the academic theater was able to construct buildings that had auditoriums well suited for spoken drama and excellent facilities for production in terms of space and equipment.

One of the first university theaters in this country was built at the University of Iowa in 1935. It included an auditorium with continental seating for 500 spectators, a double proscenium, and most important, a great deal of offstage space for shops and storage. This theater set the standards, emulated by scores of other academic institutions.

FLEXIBLE AND MULTIPLE STAGES

A persistent problem of theater buildings occupied by residential repertory companies on a permanent basis is that of providing suitable staging for plays intended for varied playing conditions—from Greek orchestra to Shakespearean thrust to nineteenth-century proscenium arch to contemporary avant garde. In general, attempts to serve all needs result in serving none well.

In 1927 Walter Gropius, a German architect noted for his leadership of the Bauhaus school, designed a "total theater" for Piscator, an experimental director who, you will remember, worked with Brecht in developing epic theater. Although Gropius' plan was never built, his design provoked a great deal of thought. He attempted to include in one structure three stage forms—proscenium, thrust, and arena. By means of mechanical equipment, the components of the building could be arranged to make any of the three stages. The thrust stage was mounted on a large circular platform that could

The Arena Stage during a performance of *Room Service,* showing the arrangement
of the setting, the entrances, and the audience surrounding the acting area.

be revolved, placing the stage in the center of the auditorium. An open platform that could be used by the actors ran around the auditorium, and behind it a series of screens provided places for projections. A wide stagehouse
that could accommodate wagons was backed by a translucent screen for rear
projections.

The Malmo Municipal Theater, built in 1941 in Sweden, is a fairly successful attempt to design a multipurpose structure. The front of the orchestra is provided with elevators, which make the area usable for a thrust
stage, for an orchestra pit, or for seating. Another interesting feature is the
flexible auditorium, which can be varied in size by the use of large, movable
panels—so that the building is suitable for large concerts and musical productions; when reduced in size, it is an effective house for spoken drama.
As a civic structure, it is exemplary because of its spacious lobbies, working
and rehearsal areas, experimental theater, and parklike setting.

Another, much more satisfactory solution to the problem of various
production conditions is the multitheater, which includes a proscenium,
thrust, and/or arena as experimental stages. Many American universities
and regional theaters have found this a satisfactory solution.

Although the Arena Stage is primarily a theater-in-the-round, it has enough flexibility in its movable seating to allow for an occasional illusionistic set such as this one for *Buried Child*.

University of Michigan's Mendelssohn Theater with a projecting semi-circular stage. Note the variety of lighting positions.

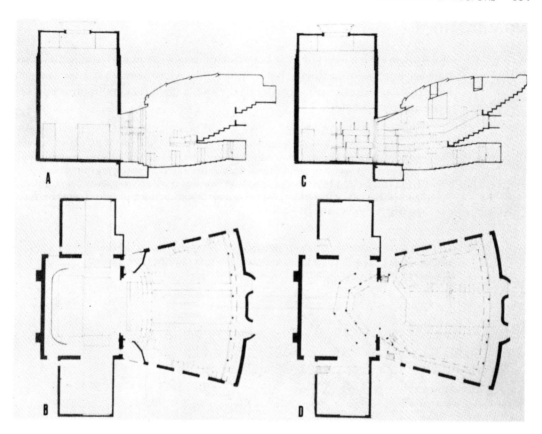

These elevations and ground plans show how the Memorial Theater at Stratford-on-Avon was changed from a proscenium arch theater to a thrust stage. A & B show the 1932 version; C & D indicate the addition of the thrust and a new gallery arrangement to accommodate an additional 576 spectators.

An excellent example of the multitheater is the National Theater in London. After 125 years of planning, it was finally opened in 1976. It includes three kinds of theater. The Olivier has a thrust stage in the corner of a two-tiered, fan-shaped auditorium that holds 1,160. The Lyttelton is an adjustable proscenium theater with continental seating for 895. Experimental productions are given in the Cottsloe, a flexible studio space with galleries around three of the four walls that range in capacity from 200 to 400, depending on the arrangement of the playing space. A most attractive feature of this plant are the supporting facilities for the audience's convenience and comfort—terraces, foyers, exhibition spaces, bars, restaurants, and parking facilities.

ARTAUD'S THEATER

We have seen how Artaud's ideas affected playwriting and acting; he also had an enormous influence on staging. His views are worth quoting at length because in them are the seeds that have since reached fruition in the experimental theater:

> The Stage—The Auditorium: We abolish the stage and the auditorium and replace them by a single site, without partition or barrier of any kind, which will become the theater of action. A direct communication will be reestablished between the spectator and the spectacle, between the actor and the spectator, from the fact that the spectator, placed in the middle of the action, is engulfed and physically affected by it. This envelopment results, in part, from the very configuration of the room itself.

Ground plan of the Olivier Theater of the National Theater in London. The large platform stage projects into the fan-shaped auditorium which seats 1160 people. The rear of the stage can be opened to give additional depth.

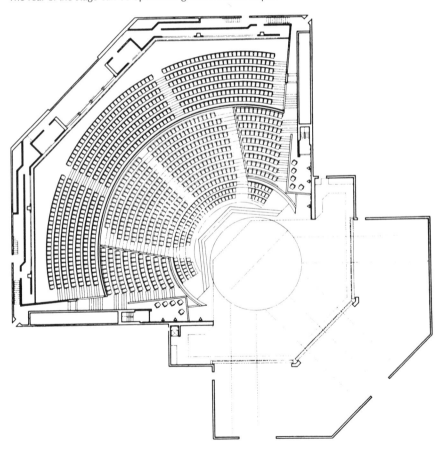

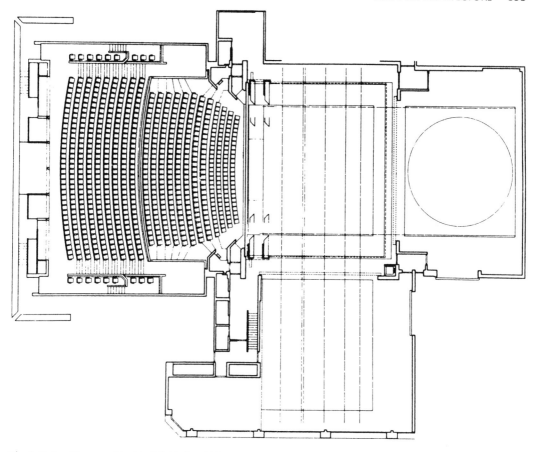

The Lyttelton Theater of the English National Theater is a proscenium arch structure
that seats 895 people in two tiers. Spacious areas in the wings and backstage, one
equipped with motorized scenery wagons. Scenery can also be flown overhead.

Thus, abandoning the architecture of present-day theaters, we shall take
some hangar or barn, which we shall have reconstructed according to processes which have culminated in the architecture of certain churches or holy
places, and of certain temples in Tibet.

In the interior of this construction special proportions of height and depth
will prevail. The hall will be enclosed by four walls, without any kind of or-
nament, and the public will be seated in the middle of the room, on the ground
floor, on mobile chairs which will allow them to follow the spectacle which will
take place all around them. In effect, the absence of a stage in the usual sense
of the word will provide for the deployment of the action in the four corners
of the room. Particular positions will be reserved for actors and action at the
four cardinal points of the room. The scenes will be played in front of white-
washed, wall-backgrounds designed to absorb the light. In addition, galleries
overhead will run around the periphery of the hall as in certain primitive

paintings. These galleries will permit the actors, whenever the action makes it necessary, to be pursued from one point in the room to another, and the action to be deployed on all levels and in all perspectives of height and depth. A cry uttered at one end of the room can be transmitted from mouth to mouth with amplifications and successive modulations all the way to the other. The action will unfold, will extend its trajectory from level to level, point to point, paroxysms will suddenly burst forth, will flare up like fires in different spots. And to speak of the spectacle's character as true illusion or of the direct and immediate influence of the action on the spectator will not be hollow words. For this diffusion of action over an immense space will oblige the lighting of a scene and the varied lighting of a performance to fall upon the public as much as upon the actors—and to the several simultaneous actions or several phases of an identical action in which the characters, swarming over each other like bees, will endure the onslaughts of the situations and the external assaults of the tempestuous elements, will correspond the physical means of lighting, of producing thunder or wind, whose repercussions the spectator will undergo.

However, a central position will be reserved which, without serving, properly speaking, as a stage, will permit the bulk of the action to be concentrated and brought to a climax whenever necessary.[3]

THEATER ARCHITECTURE REVISED

Another attempt to find new relationships between audience and players has been found in the radical revision of the buildings themselves. Performers have moved out into the audience's areas, in the auditorium, lobbies, cloakrooms, and rehearsal spaces. Spectators have found themselves on-stage or confronted by players all over the theater.

Some designers today consider it their prerogative to change the structure of the building as well as to design the stage space. John Napier, in designing *The Comedy of Errors* in 1976, extended the two top galleries of seating beyond the proscenium to surround the acting area of the stage, which became a public square in Corfu, with souvenir shops and bistros. Some of the audience occupied side tables on the stage level.

Napier made an even more radical transformation of the architecture for the musical *Cats* in 1981. The New London Theater had a spotty record as a musical hall, conference center, theater, and television studio. Napier changed the arena space into a three-sided circular seating arrangement around a raised, circular platform. A variety of ramps provided access from the stage to the auditorium so that the performers could mingle with the audience. The first four rows of seats and the acting platform were mounted on an immense turntable that moved 180 degrees when the performance began. For the New York production, it was necessary to open up the roof of the Wintergarden Theater to allow the heavenly ascension of the cat Grizabella, astride a huge tire.

Eugene Lee, in designing a double-decked framework for Baraka's *Slaveship* for the Chelsea Center Theater in New York, ripped up the seats

Peter Brook reconstructed an old Parisian proscenium arch theater for his
production of Shakespeare's *Timon of Athens*. This view from the balcony looks
down on the acting area that was formerly the orchestra floor, now cemented over.
The orchestra pit was covered with wood, except for a section that opened up to
provide an entranceway for the actors. Inside the proscenium arch, the raised stage
was replaced by a deep pit reached by a large staircase.

and leveled the floor of the auditorium. In the center, he built a larger platform set on rockers. The spectators could see into the narrow space below,
where the tortured, frightened slaves were chained. In Brazil, Victoria Garcia gutted the inside of a theater and replaced the seats with a large circular
metal tower, complete with elevators and transparent spirals for Genêt's *The
Balcony* (1970). Brook reconstructed the Théâtre des Bouffes du Nord for
his production of Shakespeare's *Timon of Athens* (1975). He took up the seats
of the orchestra and put in a concrete slab floor, which became the primary
playing area. The raised stage was removed and replaced by a pit six meters
deep, reached by a wide set of steps. The orchestra pit was covered by a
wooden platform, part of which was removed to serve as Timon's cave.
Spectators sat on rows of seats under the balcony at the sides of the playing
area. The decaying walls of the old theater remained unchanged and un-
painted to suggest Timon's decaying universe. When Brook produced *Car-*

men in 1983 at the Beaumont Theater in New York, the first thing the spectators saw when they entered was a mound of dirt and gravel in the center of the auditorium, surrounded by a board fence to convey the sense of earthiness.

FOUND SPACES

Another attempt to find greater freedom from traditional forms of production is to reject the playhouse altogether. Avant garde experimentalists wanted to get away from a theater of illusion—painted scenery and actors on display like commercial products. They believed that all aspects of pro-

Mnouchkine's Théâtre du Soleil plays in an abandoned munitions factory in Vincennes, near Paris. Spectators stand in the center or are seated in the raised gallery and watch the action on three large table platforms.

duction should make their own statements, not merely support the words of a dead text. The quest for new environments led to making performance areas out of "found spaces," adapting productions to existing structures, or performing in the open air.

Schechner's Performance Group adapted an old garage by moving scaffolding and platforms around the interior. Mnouchkine's Théâtre du Soleil occupies an abandoned cartridge factory. Stein moved from his theater in Berlin to an exhibition hall for *Peer Gynt;* Schuman's Bread and Puppet Theater plays in the streets or in the Coney Island concession hall formerly occupied by a freak show; Serban, Garcia, and Brook have staged productions in an ancient Persian monument.

In part, this exodus from the theater stems from the experimental groups' limited budget. (Antoine began the Théâtre Libre in Paris in a room over a billiard parlor, and O'Neill's early one-act plays were tried out in a

The Théâtre du Soleil during a performance of *1789* shows the multi-focused, simultaneous action and the interrelationship of spectators and players.

Provincetown living room before they were shifted to a warehouse on the wharf.)

One of the most innovative European directors is Luca Ronconi, who experiments with new uses of actors, language, and spaces. He is especially noted for his multifocus staging and simultaneity. His staging of *XX* at the Odeon in Paris took place in a set representing a two-story house with twenty rooms, in which several actors performed for about twenty spectators who could not see into the other nineteen rooms. At times, the performers changed spaces and presented another segment of the action. Finally, the partitions between the compartments began to disappear, and the actors interacted from space to space until all the walls were gone.

For Heinrich von Kleist's *Kathchen von Heilbroun*, Ronconi put the audience and the actors on barges on a lake. His celebrated production of *Orlando Furioso*, based on Ariosto's sixteenth-century poem, was first given in 1969 in Milan and then toured throughout the continent. Ronconi described the work as an "environmental spectacle." It was a loose conglomerate of events and characters, well suited for the director's penchant for lively, simultaneous action. Franco Quadri describes the staging of the Milan production:

> Ronconi designed the performance for a large space, measuring at least 120 feet by 45 feet, having two open portable stages (with projecting platforms) on the space's two shorter sides. The central space is occupied at the same time by the audience and by the actors, who for the most part, speak, gallop, and duel on wooden floats which are either bare or embellished with metal constructions: sheet-metal horses, an enormous monster which looks like the skeleton of a prehistoric animal, a hippogriff with great wings which a wooden machine raises in the air above the spectators' heads, many transparent plastic cubes forming the castle of Atlanti, and cages of gauze and plywood which at the end of the spectacle come together and enclose the audience in a labyrinth. The floats, propelled by actors who for a moment are not participating in the action, pass through the whole stage area. Their continuous movement—endangering the spectators and forcing them to move away suddenly—is a means of attack and a means of communication.[4]

Among noteworthy theater experimentalists, Grotowski rejects traditional architecture because he wants a "poor theater," free from décor, and because he insists that the emphasis should be on the actor. Grotowski calls for limited, elite audiences that are willing to go through self-analysis as they participate in the explorations of the performers. For this action, he prescribes a minimal, but variable, performance area:

> We have practically renounced the stage. The only indispensable thing is an empty area where a space can be shaped for the audience and the actors, and in a different way for each new production so that the most diverse relationships are made possible. The actors can perform in the pathways formed between spectators. . . .[5]

And so we have come full circle. Long ago, Thespis made theater from a bare space by the act of performing. So today, in many places, actors and directors, in their effort to reduce their art to its basic essentials, emphasize performance—and in the process, remind us that theater is not architecture or set design but players in action before an audience.

FILMS AND VIDEOTAPES ON THEATER ARCHITECTURE AVAILABLE

F = *Film Available;* V = *Videotape Available.*

F		*Drottingholm Court Theater*
F	V	*Shakespeare and His Stage*
F	V	*Shakespeare and the Globe*

BIBLIOGRAPHY

BECKERMAN, BERNARD. *Shakespeare at the Globe, 1599–1609.* New York: Macmillan, Inc., 1962.

BIEBER, MARGARETE. *The History of the Greek and Roman Theater.* Princeton, N.J.: Princeton University Press, 1961.

BURRIS-MEYER, HAROLD, and EDWARD COLE. *Theaters and Auditoriums,* 2nd ed. New York: Van Nostrand Reinhold Company, 1964.

GASCOIGNE, BAMBER. *World Theater: An Illustrated History.* Boston: Little, Brown & Company, 1968.

HODGES, C. WALTER. *The Globe Restored.* New York: Coward, McCann & Geoghegan, Inc., 1968.

IZENOUR, GEORGE C. *Theater Design.* New York: McGraw-Hill Book Company, 1977.

LEACROFT, RICHARD, and HELEN LEACROFT. *Theater and Playhouse.* London: Methuen, 1984.

MOLNARI, CESARE. *Theater Through the Ages.* New York: McGraw-Hill Book Company, 1975.

MULLIN, DONALD C. *The Development of the Playhouse.* Berkeley: University of California Press, 1970.

NICOLL, ALLARDYCE. *The Development of the Theater,* 5th ed. New York: Harcourt Brace Jovanovich, Inc., 1966.

SILVERMAN, MAX, and NED A. BOWMAN. *Contemporary Theater Architecture.* New York: New York Public Library, 1965.

WICKHAM, GLYNNE. *Early English Stages, 1300–1660.* New York: Columbia University Press, 1959–1963.

NOTES

1. Edward Parone, *Theater Quarterly,* Vol. 3, no. 11 (July–September 1973).

2. Michael Langham, *Theater Quarterly.*

3. Antonin Artaud, *The Theater and Its Double,* trans. Mary Caroline Richards (New York: Grove Press, Inc., 1958).

4. Franco Quadri, "Orlando Furioso," trans. Helen R. Lane, *Drama Review,* T47, 1970.

5. Jerzy Grotowski, *Towards a Poor Theater* (New York: Simon and Schuster, Inc., 1968).

12

The Audience

You may not have your name in lights on a Broadway marquee nor know the thrill and frustration of seeing your work put on stage, but nevertheless you play an important role in the theater—as a member of the audience. It is for you that the theater was built, the play written, the actors rehearsed, and the performance given. While they labor to find the precise words for their characters to speak on stage, dramatists try to anticipate your response. All too frequently you bedevil them with your fickleness because sometimes you give them the response they hope for and sometimes you sit on your hands or stay away from the theater in droves.

Although the physical environment affects the way a play is staged, it is the audience that dictates the kind of material that can be used. As Samuel Johnson observed,

> The drama's laws the patrons give,
> And we who live to please, must please to live.

A painting may be viewed by a solitary viewer, and a novel may be enjoyed alone on a cold night before a fire, but the play is a social event. Its full effect must be experienced as a group response to a live performance. Drama is a dynamic communal celebration that requires the union of all aspects of the theater—a coming together.

Most plays are written for immediate consumption; the obvious way of measuring success is at the box office. This influences the playwrights, who are aware that they must create a work that will elicit a ready response from a sufficient number of patrons to pay the bills and perhaps even show a profit. (In these days of astronomical production costs on Broadway, the play must pack the house every night for months to break even.) Most dramatists are aware of the economics of producing a winner, and they know that the popular hits are mostly musicals and lightweight comedies with little intellectual stimulation.

The list of long-run hits on Broadway indicates that fifty productions have run for over 1,100 performances. Of these, twenty-eight were musicals; nine, light comedies; three, suspense melodramas; and only two, serious plays, both by Peter Shaffer: *Equus*, number 44, and *Amadeus*, number 49.

The list of off-Broadway hits shows a larger selection from more substantial playwrights. Among the top fifty are two plays by Miller, two by Genêt, and single works by Shepard, Pirandello, Ionesco, Pinter, Euripides, Albee, and O'Neill.

However, there is evidence of the development of an increasingly mature and discriminating following in the theater and of a new openness to experimentation; this means the present-day dramatist and producer are able to find an audience for works of more than momentary interest. It should be remembered that many masters of drama in the past transcended the problems of catering to the lowest common denominator of the audience. Sophocles, Aristophanes, Shakespeare, Molière, Jonson, Lessing, Schiller, and Sheridan satisfied public taste while creating landmarks of dramatic literature. But popularity itself is no criterion of lasting value; many plays of enormous popularity are very thin, and conversely, some of the masterpieces of the theater are not major attractions. As educational, civic, and regional theaters continue to grow, they are developing audiences for all kinds of theatrical experiences, including literary, provocative, and experimental plays.

THE NATURE OF ATTENTION

To create a play and a performance that will evoke an appropriate response, it is essential for the playwright and the theater worker to know something about the nature of attention. Attention comes in short spurts. Concentration requires constant renewal because it is impossible for us to fix our attention on a single object and hold it there as we might a spotlight. Ordinarily, an audience arrives with the expectation of giving full attention to the play, but if the drama is dull and the performance monotonous, if attention is not captured and sustained, the spectators make their escape into a world of their own imagining.

There are two kinds of attention—voluntary and involuntary. Voluntary attention implies that spectators look and listen by an act of will; they make an effort. Involuntary attention, on the other hand, requires no conscious effort; it results from responding to stimuli, for example, a scream in the night, a fascinating story, or our name spoken aloud by another. Theater workers are interested in securing our involuntary attention. They employ such devices as bright lights and colors, movement, emotional stimulation, space and elevations, sound, and visual focus. Directors combat monotony by varying the groupings of characters, by changes of pace, by making sure that actors do not imitate one another's pitch patterns, by inventing business and action—in short, by every possible means of renewing attention. They aim to control and direct every instant of our attention throughout the course of the play. This is one of the director's most difficult tasks since the play, by its very nature, is a stream of complex visual and auditory stimuli; attention constantly flits from one character to another and back again. Motion-picture directors have a far greater control of the spectator's attention because of their ability to focus the camera on one object, one person, one face at a time, eliminating all extraneous elements, and to edit a film after it has been shot, ordering retakes if necessary. But stage directors must find other ways to achieve much the same effect.

A part of the problem of controlling attention is avoiding the distractions that plague a theatrical performance, such as late arrivals, rustling of programs, foot shuffling, coughs and wheezes, and the vicissitudes of production that may occur onstage—missed cues, long waits, poor costumes, obvious makeup, scenery that shakes when the door is slammed, a crooked picture, and light-reflecting surfaces. Some aspects of the production itself may destroy the audience's concentration, such as an unexpected novelty that arouses surprise and comment in the audience, scene shifts that take too long or involve too much noise, special spectacular effects, or an unexpected laugh. In a well-managed theater, every effort is made to focus and control the audience's interest so that their voluntary attention becomes involuntary as they become thoroughly engrossed in the action and the play.

THE AUDIENCE AS A CROWD

Most members of the audience come to the theater to be entertained, to be stirred emotionally, to be amused by the foibles of their fellow mortals, to be enlightened by fresh insights into the human condition, or to be in the same room with talented, interesting people.

As a reader, you simply have to pick up the text of a good play, find a quiet place, and enjoy yourself. If you are an art buff, you meander through a gallery at your own pace, pausing before a painting that arrests your attention and passing by those that do not appeal to you. But if you go to the theater, usually you must plan in advance, obtain tickets, and arrange your schedule to fit that of the performance. Then you will be herded into a darkened room, along with hundreds of strangers, most of whom you have never seen before in your life and never will again. The theater audience is usually a varied mix—all ages, occupations, backgrounds, and races. Your gathering together is mostly accidental. You are together because of one reason: You hope to find a meaningful theatrical experience.

The lights go down, the curtain opens, and you see before you a place you have never seen before occupied by a small group of make-believe people, going through an artificially contrived plot. All of you know you are being deceived. You know that the handsome room is made of painted canvas, that the gun fires only blanks, that the innocent-looking blonde lead is in litigation over her third sensational divorce, and that the murdered victim will appear smiling and bowing for the curtain call. Astonishingly enough, you and your fellow theatergoers are fully aware that you are being successfully duped, and at the end you will join in enthusiastic applause to show your appreciation of how well the deception has been carried out.

Although you came together as isolated individuals, an audience quickly becomes a group. Through willing suspension of disbelief, individual differences melt away, you become a crowd, and the nature of your response changes, too. The social psychologist Emory Bogardus, in his discussion of crowd behavior, points out, "A heightened state of suggestibility is characteristic of a crowd. The preponderance of feelings over reason heightens suggestibility. The excitement that frequently prevails in a crowd throws persons off their guard. The force of numbers is overwhelming."[1]

Thus, a theater audience loses some of its sense of personal responsibility. There is a temporary release from restraint, with the result that in a crowd people may respond to stimuli that would leave them untouched as isolated individuals. For example, they may laugh in the theater at salacious humor they would consider vulgar in their own living rooms. There is the pressure to conform, the contagion to join in. These psychological phenomena are at least a partial explanation of how the effectiveness of a play may be enhanced by a responsive audience, which willingly suspends its disbelief and succumbs to the emotions of the play.

TYPES OF AUDIENCES

Anyone experienced in theatrical production can testify to the fact that audiences vary from performance to performance. A Saturday night crowd will almost invariably outlaugh a Monday night one. A matinee audience with a preponderance of shoppers or tourists reacts quite differently from one dominated by travelers. Audiences likewise differ from place to place. A performer meets a different reception in Las Vegas than in Boston. Uni-

Spectators in an audience lose their sense of identity and become a group. Painted audience background for Chekhov's *The Good Doctor.*

(University of California, Santa Barbara. Photo: Will Swelling.)

versity theatergoers are a marked contrast to those in a community theater. Spectators may find their responses to a play varying according to the stimulation they receive from others, the way they feel, the temperature of the auditorium, and the location of their seats. They will also notice that their reactions to a motion picture in a crowded theater are not the same as their response to a film seen in the seclusion of their own home.

Different kinds of plays attract different kinds of audiences. Compare an audience that attends an opera with those at a musical comedy, or note the difference between the spectators attending a farce and a tragedy. A striking example of variation may be seen in Japan, where the archaic, restrained Noh drama is met with dignified, nearly reverent attention, whereas the popular Kabuki audience may have a noisy and enthusiastic response. Spectators at an experimental production are often a strange mixture; some are sympathetic to any kind of provocation, whereas others may remain aloof—baffled, shocked, or offended by what is going on.

As a social institution, the theater has at times served as a tribunal, propaganda agency, house of the devil, temple of worship, meeting place for disreputable characters, showcase for ostentatious display, and place for intellectual stimulation. Its status and function have depended on the audience that patronized it. Consider, for example, four representative audiences.

As Daumier in one of his famous theater prints shows, people gathered together in an audience are more susceptible to emotional response.

(Munich Theater Museum.)

The Greek Audience

The theater of Greece was a religious institution, which every free male attended during the two main festivals; the Lenaia, primarily a local celebration since the seas were rough for travel in winter, was especially important for comedy. Since most of the audience were Athenians, Aristophanes took great delight in satirizing local situations and prominent people, and even the audience itself. The City Dionysia, which offered competition in tragedies, satyr plays, and choral singing, was a more serious occasion, though still a celebration. The audience came to share in the great searching problems of mankind—problems that elevated the human spirit through suffering.

Athenian audiences were remarkable because of their great zest for living and thinking. Art, literature, philosophy, and logic were not mere subjects of contemplation for them. They were an active, inquiring people with an unquenchable thirst for learning. Because their interests and tastes ranged widely, their infrequent dramatic productions could accommodate

Greek vase painting showing ancient spectators actively involved in cheering their favorites during a horse race. The Greek theater audience was similarly disposed to a lively response to dramatic productions.

(Photo: D. A. Harissiadis.)

the tragic grandeur of Aeschylus and the comic irreverence of Aristophanes—whose uninhibited shafts of ridicule are a commentary on the amazing tolerance of Greek society.

The Greeks were a knowledgeable audience, steeped in their literary heritage, with keen ears for the rhythm and texture of language, and so thoroughly familiar with the plays of their time that they could identify specific passages of Euripidean and Aeschylean dialogue in Aristophanes' comedy *The Frogs*. Such an audience invited dramas of great ideas and magnificent language. The culture that produced the idea of the golden mean—moderation in all things—led to a drama that was clear and logically organized and usually free from the excesses of pathos and sentiment. The Athenians' search for truth in life resulted in drama that was unflinchingly and relentlessly honest in confronting evil, suffering, and catastrophe. Their intellectual tolerance and sense of balance enabled them to see the sense and nonsense of the Aristophanic satire that scathingly attacked the follies of the time. The Athenians of the fifth century B.C. were astonishingly civilized human beings, and their level of culture is nowhere reflected so admirably as in the dramas created for their pleasure and edification.

The Elizabethan Audience

Like the Greeks, the Elizabethans had an enormous enthusiasm for life. Shakespeare's time was one of remarkable intellectual ferment, with great interest in language, literature, music, and politics. The Elizabethans viewed

Looking through the gateway of the parodus in the ancient theater of Epidaurus which seated about 16,000 spectators. Summer festival productions are given here and in Athens.

An audience at the Globe Theater as visualized by C. Walter Hodges in *Shakespeare's Theater*. This view, looking toward the stage, shows groundlings standing in the pit, while other spectators are seated in the galleries. Hodges' drawing conveys the intimacy that characterized the Elizabethan playhouse.

human beings as creatures of great potential. The spirit of the times was positive, dynamic, tumultuous.

The theater reflected the climate of the age. More than 30,000 customers a week flocked to see half a dozen professional, competing companies in London offer the richest concentration of dramatic fare the world has ever known. The theater appealed to the public's taste for pageantry and action, which elsewhere manifested itself in masques, processionals, and bear-baiting. The plays capitalized on the audience's interest in language, and the Elizabethan playwright enthusiastically followed the practice of medieval drama in putting as much vigorous and vivid action onstage as possible. Such a combination of words and action enlarged the appeal of drama so that all the motley audience could find something to suit its pleasure in the play. For the groundlings, there was exciting and violent action and raucous comedy. For the discriminating, there was delight in the magnificent language and food for thought in the elevated ideas. The Elizabethan audience's interests and tastes covered a wide range, and for it the playwright wrote both serious and comic dramas that were full-bodied, exuberant images of a turbulent and heady age.

The Restoration Audience

The Restoration audience offers a sharp contrast to the Elizabethan. When Charles II returned to the throne, the theater became the preoccupation of the court. The audience was made up of fashionable wits, fops, beaux, par-

James Wright visualizes an eighteenth century English audience in rustic surroundings from the backstage. This may be a scene from *Macbeth* during the sensational entrance of the three witches. Notice the by-play of some individuals in the audience.

(Theater Annual, 1906.)

asites, and women of easy virtue. So limited was the audience that only two theaters were active in London, despite the fact that the population had doubled since Elizabethan times. For twelve years, one theater was sufficient to accommodate this narrow following. It was a plaything for fashionable people. Such patronage resulted in drama that was artificial and deliberately unconcerned with the stern realities of life. When the Restoration playwright attempted to write serious heroic dramas, the result was exaggerated and false pseudoclassical plays, full of excessive emotion. The special achievement of the period was high comedy, which dealt with the foibles of social conduct rather than ethics. Puritan morality was satirized. Comedies dealt with the complications of intrigue and the defects of manners. The level of the playwrights' subject matter was offset by their brilliant use of language. They achieved a high polish in their repartee and their eloquence of style. The limited audience allowed the playwright to capitalize on personal invective and local and timely allusions. Restoration comedy is a particularly explicit example of the effect of an audience on the drama.

Thus we see that people come to the theater for a variety of purposes and that they constitute a vital force on the writing and production of plays.

The Modern Audience

Part of the driving force toward a new theater was the dissatisfaction with the audience-actor relationship. Brecht and Artaud were outspoken about the need for new kinds of audiences, suitable for their concepts of theater. Although they represented entirely different points of view, both made an enormous impact on the changing view of what the audience in the theater should be.

Brecht was dedicated to finding a new actor-audience relationship based on an objective attitude. At the center of his dramatic theory was the idea of "alienation," which rejected the emotional attachment of the Stanislavski illusionistic theater; Brecht believed this theater lulled the spectators into a fantasy land of make-believe and shut off the rational, critical judgments necessary for evaluating the social problems put before them.

Brecht makes this contrast between realistic, "dramatic" theater and his epic theater:

> The audience in the dramatic theater says: Yes, I have felt that way too.—That's how I am.—That is only natural.—That will always be so.—This person's suffering shocks me because he has no way out. This is great art: everything in it is self-evident.—I weep with the weeping, I laugh with the laughing.
> The audience in the epic theater says: I wouldn't have thought that.—People shouldn't do things like that.—That's extremely odd, almost unbelievable.—This has to stop.—This person's suffering shocks me, because there might be a way out for him.—This is great art: nothing in it is self-evident.—I laugh over the weeping, and I weep over the laughing.[2]

Max Reinhardt in Berlin in 1919 brought the actors and the audience into the same room in the Grosses Schauspielhaus in this vast auditorium that wrapped around the playing area. Note the performers in the audience area.
(Munich Theater Museum.)

At the other end of the spectrum, Artaud, in *The Theater and Its Double,* called for a radical departure that would place the audience and the actors in the same space, sharing a common experience that would completely engage the spectators in a communal ceremony. Artaud describes the desired response:

> It is a question, then, of making the theater, in the proper sense of the word, a function; something as localized and as precise as the circulation of the blood in the arteries or the apparently chaotic development of dream images in the brain, and this is to be accomplished through involvement, a genuine enslavement of the attention.[3]

Perhaps, the most notable example of Artaud's influence was Brook's *Marat/Sade* production at the Royal Shakespeare Theater (pp. 243–44). Artaud's notion of a "theater of cruelty" made an important impact, especially in some of the highly inventive offerings in the new theater.

Although the actor was at the matrix of the Polish Laboratory Theater, Grotowski was also dedicated to developing a special kind of audience, which came to a performance as serious participants in a demanding experience. Working without the customary technical support of scenery, costuming, lighting, or even makeup, the Laboratory actors gave themselves

An audience gathers for a performance in the Olivier Theater, a part of the National Theater in London.

(Architectural Press, Ltd., London.)

fully to the performance with a kind of religious fervor. Grotowski, like Artaud, sought a special kind of involvement:

> We do not cater to the man who goes to the theater to satisfy a social need for contact with culture: in other words, to have something to talk about to his friends and be able to say that he has seen this or that play and that it was

interesting. We are concerned with the spectator who has genuine spiritual needs and who really wishes, through confrontation with the performance, to analyze himself . . . toward a search for the truth about himself and his mission in life.[4]

Grotowski was keenly interested in controlling the audience as well as the players, and he often specified the place of performance and the number of spectators to be admitted. An example of how he included the audience in his production design for the *Acropolis* is described by James Roose-Evans:

The production is set on a large rectangular stage standing in the middle of the audience. The platform is piled high with scrap metal. A ragged violinist appears and summons the rest of the cast, who hobble on in sacks and wooden boots. The action takes the form of daydreams in the breaks, between work. The seven actors attack the mound of rusting metal, hammering in unison, and fixing twisted pipes to struts over the audience's heads. The audience,

Grotowski's Polish Laboratory Theater during a performance of *The Constant Prince,* designed by Jerzy Gurawski. The director deliberately restricted the size of the audience, and in this instance, kept it behind a fenced enclosure that surrounded the playing area.

however, is not involved. They represent the dead. . . . At the end of *Acropolis* there is an ecstatic procession following the image of the Saviour (a headless corpse) into a paradise which is also the extermination chamber.[5]

It was inevitable that the rebellion in the 1960s in this country should include new views of the audience, stemming not only from Brecht, Artaud, and Grotowski but also from experimental groups with their own original ideas. Disdainfully opposed to the "canned entertainment" of movies and television, as well as popular Broadway hits aimed at bored or tired business people, the new theater workers wanted to capitalize on live, kinetic, highly energized performances that could jolt the spectators out of their seats. Director Tom O'Horgan, who gave the new audience the tribal rock musical *Hair,* described his view of the way to handle an audience: "You have to keep nudging the audience; to say, 'You're alive. You do exist, right now.' You try to make the audience feel that it's not something that's nailed to a chair."

One of the striking features of the Living Theater was Beck's strenuous efforts to engage the audience as participants in a form of political activism. As a part of the performance, the actors encroached on the audience's area. For example, before the plays began, actors in street clothes circulated in the auditorium, sometimes buttonholing individuals directly, sometimes in warm-up exercises. Audiences were invited onstage, where they might join in a pile of bodies of other spectators and performers in a communal gesture. Or spectators joined a circle with the actors onstage, moving and chanting as one voice. At the end of the performance, the cast would at times come down the aisles and invite the audience to join them in the streets in celebrations that occasionally led to protest marches, demonstrations, or riots. In some instances, Beck's intentions were successfully realized, and audiences freely participated in the action; but at other times, the blatant aggression was counterproductive.

Chaikin's Open Theater began as a private workshop for actors exploring their potential for new ways of working, but inevitably actors need a response to test the effectiveness of their playing. At first, the public was admitted to observe workshops of improvisations and exercises, but the need was felt to create a full-scale production. The Open Theater did not attract an ordinary audience, looking for momentary diversion. People came to share an experience or to see new ways of performing.

Chaikin's workshop and his book were centered on *The Actor's Presence.* He was acutely concerned with developing ensemble play or interrelationships of one actor with another and with the group. But his sensitivity also expanded to include the audience:

> The confrontation is with that delicate but powerful pulse of people assembled in the same room. For this reason, it is the rhythm and dynamic responses, rather than the confrontation of attitudes between the actor and the audience, which is important. This special task is possible in the particular context of the

anonymous intimacy between players and audience, and through it the main theme, which is the confrontation of our mortality.[6]

Schechner, under the strong influence of Grotowski's Laboratory Theater and its methods, aimed at involving the audience in communal events with the Performance Group. In his production notebook, Schechner described the objectives of his productions: "No longer a theater of telling a story—or even doing a story. But doing/showing something, here and now. The audience as partner-participant."

In an attempt to enlist the audience in the performances, some of which were intended to be rites or celebrations, the Group members would usher their patrons into the theater one at a time, invite them to remove their shoes, and ask for donations of small pieces of paper that were later burned during a ritualistic fire in the performance. At times, during key speeches, actors faced the audience and talked to them directly, rather than to their fellow performers.

The radically slanted San Francisco Mime Troupe views its audience as a potential human resource to mobilize in its battle against social injustice. The Troupe specializes in broad comedy and sharp satire, using both as weapons for promoting social change. It works in parks, marketplaces, fairgrounds, and any other place it can gather up a crowd. Because it depends so heavily on the skills of the performers to capture casual onlookers and make them into an audience, the Mime Troupe has developed a spontaneous, broad style of playing, necessary for its kind of theater.

Schumann's Bread and Puppet Theater is also a street theater, working wherever it can find an audience, but its purpose is quite different from the Mime Troupe. Although its huge, awesome puppets frequently appeared in parades and protest marches during the time of the Vietnam war, its underlying drive seems to be toward a restoration of a traditional moral order and beneficent humanism. Because it performs without ticket sales or in a regular place for playing, Schumann's theater performs with childlike clarity and simplicity, making its points with impressive images and gestures.

The audience of the new theater very often sees a different kind of drama than the theatergoer in the commercial playhouse. The story line gives way to sensory experience often multilayered, with multifocused and simultaneous action. Instead of following clearly defined characters involved in a plot, spectators respond to the moment-by-moment stimuli that impinge on them. They are interested in what is happening now, rather than what will happen next. Lighting, scenic effects, film, projections, and sound are often used as separate entities as well as for support. The theater worker operates in a world of permissiveness since there are almost no barriers on subject matter, nudity, obscenity, and behavior. Anything goes. As a result, there is a good deal of straining for effect and an exaggerated use

Director Adrian Hall, in this production of *Billy Budd* at the Trinity Square
Repertory Company, Providence, brought the action out into the audience. Eugene
Lee's setting provided a flexible environment with a shipyard atmosphere.

of novelty and sensational devices, often without control or taste.

Once upon a time, when you went to the theater, you settled back in
the darkness and drifted off to some never-never land in a vicarious adventure that freed you from your mundane cares. Now you may sit on the floor
or in bleachers or on scaffolding, with no assurance you will remain aloof
from the show. You may be invited to participate in a group exercise; you
may be queried or argued with; you may be teased, insulted, fondled, whis-
pered to, embraced. Experimental performance seeks immediacy, intensity,
and exuberance in an effort to reach all levels of your consciousness. These
changes are directed at the narrow concept of drama as middle- and upper-
class amusement and toward theater as a means of enlightenment and release, a place of celebration, fulfillment, and wonder.

Luca Ronconi's production of *Orlando Furioso* first played in Italy, then elsewhere in Europe and America, where it made a strong impression because of its theatricalized style. Wheeled platforms were rolled into open spaces and became the centers of action which the audience followed.

OPPORTUNITIES FOR THE AUDIENCE

In this country, we have no permanent dramatic tradition, no national theater, no classical repertory of American plays. We do have a rich history of professional theatrical activity, especially before World War I. At the turn of the century, more than 300 traveling companies brought stars and productions to every corner of the country, but the coming of film and television has taken over much of the public's hunger for popular entertainment.

Even in New York City theatrical conditions are not encouraging. In 1929, there were seventy-five theaters that offered 233 new shows in a single season. Now, there are approximately a third of the playhouses remaining and only about thirty-five new offerings each year—and they are mostly musicals, revivals, or foreign plays. Increased production costs and soaring ticket prices do not make the Broadway situation any brighter.

In London, more than forty theaters offer a wide variety of fare that features the two jewels of the British crown, the Royal Shakespeare Company and the National Theater, both occupying excellent new facilities for performances at half the admission price of New York theaters. The two leading companies are supported by substantial government subsidies, as are about thirty other English theaters, many of whom are repertory companies.

The virtue of a residential repertory company is that a theater can have a stabilized, continuous program with a full complement of actors, technicians, and management personnel to offer a diversified bill of plays—revivals of the classics, experimental styles of productions, and new plays. Such a company develops an audience that is willing to take the risk of seeing new and innovative performances, and it reduces the box-office pressure from management. Because of the diversification of the repertory system, the English theater has an enormous advantage in training new talent in all aspects of production. It is no wonder that more than 2 million American tourists visit the English theaters in the summer and account for 80 percent of their business.

In the United States, we took a brief fling at government-subsidized theater as a means of combatting unemployment in 1935. The Federal Theater Project, under Hallie Flanagan, employed more than 10,000 theater workers and brought plays to audiences in forty states. It developed a highly theatricalized style of production, "the living newspaper," which were dramatic documentaries of scenes and excerpts of speeches and articles, resembling Brecht's epic theater in form. One of its productions, Sinclair Lewis' *It Can't Happen Here* (1936), played simultaneously in twenty-one theaters throughout the country to people paying admission prices from a dime to a dollar. When the project was forced to close because Congress felt the plays were too political in tone, it is estimated that one-fourth of the entire population had seen live theater, most for the first time.

To fill the vacuum left by the Broadway theatrical decline since World War II, the off-Broadway movement has made an important contribution. Newcomers searching for a place to train and exhibit their talents began forming groups, which usually occupied small houses, to be able to negotiate with unions for actors and stagehands. Limited by scanty resources, they made theaters of old movie houses, lofts, cafés, and churches. Their efforts followed the pattern of two early experimental companies, the Provincetown Playhouse and the Washington Square Players, which had as early as 1916 served as showcases for promising talent. From the Provincetown Players came such outstanding figures as Eugene O'Neill and Robert Edmond Jones, America's foremost playwright and designer. The Washington Square Players became the Theater Guild, which played to subscription audiences and gave to New York a high standard of production of innovative and noncommercial plays.

Following these two examples, the burgeoning off-Broadway theaters of the 1950s and 1960s proved to be excellent training grounds and showcases for new actors, including Dustin Hoffman, Al Pacino, George C. Scott, Geraldine Page, Meryl Streep, and William Hurt. It also was an important development for attracting and conditioning new audiences open to fresh approaches.

In 1959, another movement began with the introduction of off-off-Broadway theaters that were not primarily "farm clubs" for training rookies for the big leagues of Broadway. The new movement was more inclined to develop its own kind of theater without one eye on the scouts and critics. These venturesome theater workers wanted their own identity, and although audiences' acceptance was appreciated, their goal was not box office nor the ambition to become part of the "show-biz" scene. Off-off-Broadway began with Joe Chino's Coffee House, followed by Ellen Stewart's Café La Mama.

Both these theaters were dedicated to giving new writers a chance to be heard without worrying about the commercial feasibility of their work. They provided opportunities for dozens of playwrights to see their plays in performance before audiences, an invaluable experience for the writer. Now there are more than 200 off-off-Broadway groups, playing all kinds of material under all kinds of conditions. The New York example has been followed in most of the major cities of the country. This expansion has been a healthy one for bringing into the theater adventuresome spectators, many of whom are dissatisfied with Broadway policies and prices. They welcome the opportunity to be a part of the debuts of promising and interesting newcomers.

Meanwhile, the regional theater has become a potent force, with more than 150 nonprofit professional groups that are developing their own talent and audiences. There are now more actors making a living on stages outside of New York than on Broadway. A significant number of regional theaters have earned excellent reputations for their outstanding productions and for developing new directors, actors, designers, and playwrights. Audiences no longer depend on Broadway to see an interesting play, well mounted and professionally produced. Regional theaters are building their own audiences. The Chicago Goodman Theater has 20,000 subscribers; the Arena Theater of Washington, D.C., and the Louisville Actors' Theater each have 18,000; and the San Diego Old Globe Theater has a whopping 48,000. Most of the plays now appearing on Broadway were first performed in regional theaters.

Augmenting the professional scene is an impressive number of college and university theaters, many of them with exemplary physical plants. They offer extensive training in all phases of dramatic literature and production, supplemented by ambitious programs of theatrical performances. At least forty of them sustain resident companies.

You may be a student in such a university with all of the opportunities it affords. Or if dramatic arts is not a major offering, you are sure to find on your campus courses and activities related to the theater that will give you a chance to try your hand at acting, painting scenery, running lights, writing a play, or taking tickets—an opportunity that is sure to leave its mark because the theater is a beguiling creature, and once she smiles on you, she will be difficult to ignore.

BIBLIOGRAPHY

BLAU, HERBERT. *The Impossible Theater: A Manifesto.* New York: Macmillan, Inc., 1964.

CORRIGAN, ROBERT. *The Making of the Theater.* Glenview, Ill.: Scott, Foresman & Company, 1981.

LEE, VERA G. *Quest for a Public, French Popular Theater Since 1945.* Cambridge, Mass.: Schenckman Publishing Company, Inc., 1970.

McLUHAN, MARSHALL. *Understanding Media.* New York: McGraw-Hill Book Company, 1964.

SCHECHNER, RICHARD. *Public Domain.* Indianapolis: The Bobbs-Merrill Co., Inc., 1969.

SONTAG, SUSAN. *Against Interpretation.* New York: Farrar, Straus & Giroux, Inc., 1966.

STYAN, J. L. *Drama, Stage and Audience.* Cambridge, Eng.: Cambridge University Press, 1975.

YURKA, BLANCHE. *Dear Audience: A Guide to the Enjoyment of the Theater.* Englewood Cliffs, N.J.: Prentice-Hall, Inc., 1959.

NOTES

1. Emory Bogardus, *Sociology* (New York: Macmillan, Inc., 1949).

2. Bertolt Brecht, "Theater for Learning or Theater for Pleasure," trans. Edith Anderson, *Mainstream,* 11 (June 1958).

3. Antonin Artaud, *The Theater and Its Double* (New York: Grove Press, Inc., 1958).

4. Jerzy Grotowski, quoted in *Time,* October 24, 1969.

5. James Roose-Evans, *The Experimental Theater* (New York: Universe Books, 1970).

6. Joseph Chaikin, "Closing the Open Theater," *Theater Quarterly,* November 1974–January 1975.

General Bibliography

ARNOTT, PETER. *The Theater in Its Time*. Boston: Little, Brown & Company, 1981.

BENTLEY, ERIC. *The Life of the Drama*. New York: Barnes & Noble, 1967.

BIGSBY, C.W.E. *Twentieth Century American Drama*, 3 vols. New York: Cambridge University Press, 1982–1985.

BROCKETT, OSCAR G. *The Essential Theater*. New York: Holt, Rinehart & Winston, 1980.

———. *Modern Theater: Realism & Naturalism to the Present*. Boston: Allyn & Bacon, Inc., 1982.

CHINOY, HELEN KRICH, and LINDA WALSH JENKINS. *Women in American Theater: Careers, Images, Movements*. New York: Crown Publishers, 1982.

CORRIGAN, ROBERT. *The World of the Theater*. Glenview, Ill.: Scott, Foresman & Company, 1979.

ESSLIN, MARTIN, ed. *The Encyclopedia of World Theater*. New York: Charles Scribner's Sons, 1977.

GREENBERG, JAN. *Theater Careers: A Comprehensive Guide to Non-Acting Careers in the Theater*. New York: Holt, Rinehart & Winston, 1980.

HARTNOLL, PHYLLIS. *The Oxford Companion to the Theater*. New York: Oxford University Press, 1967.

HUERTA, JORGE A. *Chicano Theater*. Ypsilanti, Mich.: Themes & Forms, 1982.

MALPEDE, KAREN, ED. *Women in the Theater: Compassion and Hope*. New York: Drama Book Publishers, 1983.

MARRANCA, BONNIE. *American Playwrights: A Critical Survey*. New York: Drama Book Publishers, 1981.

MITCHELL, LOFTEN. *Black Drama: The Story of the American Negro in the Theater*. New York: Hawthorne Books, 1967.

NICOLL, ALLARDYCE. *The Developments of the Theater*. London: Harrap, 1966.

TAYLOR, J. R. *The Penguin Dictionary of the Theater*. London: Penguin Books, 1966.

VINSON, JAMES, ed. *Contemporary Dramatists*. New York: St. Martin's Press, 1977.

WALKER, ETHEL PITTS. *The Theater of Black Americans*. Englewood Cliffs, N.J.: Prentice-Hall, Inc., 1980.

FILMS OF PLAYS AND MUSICALS
AVAILABLE ON VIDEOTAPE CASSETTES

Note: This list is constantly growing. Consult your local videotape outlet for rental and sales.

Abe Lincoln in Illinois	*Arsenic and Old Lace*
Amadeus	*Barefoot in the Park*
Annie	*Becket*

Bell, Book and Candle
Betrayal
The Boys in the Band
Bus Stop
Butterflies Are Free
Bye Bye Birdie
Cabaret
Cactus Flower
California Suite
Cat on a Hot Tin Roof
The Count of Monte Cristo
Country Girl
Cyrano de Bergerac
Deathtrap
Dinner at Eight
A Doll's House
The Dresser
Educating Rita
Fiddler on the Roof
A Funny Thing Happened on the Way to the Forum
Gaslight
Golden Boy
Guys and Dolls
Hair
His Girl Friday
The King and I
Hello Dolly
Hobson's Choice
Home of the Brave
The Inspector General
I Ought to Be in Pictures
The Lion in Winter
Long Day's Journey Into Night
Look Back in Anger
Macbeth
Mame
A Man for All Seasons
A Midsummer Night's Dream
Mister Roberts

My Fair Lady
Night Must Fall
No Time for Sergeants
The Odd Couple
Oh Dad, Poor Dad
Oklahoma
On Golden Pond
Our Town
Pajama Game
The Petrified Forest
The Philadelphia Story
The Pirates of Penzance
Plaza Suite
Pride and Prejudice
The Prisoner of Zenda
Romantic Comedy
Romeo and Juliet
Room Service
Same Time, Next Year
Separate Tables
The Seven Year Itch
Sleuth
The Soldier's Play (Story)
Sorry, Wrong Number
South Pacific
State of the Union
Streamers
A Streetcar Named Desire
The Sunshine Boys
Sweeney Todd
The Taming of the Shrew
The Tempest
That Championship Season
The Trojan Women
Wait Until Dark
West Side Story
Who's Afraid of Virginia Woolf?
Whose Life Is It Anyway?
The Winslow Boy
The Witness for the Prosecution

Glossary

(The reader should also refer to the Index, since many terms are given extended treatment in the text.)

Acting area. Traditionally, that part of the theater occupied by the performers. Usually the stage, but in experimental productions it may be any area used by the actor.

Aesthetic distance. The physical and psychological detachment between a work of art and those who respond to it. Experimentalists are now trying to eliminate this area of separation.

Alienation. A technique used by Bertolt Brecht in his "epic dramas" to negate the emotional involvement of his audience to make an intellectual appeal for his message.

Antagonist. The character or force in opposition to the protagonist or hero.

Apron. The forestage extending beyond the proscenium arch.

Arena stage. An arrangement for "central staging" of plays with the acting area in the middle of the room, surrounded by the audience.

Aside. A dramatic convention in which the actor speaks private thoughts aloud, unnoticed by the other actors.

Automatism. A comic theory based on mechanical repetition. *See* Bergson in Index.

Backing. Stage scenery used to mask the openings to prevent the audience from seeing the offstage areas.

Beat. A basic unit for rehearsal.

Blocking. The director's organization of the stage movements of the cast.

Bourgeois drama. Pseudoserious plays involving middle-class society, with the general emphasis on pathos and morality.

Business. The individual actions of the characters in a play, for example, taking a drink, smoking a pipe, writing a letter.

Catharsis. The act of purging, cleansing, or purifying, usually associated with tragedy.

Chorus. In Greek drama a group, varying in size from 12 to 50, that recited lines in unison. As the first element to develop in Greek drama, it provided information and, in its most elaborate state, commentary on past actions and forebodings about future ones. With the invention of the second and third actors, the chorus gradually became less important.

Classical drama. Usually refers to the dramas of ancient Greece and Rome. *See also* Neoclassicism.

Climax. The strongest point of emotional tension. Most plays have a series of climaxes culminating in a major climax.

Comedy. Drama designed to amuse the audience, often showing human frailties and foibles; usually ends happily.

Comedy of humours. Comedy of character based on a dominant trait, such as greed or jealousy. Popularized by the Elizabethan playwright Ben Jonson.

Comedy of manners. Social comedy wittily satirizing characters in terms of their shortcomings as measured against a specific code of conduct, for example, *The School for Scandal.*

Commedia dell'arte. Improvised Italian comedy of the sixteenth, seventeenth, and eighteenth centuries put together out of stock roles in formula situations. Performed by small companies of professional actors who were very popular all over Europe.

Confidant(e). A minor character paired with a major one, who shares the latter's confidences, usually for expository purposes.

Constructivism. An approach to staging developed by the Russians in the 1920s that was antidecorative, antiillusionistic. The setting was a framework for action.

Conventions. Common agreements between theater worker and spectator concerning the manner of production, that is, certain "ground rules" that determine how the game is played, for example, the physical separation of actor and spectator.

Crisis. A time of decision; a turning point.

Cycle plays. Medieval plays dealing with scriptural stories from the Creation to the Last Judgment.

Cyclorama. Drapery or canvas usually hung in a half circle to mask the wings and backstage areas. It often represents the sky, or it may be a simple drapery.

Denouement. The resolution or unraveling of a plot so that an equilibrium is usually restored.

Deus ex machina. In the Greek theater, a "god from a machine"; a mechanical device used for the intervention of some outside agent to resolve the plot. As a general term, it refers to the intervention of any outside force to bring about a desired end.

Diction. Aristotle's fourth element—the language of the play; the words that the actors speak.

Discovery. The revelation of important information about the characters, their motivations, feelings, and relationships. Discovery is often accompanied by recognition (*anagnorisis*), when a character learns the truth about him- or herself.

Doubling. One actor playing more than one character in a single play. In the ancient Greek theater, the actor usually doubled.

Downstage. The area of the stage closest to the audience.

Drame. Any play that deals seriously with themes, characters, and ideas of the present day.

Dress rehearsal. A rehearsal conducted under complete performance conditions, including all technical aspects.

Eccyclema. A movable platform in the Greek theater thought to have been positioned in the central opening of the *skene,* usually to show corpses.

Empathy. Literally, "feeling into"; the imitative motor response of the spectator.

Environmental theater. The performers play around, above, behind, and among the spectators. Any environment can be used

as a theater that has enough space for performing and viewing. Often takes place in "found spaces."

Epic theater. The nonillusionistic theater of Piscator and Brecht, dealing with broad themes, with loosely organized plots presented in a frankly theatrical style.

Exposition. Dramatic techniques for acquainting the audience with antecedent information and background material.

Expressionism. A style of drama that attempts to present "inner reality," the person beneath the skin. Often distorts the normal to present symbolic action in dreamlike sequences.

Farce. Low comedy, written for amusement, usually emphasizing physical action.

Flat. The most useful element of stage scenery, consisting of a wooden frame generally covered with muslin or canvas to represent walls.

High comedy. A general term referring to comedy that evokes thoughtful laughter through its concern with character, ideas, and dialogue.

Histrionic sensibility. The spectator's ability to perceive and discriminate actions and visual symbols, just as in music the trained ear discriminates sounds.

Illusionistic theater. Any theater that attempts to create the effect of an actual experience—authentic places, real people, and genuine situations.

Imagery. Communication by means of concrete and particular meanings through language devices such as metaphors, similes, and clusters of related words.

Improvisation. Spontaneous invention by the performers of actions, dialogue, and characters usually around a basic idea, situation, or theme. Although widely used for actors' rehearsal and training, it is now employed in happenings, performances, and other experimental forms of theater.

Incongruity. A comic theory based on contrast.

Irony. A discrepancy between what a character plans or anticipates and what actually occurs.

Linear plot. A plot that follows a carefully articulated sequence of action generally organized in chronological order.

Magnitude. The elevation that Aristotle says should characterize tragedy. May refer to character, thought, diction, and spectacle.

Mask. To conceal the backstage, wings, or flies from the spectator's view.

Melodrama. Pseudoserious drama that is played at the game level, employing exciting action aimed at audience involvement. Usually ends with poetic justice. Popular in nineteenth century but still stageworthy in present-day mystery and suspense plays.

Method acting. Stanislavski attempted to devise a systematic approach that enabled actors to gain more control over themselves and their performance. Involves control of the voice and body, the "correct state of being" onstage, and inner psychological response as the basis for outer physical actions.

Mise-en-scène. All of the visual aspects of the staged production.

Mixed media performances. Experiments that may involve a combination of the arts and technical equipment, such as tapes, slides, and films.

Motivation. Logical justification, or the giving of plausible reasons, for the behavior of the characters in a play.

Myth. Archetypal stories that suggest widespread cultural beliefs, events, and feelings.

Naturalism. An exaggerated form of realism that emphasizes a sordid and deterministic view of life. First appeared in France in the late nineteenth century as a response to the scientific revolution.

Neoclassicism. An attempt in the sixteenth, seventeenth, and eighteenth centuries to "regularize" dramatic techniques by following scrupulously what were thought to be practices of the ancients, e.g., adherence to the "unities," use of a chorus, preservation of "decorum" in language and action, avoiding acts of violence onstage, and use of only royal or noble characters.

Objective. A dramatic character's goal.

Open stage. Sometimes an attempt to break away from the proscenium arch theater to play as close as possible to the audience. Also, experimental productions freed from the strictures of a prepared script.

Orchestra. In the fifth-century B.C. Greek theater, the large circle (approximately 22 meters across) that served as the playing area. Located between the *theatron* and the *skene*.

Pathos. The "suffering" aspect of drama, especially that quality that evokes pity.

Peripetia. In ancient Greek tragedy a reversal, usually in the protagonist's fortunes.

Pity and fear. The emotions aroused and purged in tragedy. Pity goes beyond pathos to include compassion and shared grief; fear goes beyond fright to include awe and wonder.

Plot. The structure of the incidents; the formative agent of drama; dramatic composition.

Point of attack. The moment in a play when a precipitating force sets the mechanism in motion and disrupts the equilibrium; the first complication.

Practical. Functional, utilitarian; for example, doors and windows that are workable, not simply decorative.

Presentational staging. Production that is frankly theatrical, free from the illusion of reality. The performer confronts the audience directly.

Probability. An attempt by the playwright to establish credibility or, as Aristotle says, to make the action of a play seem "necessary and probable."

Project. Vocally, increasing the volume so as to be heard by the entire audience; technically, showing enlarged slides or films on backgrounds as a part of the scenery.

Prologue. The introduction to a play, sometimes a monologue delivered by an actor directly to the audience. In classical drama, that part of the play preceding the chorus's entrance.

Properties (props). Includes objects used by the actors in the production of a play, such as letters, weapons, food.

Proscenium arch. The architectural frame through which the spectator views the stage.

Protagonist. The chief character in a play.

Purgation. *See* Catharsis.

Rake. To slant the stage floor so that it is higher away from the audience to aid in the perspective illusion. Also, the slant of the auditorium floor, designed to give all of the audience a good view.

Realism. Drama that attempts to establish authenticity through the use of the observed facts of daily existence.

Recognition. *See* Discovery.

Representational staging. Production that imitates experience, that seeks to create the illusion of reality.

Reversal. An Aristotelian critical term (*peripetia*) referring to a sudden change in the fortunes of the protagonist.

Ritual. Social customs, events, and ceremonies whose repeated actions are directed toward specific goals.

Romanticism. Concerns itself with adventurous, emotionally loaded characters in remote and exotic circumstances; in contrast to classical drama.

Satire comedy. Uses wit as a weapon to correct antisocial behavior.

Scenario. The skeletal outline of the plot.

Setting. The scenic environment of the action.

Skene. Originally a small hut at the back of the orchestra in the Greek theater, which later became the stagehouse.

"Slice of life." Attempt to give the impression of unorganized actuality without an apparent beginning, middle, or end. Used principally in naturalistic drama.

Soliloquy. A "solo" speech of a single character, which is usually taken to be introspective analysis; a character's internal thoughts.

Spectacle. The visual aspects of a produced play.

Spine. Stanislavski's idea of "line of through-action" of an acting role. A means of connecting motivations and objectives of all parts of a play.

Stage left or right. Left or right side of the stage from the actor's point of view facing the audience.

Stylization. Theatrical production that usually emphasizes the visual aspects and the manner of performing.

Subtext. Interaction beneath the surface of the spoken language of a play.

Surrealism. A literary movement that began in France in the 1920s, exploiting the irrational and unconscious with emphasis on dreams.

Sympathetic magic. Primitive ceremonies used in an attempt to enlist the help of the gods by enacting the desired objectives.

Theatricalism. The direct use of all aspects of the theater to exploit the play as a staged work.

Theatron. The seating area in the Greek theater.

Theme. The general subject of the playwrights' concern; their interpretation of the meaning of their action.

Thought. Aristotle's third element. The reasoning aspect of drama—the argument, the theme, the meaning.

Thrust stage. A platform or "open stage" projecting into the auditorium, bringing the performer in close proximity to the audience.

Tracking. An approach to performance in which several elements develop simultaneously in parallel tracks, such as music, images, and mime. The elements may remain separate from one another.

Tragic flaw. An Aristotelian concept of an "error in judgment," or missing the mark. A frailty in an otherwise good and prominent character that accounts for his or her downfall.

Tragic hero. The central figure in a tragedy. Aristotle described the hero as a prominent person "not pre-eminently virtuous and just, whose misfortune is brought upon him not by vice and depravity but by some error of judgment."

Tragicomedy. That form of drama that is serious and evokes apprehension for the fate of the protagonist but ends happily.

Transactions. An approach to action through the "games theory" of Eric Berne, which analyzes behavior in terms of the social, or overt, level and the psychological, or concealed, level.

Unity of action. Aristotle stipulated that all parts of a plot should be essential and organic to make a complete whole, free from digressions or subplots.

Unity of place. All action occurs in a single locale. By convention, the Greeks usually observed this unity.

Unity of time. The action of a play takes place, as Aristotle suggested, "within the single revolution of the sun." Covers a short span of time.

Upstage. The acting area farthest from the audience.

"Well-made play." Dramatic technique associated with French playwrights Scribe and Sardou in which all aspects of plot are carefully worked out in a logical cause-and-effect relationship.

Wings. The area offstage of the acting area.

Index

KING ALFRED'S COLLEGE
LIBRARY